ASSASSINATION CLASSROOM

YUSEI MATSUI

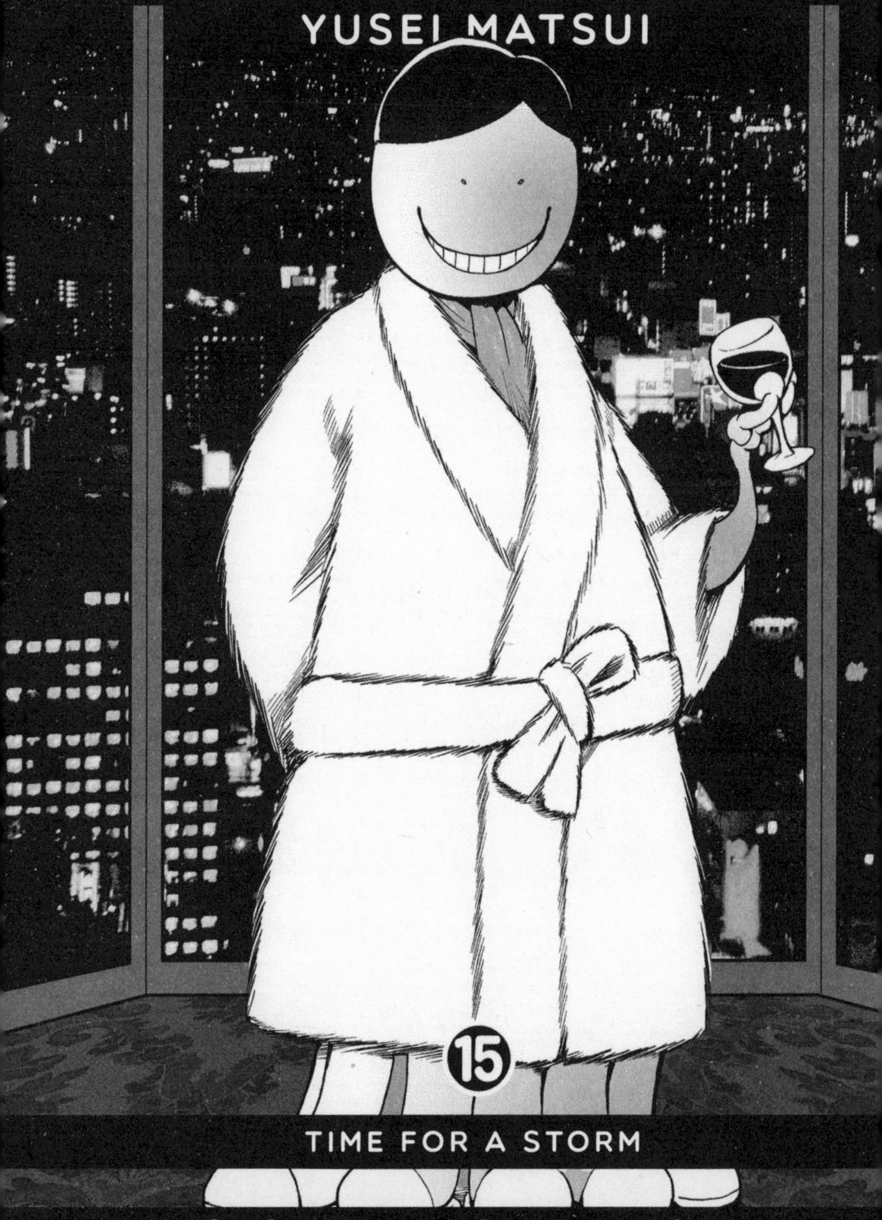

15

TIME FOR A STORM

SHONEN JUMP ADVANCED

Koro Tribune

December Issue ②

Published by: Class 3-E Newspaper Staff

Although we have data on his weaknesses, we are still far from assassinating Koro Sensei...

I EXPECT TO SEE THE BEST ASSASSINATION YOU CAN POSSIBLY DO.
MAKE THE MOST OUT OF YOUR KNOWLEDGE, INGENUITY AND HARD WORK.
THAT IS WHAT I ENJOY SEEING MORE THAN ANYTHING IN THIS WORLD.

Story Thus Far

Kunugigaoka Junior High, Class 3-E is a class led by a monster who has disintegrated the moon and is planning to do the same thing to Earth next year in March.

Even the armies of the world, with the latest technology, can't kill the super creature Koro Sensei and collect the maximum thirty billion yen (300 million dollar) bounty! So it comes down to his students, the so-called "End Class." Thanks to Koro Sensei's dedication to them, they grow to become fine students who can even outshine the top students in their school. Likewise, their martial skills rapidly improve with the help of Mr. Karasuma from the Ministry of Defense, molding them into a professional team of assassins. The second semester has gone by and the clock is ticking. Will they be able to successfully assassinate Koro Sensei?!

Is Koro Sensei in big trouble?!

RM
MM
I WON'T BE NEEDING YOU TO TEACH THE STUDENTS ANYMORE.
DISMISSAL NOTICE
BL
SO I'M GOING TO PERSONALLY KILL YOU—RIGHT HERE AND NOW.

Koro Sensei

A mysterious, man-made, octopus-like creature whose name is a play on the words "koro senai," which means "can't kill." He is capable of flying at Mach 20 and his versatile tentacles protect him from attacks and aid him in everyday activities. Nobody knows who created him or why he wants to teach Class 3-E, but he has proven to be an extremely capable instructor.

Kaede Kayano

Class E student. She's the one who named Koro Sensei. She sits at the desk next to Nagisa, and they seem to get along well.

Uh-huh.

Nagisa Shiota

Class E student. Skilled at information gathering, he has been taking notes on Koro Sensei's weaknesses. He has a hidden talent for assassinations and even the Assassin Broker Lovro sees his potential.

Fan service.♥

C'MON
LET'S EAT SOMEWHERE A LITTLE MORE PRIVATE...
I'M GETTING IDEAS...

Tomohito Sugino

An athlete who's good at baseball and sports in general. But not just sports, he's quite skilled at other things too—and not just video games. Unfortunately, he's such a gamer that he has a hard time breaking the ice with Yukiko...

pick up!

Karma Akabane

Class E student. A natural genius who gets top grades too. His failure in the final exam of the first semester has forced his to grow up and take things a bit more seriously.

Tadaomi Karasuma

Member of the Ministry of Defense and the Class E students' P.E. teacher. Though serious in his duties, he has been successful in building a good relationship with his students.

Yukiko Kanzaki

She got demoted to Class E after becoming a juvenile delinquent to rebel against her domineering father. With the help of Koro Sensei, she's gotten over her problems. She has no idea that Sugino has a crush on her.

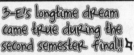
3-E's longtime dream came true during the second semester final!!

We've finally beaten the students at the main school building! Now many of us Class E students are aiming for high schools that are more competitive than Kunugigaoka. We have a bright future ahead of us...as long as the world doesn't get disintegrated.

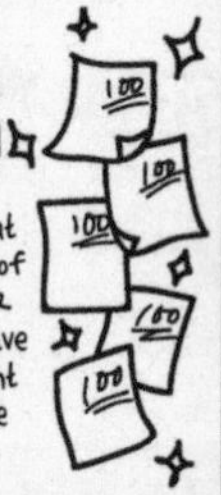

Irina Jelavich

A sexy assassin hired as an English teacher. She's known for using her "womanly charms" to get close to a target. She often flirts with Karasuma, but hasn't had any success so far.

We'll take you to the depths of hell if you want!

Minimum Fare 666 yen

Gakuho Asano

The principal of Kunugigaoka Academy, who built this academically competitive school based on his faith in rationality and hierarchy.

Assassination Class Roster

Always assassinate your target using a method that brings a smile to your face.

I am open for assassinations at any time. But don't let them get in the way of your studying.

I won't harm students who try to assassinate me. But if your skills are rusty, expect a good scrubbing.

Teacher Koro Sensei
Teacher Tadaomi Karasuma
Teacher Irina Jelavich
E-4 Hinata Okano
E-2 Yuma Isogai
E-10 Hinano Kurahashi
E-9 Masayoshi Kimura
E-17 Rio Nakamura
E-23 Koki Mimura
E-25 Toka Yada
E-14 Kotaro Takebayashi
E-19 Rinka Hayami
E-3 Taiga Okajima
E-8 Yukiko Kanzaki
E-26 Taisei Yoshida
E-5 Manami Okuda
E-15 Ryunosuke Chiba
E-18 Kirara Hazama
E-24 Takuya Muramatsu
E-1 Karma Akabane
E-16 Ryoma Terasaka

Kunugigaoka Junior High

3-E

Koro Sensei Class

Seating Arrangement

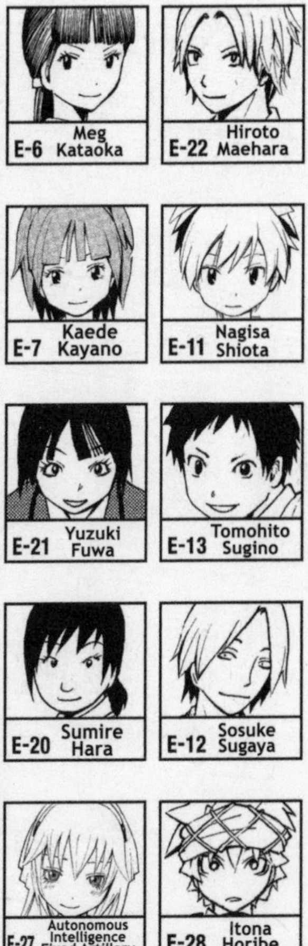

E-6 Meg Kataoka
E-22 Hiroto Maehara
E-7 Kaede Kayano
E-11 Nagisa Shiota
E-21 Yuzuki Fuwa
E-13 Tomohito Sugino
E-20 Sumire Hara
E-12 Sosuke Sugaya
E-27 Autonomous Intelligence Fixed Artillery
E-28 Itona Horibe

Individual Statistics

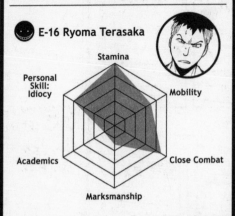

E-16 Ryoma Terasaka

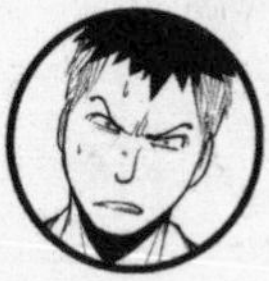

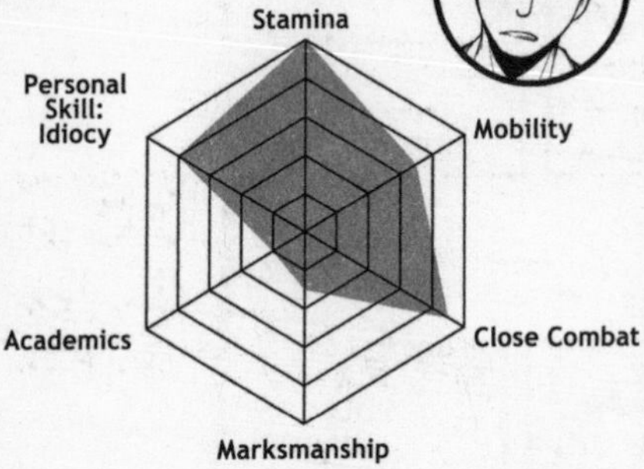

Stamina
Mobility
Close Combat
Marksmanship
Academics
Personal Skill: Idiocy

E-17 Rio Nakamura

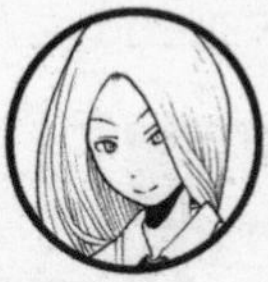

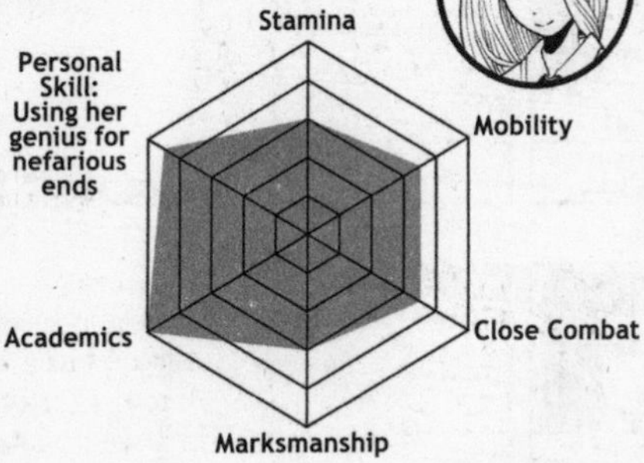

Stamina
Mobility
Close Combat
Marksmanship
Academics
Personal Skill: Using her genius for nefarious ends

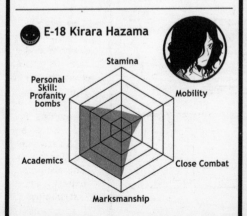

E-18 Kirara Hazama

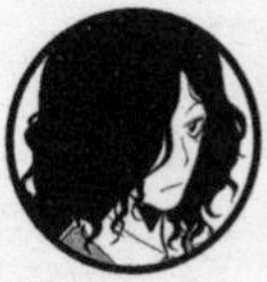

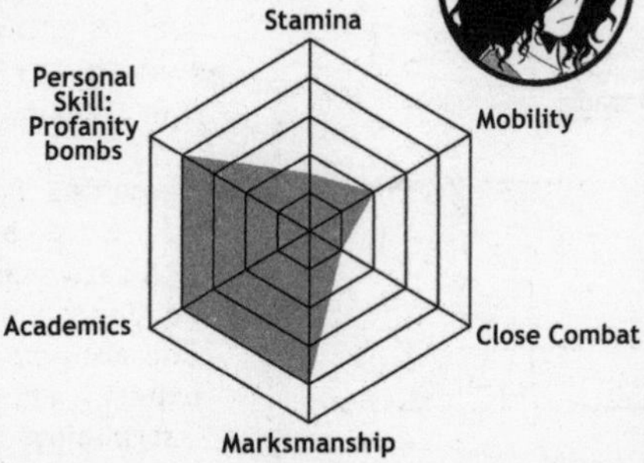

Stamina
Mobility
Close Combat
Marksmanship
Academics
Personal Skill: Profanity bombs

A S S A S S I N A T I O N
CLASSROOM 15 CONTENTS

(ANSWER SHEET)

| Grade | 3 | Class | E | Name | CONTENTS | Score | |

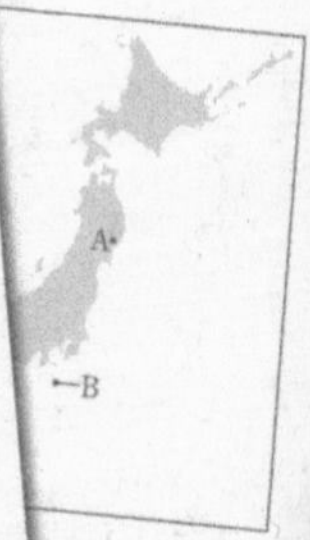

map of the
palaces of
katakana

and also

which
is C
ictor

presentations. The illustration
of each country. Fill in the names of the countries.

(2): Answer the following question
about B.

① Name the person who wrote a poem
about his love for his younger brother
who went off to war.

Class 125 Time To Be Perfect

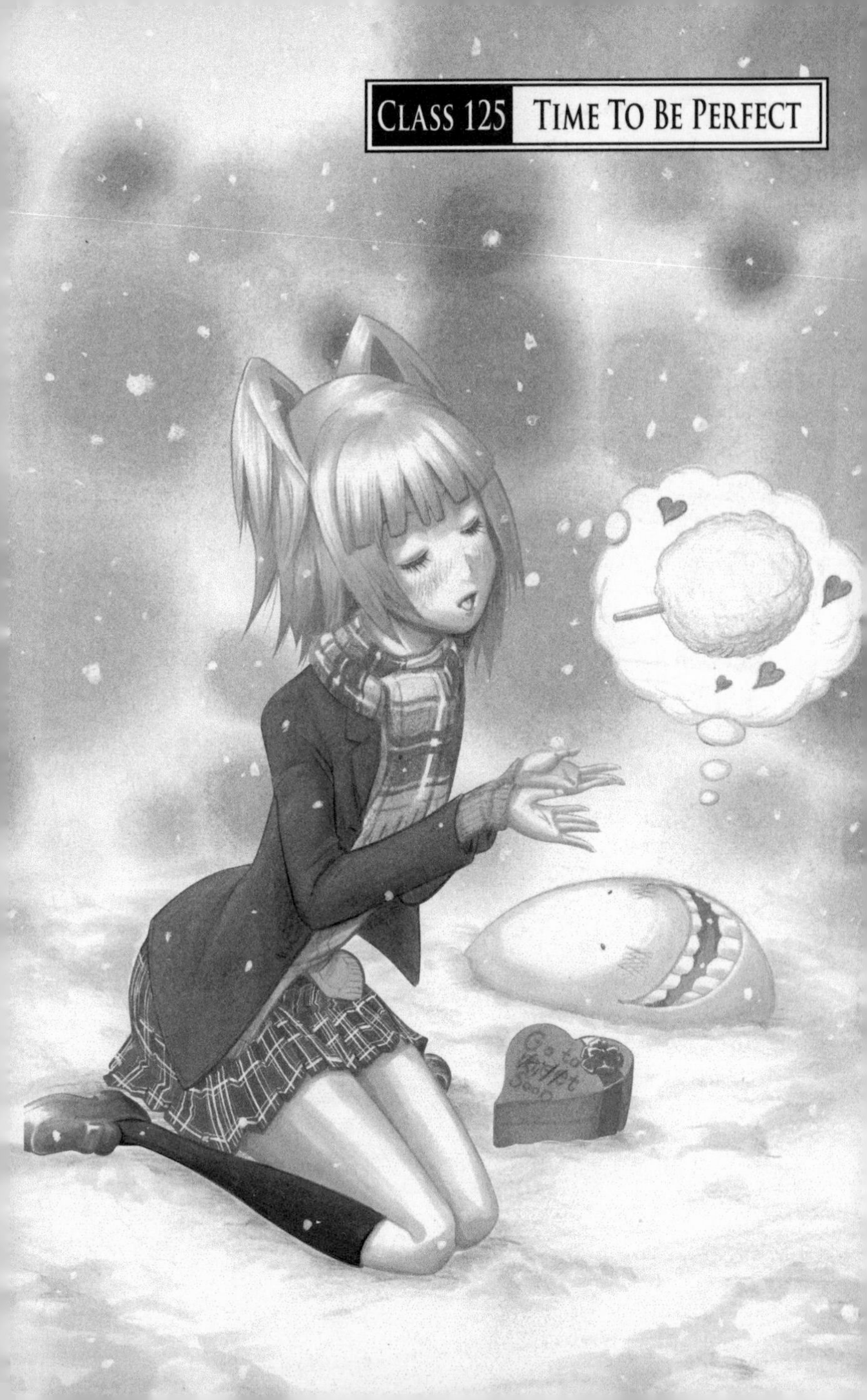

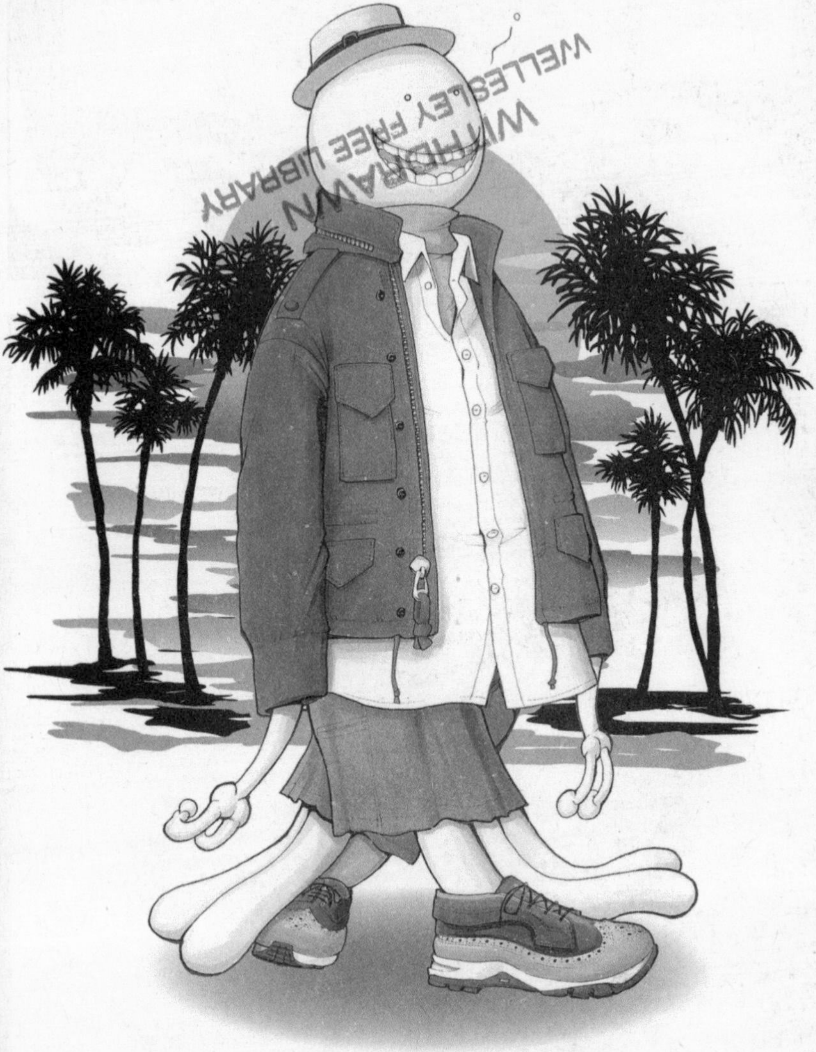

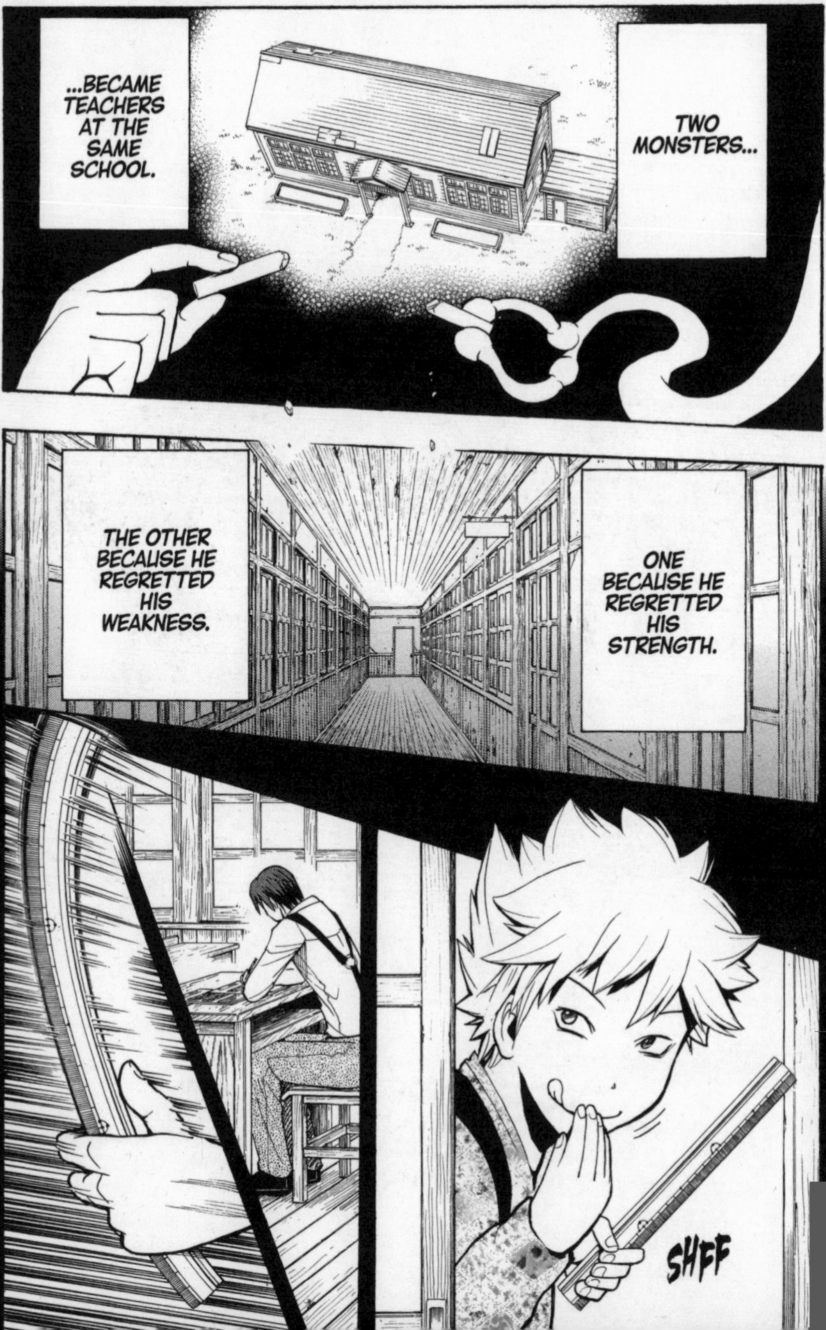
TWO MONSTERS...
...BECAME TEACHERS AT THE SAME SCHOOL.
ONE BECAUSE HE REGRETTED HIS STRENGTH.
THE OTHER BECAUSE HE REGRETTED HIS WEAKNESS.
SHFF

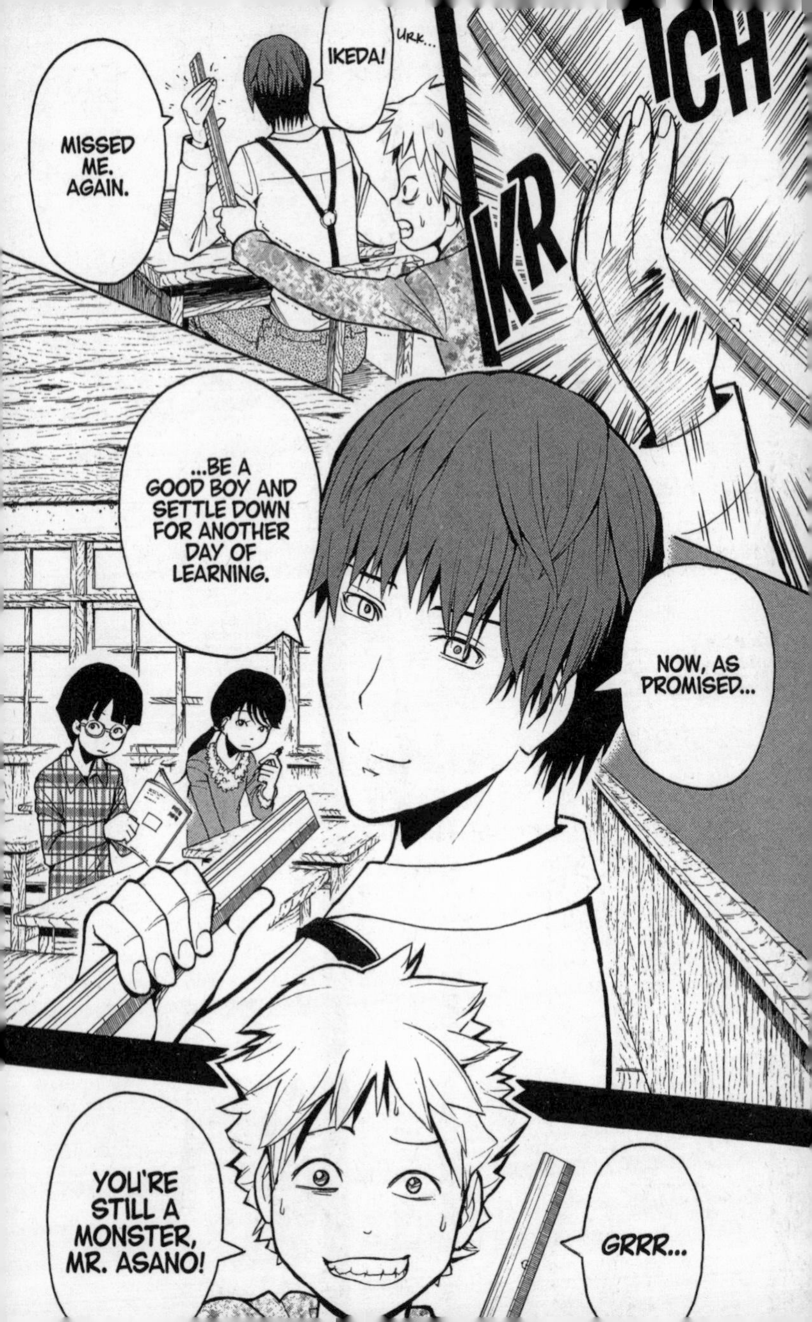
KR
ICH
URK...
IKEDA!
MISSED ME. AGAIN.
NOW, AS PROMISED...
...BE A GOOD BOY AND SETTLE DOWN FOR ANOTHER DAY OF LEARNING.
GRRR...
YOU'RE STILL A MONSTER, MR. ASANO!

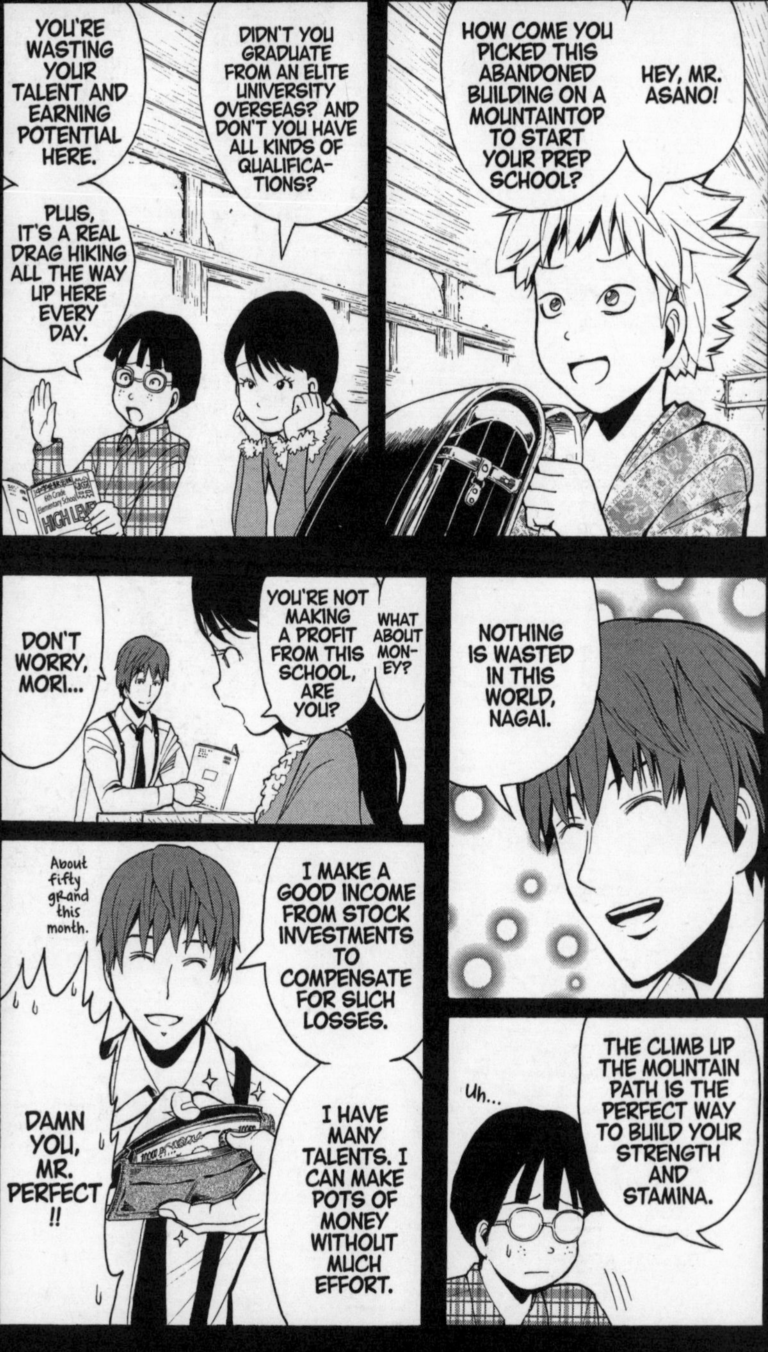
HEY, MR. ASANO!
HOW COME YOU PICKED THIS ABANDONED BUILDING ON A MOUNTAINTOP TO START YOUR PREP SCHOOL?
DIDN'T YOU GRADUATE FROM AN ELITE UNIVERSITY OVERSEAS? AND DON'T YOU HAVE ALL KINDS OF QUALIFICA-TIONS?
YOU'RE WASTING YOUR TALENT AND EARNING POTENTIAL HERE.
PLUS, IT'S A REAL DRAG HIKING ALL THE WAY UP HERE EVERY DAY.
6th Grade Elementary School HIGH LEVEL
NOTHING IS WASTED IN THIS WORLD, NAGAI.
THE CLIMB UP THE MOUNTAIN PATH IS THE PERFECT WAY TO BUILD YOUR STRENGTH AND STAMINA.
Uh...
WHAT ABOUT MON-EY?
YOU'RE NOT MAKING A PROFIT FROM THIS SCHOOL, ARE YOU?
DON'T WORRY, MORI...
I MAKE A GOOD INCOME FROM STOCK INVESTMENTS TO COMPENSATE FOR SUCH LOSSES.
About fifty grand this month.
I HAVE MANY TALENTS. I CAN MAKE POTS OF MONEY WITHOUT MUCH EFFORT.
DAMN YOU, MR. PERFECT!!

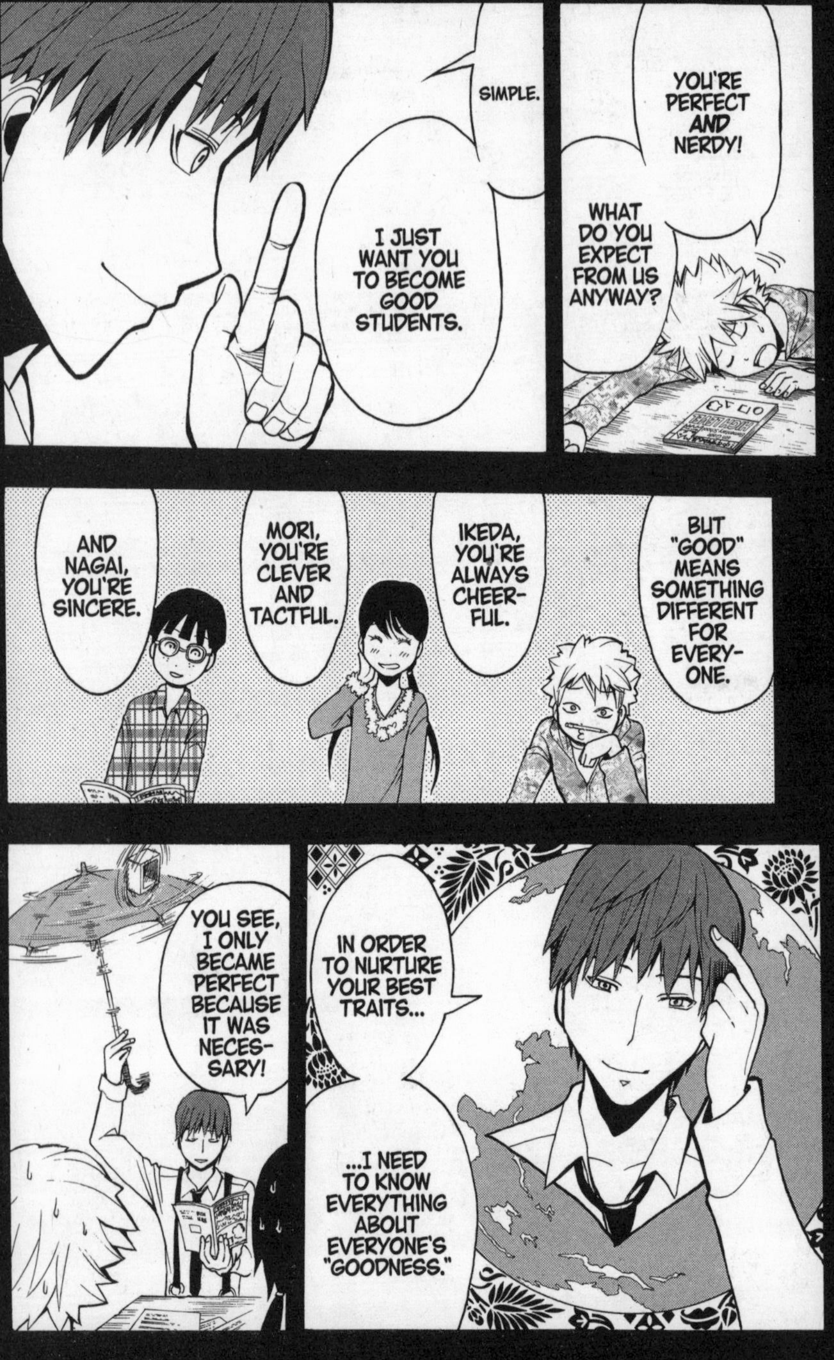
YOU'RE PERFECT AND NERDY!
WHAT DO YOU EXPECT FROM US ANYWAY?
SIMPLE.
I JUST WANT YOU TO BECOME GOOD STUDENTS.
BUT "GOOD" MEANS SOMETHING DIFFERENT FOR EVERY-ONE.
IKEDA, YOU'RE ALWAYS CHEER-FUL.
MORI, YOU'RE CLEVER AND TACTFUL.
AND NAGAI, YOU'RE SINCERE.
IN ORDER TO NURTURE YOUR BEST TRAITS...
...I NEED TO KNOW EVERYTHING ABOUT EVERYONE'S "GOODNESS."
YOU SEE, I ONLY BECAME PERFECT BECAUSE IT WAS NECES-SARY!

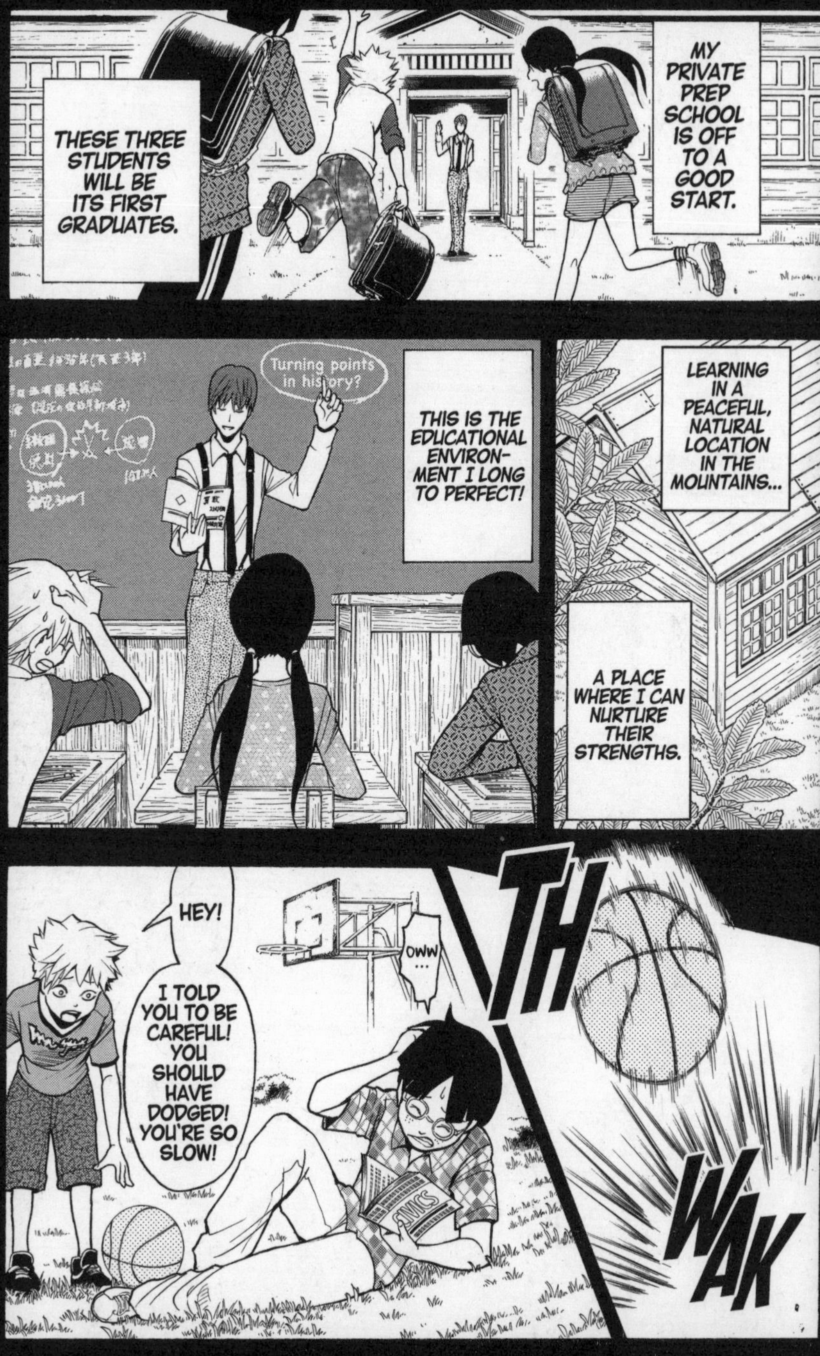
MY PRIVATE PREP SCHOOL IS OFF TO A GOOD START.
THESE THREE STUDENTS WILL BE ITS FIRST GRADUATES.
LEARNING IN A PEACEFUL, NATURAL LOCATION IN THE MOUNTAINS...
A PLACE WHERE I CAN NURTURE THEIR STRENGTHS.
THIS IS THE EDUCATIONAL ENVIRONMENT I LONG TO PERFECT!
Turning points in history?
THWAK
OWW...
HEY!
I TOLD YOU TO BE CAREFUL! YOU SHOULD HAVE DODGED! YOU'RE SO SLOW!
CIVICS

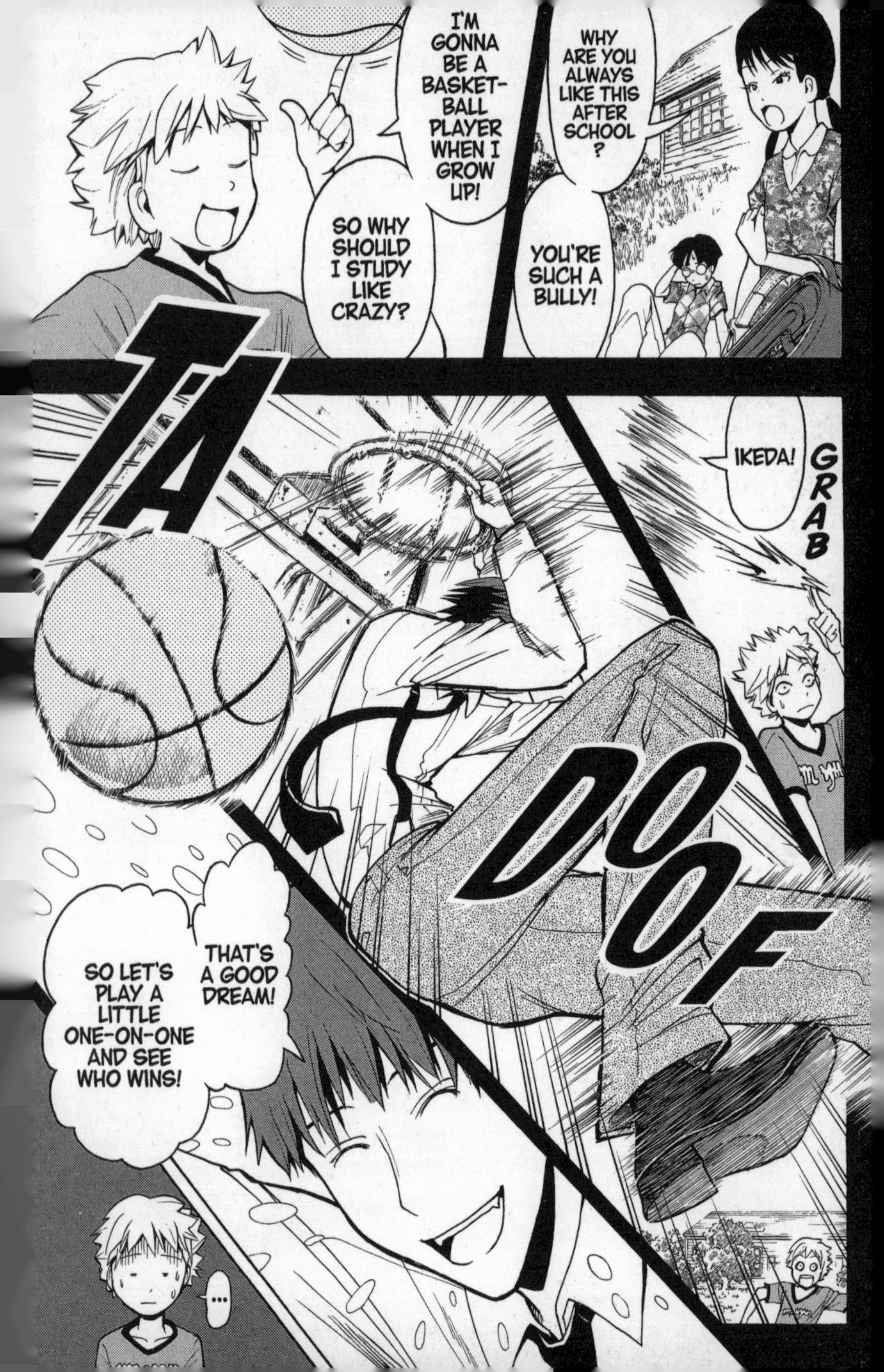
WHY ARE YOU ALWAYS LIKE THIS AFTER SCHOOL?
YOU'RE SUCH A BULLY!
I'M GONNA BE A BASKETBALL PLAYER WHEN I GROW UP!
SO WHY SHOULD I STUDY LIKE CRAZY?
IKEDA!
GRAB
TA
DOOF
THAT'S A GOOD DREAM!
SO LET'S PLAY A LITTLE ONE-ON-ONE AND SEE WHO WINS!
...

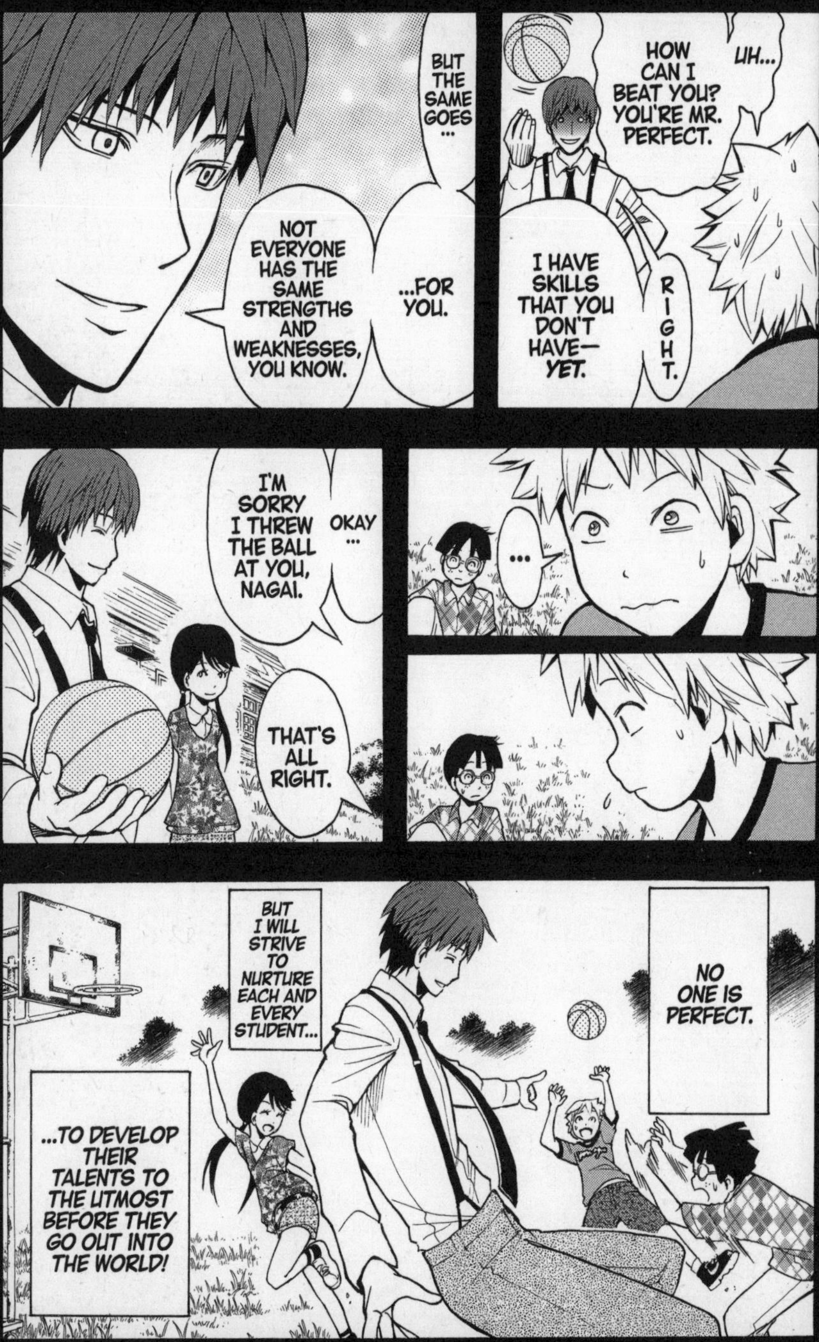
UH...
HOW CAN I BEAT YOU? YOU'RE MR. PERFECT.
I HAVE SKILLS THAT YOU DON'T HAVE—*YET.*
RIGHT.
BUT THE SAME GOES...
...FOR YOU.
NOT EVERYONE HAS THE SAME STRENGTHS AND WEAKNESSES, YOU KNOW.
...
I'M SORRY I THREW THE BALL AT YOU, NAGAI.
OKAY...
THAT'S ALL RIGHT.
NO ONE IS PERFECT.
BUT I WILL STRIVE TO NURTURE EACH AND EVERY STUDENT...
...TO DEVELOP THEIR TALENTS TO THE UTMOST BEFORE THEY GO OUT INTO THE WORLD!

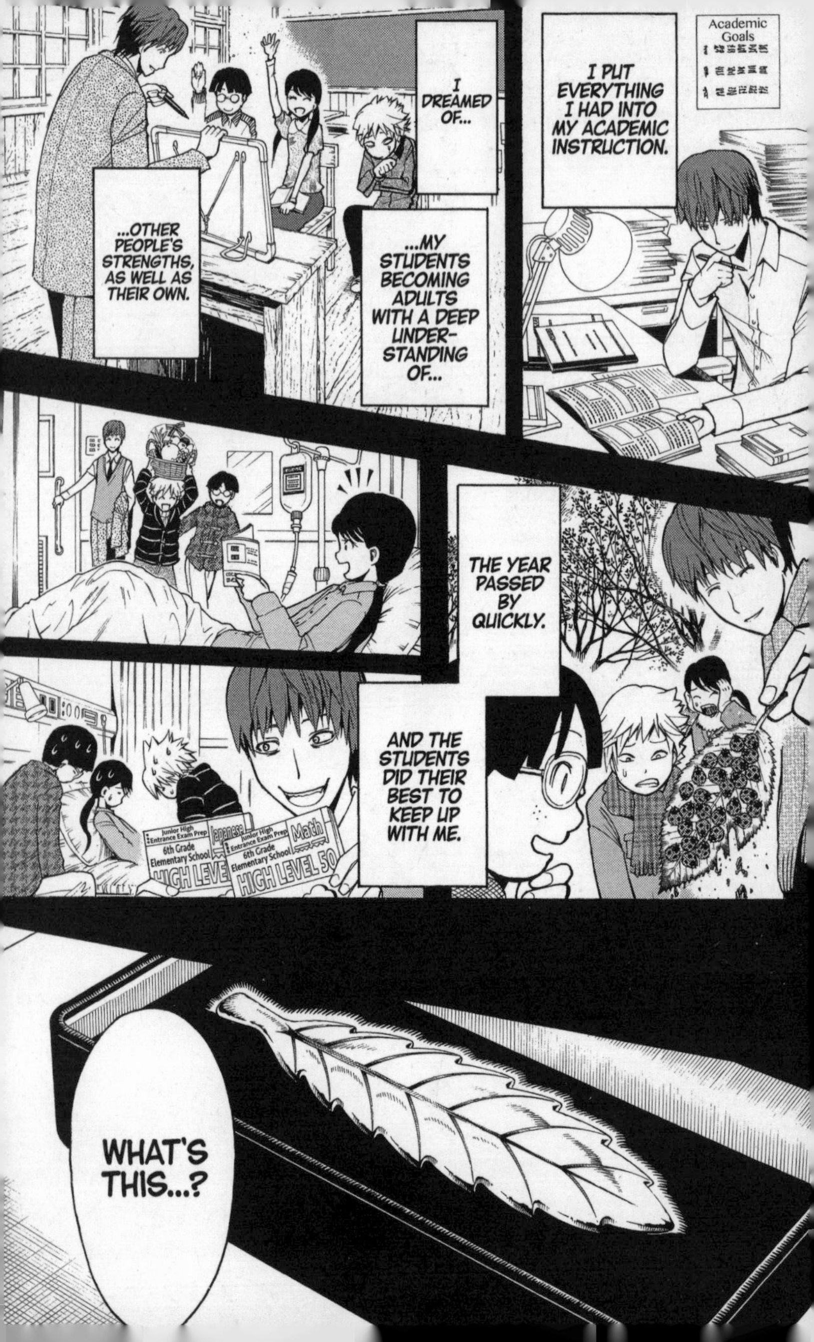
Academic Goals
I PUT EVERYTHING I HAD INTO MY ACADEMIC INSTRUCTION.
I DREAMED OF...
...MY STUDENTS BECOMING ADULTS WITH A DEEP UNDER-STANDING OF...
...OTHER PEOPLE'S STRENGTHS, AS WELL AS THEIR OWN.
THE YEAR PASSED BY QUICKLY.
AND THE STUDENTS DID THEIR BEST TO KEEP UP WITH ME.
Junior High Entrance Exam Prep Math 6th Grade Elementary School HIGH LEVEL 50
Junior High Entrance Exam Prep Japanese 6th Grade Elementary School HIGH LEVE
WHAT'S THIS...?

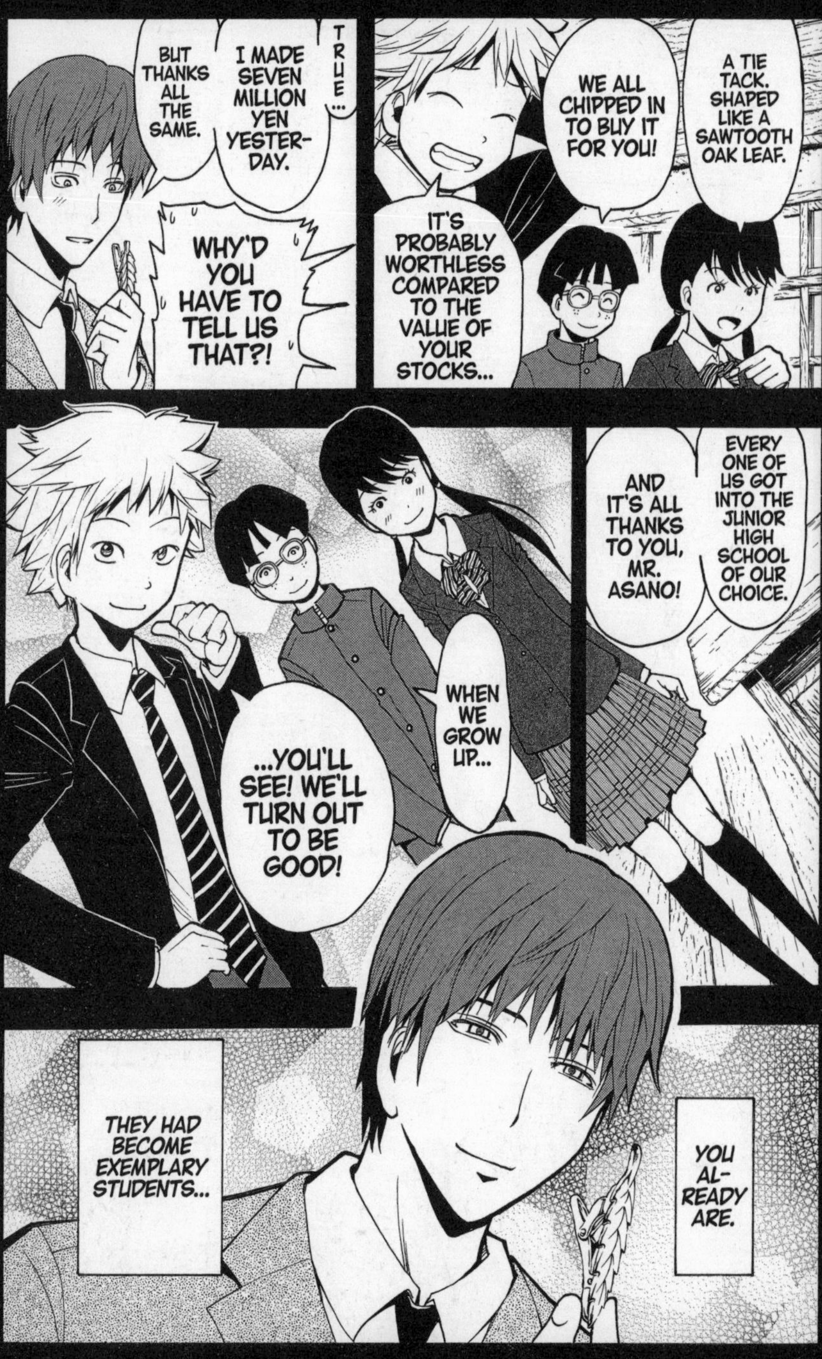
A TIE TACK. SHAPED LIKE A SAWTOOTH OAK LEAF.
WE ALL CHIPPED IN TO BUY IT FOR YOU!
IT'S PROBABLY WORTHLESS COMPARED TO THE VALUE OF YOUR STOCKS...
TRUE...
I MADE SEVEN MILLION YEN YESTERDAY.
BUT THANKS ALL THE SAME.
WHY'D YOU HAVE TO TELL US THAT?!
EVERY ONE OF US GOT INTO THE JUNIOR HIGH SCHOOL OF OUR CHOICE.
AND IT'S ALL THANKS TO YOU, MR. ASANO!
WHEN WE GROW UP...
...YOU'LL SEE! WE'LL TURN OUT TO BE GOOD!
YOU ALREADY ARE.
THEY HAD BECOME EXEMPLARY STUDENTS...

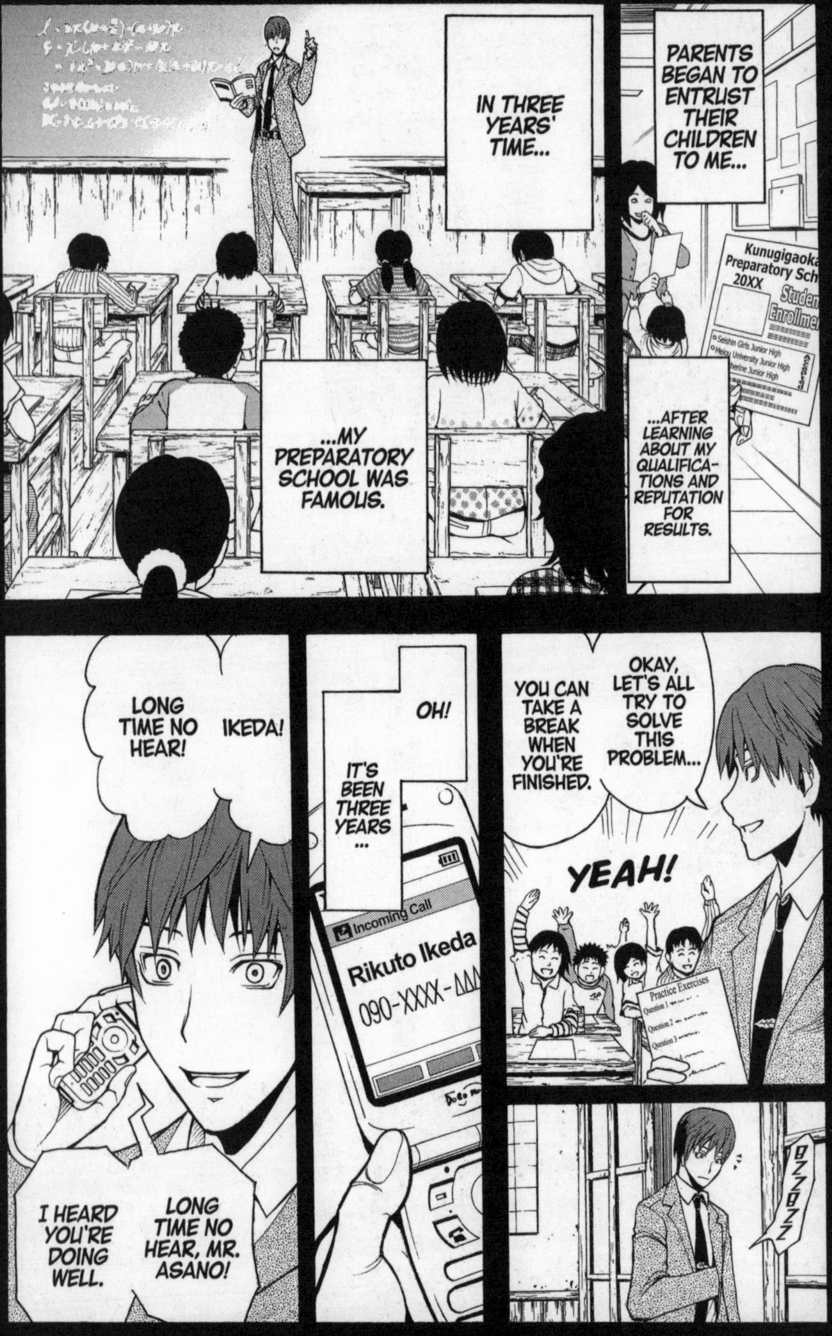
PARENTS BEGAN TO ENTRUST THEIR CHILDREN TO ME...
...AFTER LEARNING ABOUT MY QUALIFICA-TIONS AND REPUTATION FOR RESULTS.
Kunugigaoka Preparatory Sch
20XX
Studen
Enrollme
Seishin Girls Junior High
Meiou University Junior High
therine Junior High
IN THREE YEARS' TIME...
...MY PREPARATORY SCHOOL WAS FAMOUS.
OKAY, LET'S ALL TRY TO SOLVE THIS PROBLEM...
YOU CAN TAKE A BREAK WHEN YOU'RE FINISHED.
YEAH!
Practice Exercises
Question 1
Question 2
Question 3
BZZBZZ
OH!
IT'S BEEN THREE YEARS...
Incoming Call
Rikuto Ikeda
090-XXXX-ΔΔΔ
IKEDA!
LONG TIME NO HEAR!
LONG TIME NO HEAR, MR. ASANO!
I HEARD YOU'RE DOING WELL.

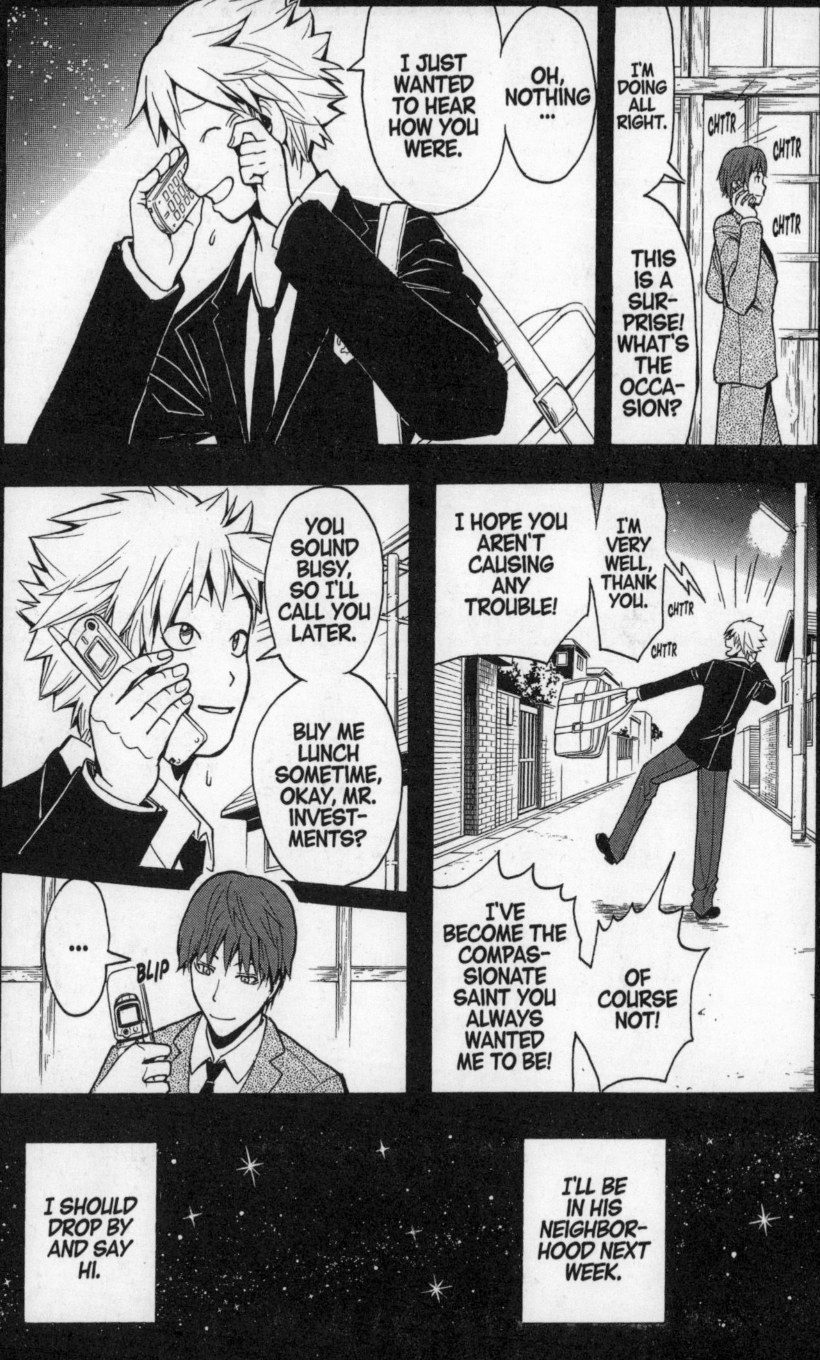
I'M DOING ALL RIGHT.
CHTTR
CHTTR
CHTTR
THIS IS A SURPRISE! WHAT'S THE OCCASION?
OH, NOTHING...
I JUST WANTED TO HEAR HOW YOU WERE.
I'M VERY WELL, THANK YOU.
I HOPE YOU AREN'T CAUSING ANY TROUBLE!
CHTTR
CHTTR
OF COURSE NOT!
I'VE BECOME THE COMPASSIONATE SAINT YOU ALWAYS WANTED ME TO BE!
YOU SOUND BUSY, SO I'LL CALL YOU LATER.
BUY ME LUNCH SOMETIME, OKAY, MR. INVESTMENTS?
...
BLIP
I'LL BE IN HIS NEIGHBORHOOD NEXT WEEK.
I SHOULD DROP BY AND SAY HI.

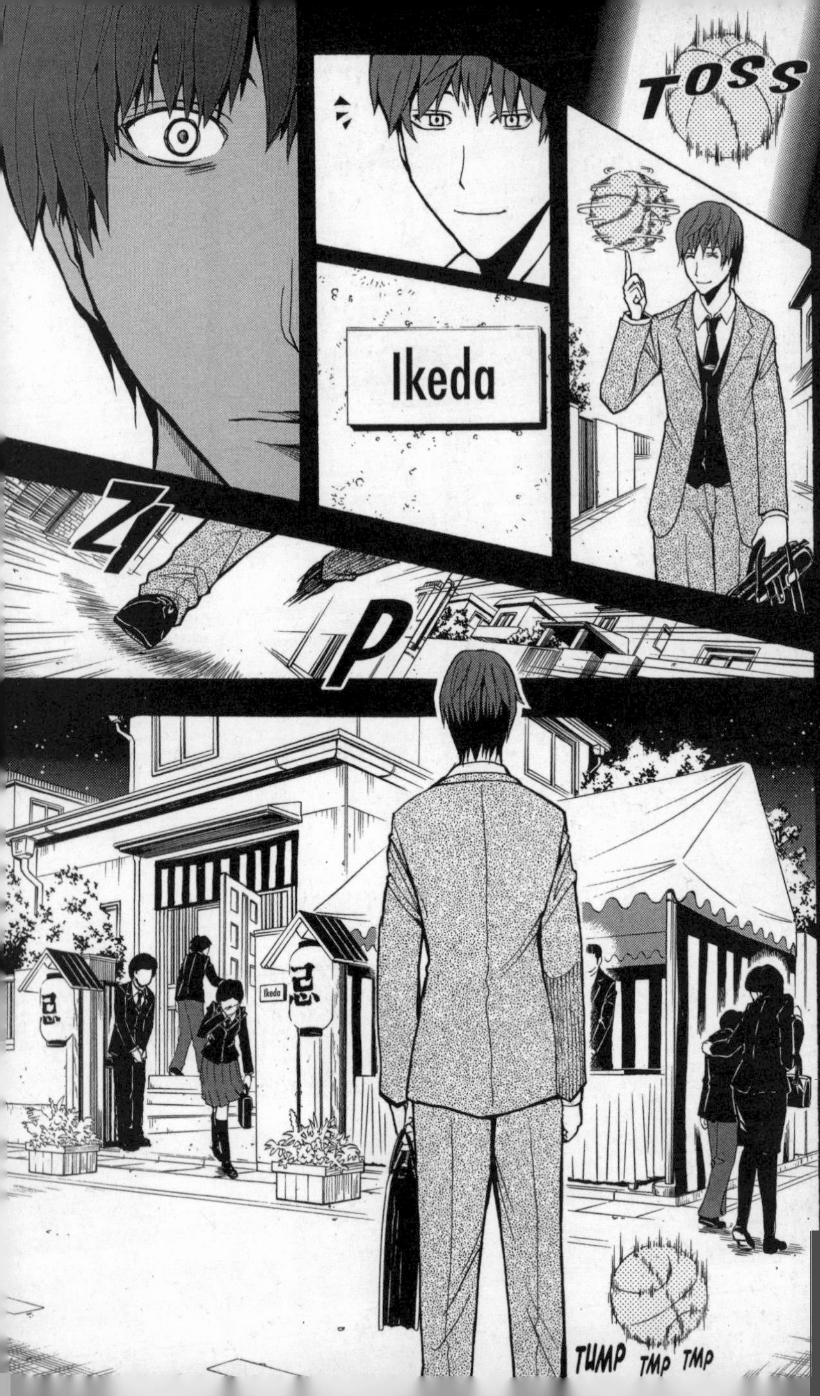

TOSS
Ikeda
ZI
P
Ikeda
TUMP TMP TMP

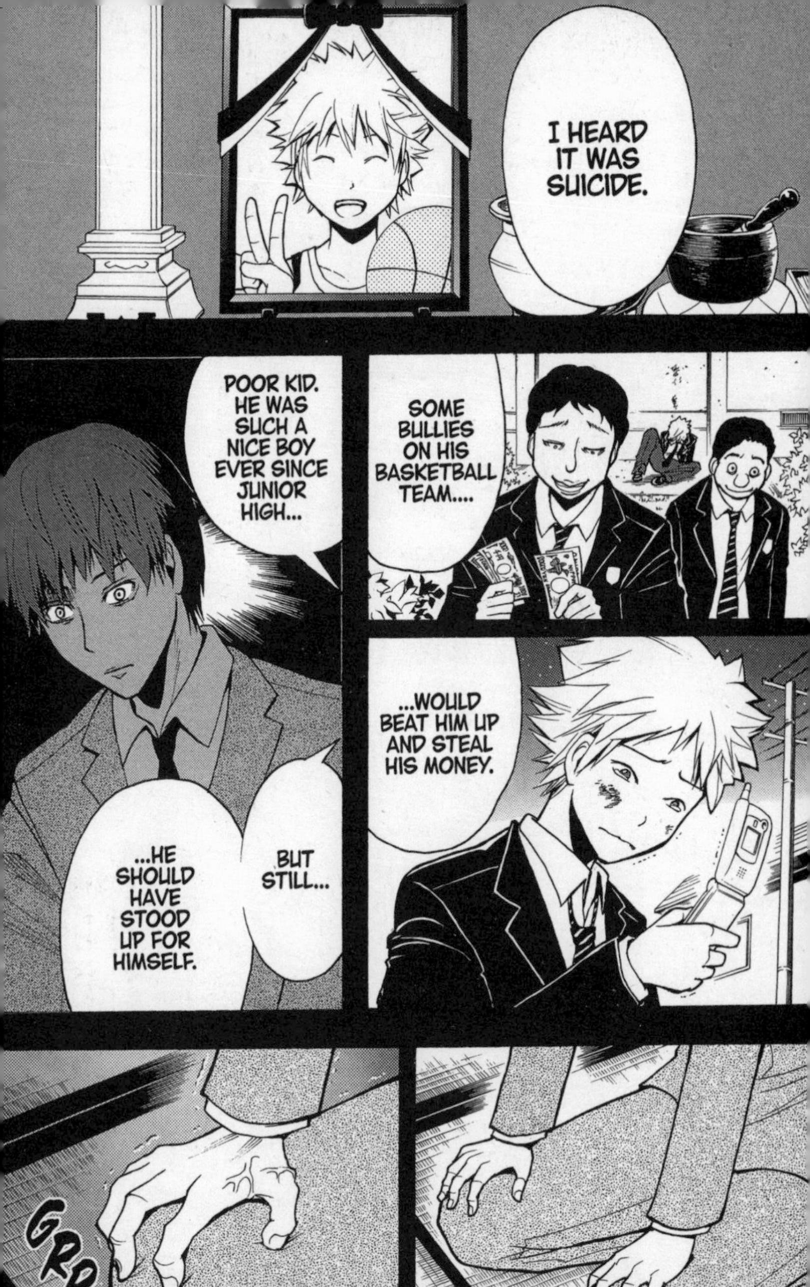
I HEARD IT WAS SUICIDE.
SOME BULLIES ON HIS BASKETBALL TEAM....
...WOULD BEAT HIM UP AND STEAL HIS MONEY.
POOR KID. HE WAS SUCH A NICE BOY EVER SINCE JUNIOR HIGH...
BUT STILL...
...HE SHOULD HAVE STOOD UP FOR HIMSELF.
GRP

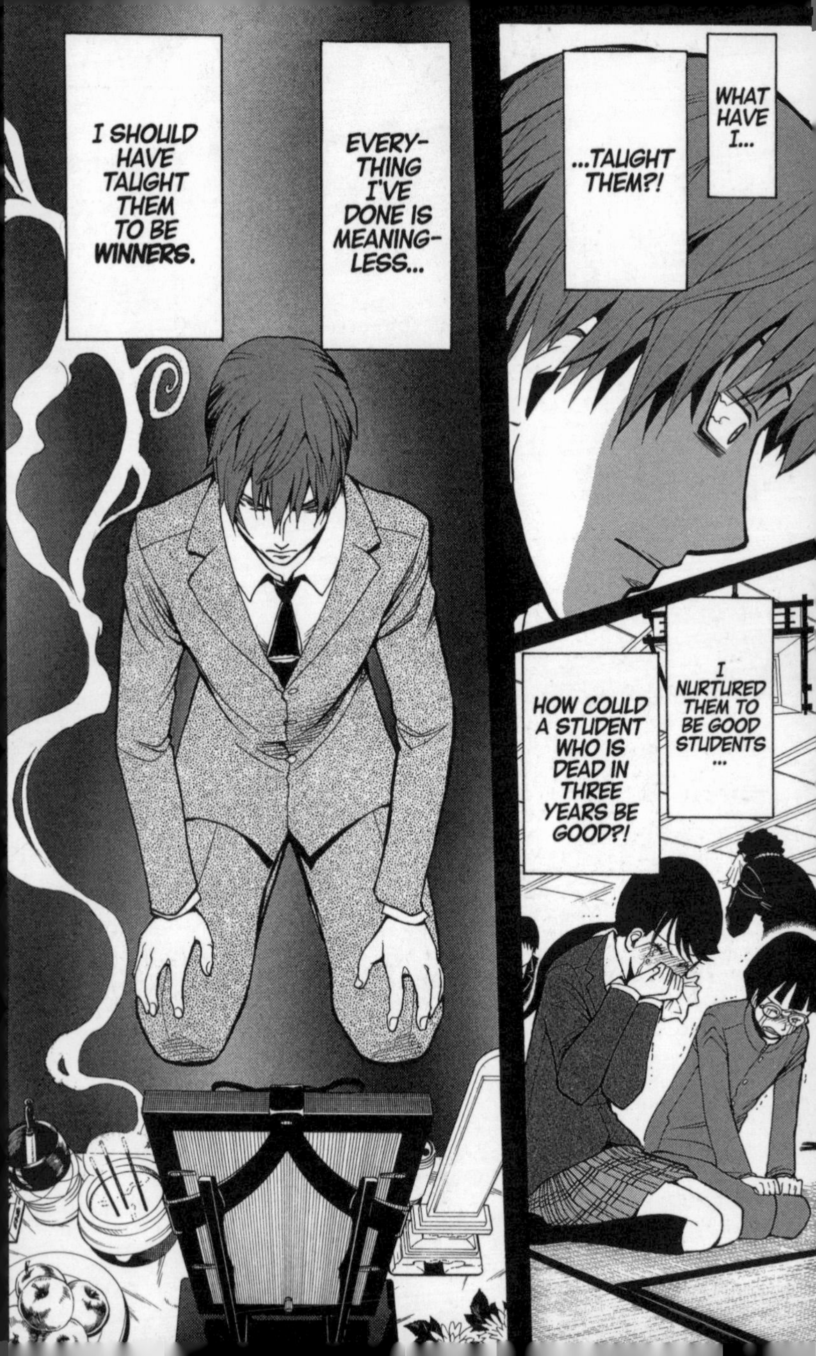
WHAT HAVE I...
...TAUGHT THEM?!
I NURTURED THEM TO BE GOOD STUDENTS...
HOW COULD A STUDENT WHO IS DEAD IN THREE YEARS BE GOOD?!
EVERYTHING I'VE DONE IS MEANINGLESS...
I SHOULD HAVE TAUGHT THEM TO BE WINNERS.

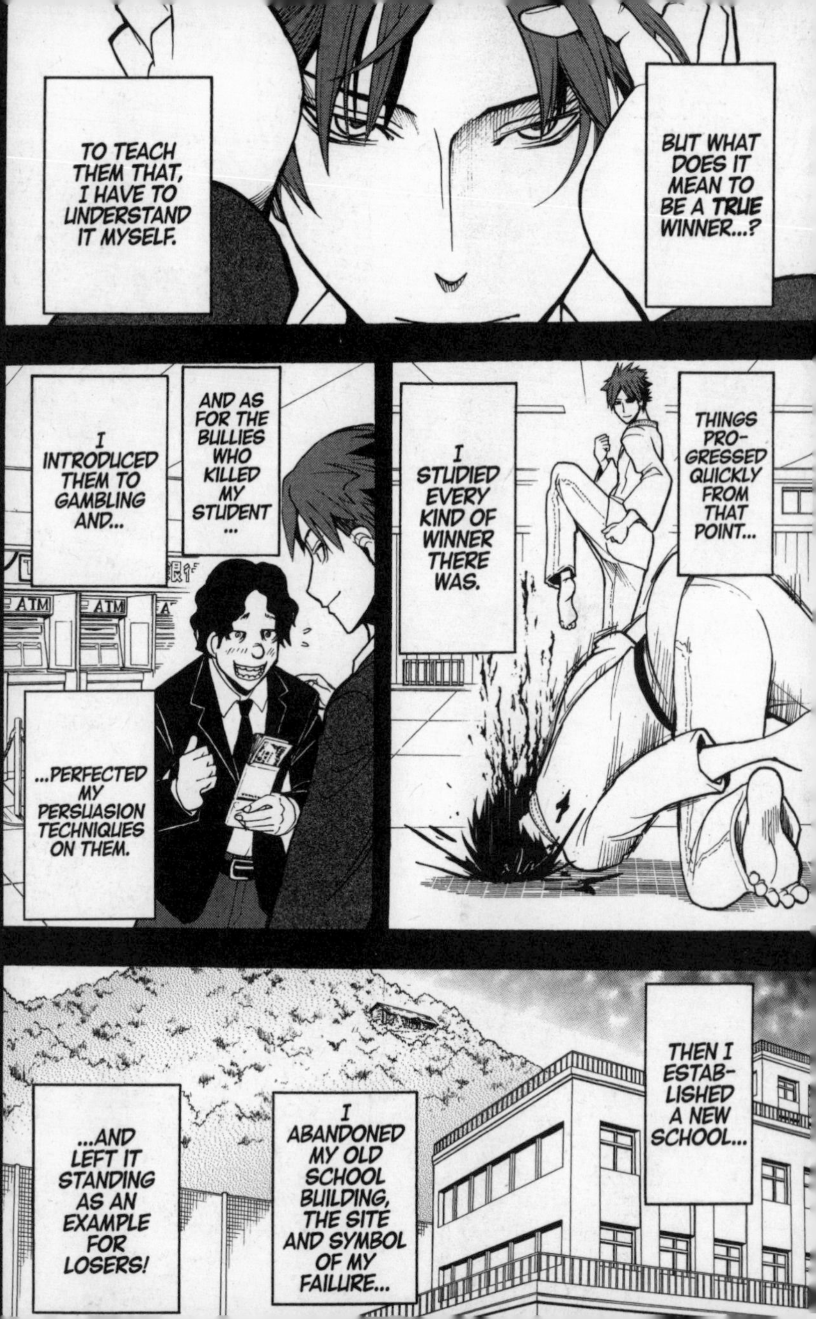
BUT WHAT DOES IT MEAN TO BE A **TRUE** WINNER...?
TO TEACH THEM THAT, I HAVE TO UNDERSTAND IT MYSELF.
THINGS PRO-GRESSED QUICKLY FROM THAT POINT...
I STUDIED EVERY KIND OF WINNER THERE WAS.
AND AS FOR THE BULLIES WHO KILLED MY STUDENT...
I INTRODUCED THEM TO GAMBLING AND...
ATM
ATM
...PERFECTED MY PERSUASION TECHNIQUES ON THEM.
THEN I ESTAB-LISHED A NEW SCHOOL...
I ABANDONED MY OLD SCHOOL BUILDING, THE SITE AND SYMBOL OF MY FAILURE...
...AND LEFT IT STANDING AS AN EXAMPLE FOR LOSERS!

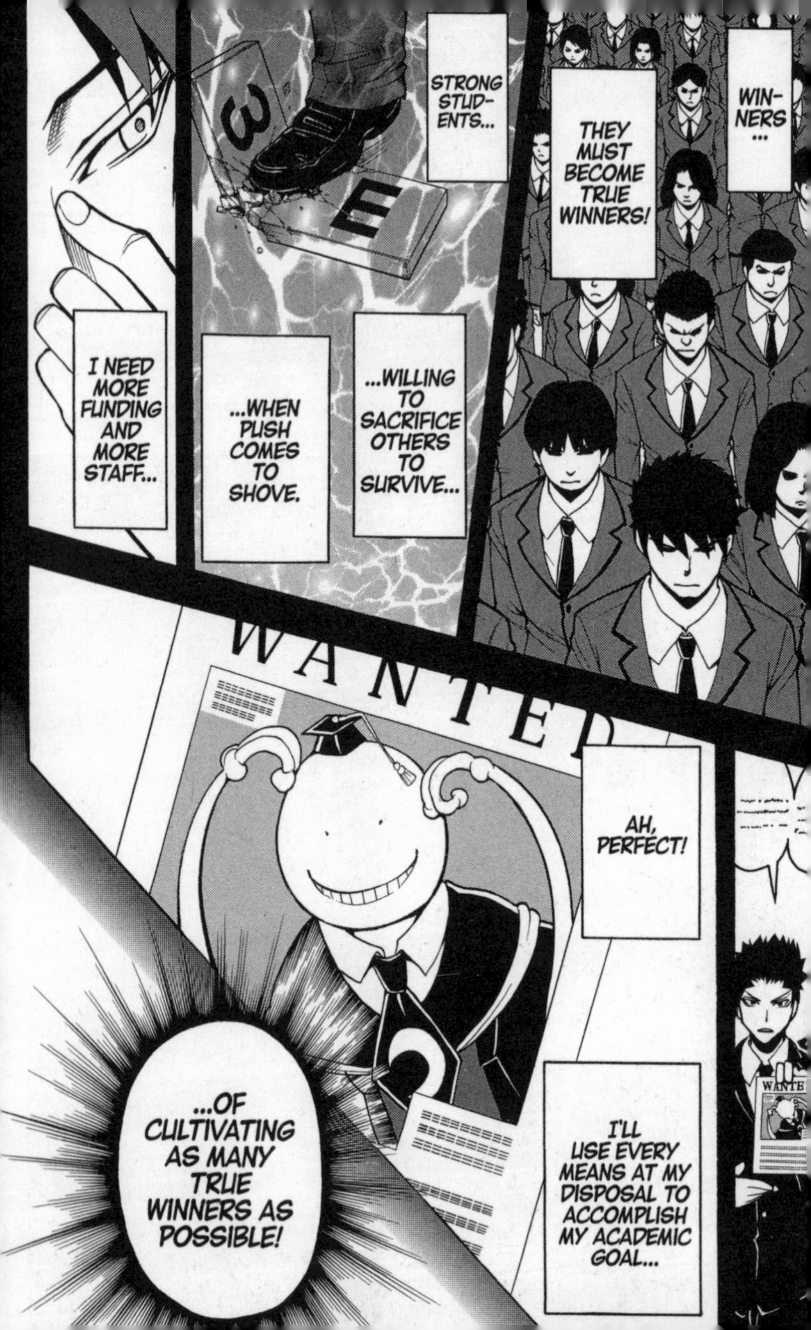
WIN-NERS...
THEY MUST BECOME TRUE WINNERS!
STRONG STUD-ENTS...
...WILLING TO SACRIFICE OTHERS TO SURVIVE...
...WHEN PUSH COMES TO SHOVE.
I NEED MORE FUNDING AND MORE STAFF...
AH, PERFECT!
WANTED
I'LL USE EVERY MEANS AT MY DISPOSAL TO ACCOMPLISH MY ACADEMIC GOAL...
...OF CULTIVATING AS MANY TRUE WINNERS AS POSSIBLE!

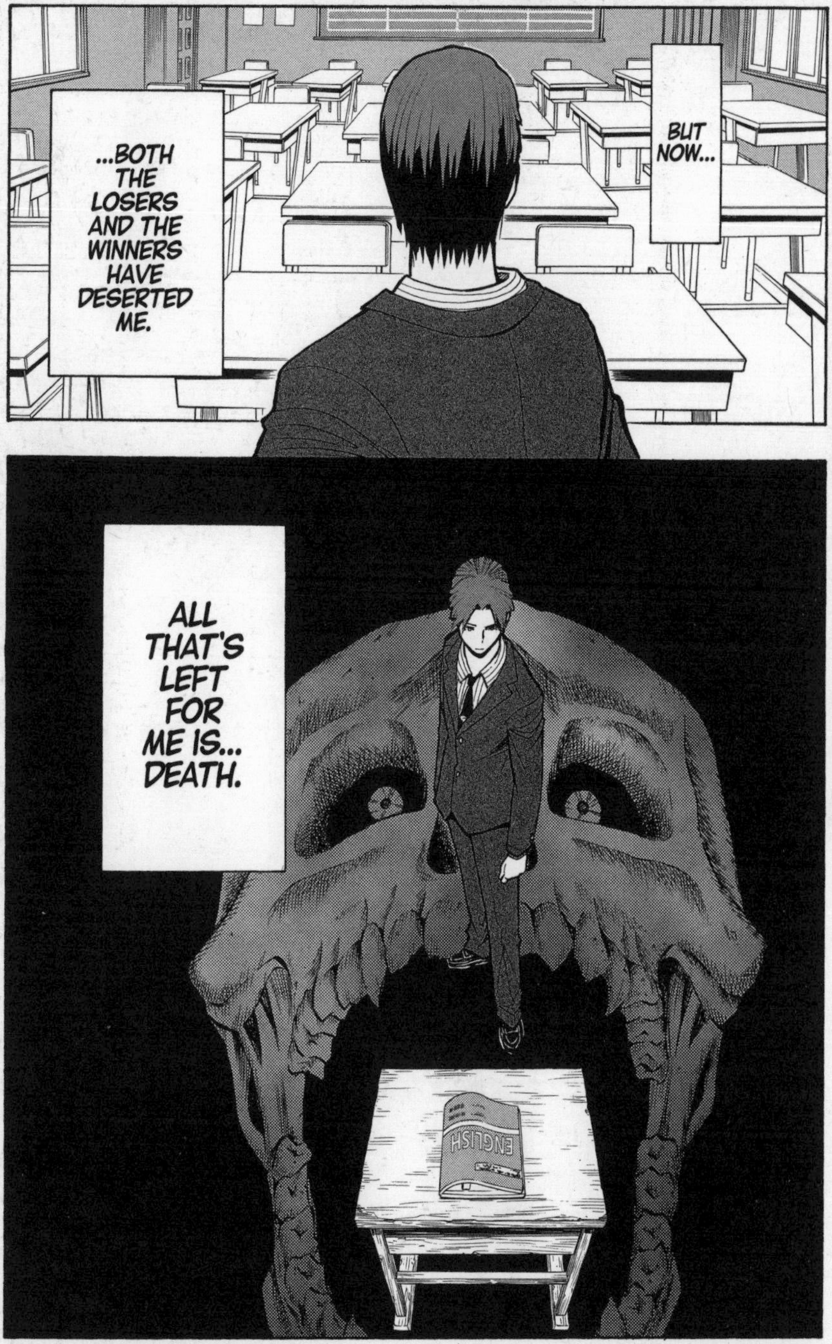
BUT NOW...
...BOTH THE LOSERS AND THE WINNERS HAVE DESERTED ME.
ALL THAT'S LEFT FOR ME IS... DEATH.

E-28 ITONA HORIBE

- BIRTHDAY: MARCH 31
- HEIGHT: 5' 3"
- WEIGHT: 117 LBS.
- FAVORITE SUBJECT: SCIENCE
- LEAST FAVORITE SUBJECT: CIVICS
- HOBBY/SKILLS: MECHANICAL ENGINEERING
- FUTURE GOAL: TO GET HIS PARENTS' FACTORY BACK
- MOST HIGH-TECH MACHINE OF HIS ITONA SERIES IS: ITONA VIII (FULLY AUTOMATIC STEALTH DRONE)
- HIS PRIZE POSSESSION: ITONA I (SCRAP)

Class 126 Time to Let Live

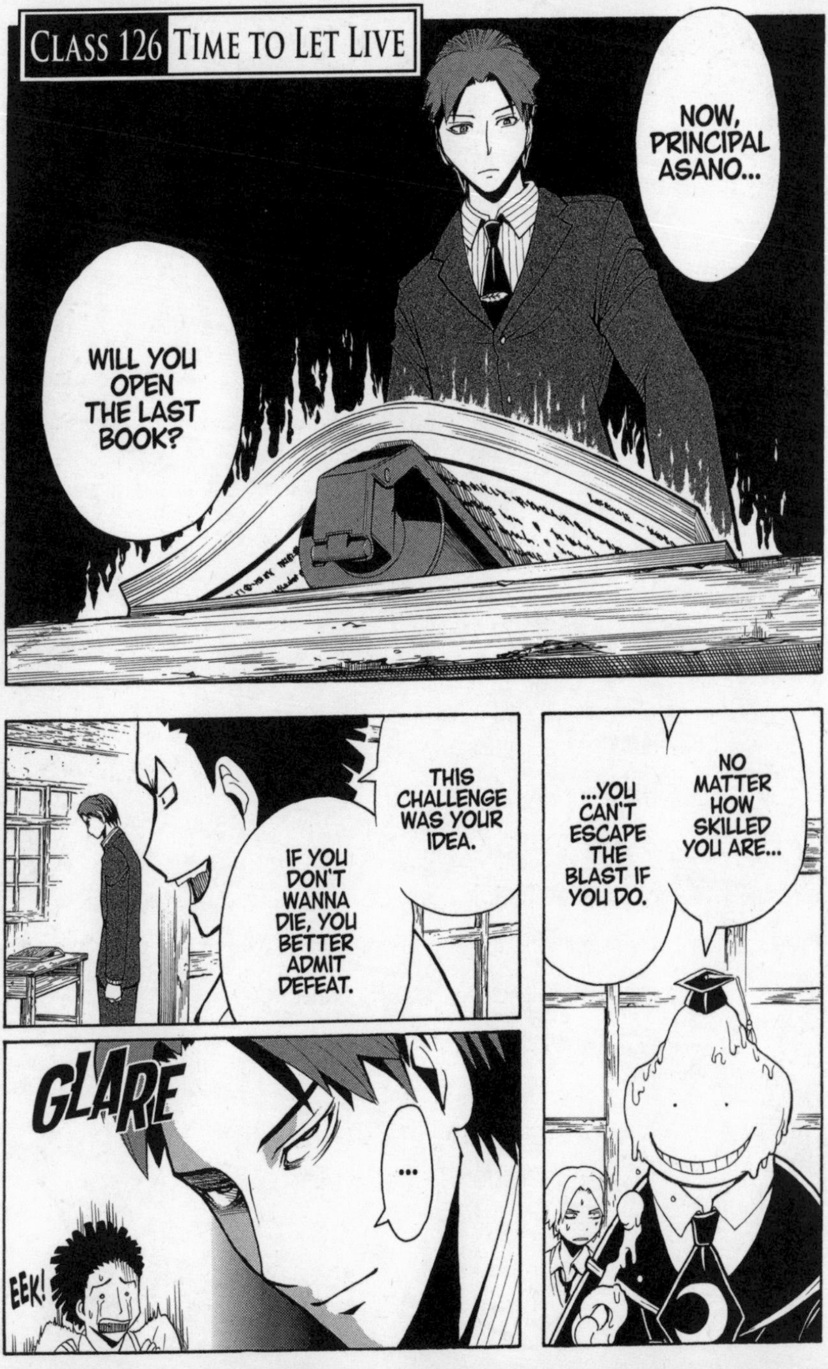
NOW, PRINCIPAL ASANO...
WILL YOU OPEN THE LAST BOOK?
NO MATTER HOW SKILLED YOU ARE...
...YOU CAN'T ESCAPE THE BLAST IF YOU DO.
THIS CHALLENGE WAS YOUR IDEA.
IF YOU DON'T WANNA DIE, YOU BETTER ADMIT DEFEAT.
GLARE
...
EEK!

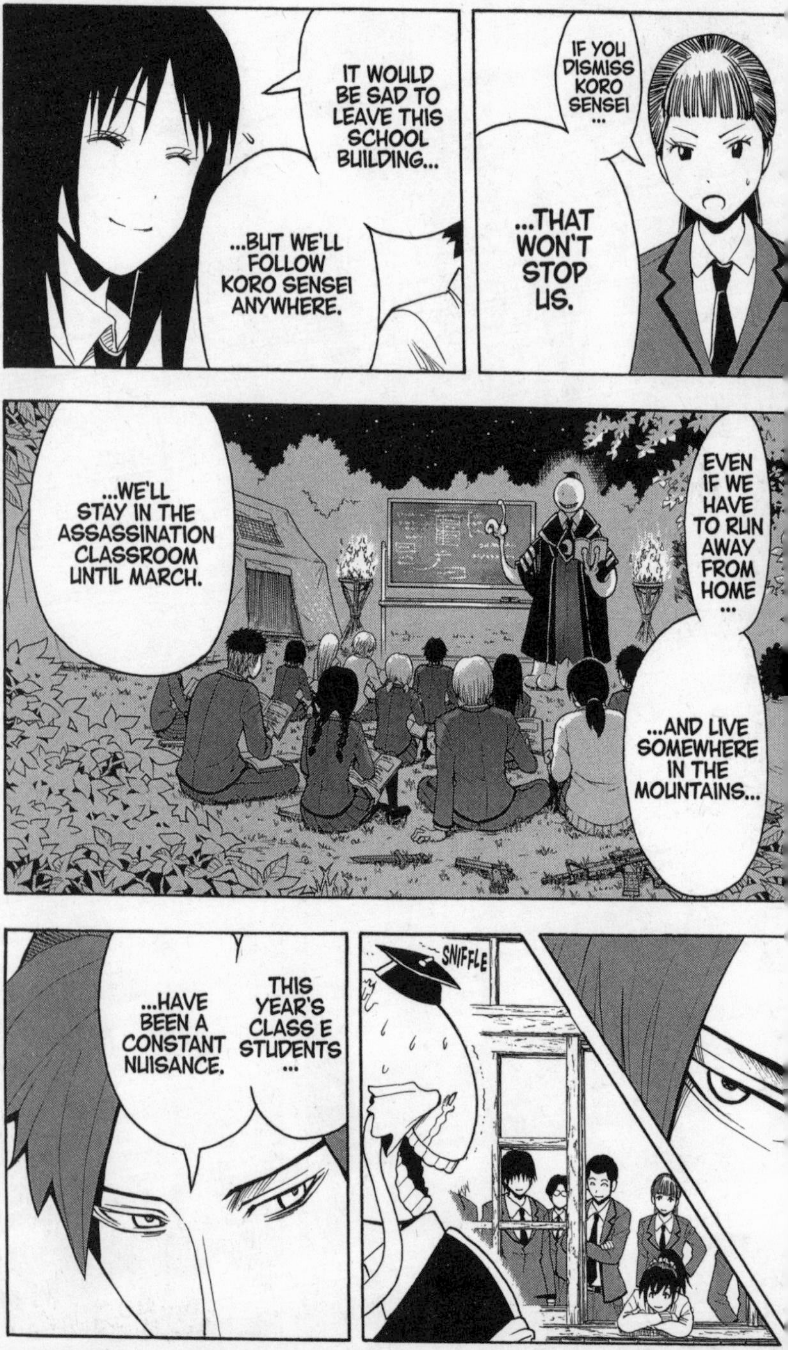
IF YOU DISMISS KORO SENSEI ...
...THAT WON'T STOP US.
IT WOULD BE SAD TO LEAVE THIS SCHOOL BUILDING...
...BUT WE'LL FOLLOW KORO SENSEI ANYWHERE.
EVEN IF WE HAVE TO RUN AWAY FROM HOME ...
...AND LIVE SOMEWHERE IN THE MOUNTAINS...
...WE'LL STAY IN THE ASSASSINATION CLASSROOM UNTIL MARCH.
SNIFFLE
THIS YEAR'S CLASS E STUDENTS ...
...HAVE BEEN A CONSTANT NUISANCE.

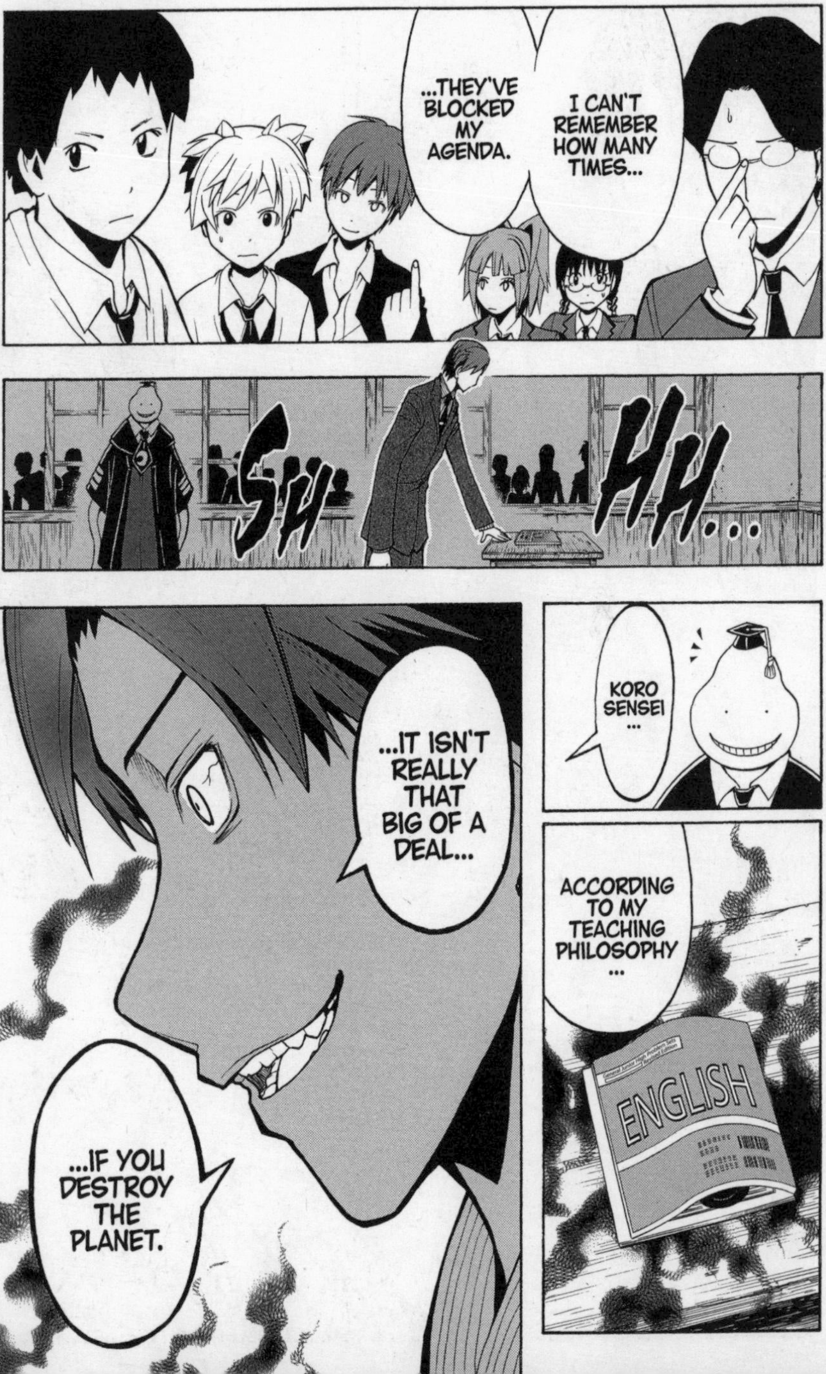
I CAN'T REMEMBER HOW MANY TIMES...
...THEY'VE BLOCKED MY AGENDA.
SH
HH...
KORO SENSEI ...
ACCORDING TO MY TEACHING PHILOSOPHY ...
ENGLISH
...IT ISN'T REALLY THAT BIG OF A DEAL...
...IF YOU DESTROY THE PLANET.

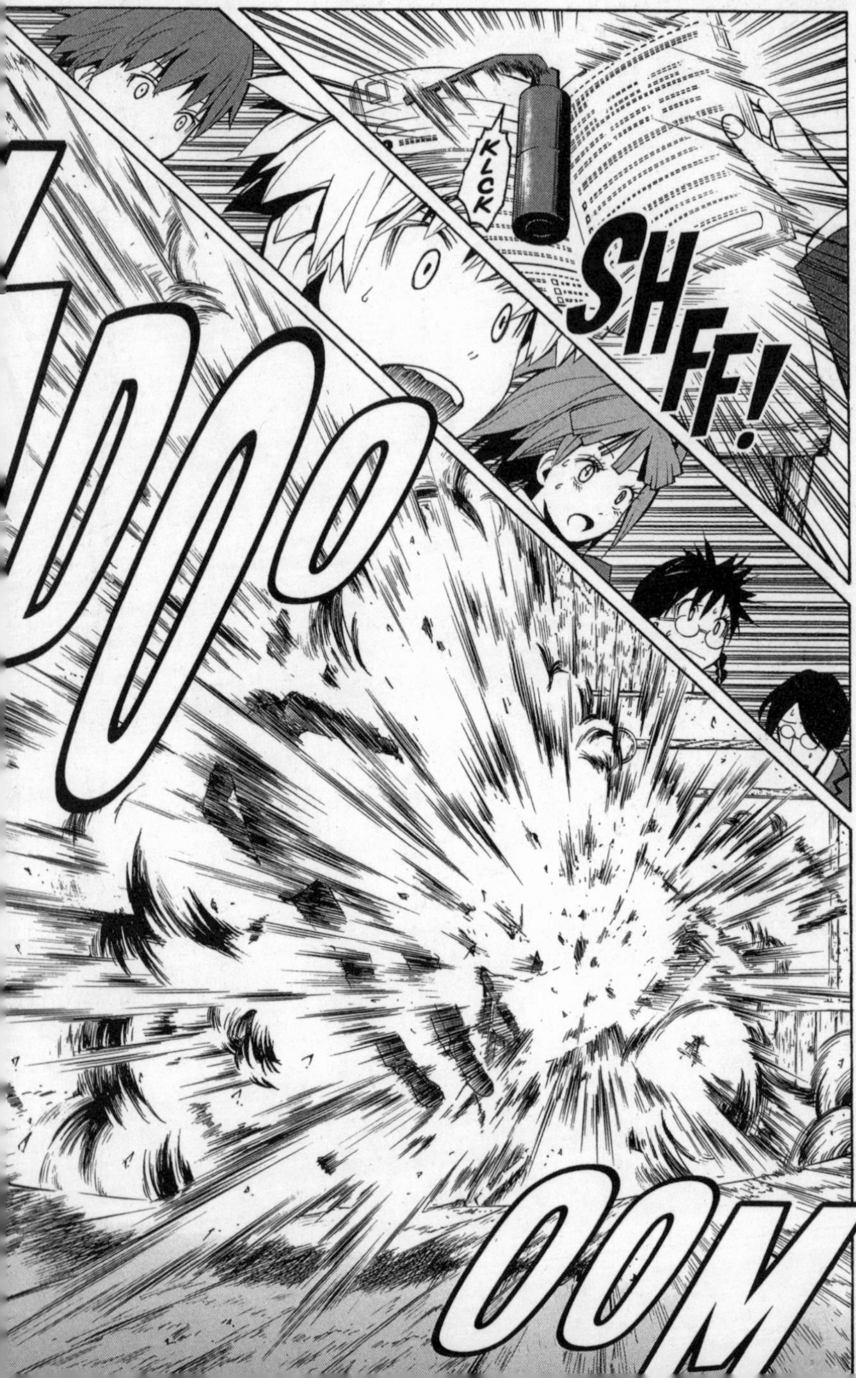
SHFF!
KLCK
OOM

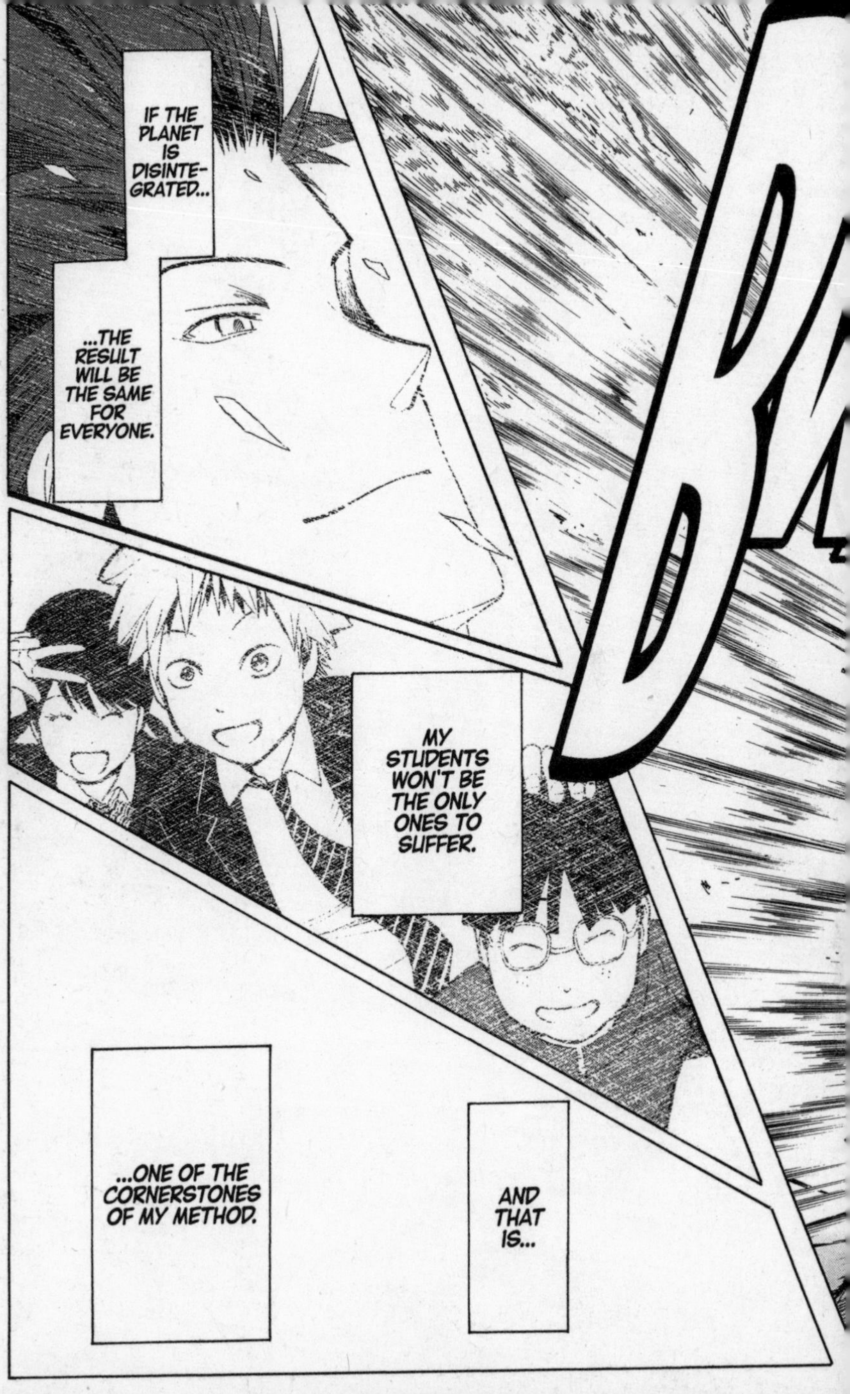
IF THE PLANET IS DISINTE-GRATED...
...THE RESULT WILL BE THE SAME FOR EVERYONE.
MY STUDENTS WON'T BE THE ONLY ONES TO SUFFER.
AND THAT IS...
...ONE OF THE CORNERSTONES OF MY METHOD.

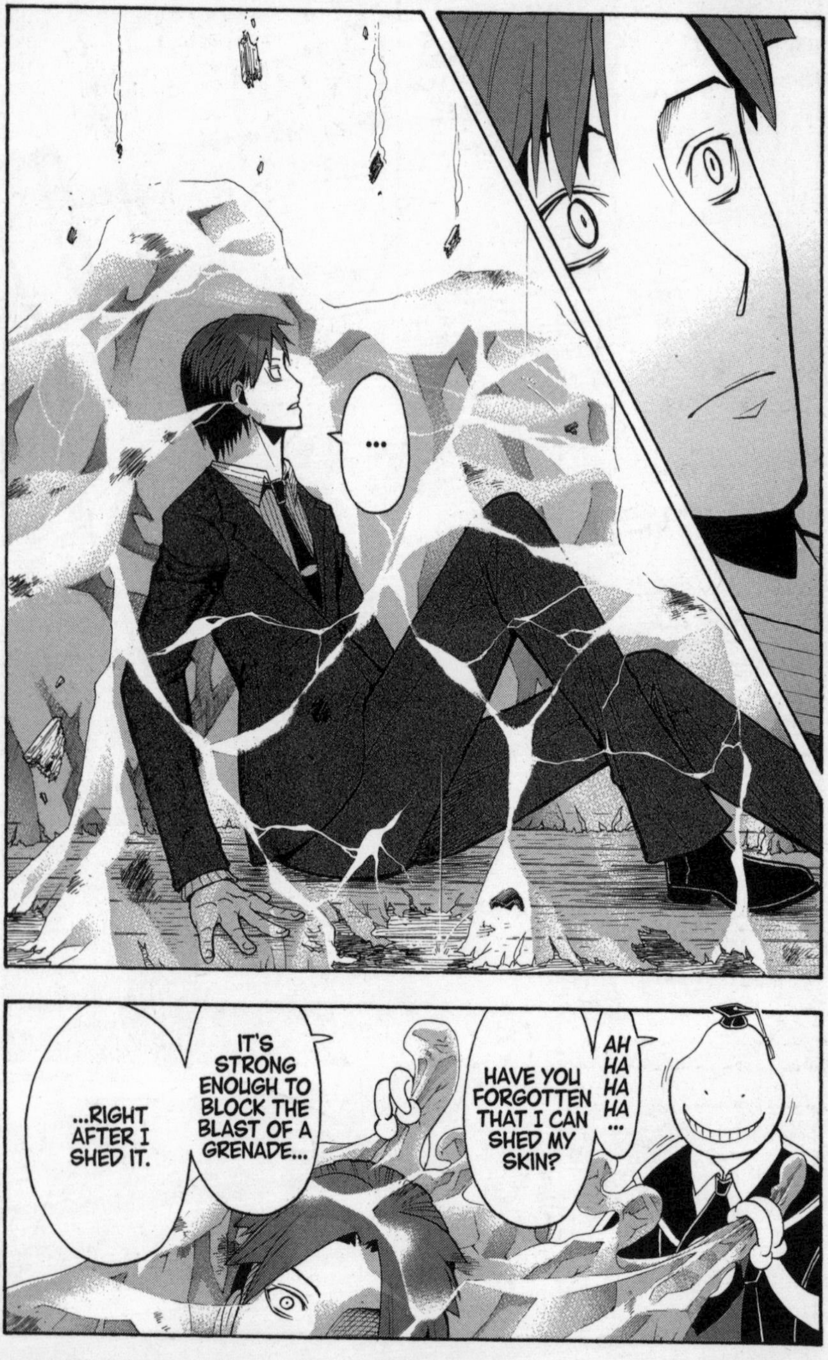
...
AH HA HA HA...
HAVE YOU FORGOTTEN THAT I CAN SHED MY SKIN?
IT'S STRONG ENOUGH TO BLOCK THE BLAST OF A GRENADE...
...RIGHT AFTER I SHED IT.

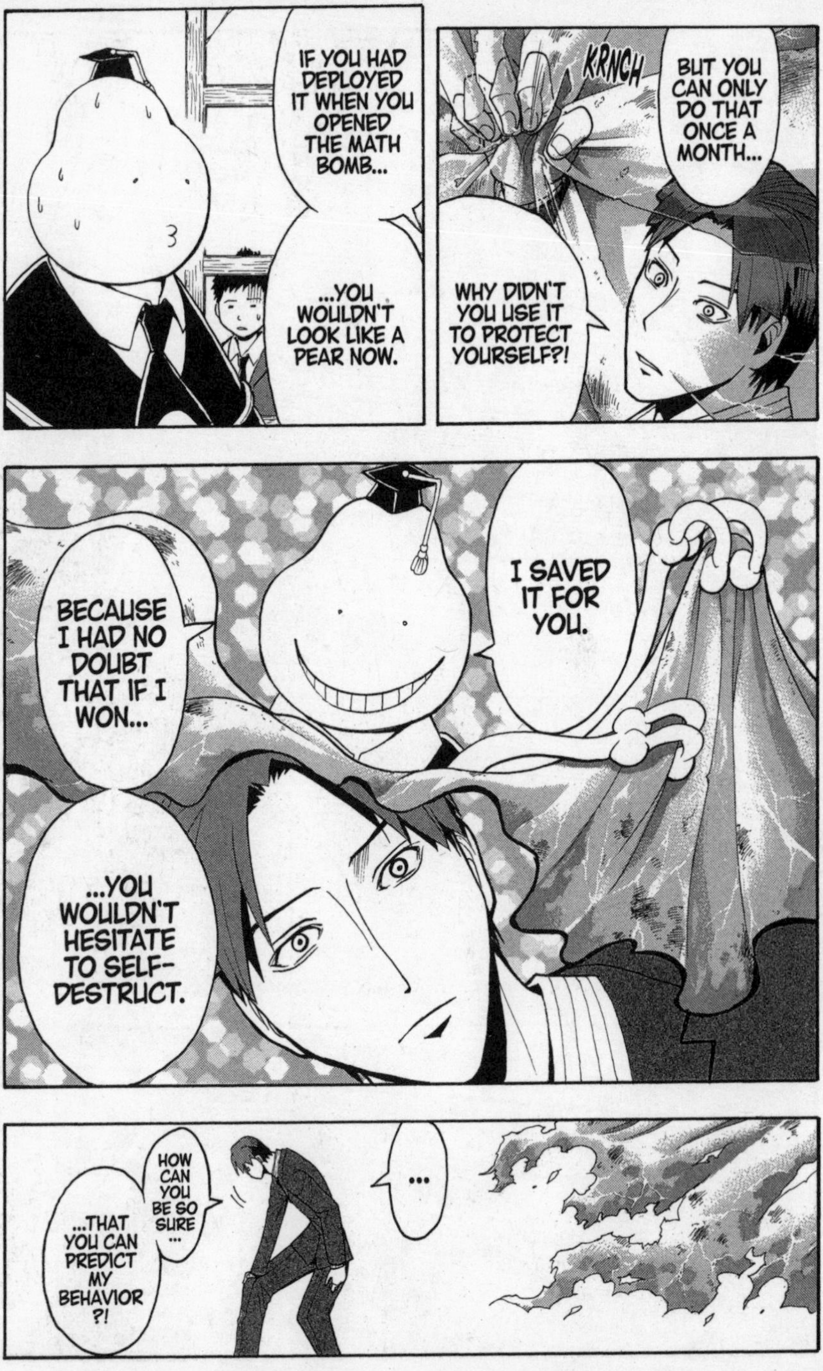
KRNCH
BUT YOU CAN ONLY DO THAT ONCE A MONTH...
WHY DIDN'T YOU USE IT TO PROTECT YOURSELF?!
IF YOU HAD DEPLOYED IT WHEN YOU OPENED THE MATH BOMB...
...YOU WOULDN'T LOOK LIKE A PEAR NOW.
I SAVED IT FOR YOU.
BECAUSE I HAD NO DOUBT THAT IF I WON...
...YOU WOULDN'T HESITATE TO SELF-DESTRUCT.
...
HOW CAN YOU BE SO SURE...
...THAT YOU CAN PREDICT MY BEHAVIOR?!

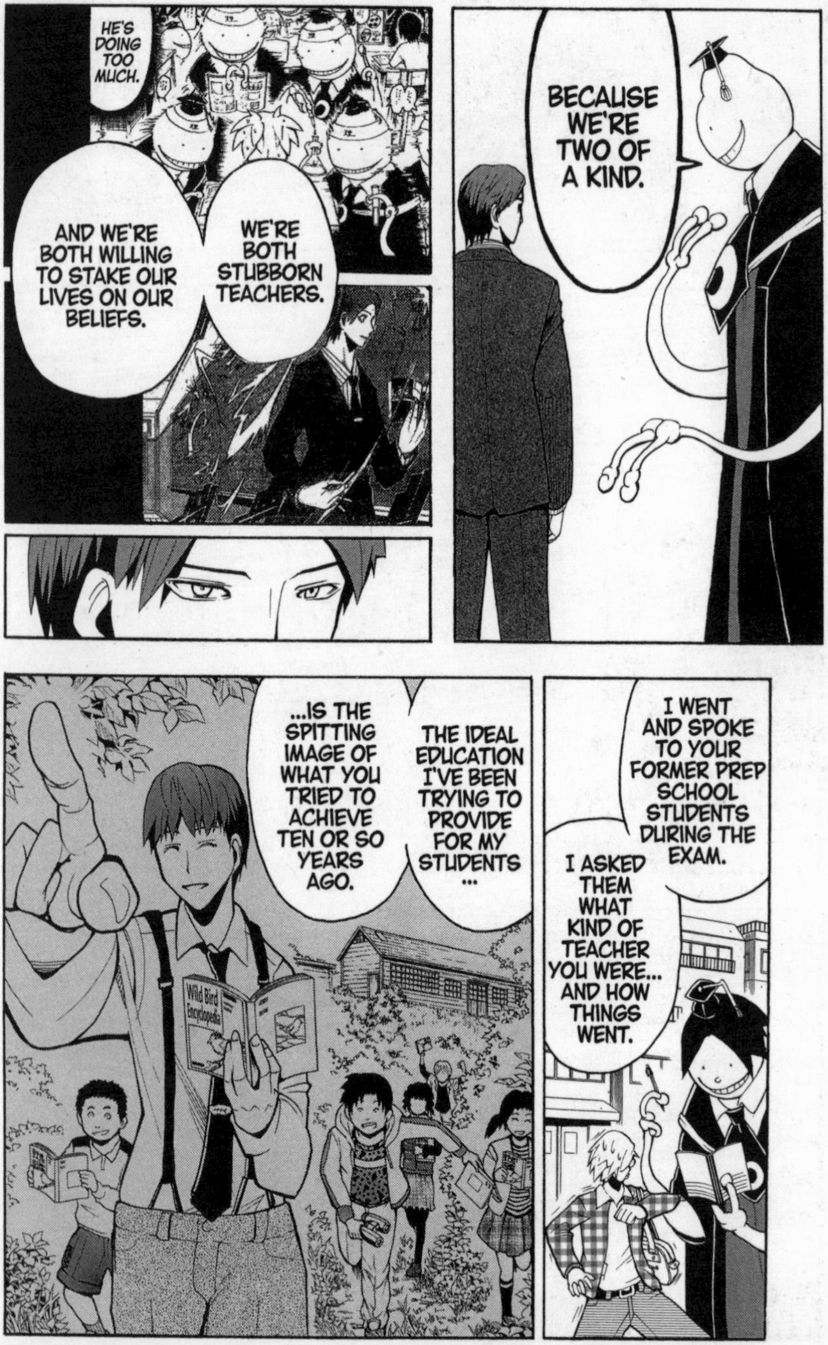
BECAUSE WE'RE TWO OF A KIND.
HE'S DOING TOO MUCH.
WE'RE BOTH STUBBORN TEACHERS.
AND WE'RE BOTH WILLING TO STAKE OUR LIVES ON OUR BELIEFS.
I WENT AND SPOKE TO YOUR FORMER PREP SCHOOL STUDENTS DURING THE EXAM.
I ASKED THEM WHAT KIND OF TEACHER YOU WERE... AND HOW THINGS WENT.
THE IDEAL EDUCATION I'VE BEEN TRYING TO PROVIDE FOR MY STUDENTS ...
...IS THE SPITTING IMAGE OF WHAT YOU TRIED TO ACHIEVE TEN OR SO YEARS AGO.
Wild Bird Encyclopedia

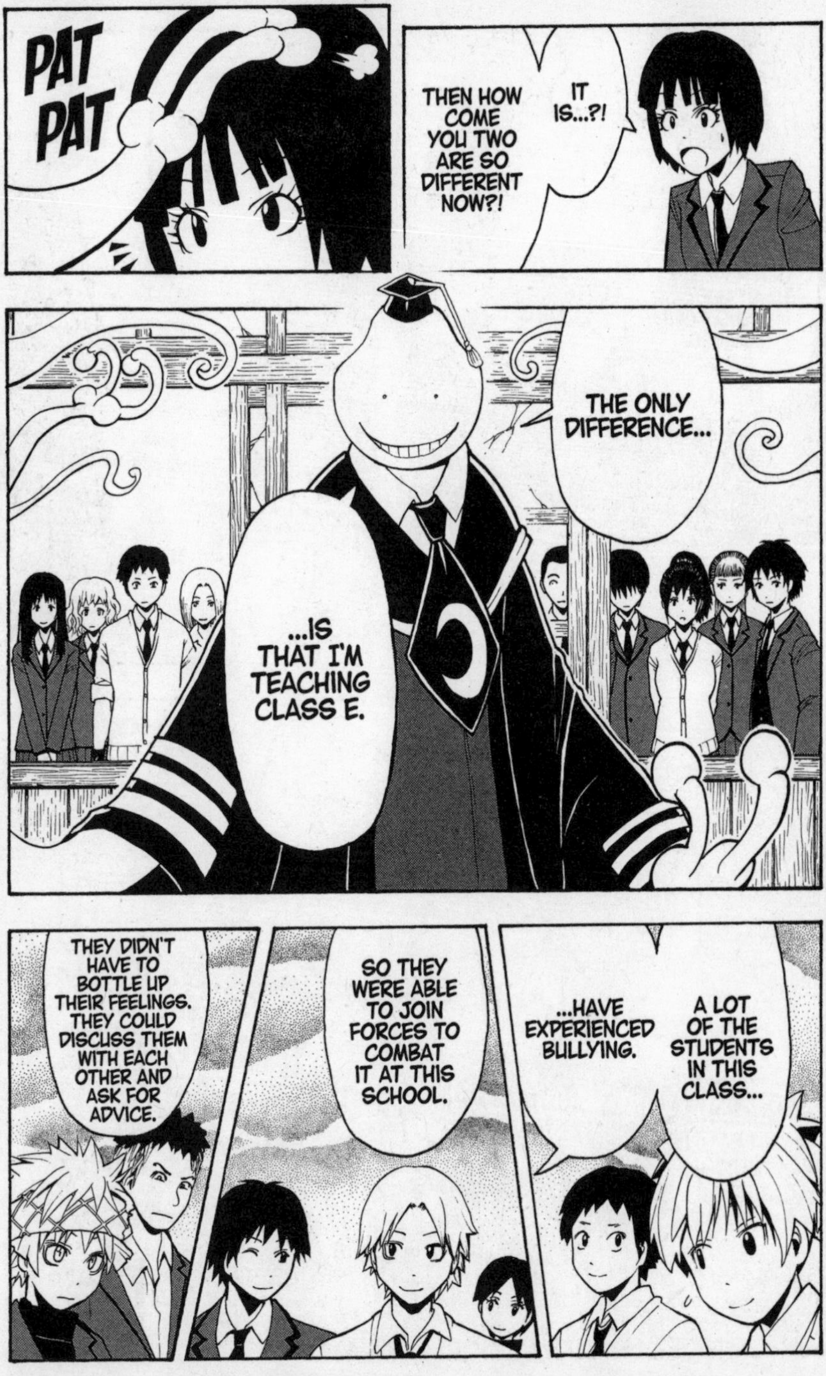
IT IS...?!
THEN HOW COME YOU TWO ARE SO DIFFERENT NOW?!
PAT PAT
THE ONLY DIFFERENCE...
...IS THAT I'M TEACHING CLASS E.
A LOT OF THE STUDENTS IN THIS CLASS...
...HAVE EXPERIENCED BULLYING.
SO THEY WERE ABLE TO JOIN FORCES TO COMBAT IT AT THIS SCHOOL.
THEY DIDN'T HAVE TO BOTTLE UP THEIR FEELINGS. THEY COULD DISCUSS THEM WITH EACH OTHER AND ASK FOR ADVICE.

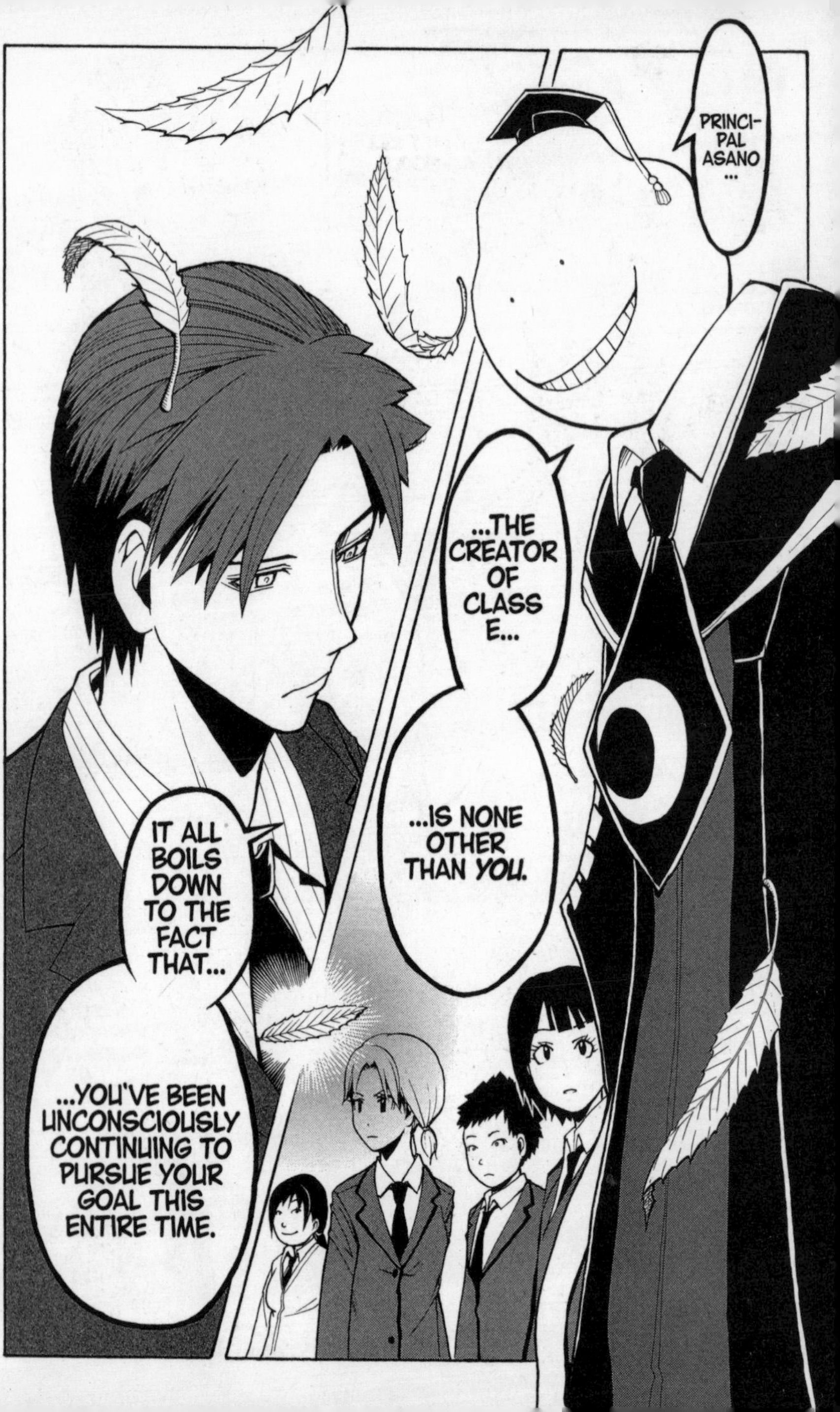
PRINCIPAL ASANO...
...THE CREATOR OF CLASS E...
...IS NONE OTHER THAN *YOU.*
IT ALL BOILS DOWN TO THE FACT THAT...
...YOU'VE BEEN UNCONSCIOUSLY CONTINUING TO PURSUE YOUR GOAL THIS ENTIRE TIME.

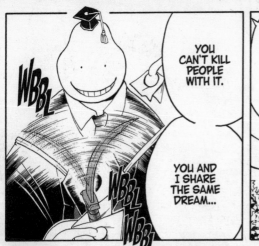

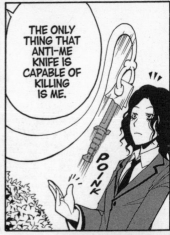

THE ONLY THING THAT ANTI-ME KNIFE IS CAPABLE OF KILLING IS ME.
POINK
YOU CAN'T KILL PEOPLE WITH IT.
WBBL
YOU AND I SHARE THE SAME DREAM...
WBBL
WBBL
AND THAT IS TO TEACH PEOPLE TO LIVE, NOT DIE.
LET'S CONTINUE TO DO THAT...
...TOGETHER.

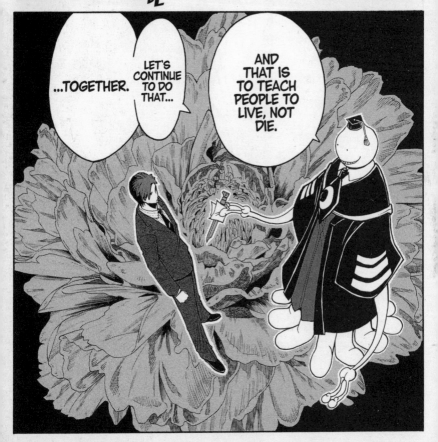

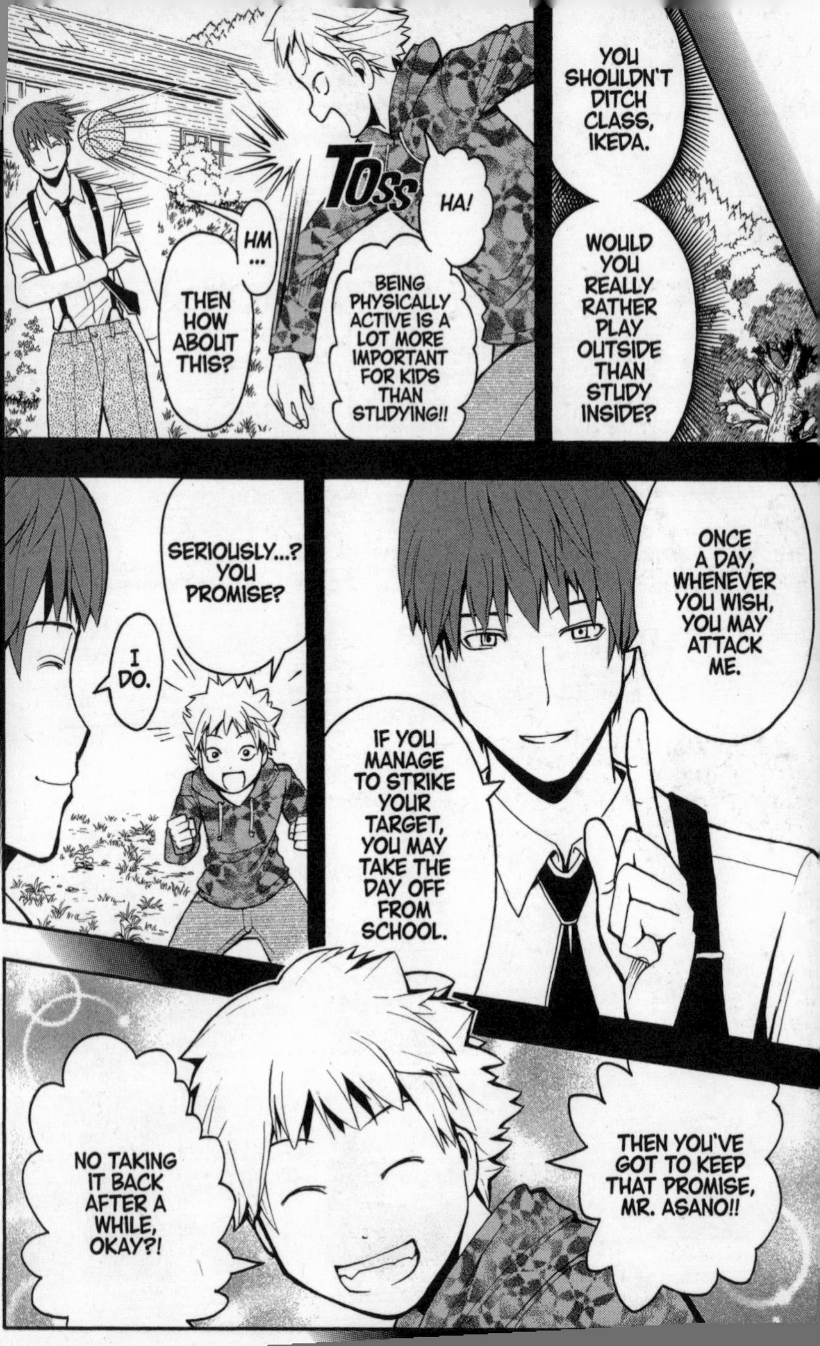
YOU SHOULDN'T DITCH CLASS, IKEDA.
WOULD YOU REALLY RATHER PLAY OUTSIDE THAN STUDY INSIDE?
TOSS
HA!
BEING PHYSICALLY ACTIVE IS A LOT MORE IMPORTANT FOR KIDS THAN STUDYING!!
HM...
THEN HOW ABOUT THIS?
ONCE A DAY, WHENEVER YOU WISH, YOU MAY ATTACK ME.
IF YOU MANAGE TO STRIKE YOUR TARGET, YOU MAY TAKE THE DAY OFF FROM SCHOOL.
SERIOUSLY...? YOU PROMISE?
I DO.
THEN YOU'VE GOT TO KEEP THAT PROMISE, MR. ASANO!!
NO TAKING IT BACK AFTER A WHILE, OKAY?!

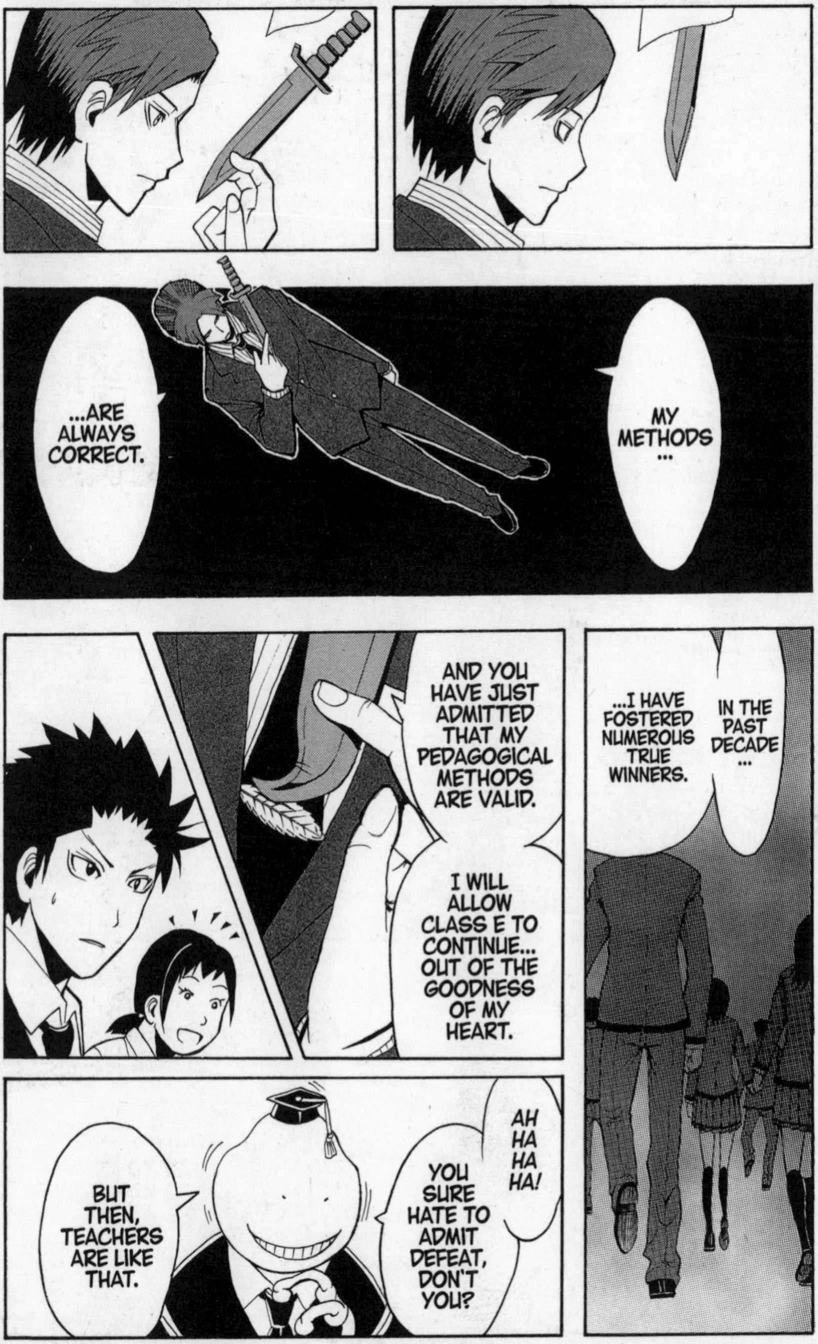
MY METHODS...
...ARE ALWAYS CORRECT.
IN THE PAST DECADE...
...I HAVE FOSTERED NUMEROUS TRUE WINNERS.
AND YOU HAVE JUST ADMITTED THAT MY PEDAGOGICAL METHODS ARE VALID.
I WILL ALLOW CLASS E TO CONTINUE... OUT OF THE GOODNESS OF MY HEART.
AH HA HA HA!
YOU SURE HATE TO ADMIT DEFEAT, DON'T YOU?
BUT THEN, TEACHERS ARE LIKE THAT.

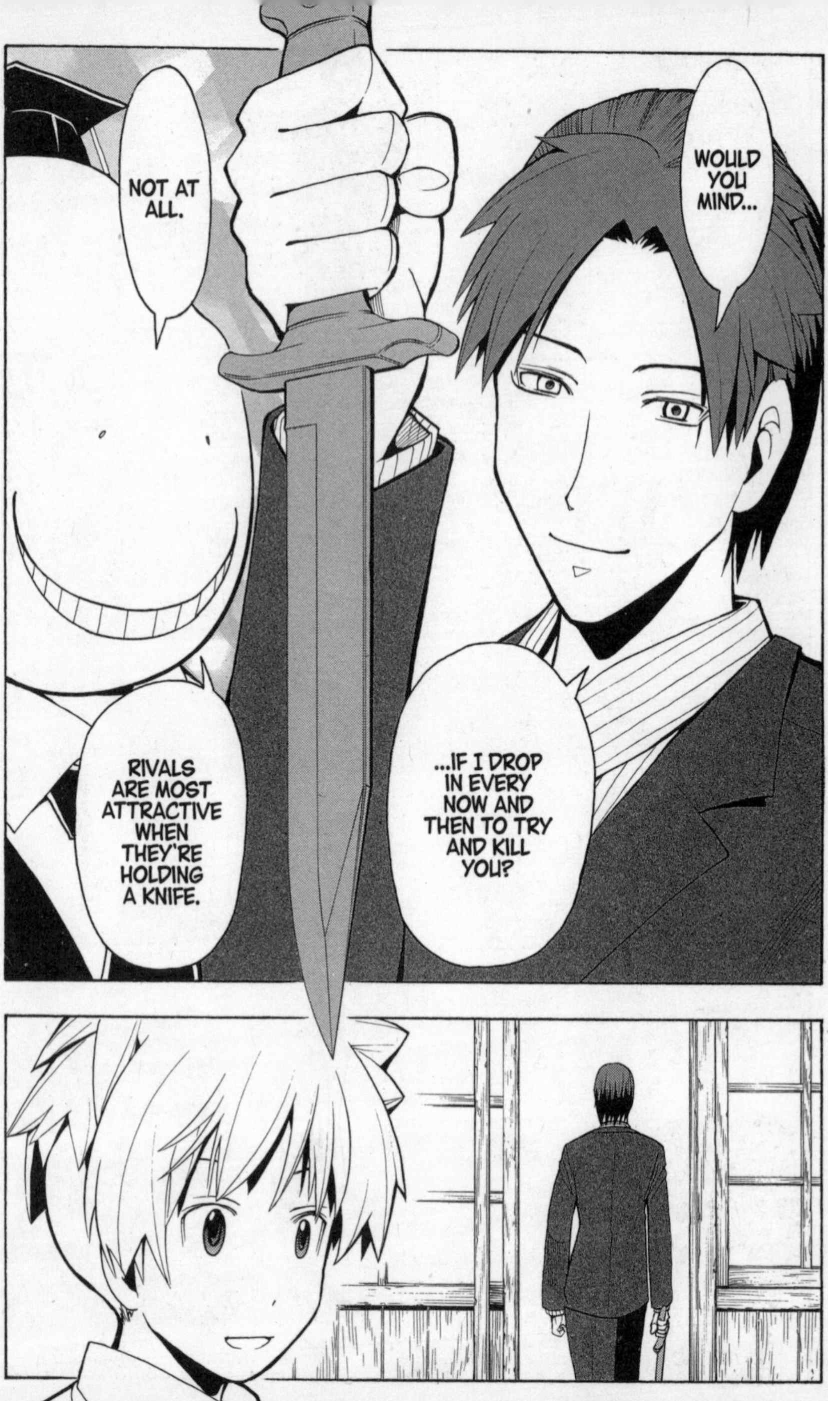
WOULD YOU MIND...
...IF I DROP IN EVERY NOW AND THEN TO TRY AND KILL YOU?
NOT AT ALL.
RIVALS ARE MOST ATTRACTIVE WHEN THEY'RE HOLDING A KNIFE.

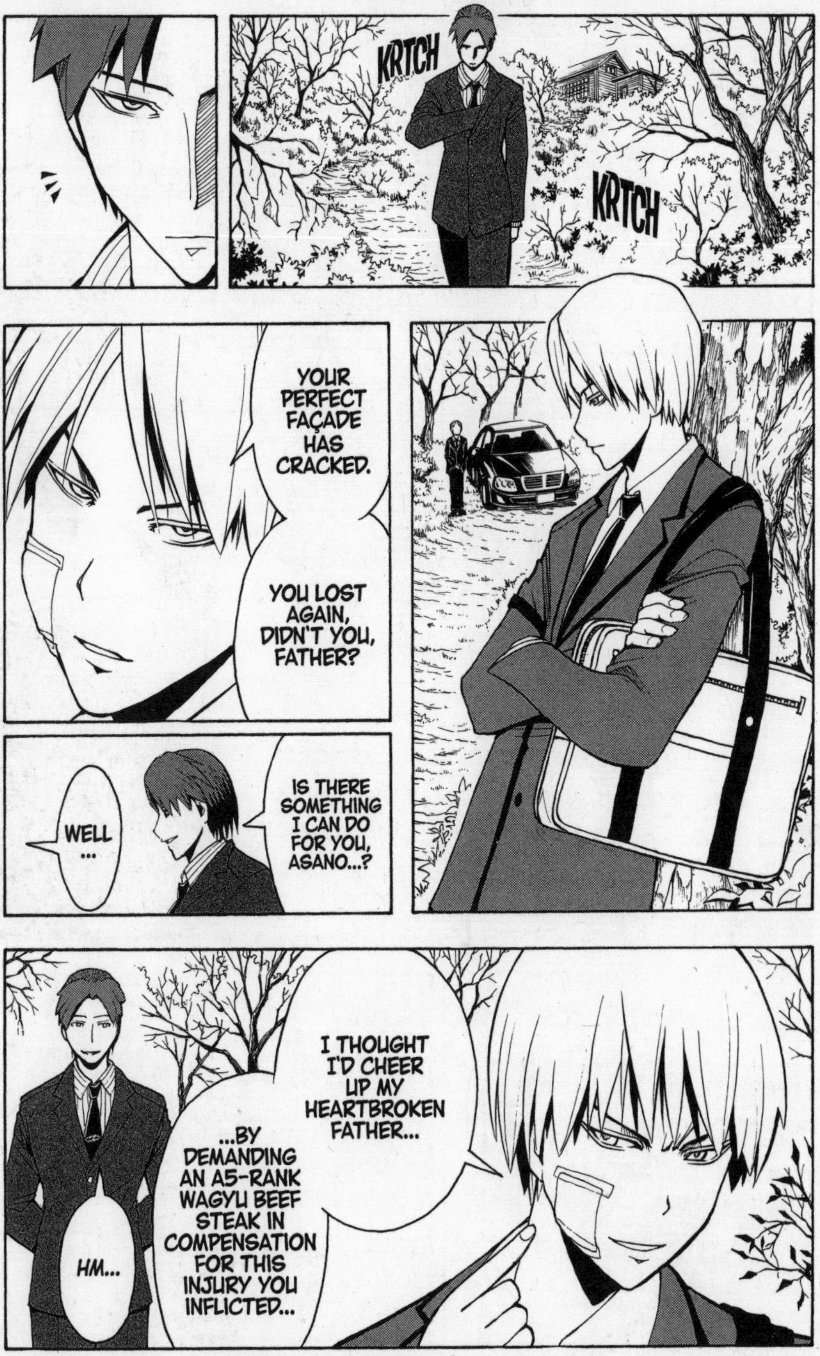
KRTCH
KRTCH
YOUR PERFECT FAÇADE HAS CRACKED.
YOU LOST AGAIN, DIDN'T YOU, FATHER?
IS THERE SOMETHING I CAN DO FOR YOU, ASANO...?
WELL ...
I THOUGHT I'D CHEER UP MY HEARTBROKEN FATHER...
...BY DEMANDING AN A5-RANK WAGYU BEEF STEAK IN COMPENSATION FOR THIS INJURY YOU INFLICTED...
HM...

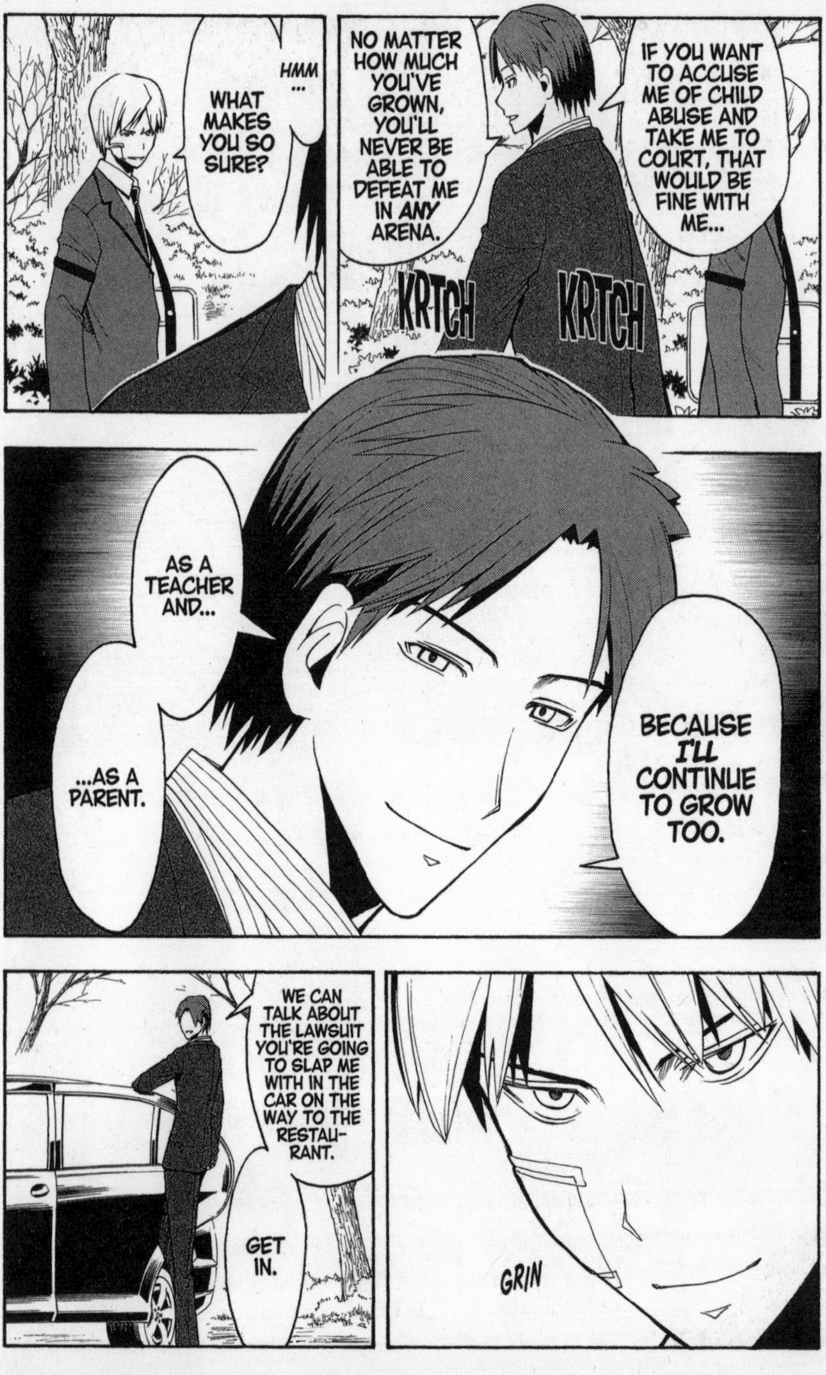
IF YOU WANT TO ACCUSE ME OF CHILD ABUSE AND TAKE ME TO COURT, THAT WOULD BE FINE WITH ME...
NO MATTER HOW MUCH YOU'VE GROWN, YOU'LL NEVER BE ABLE TO DEFEAT ME IN *ANY* ARENA.
KRTCH
KRTCH
HMM ...
WHAT MAKES YOU SO SURE?
BECAUSE *I'LL* CONTINUE TO GROW TOO.
AS A TEACHER AND...
...AS A PARENT.
GRIN
WE CAN TALK ABOUT THE LAWSUIT YOU'RE GOING TO SLAP ME WITH IN THE CAR ON THE WAY TO THE RESTAU-RANT.
GET IN.

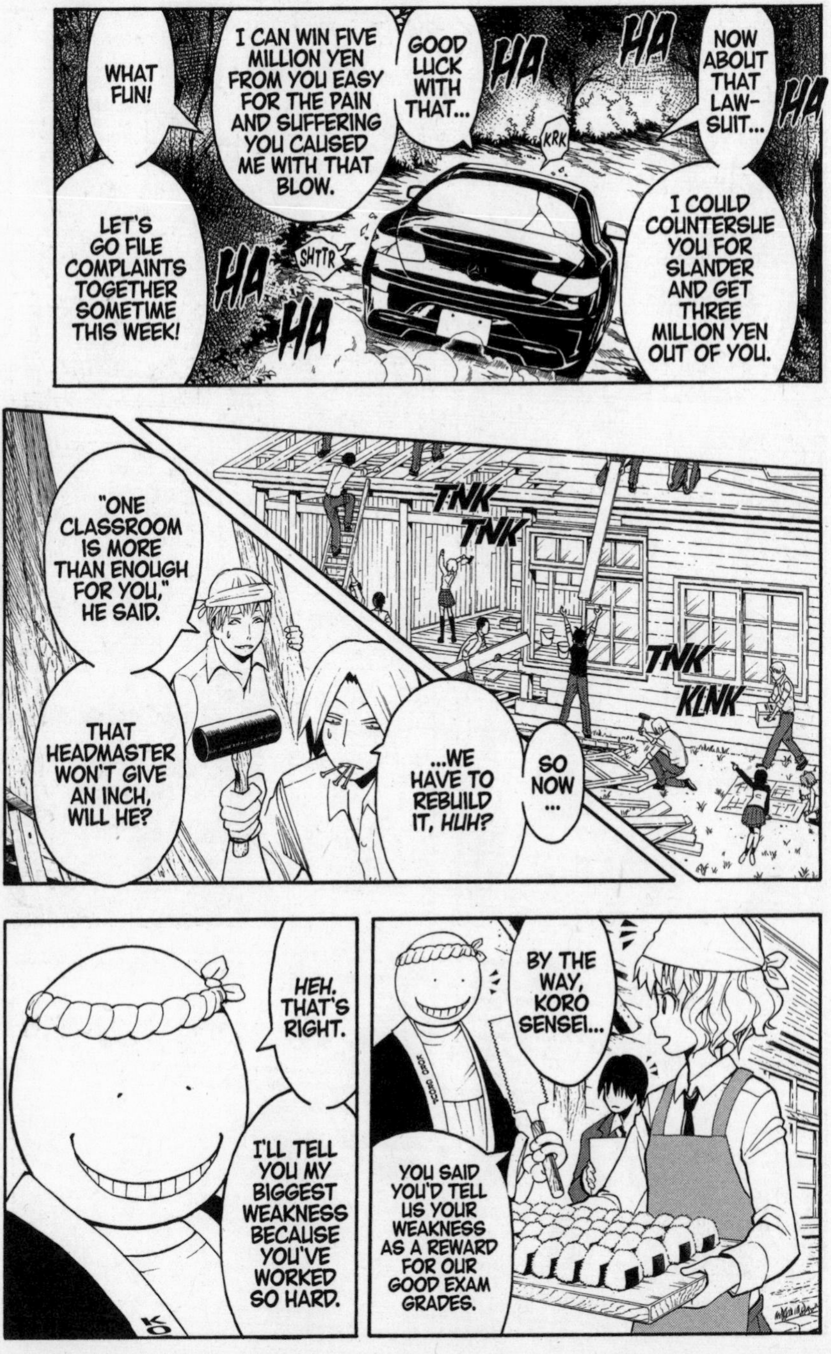

NOW ABOUT THAT LAW-SUIT...
I COULD COUNTERSUE YOU FOR SLANDER AND GET THREE MILLION YEN OUT OF YOU.
HA
HA
HA
GOOD LUCK WITH THAT...
KRK
I CAN WIN FIVE MILLION YEN FROM YOU EASY FOR THE PAIN AND SUFFERING YOU CAUSED ME WITH THAT BLOW.
SHTTR
WHAT FUN!
LET'S GO FILE COMPLAINTS TOGETHER SOMETIME THIS WEEK!
HA
HA
TNK
TNK
TNK
KLNK
SO NOW...
...WE HAVE TO REBUILD IT, HUH?
"ONE CLASSROOM IS MORE THAN ENOUGH FOR YOU," HE SAID.
THAT HEADMASTER WON'T GIVE AN INCH, WILL HE?
BY THE WAY, KORO SENSEI...
YOU SAID YOU'D TELL US YOUR WEAKNESS AS A REWARD FOR OUR GOOD EXAM GRADES.
HEH. THAT'S RIGHT.
I'LL TELL YOU MY BIGGEST WEAKNESS BECAUSE YOU'VE WORKED SO HARD.

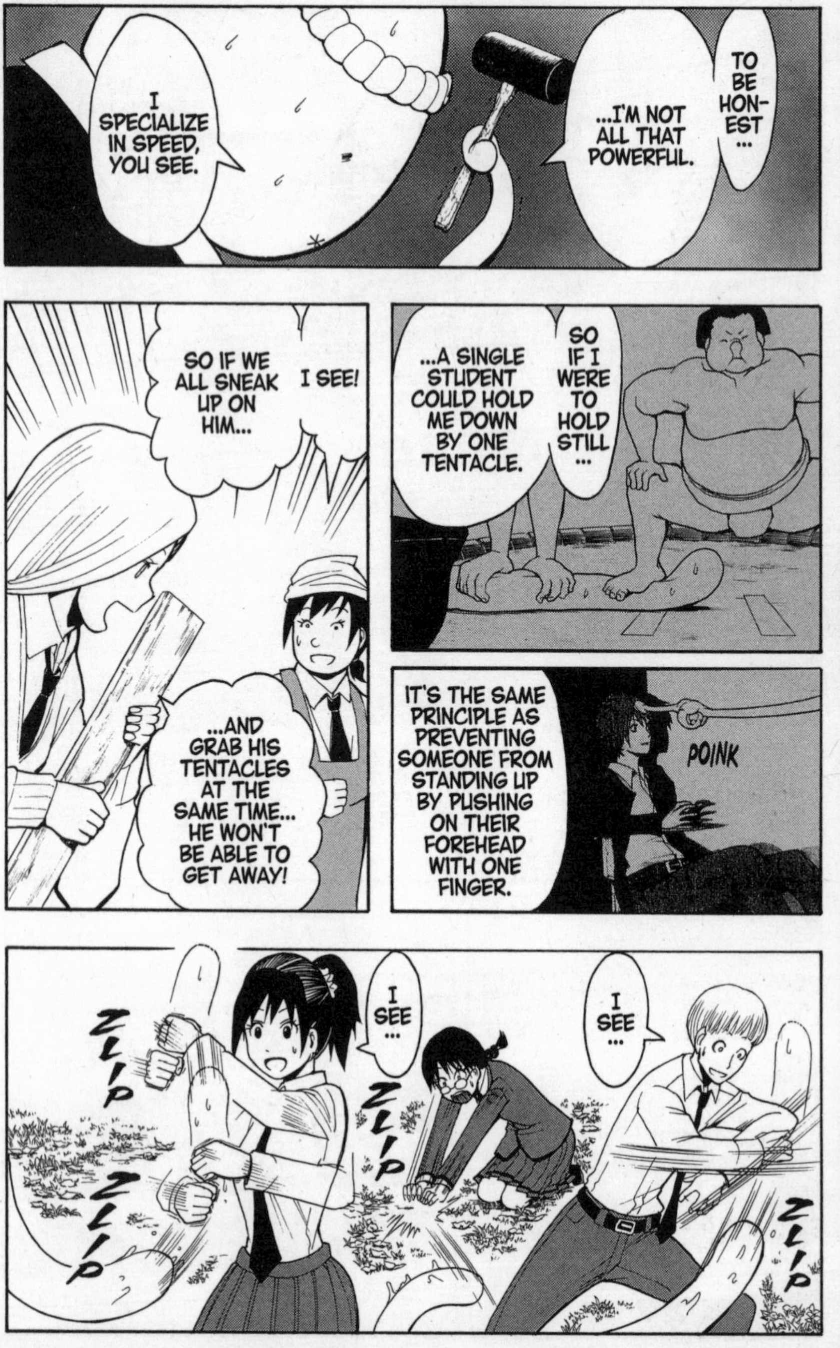
TO BE HON-EST...
...I'M NOT ALL THAT POWERFUL.
I SPECIALIZE IN SPEED, YOU SEE.
SO IF I WERE TO HOLD STILL...
...A SINGLE STUDENT COULD HOLD ME DOWN BY ONE TENTACLE.
IT'S THE SAME PRINCIPLE AS PREVENTING SOMEONE FROM STANDING UP BY PUSHING ON THEIR FOREHEAD WITH ONE FINGER.
POINK
I SEE!
SO IF WE ALL SNEAK UP ON HIM...
...AND GRAB HIS TENTACLES AT THE SAME TIME... HE WON'T BE ABLE TO GET AWAY!
I SEE...
ZLIP
I SEE...
ZLIP
ZLIP
ZLIP

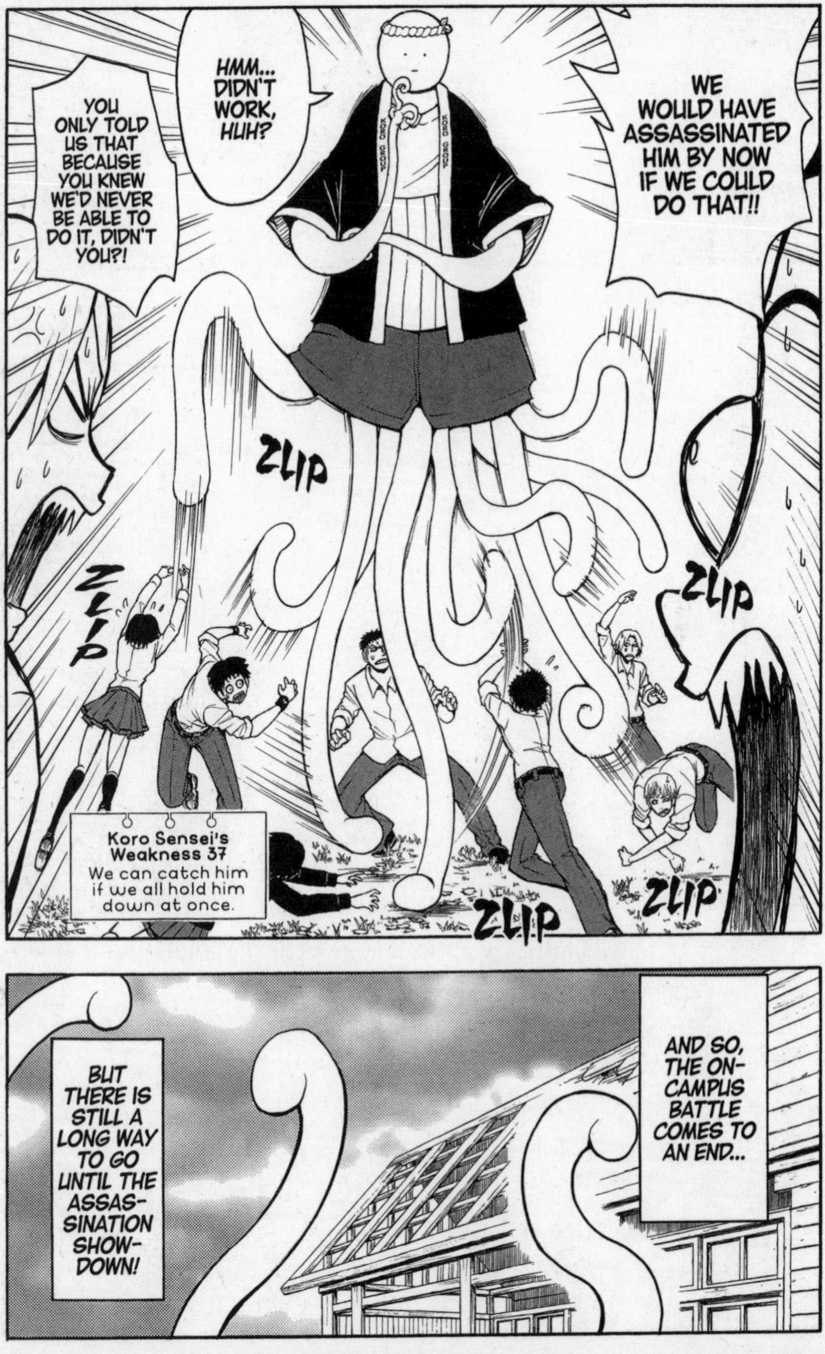
WE WOULD HAVE ASSASSINATED HIM BY NOW IF WE COULD DO THAT!!
HMM... DIDN'T WORK, HUH?
YOU ONLY TOLD US THAT BECAUSE YOU KNEW WE'D NEVER BE ABLE TO DO IT, DIDN'T YOU?!
ZLIP
ZLIP
ZLIP
Koro Sensei's Weakness 37
We can catch him if we all hold him down at once.
ZLIP
ZLIP
AND SO, THE ON-CAMPUS BATTLE COMES TO AN END...
BUT THERE IS STILL A LONG WAY TO GO UNTIL THE ASSAS-SINATION SHOW-DOWN!

GAKUHO ASANO

🌑 BIRTHDAY: APRIL 12 (41 YEARS OLD)

🌑 HEIGHT: 6'

🌑 WEIGHT: 168 LBS.

🌑 CAREER HISTORY: HARVARD UNIVERSITY GRADUATE

→ KUNUGIGAOKA PREPARATORY SCHOOL HEADMASTER

→ KUNUGIGAOKA ACADEMY CHAIRMAN OF THE BOARD

🌑 HOBBY/SKILL: EDUCATION, BUSINESS MANAGEMENT

🌑 MOTTO: "LIVE AS IF YOU WERE TO DIE TOMORROW. LEARN AS IF YOU WERE TO LIVE FOREVER." (—GANDHI, ACTUALLY)

🌑 QUALIFICATIONS: TOO MANY TO NOTE HERE

🌑 CERTIFICATIONS AND LICENSES HE STUDIED FOR AND ACQUIRED OVER THE THREE-DAY WEEKEND THIS YEAR: VEGETABLE SOMMELIER, COLOR COORDINATOR, JUMBO JET PILOT'S LICENSE

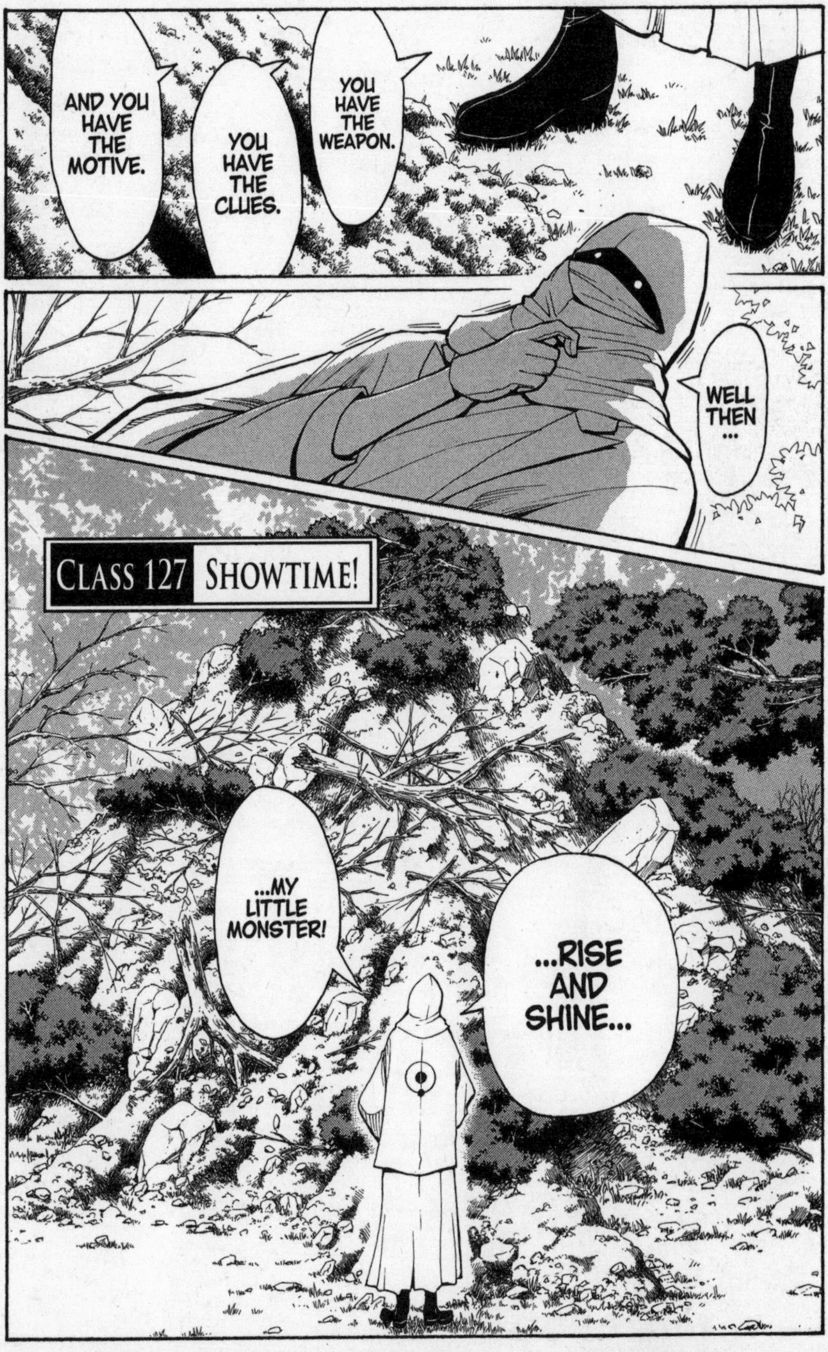
YOU HAVE THE WEAPON.
YOU HAVE THE CLUES.
AND YOU HAVE THE MOTIVE.
WELL THEN ...
CLASS 127 SHOWTIME!
...RISE AND SHINE...
...MY LITTLE MONSTER!

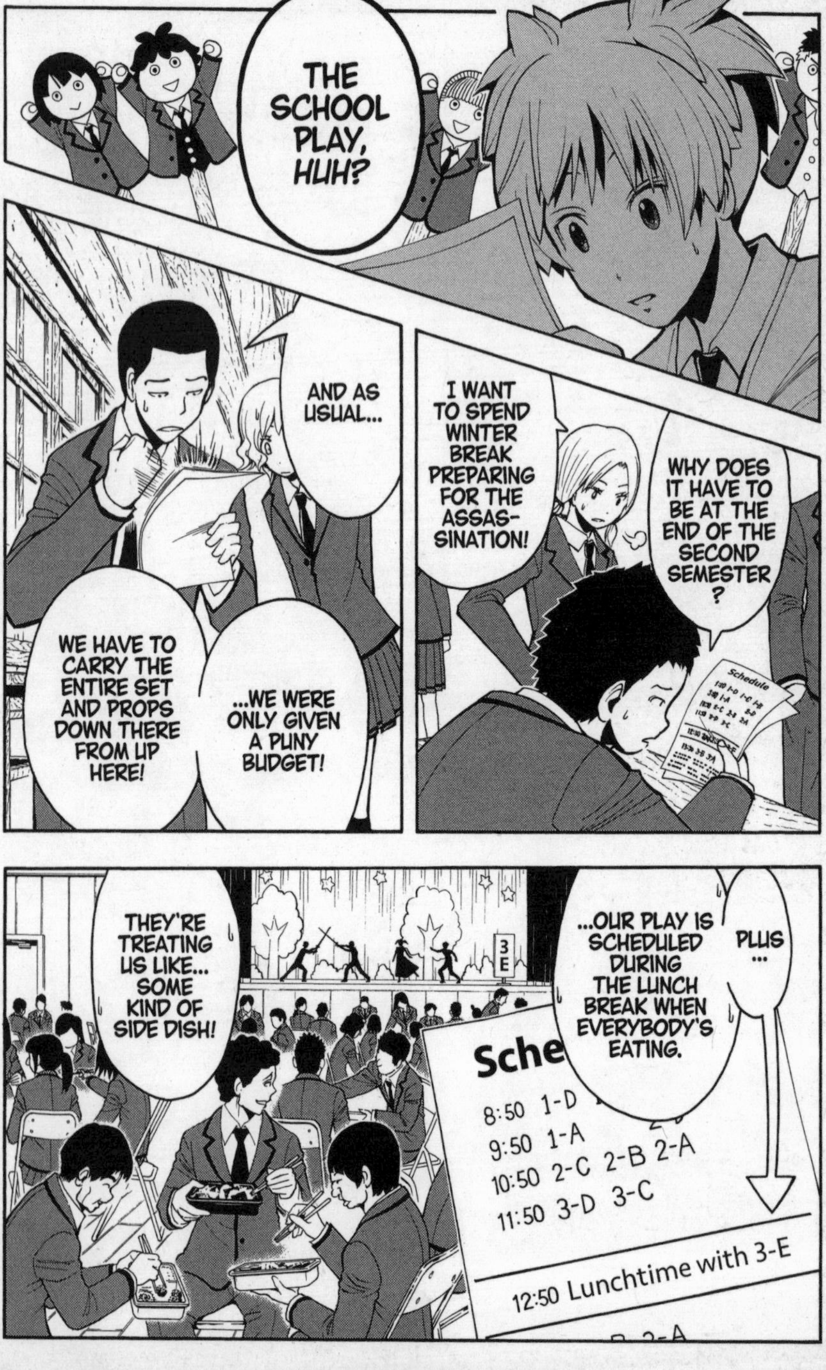
THE SCHOOL PLAY, HUH?
WHY DOES IT HAVE TO BE AT THE END OF THE SECOND SEMESTER?
I WANT TO SPEND WINTER BREAK PREPARING FOR THE ASSAS-SINATION!
Schedule
AND AS USUAL...
...WE WERE ONLY GIVEN A PUNY BUDGET!
WE HAVE TO CARRY THE ENTIRE SET AND PROPS DOWN THERE FROM UP HERE!
PLUS...
...OUR PLAY IS SCHEDULED DURING THE LUNCH BREAK WHEN EVERYBODY'S EATING.
3E
THEY'RE TREATING US LIKE... SOME KIND OF SIDE DISH!
Sche
8:50 1-D
9:50 1-A
10:50 2-C 2-B 2-A
11:50 3-D 3-C
12:50 Lunchtime with 3-E

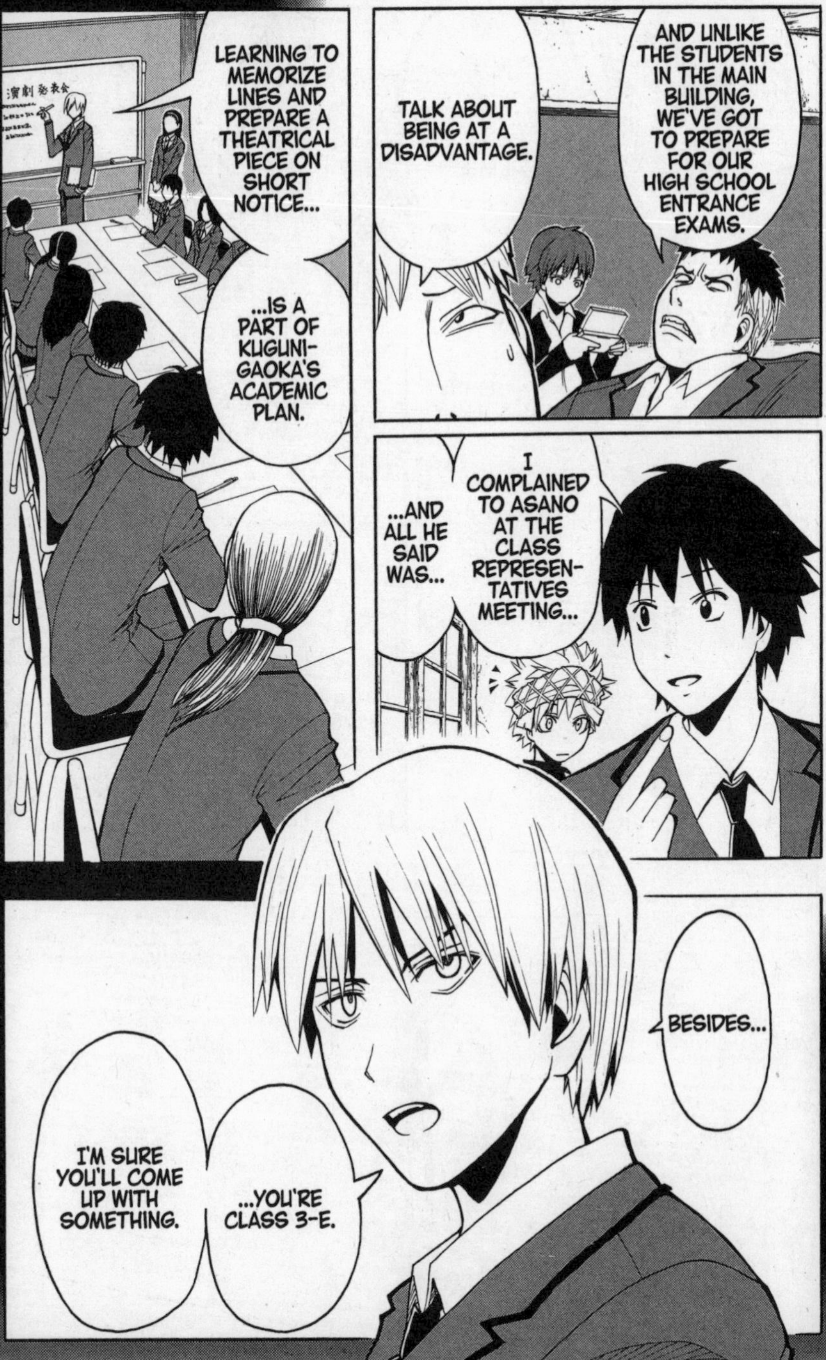
AND UNLIKE THE STUDENTS IN THE MAIN BUILDING, WE'VE GOT TO PREPARE FOR OUR HIGH SCHOOL ENTRANCE EXAMS.
TALK ABOUT BEING AT A DISADVANTAGE.
I COMPLAINED TO ASANO AT THE CLASS REPRESEN-TATIVES MEETING...
...AND ALL HE SAID WAS...
演劇発表会
LEARNING TO MEMORIZE LINES AND PREPARE A THEATRICAL PIECE ON SHORT NOTICE...
...IS A PART OF KUGUNI-GAOKA'S ACADEMIC PLAN.
BESIDES...
...YOU'RE CLASS 3-E.
I'M SURE YOU'LL COME UP WITH SOMETHING.

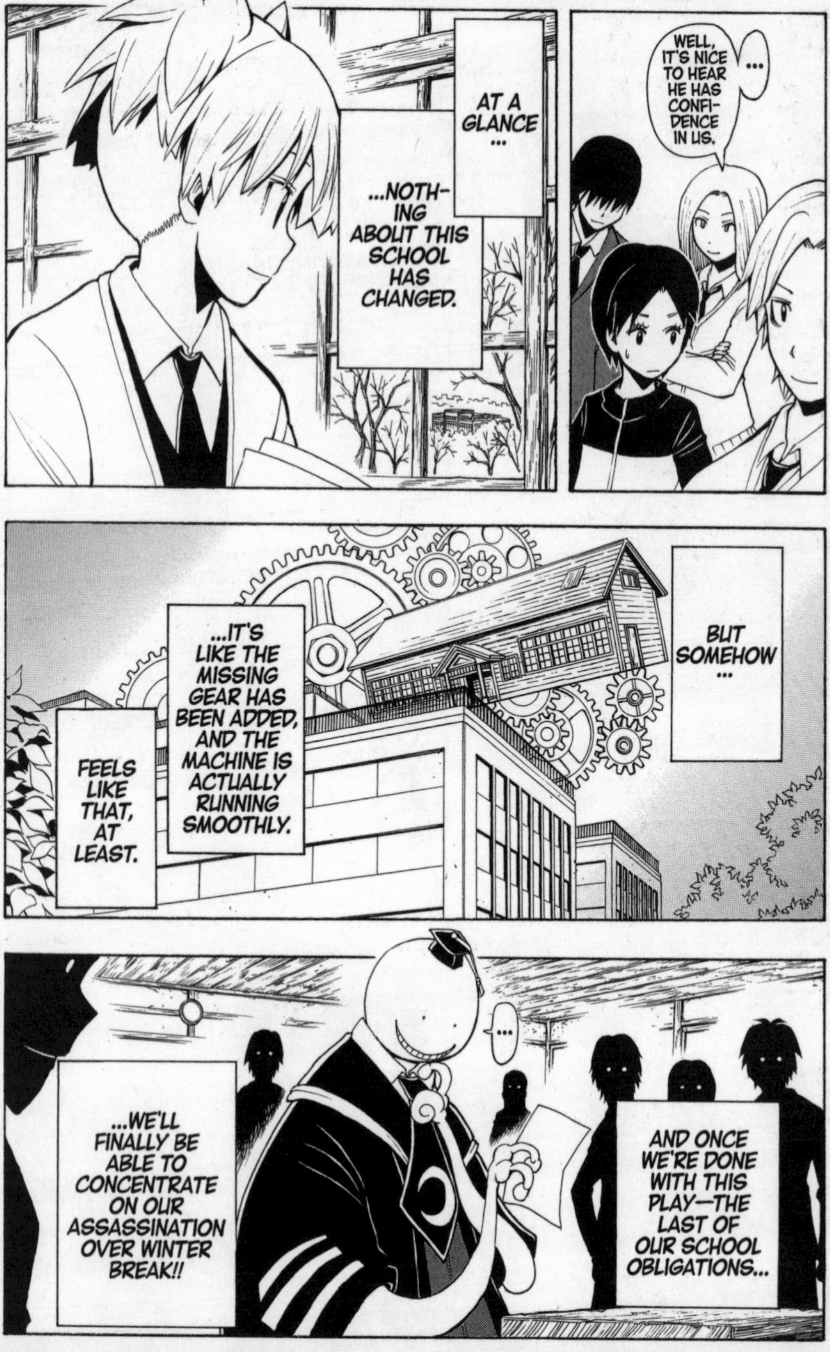
...
WELL, IT'S NICE TO HEAR HE HAS CONFIDENCE IN US.
AT A GLANCE...
...NOTHING ABOUT THIS SCHOOL HAS CHANGED.
BUT SOMEHOW...
...IT'S LIKE THE MISSING GEAR HAS BEEN ADDED, AND THE MACHINE IS ACTUALLY RUNNING SMOOTHLY.
FEELS LIKE THAT, AT LEAST.
...
AND ONCE WE'RE DONE WITH THIS PLAY—THE LAST OF OUR SCHOOL OBLIGATIONS...
...WE'LL FINALLY BE ABLE TO CONCENTRATE ON OUR ASSASSINATION OVER WINTER BREAK!!

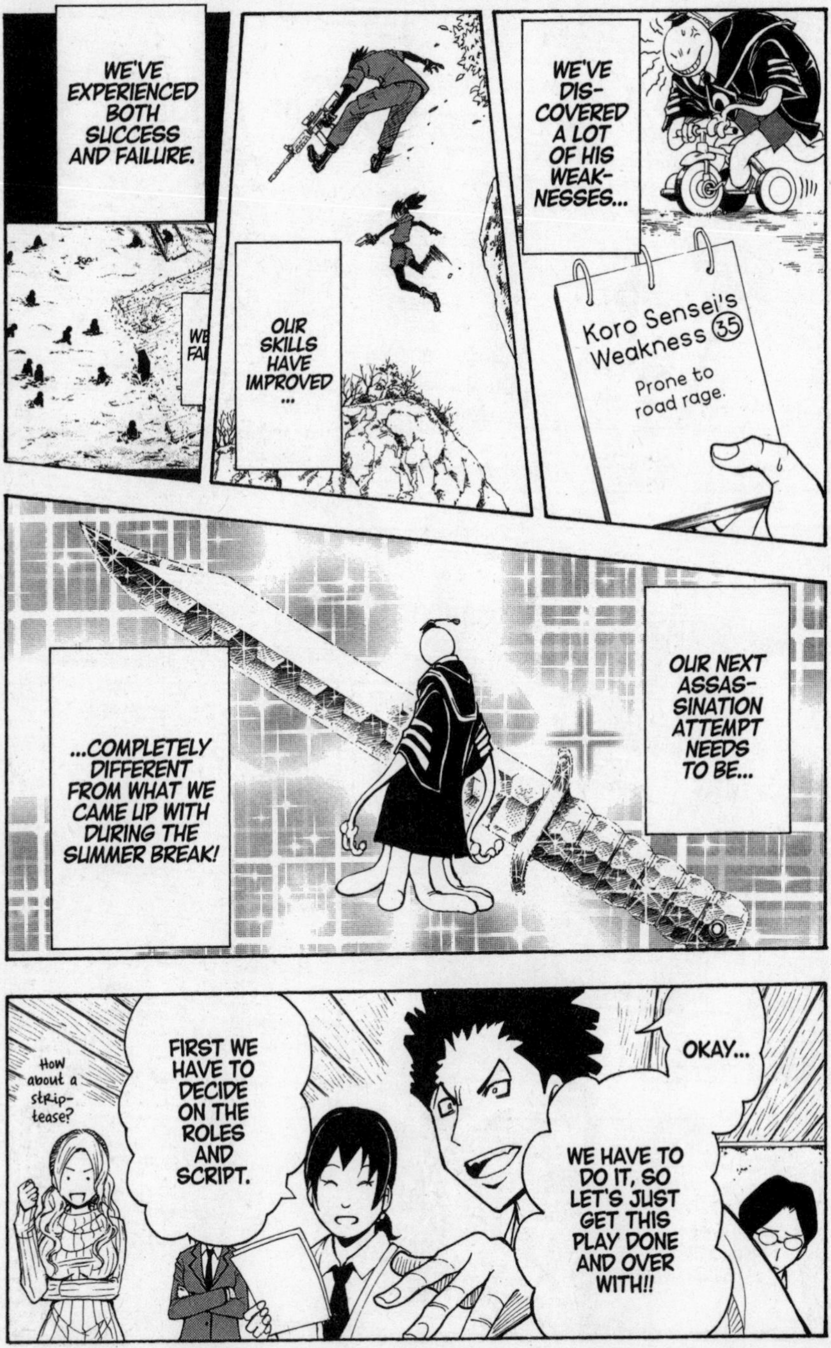
WE'VE DISCOVERED A LOT OF HIS WEAKNESSES...
Koro Sensei's Weakness 35
Prone to road rage.
OUR SKILLS HAVE IMPROVED ...
WE'VE EXPERIENCED BOTH SUCCESS AND FAILURE.
OUR NEXT ASSASSINATION ATTEMPT NEEDS TO BE...
...COMPLETELY DIFFERENT FROM WHAT WE CAME UP WITH DURING THE SUMMER BREAK!
OKAY...
WE HAVE TO DO IT, SO LET'S JUST GET THIS PLAY DONE AND OVER WITH!!
FIRST WE HAVE TO DECIDE ON THE ROLES AND SCRIPT.
How about a striptease?

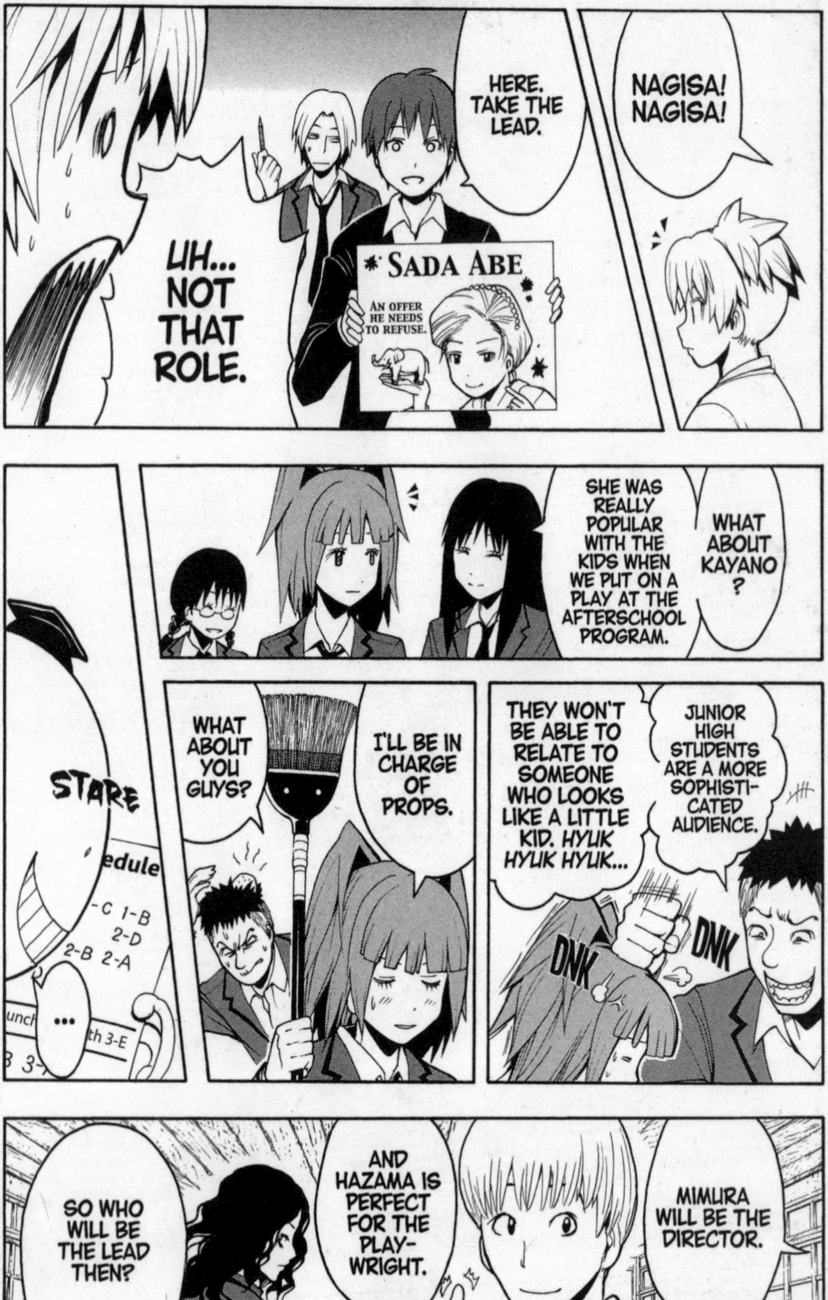
NAGISA! NAGISA!
HERE. TAKE THE LEAD.
SADA ABE
AN OFFER HE NEEDS TO REFUSE.
UH... NOT THAT ROLE.
WHAT ABOUT KAYANO?
SHE WAS REALLY POPULAR WITH THE KIDS WHEN WE PUT ON A PLAY AT THE AFTERSCHOOL PROGRAM.
JUNIOR HIGH STUDENTS ARE A MORE SOPHISTICATED AUDIENCE.
THEY WON'T BE ABLE TO RELATE TO SOMEONE WHO LOOKS LIKE A LITTLE KID. HYUK HYUK HYUK...
DNK
DNK
I'LL BE IN CHARGE OF PROPS.
WHAT ABOUT YOU GUYS?
STARE
...
MIMURA WILL BE THE DIRECTOR.
AND HAZAMA IS PERFECT FOR THE PLAYWRIGHT.
SO WHO WILL BE THE LEAD THEN?

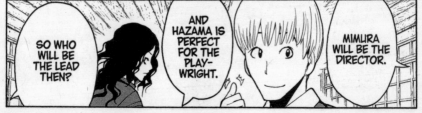

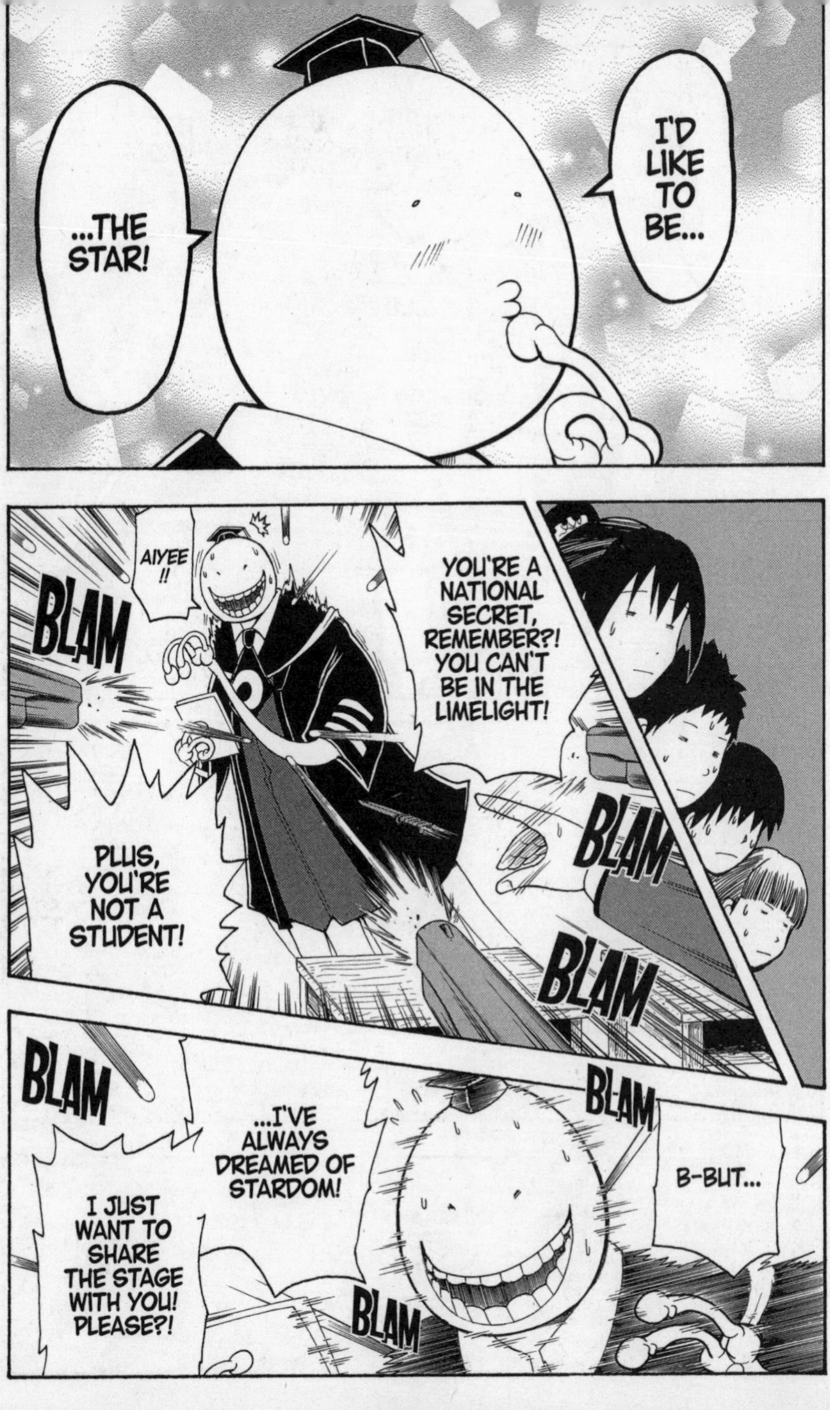
I'D LIKE TO BE...
...THE STAR!
YOU'RE A NATIONAL SECRET, REMEMBER?! YOU CAN'T BE IN THE LIMELIGHT!
BLAM
BLAM
AIYEE!!
BLAM
PLUS, YOU'RE NOT A STUDENT!
B-BUT...
BLAM
...I'VE ALWAYS DREAMED OF STARDOM!
BLAM
I JUST WANT TO SHARE THE STAGE WITH YOU! PLEASE?!
BLAM

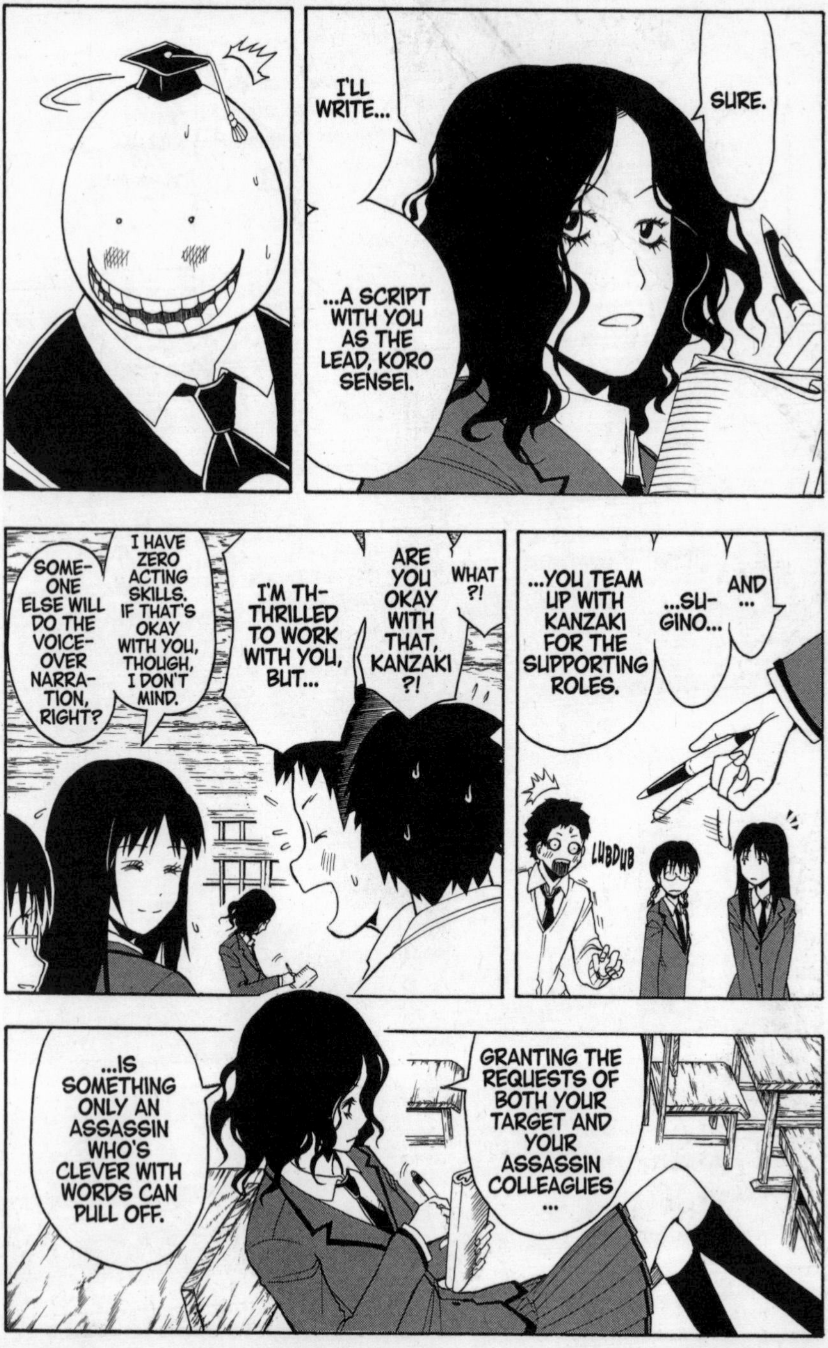
SURE.
I'LL WRITE...
...A SCRIPT WITH YOU AS THE LEAD, KORO SENSEI.
AND...
...SU-GINO...
...YOU TEAM UP WITH KANZAKI FOR THE SUPPORTING ROLES.
LUBDUB
WHAT?!
ARE YOU OKAY WITH THAT, KANZAKI?!
I'M TH-THRILLED TO WORK WITH YOU, BUT...
I HAVE ZERO ACTING SKILLS. IF THAT'S OKAY WITH YOU, THOUGH, I DON'T MIND.
SOME-ONE ELSE WILL DO THE VOICE-OVER NARRA-TION, RIGHT?
GRANTING THE REQUESTS OF BOTH YOUR TARGET AND YOUR ASSASSIN COLLEAGUES...
...IS SOMETHING ONLY AN ASSASSIN WHO'S CLEVER WITH WORDS CAN PULL OFF.

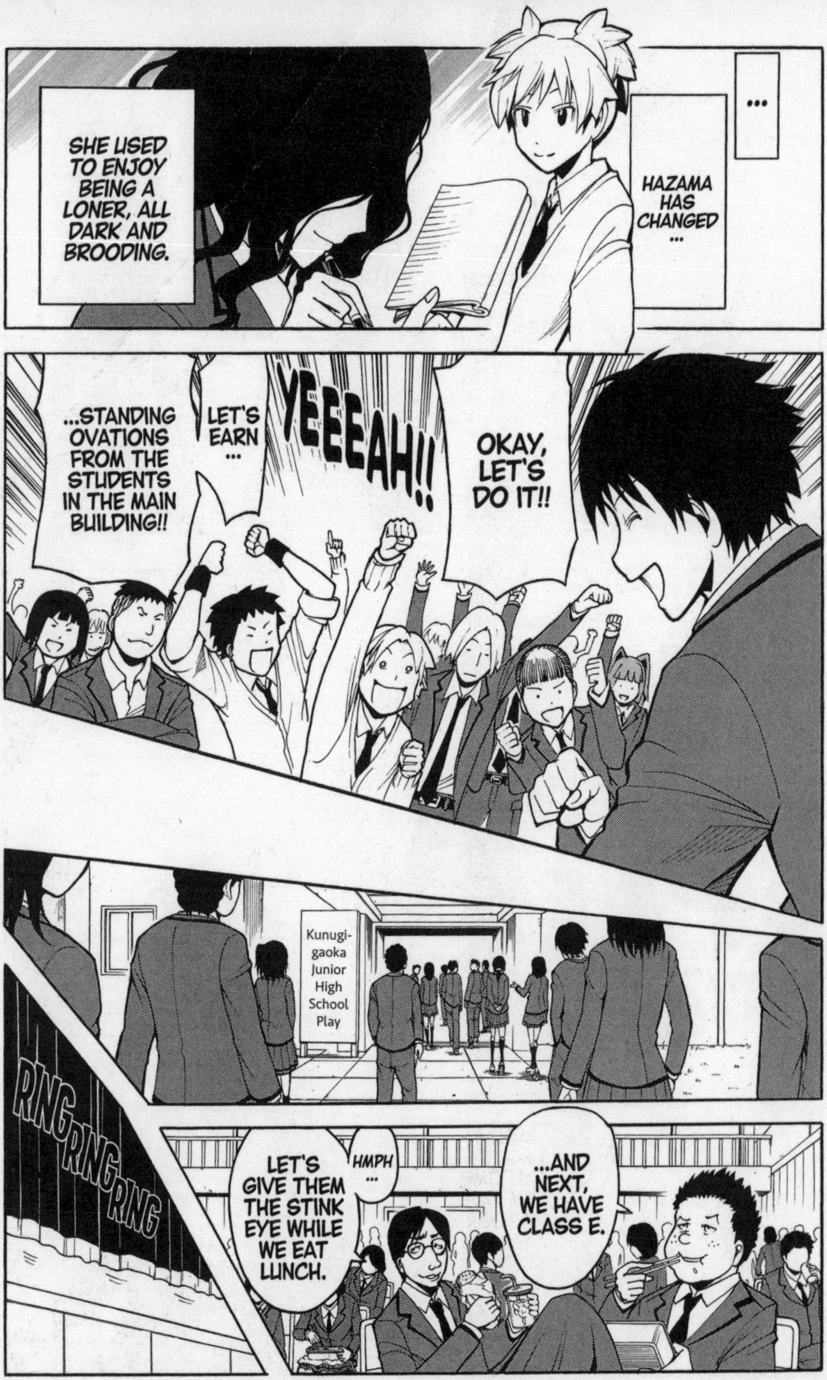
...
HAZAMA HAS CHANGED...
SHE USED TO ENJOY BEING A LONER, ALL DARK AND BROODING.
OKAY, LET'S DO IT!!
YEEEAH!!
LET'S EARN...
...STANDING OVATIONS FROM THE STUDENTS IN THE MAIN BUILDING!!
Kunugigaoka Junior High School Play
RINGRINGRINGRING
...AND NEXT, WE HAVE CLASS E.
HMPH...
LET'S GIVE THEM THE STINK EYE WHILE WE EAT LUNCH.

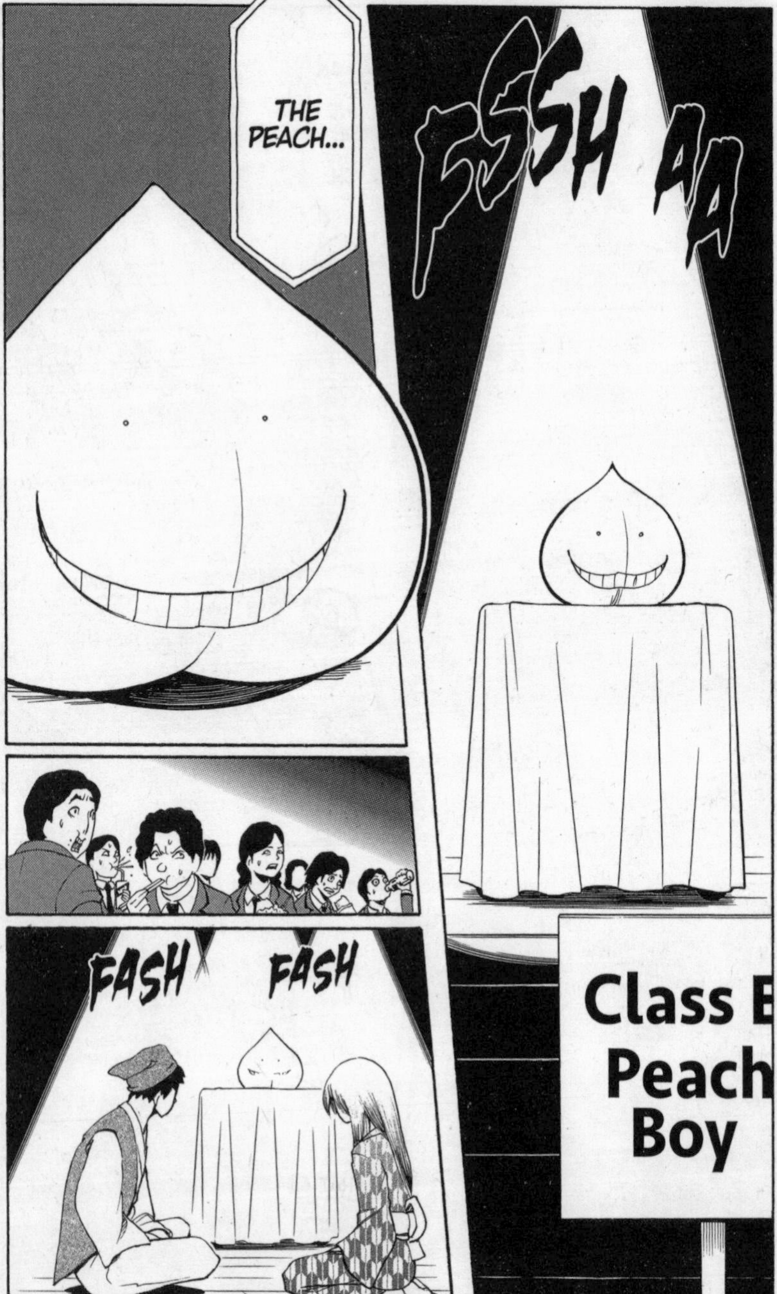
FSSH AA
Class E
Peach
Boy
THE PEACH...
FASH
FASH

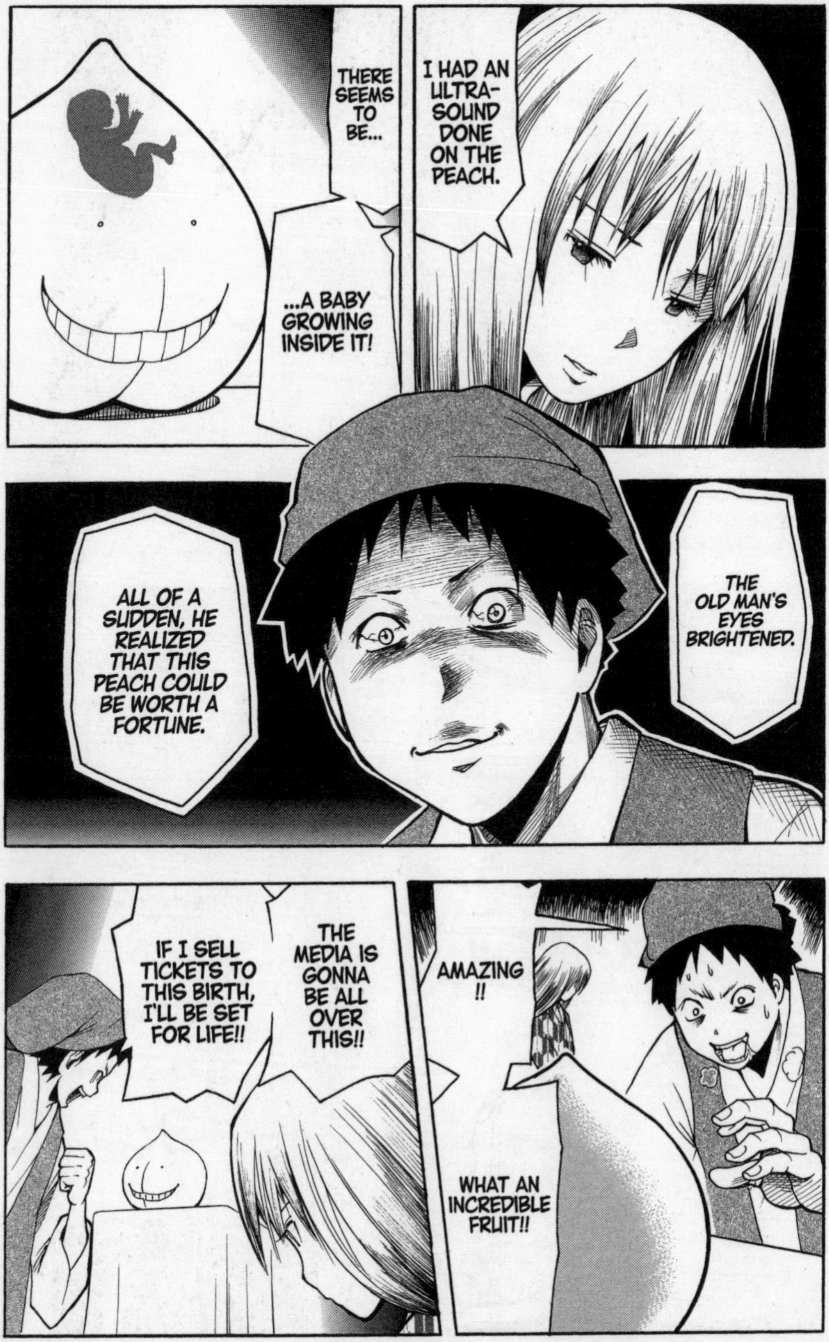
I HAD AN ULTRA-SOUND DONE ON THE PEACH.
THERE SEEMS TO BE...
...A BABY GROWING INSIDE IT!
THE OLD MAN'S EYES BRIGHTENED.
ALL OF A SUDDEN, HE REALIZED THAT THIS PEACH COULD BE WORTH A FORTUNE.
AMAZING!!
WHAT AN INCREDIBLE FRUIT!!
THE MEDIA IS GONNA BE ALL OVER THIS!!
IF I SELL TICKETS TO THIS BIRTH, I'LL BE SET FOR LIFE!!

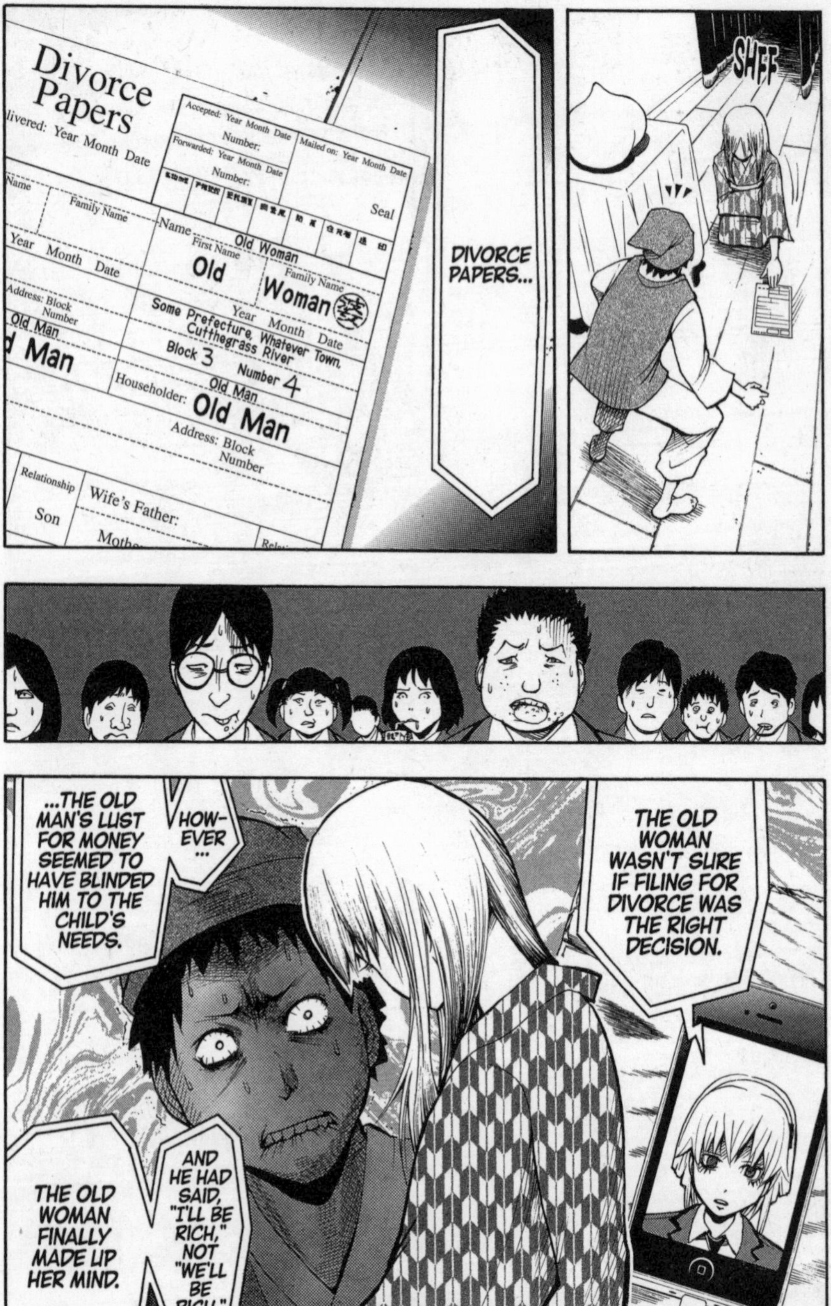
SHFF
Divorce Papers
Delivered: Year Month Date
Accepted: Year Month Date
Number:
Forwarded: Year Month Date
Number:
Mailed on: Year Month Date
Seal
Name
Family Name
Year Month Date
Address: Block Number
Old Man
d Man
Name
First Name
Old Woman
Old
Family Name
Woman
Year Month Date
Some Prefecture, Whatever Town, Cutthegrass River
Block 3
Number 4
Old Man
Householder: Old Man
Address: Block Number
Relationship
Son
Wife's Father:
DIVORCE PAPERS...
THE OLD WOMAN WASN'T SURE IF FILING FOR DIVORCE WAS THE RIGHT DECISION.
HOW-EVER...
...THE OLD MAN'S LUST FOR MONEY SEEMED TO HAVE BLINDED HIM TO THE CHILD'S NEEDS.
AND HE HAD SAID, "I'LL BE RICH," NOT "WE'LL BE RICH."
THE OLD WOMAN FINALLY MADE UP HER MIND.

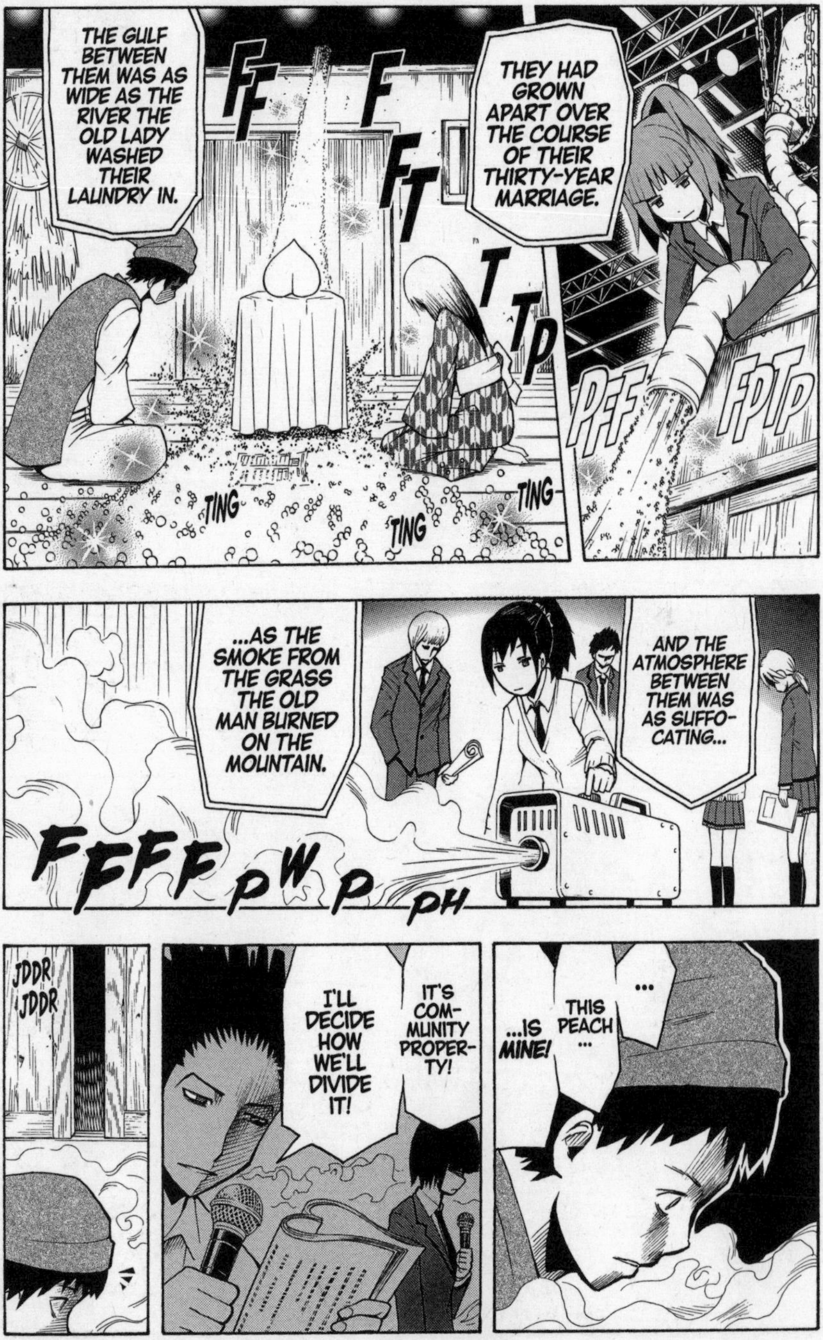
PFF
FPTP
THEY HAD GROWN APART OVER THE COURSE OF THEIR THIRTY-YEAR MARRIAGE.
FF F FT T TP
THE GULF BETWEEN THEM WAS AS WIDE AS THE RIVER THE OLD LADY WASHED THEIR LAUNDRY IN.
TING
TING
TING
AND THE ATMOSPHERE BETWEEN THEM WAS AS SUFFOCATING...
...AS THE SMOKE FROM THE GRASS THE OLD MAN BURNED ON THE MOUNTAIN.
FFFFPWPPH
...
THIS PEACH ...
...IS MINE!
IT'S COMMUNITY PROPERTY!
I'LL DECIDE HOW WE'LL DIVIDE IT!
JDDR JDDR

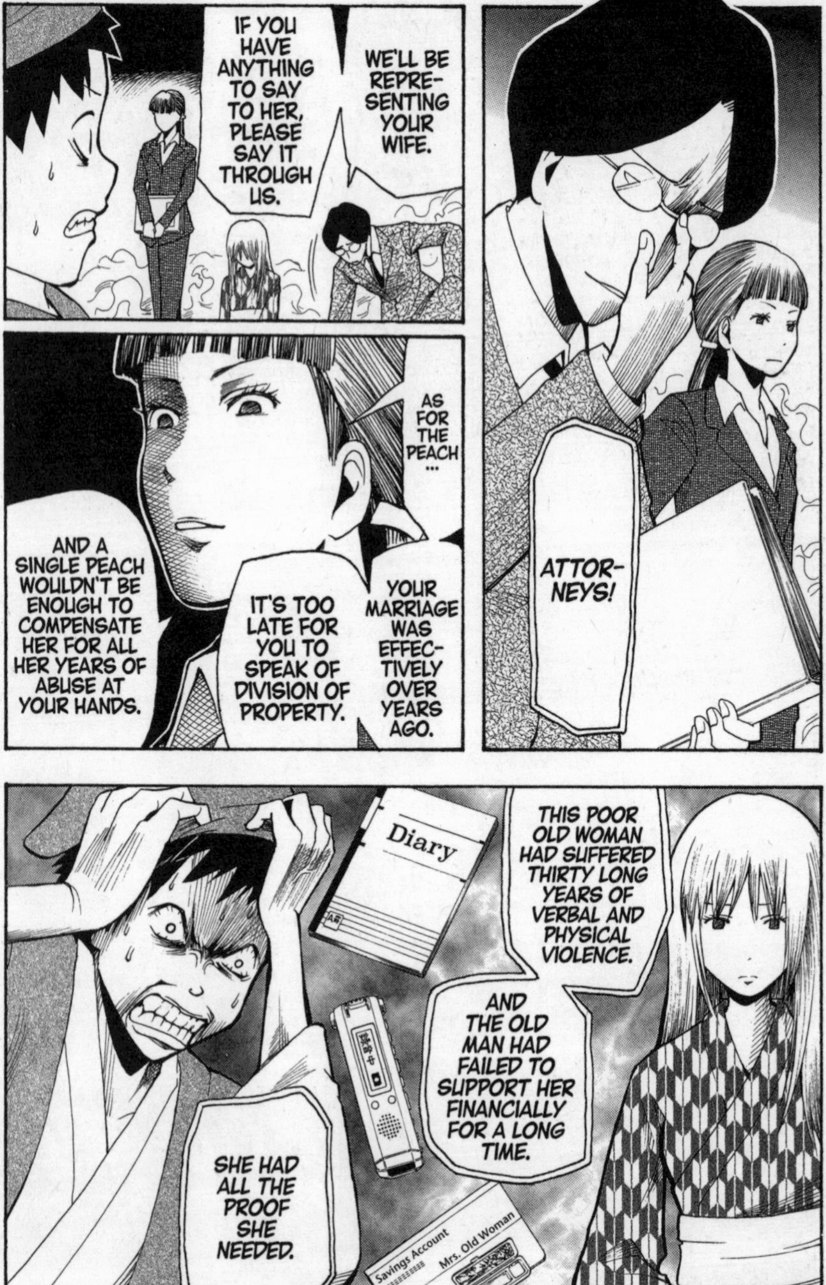
ATTORNEYS!
WE'LL BE REPRESENTING YOUR WIFE.
IF YOU HAVE ANYTHING TO SAY TO HER, PLEASE SAY IT THROUGH US.
AS FOR THE PEACH...
YOUR MARRIAGE WAS EFFECTIVELY OVER YEARS AGO.
IT'S TOO LATE FOR YOU TO SPEAK OF DIVISION OF PROPERTY.
AND A SINGLE PEACH WOULDN'T BE ENOUGH TO COMPENSATE HER FOR ALL HER YEARS OF ABUSE AT YOUR HANDS.
Diary
THIS POOR OLD WOMAN HAD SUFFERED THIRTY LONG YEARS OF VERBAL AND PHYSICAL VIOLENCE.
AND THE OLD MAN HAD FAILED TO SUPPORT HER FINANCIALLY FOR A LONG TIME.
SHE HAD ALL THE PROOF SHE NEEDED.
Savings Account
Mrs. Old Woman

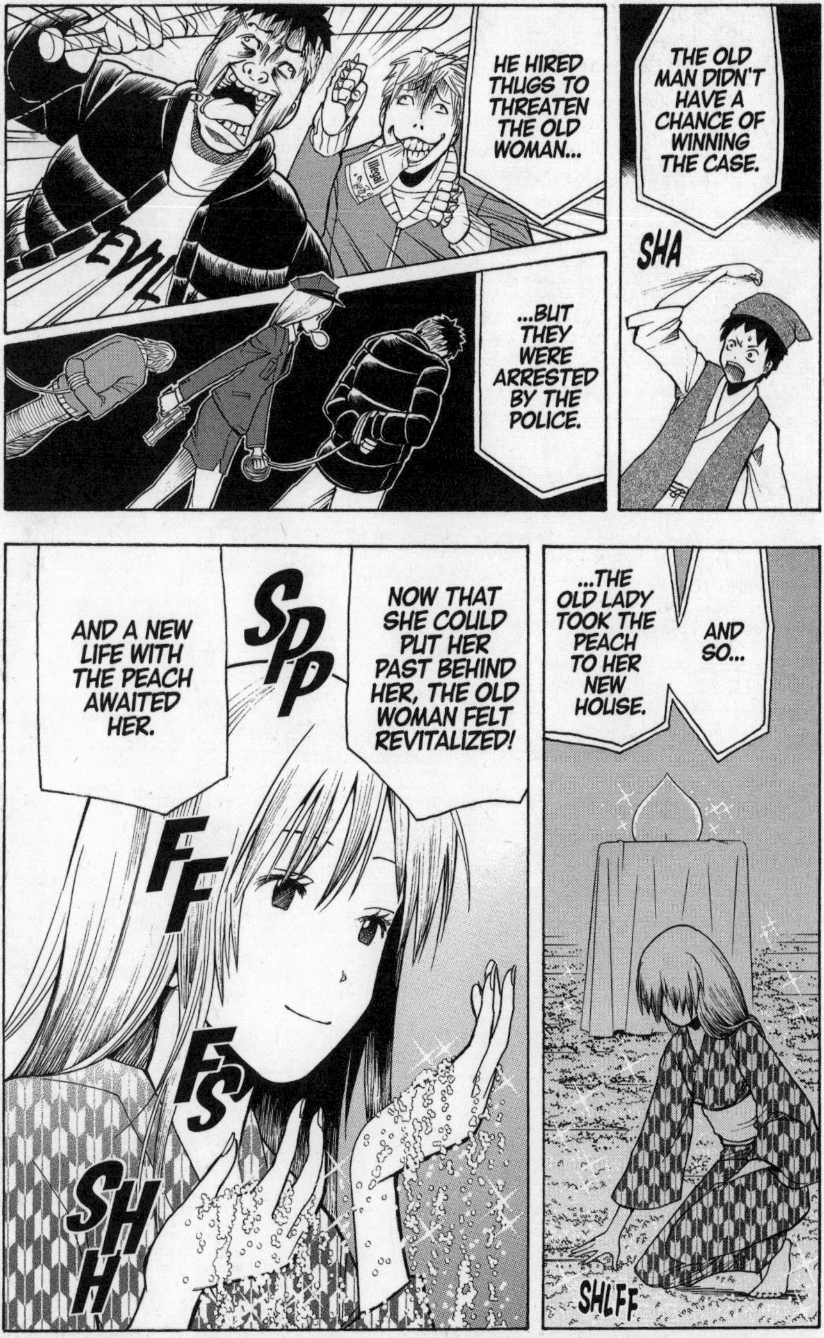
THE OLD MAN DIDN'T HAVE A CHANCE OF WINNING THE CASE.
SHA
HE HIRED THUGS TO THREATEN THE OLD WOMAN...
EVIL
Illegal
...BUT THEY WERE ARRESTED BY THE POLICE.
AND SO...
...THE OLD LADY TOOK THE PEACH TO HER NEW HOUSE.
SHLFF
NOW THAT SHE COULD PUT HER PAST BEHIND HER, THE OLD WOMAN FELT REVITALIZED!
AND A NEW LIFE WITH THE PEACH AWAITED HER.
SPP
FF
FS
SHH

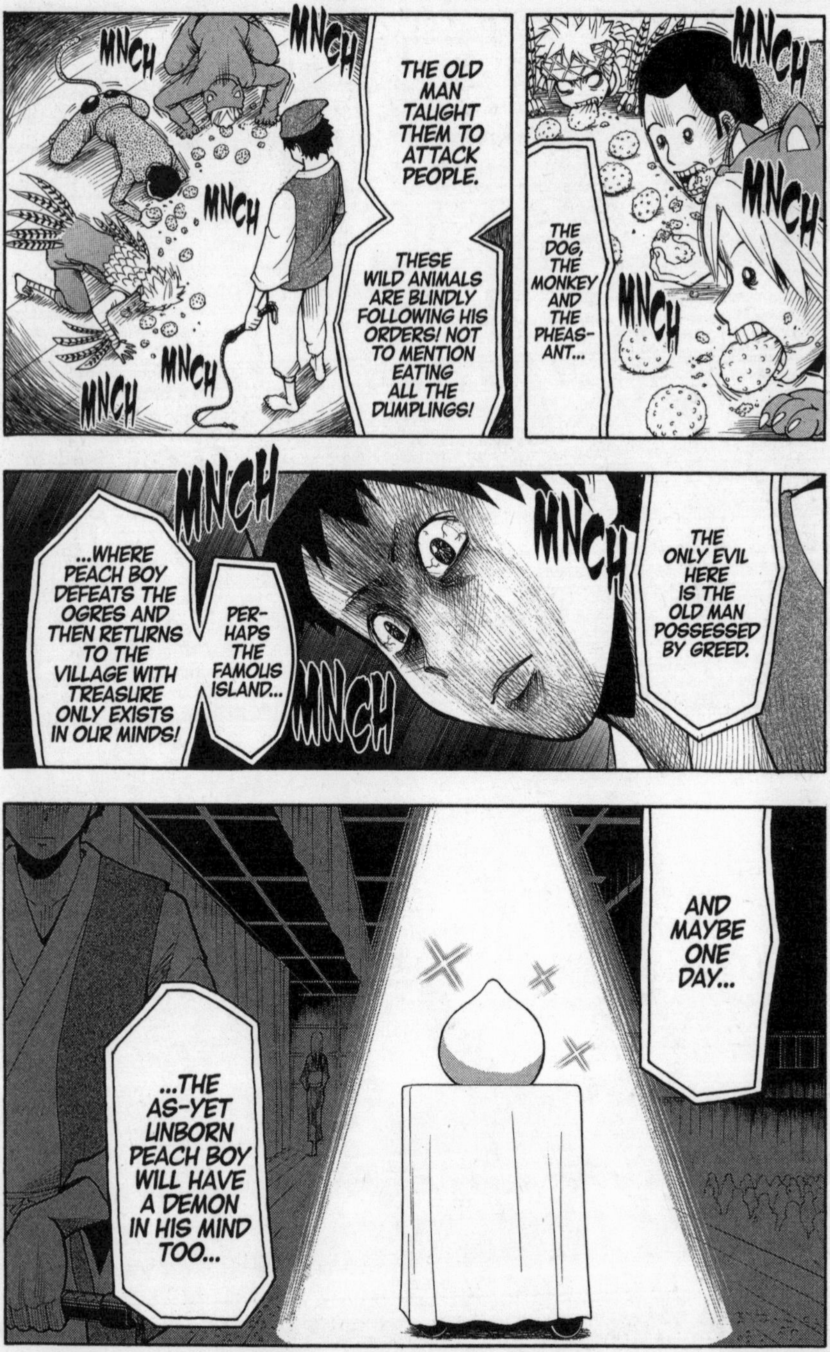
MNCH
MNCH
THE DOG, THE MONKEY AND THE PHEAS-ANT...
MNCH
MNCH
THE OLD MAN TAUGHT THEM TO ATTACK PEOPLE.
THESE WILD ANIMALS ARE BLINDLY FOLLOWING HIS ORDERS! NOT TO MENTION EATING ALL THE DUMPLINGS!
MNCH
MNCH
MNCH
MNCH
MNCH
THE ONLY EVIL HERE IS THE OLD MAN POSSESSED BY GREED.
MNCH
MNCH
PER-HAPS THE FAMOUS ISLAND...
...WHERE PEACH BOY DEFEATS THE OGRES AND THEN RETURNS TO THE VILLAGE WITH TREASURE ONLY EXISTS IN OUR MINDS!
MNCH
AND MAYBE ONE DAY...
...THE AS-YET UNBORN PEACH BOY WILL HAVE A DEMON IN HIS MIND TOO...

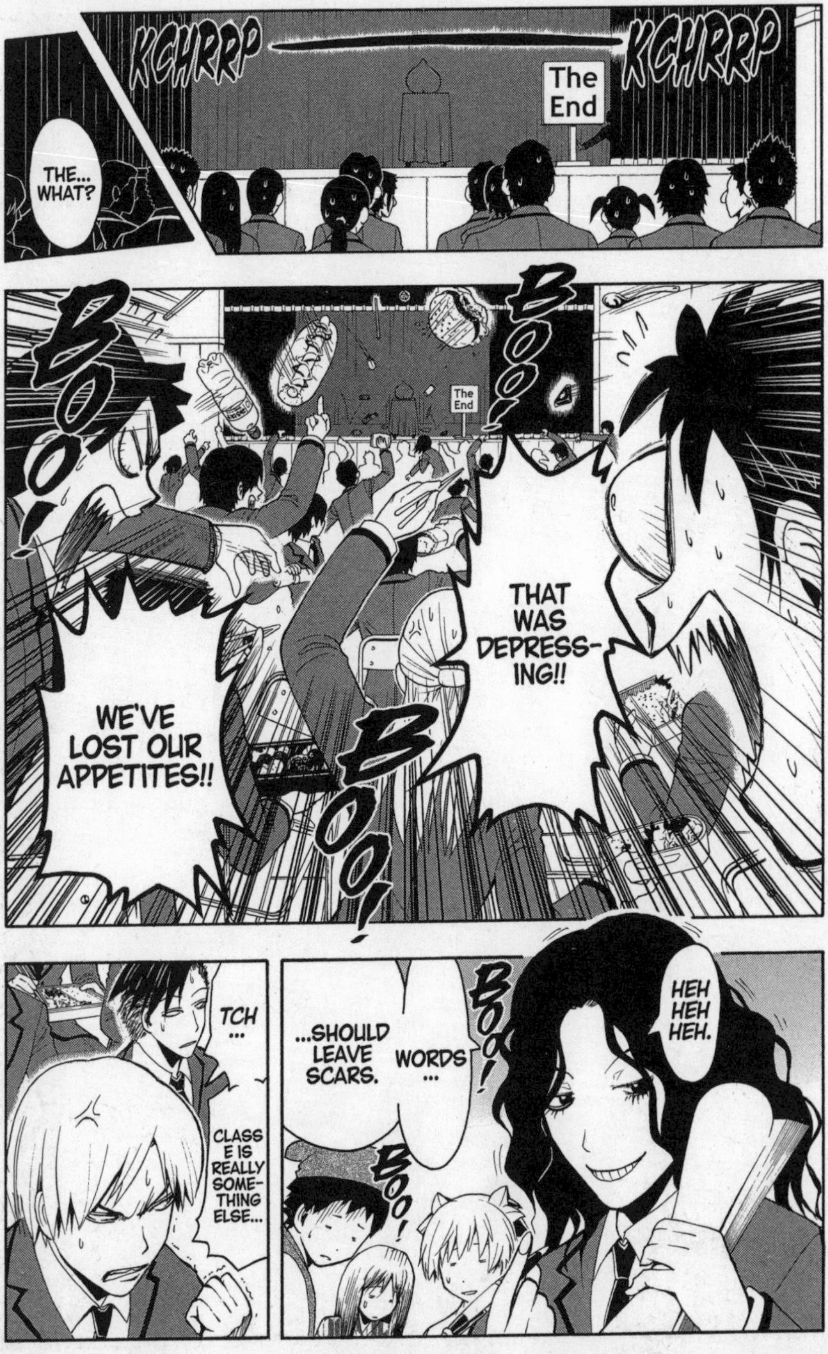
KCHRRP
The End
KCHRRP
THE... WHAT?
BOOO!
The End
BOOO!
THAT WAS DEPRESSING!!
BOOO!
WE'VE LOST OUR APPETITES!!
HEH HEH HEH.
BOO!
WORDS...
...SHOULD LEAVE SCARS.
BOO!
TCH...
CLASS E IS REALLY SOMETHING ELSE...

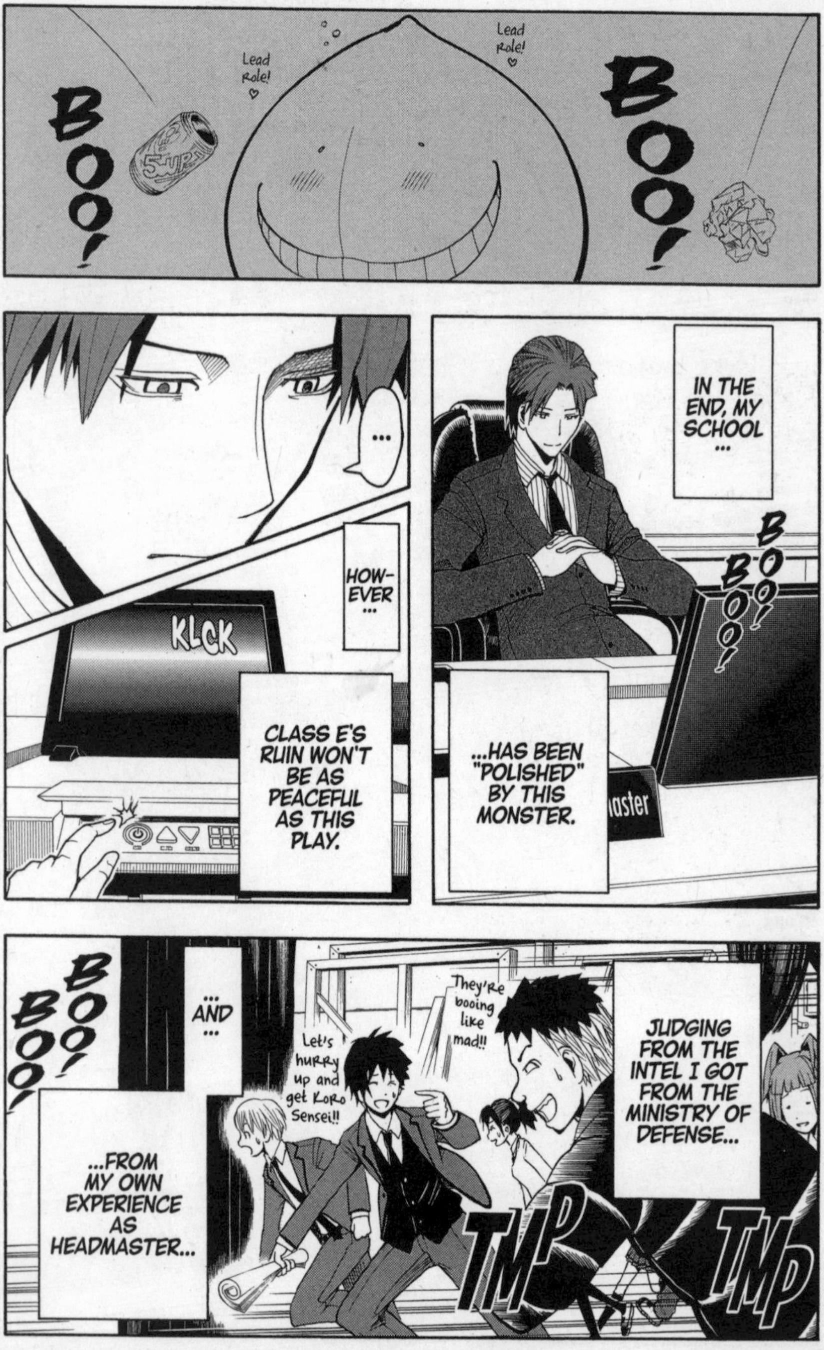
BOO!
Lead role!
Lead role!
BOO!
IN THE END, MY SCHOOL ...
BOO! BOO!
...HAS BEEN "POLISHED" BY THIS MONSTER.
...
HOW-EVER ...
KLCK
CLASS E'S RUIN WON'T BE AS PEACEFUL AS THIS PLAY.
JUDGING FROM THE INTEL I GOT FROM THE MINISTRY OF DEFENSE...
They're booing like mad!!
Let's hurry up and get Koro Sensei!!
... AND ...
BOO! BOO!
...FROM MY OWN EXPERIENCE AS HEADMASTER...
TMP
TMP

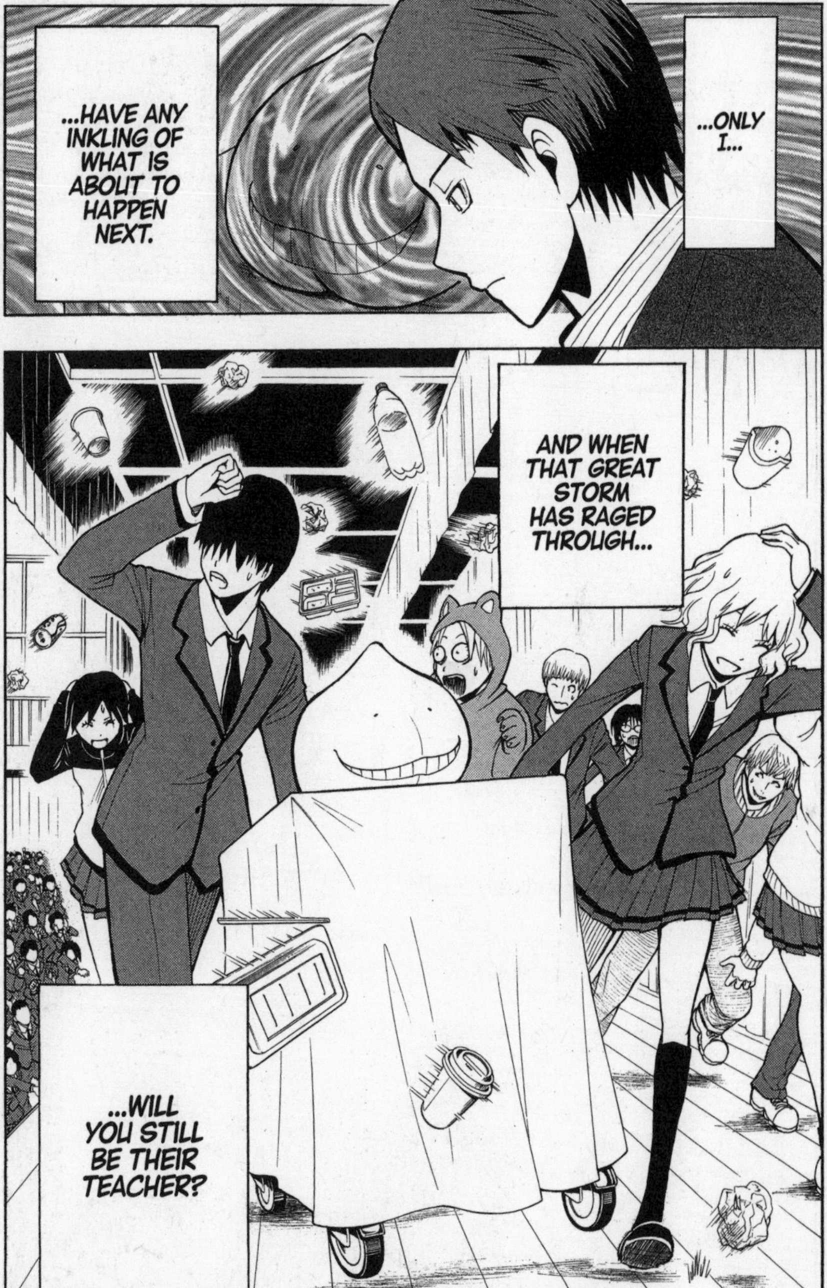
...ONLY I...
...HAVE ANY INKLING OF WHAT IS ABOUT TO HAPPEN NEXT.
AND WHEN THAT GREAT STORM HAS RAGED THROUGH...
...WILL YOU STILL BE THEIR TEACHER?

After the
end of the
on-campus
battle...

...he was
demoted
to Class E
because
he wasn't
needed
anymore.

Kunugigaoka
School Mascot
Kunudon

CLASS 128 TIME FOR A STORM

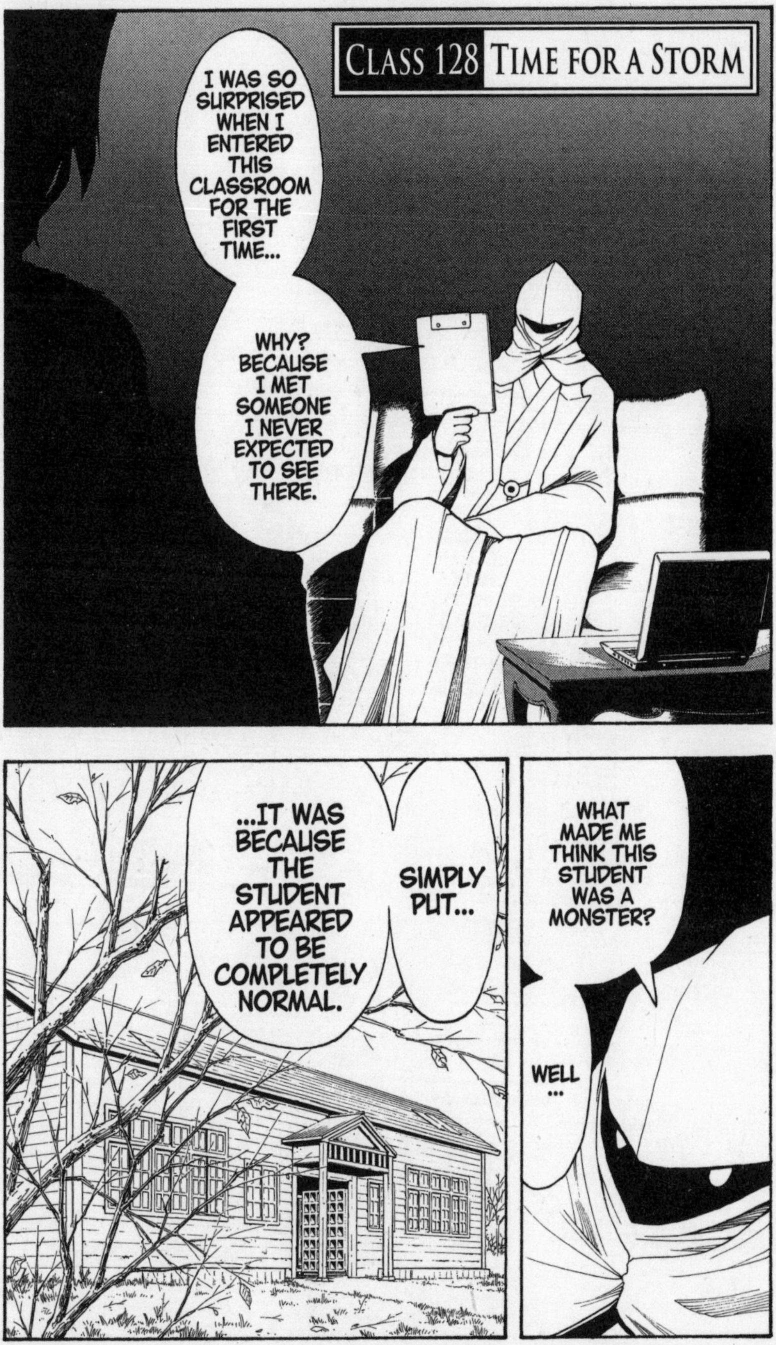
I WAS SO SURPRISED WHEN I ENTERED THIS CLASSROOM FOR THE FIRST TIME...
WHY? BECAUSE I MET SOMEONE I NEVER EXPECTED TO SEE THERE.
WHAT MADE ME THINK THIS STUDENT WAS A MONSTER?
WELL ...
SIMPLY PUT...
...IT WAS BECAUSE THE STUDENT APPEARED TO BE COMPLETELY NORMAL.

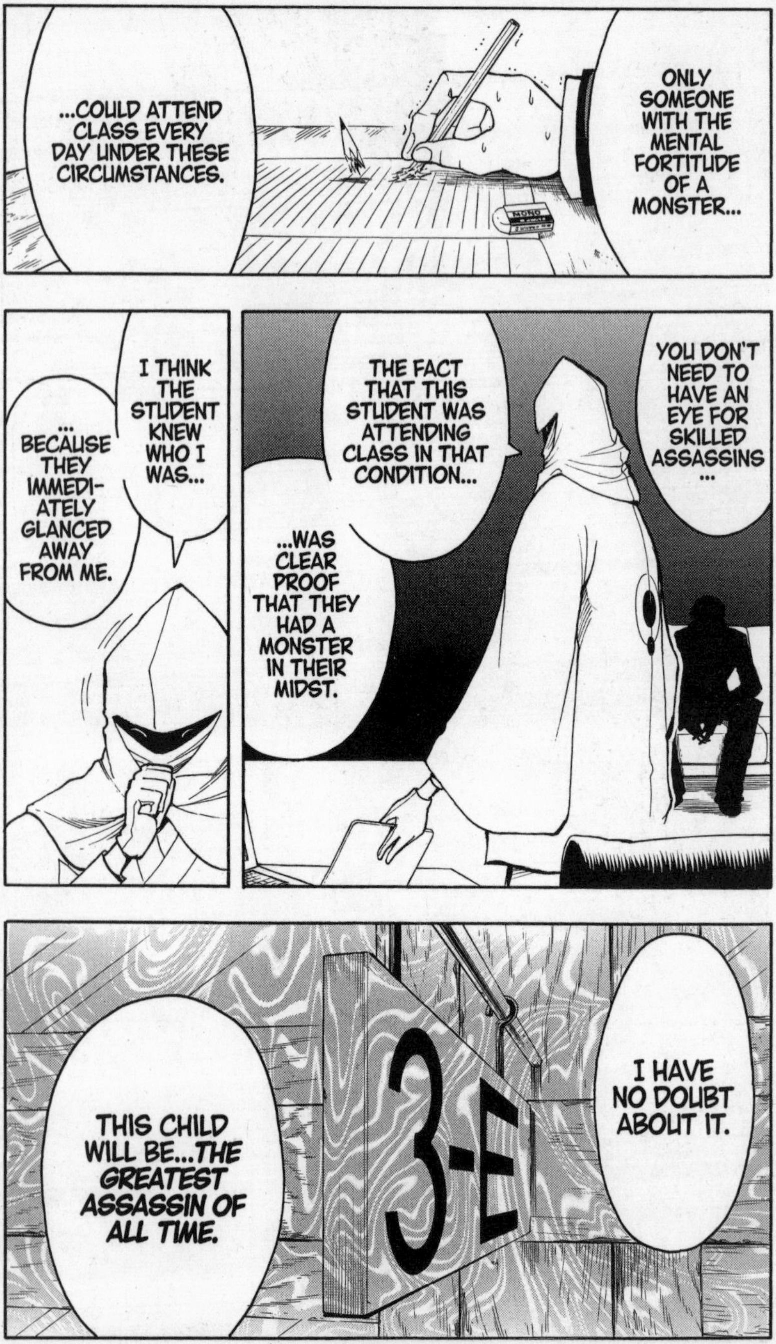
ONLY SOMEONE WITH THE MENTAL FORTITUDE OF A MONSTER...
...COULD ATTEND CLASS EVERY DAY UNDER THESE CIRCUMSTANCES.
YOU DON'T NEED TO HAVE AN EYE FOR SKILLED ASSASSINS...
THE FACT THAT THIS STUDENT WAS ATTENDING CLASS IN THAT CONDITION...
...WAS CLEAR PROOF THAT THEY HAD A MONSTER IN THEIR MIDST.
I THINK THE STUDENT KNEW WHO I WAS...
...BECAUSE THEY IMMEDIATELY GLANCED AWAY FROM ME.
I HAVE NO DOUBT ABOUT IT.
3-E
THIS CHILD WILL BE...*THE GREATEST ASSASSIN OF ALL TIME.*

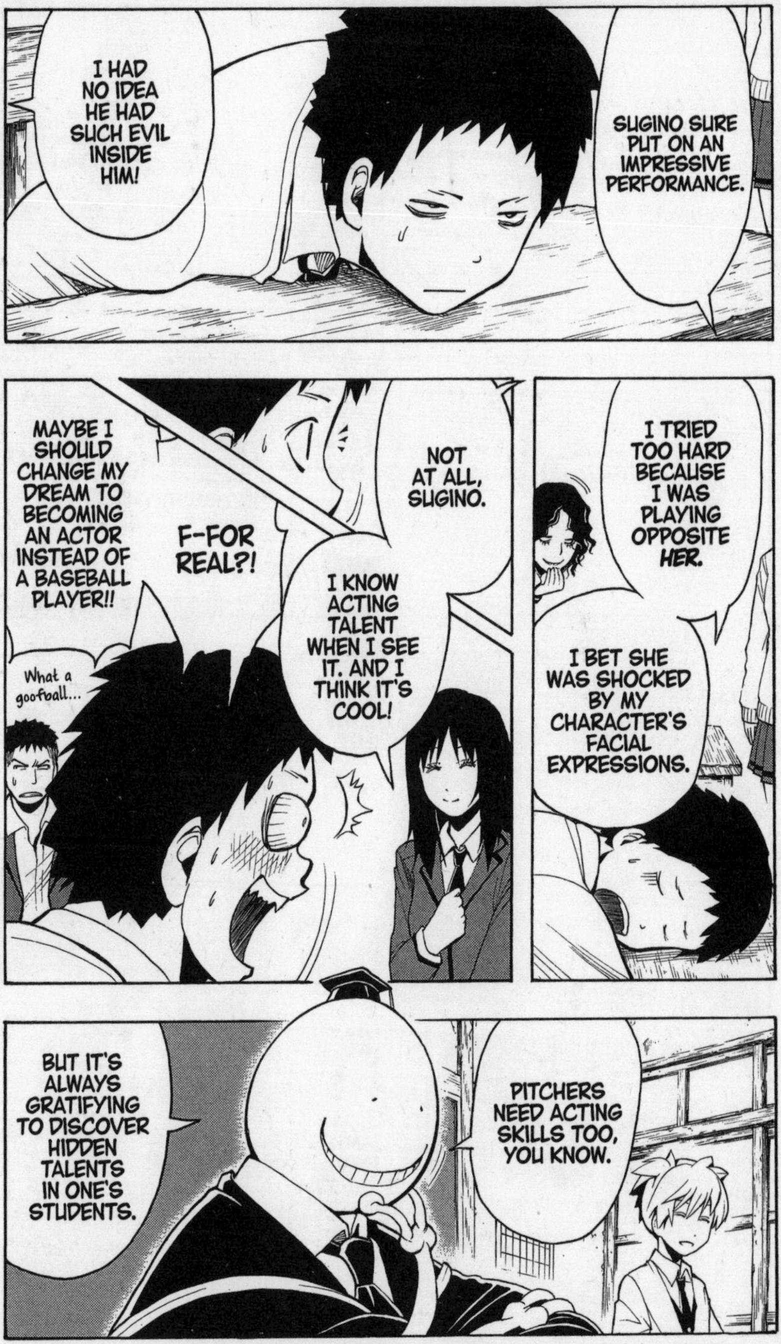
SUGINO SURE PUT ON AN IMPRESSIVE PERFORMANCE.
I HAD NO IDEA HE HAD SUCH EVIL INSIDE HIM!
I TRIED TOO HARD BECAUSE I WAS PLAYING OPPOSITE HER.
I BET SHE WAS SHOCKED BY MY CHARACTER'S FACIAL EXPRESSIONS.
NOT AT ALL, SUGINO.
I KNOW ACTING TALENT WHEN I SEE IT. AND I THINK IT'S COOL!
F-FOR REAL?!
MAYBE I SHOULD CHANGE MY DREAM TO BECOMING AN ACTOR INSTEAD OF A BASEBALL PLAYER!!
What a goofball...
PITCHERS NEED ACTING SKILLS TOO, YOU KNOW.
BUT IT'S ALWAYS GRATIFYING TO DISCOVER HIDDEN TALENTS IN ONE'S STUDENTS.

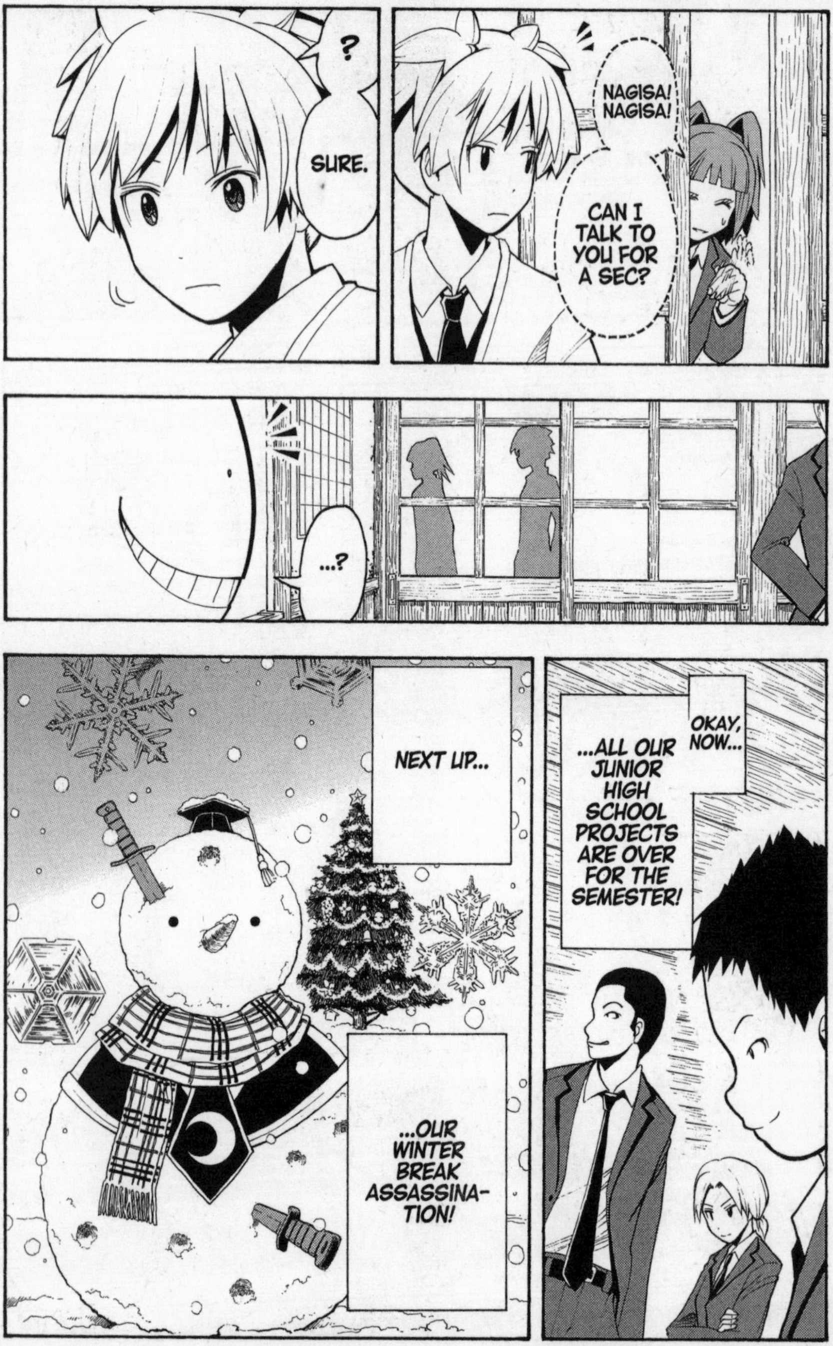
NAGISA! NAGISA!
CAN I TALK TO YOU FOR A SEC?
?
SURE.
...?
OKAY, NOW...
...ALL OUR JUNIOR HIGH SCHOOL PROJECTS ARE OVER FOR THE SEMESTER!
NEXT UP...
...OUR WINTER BREAK ASSASSINATION!

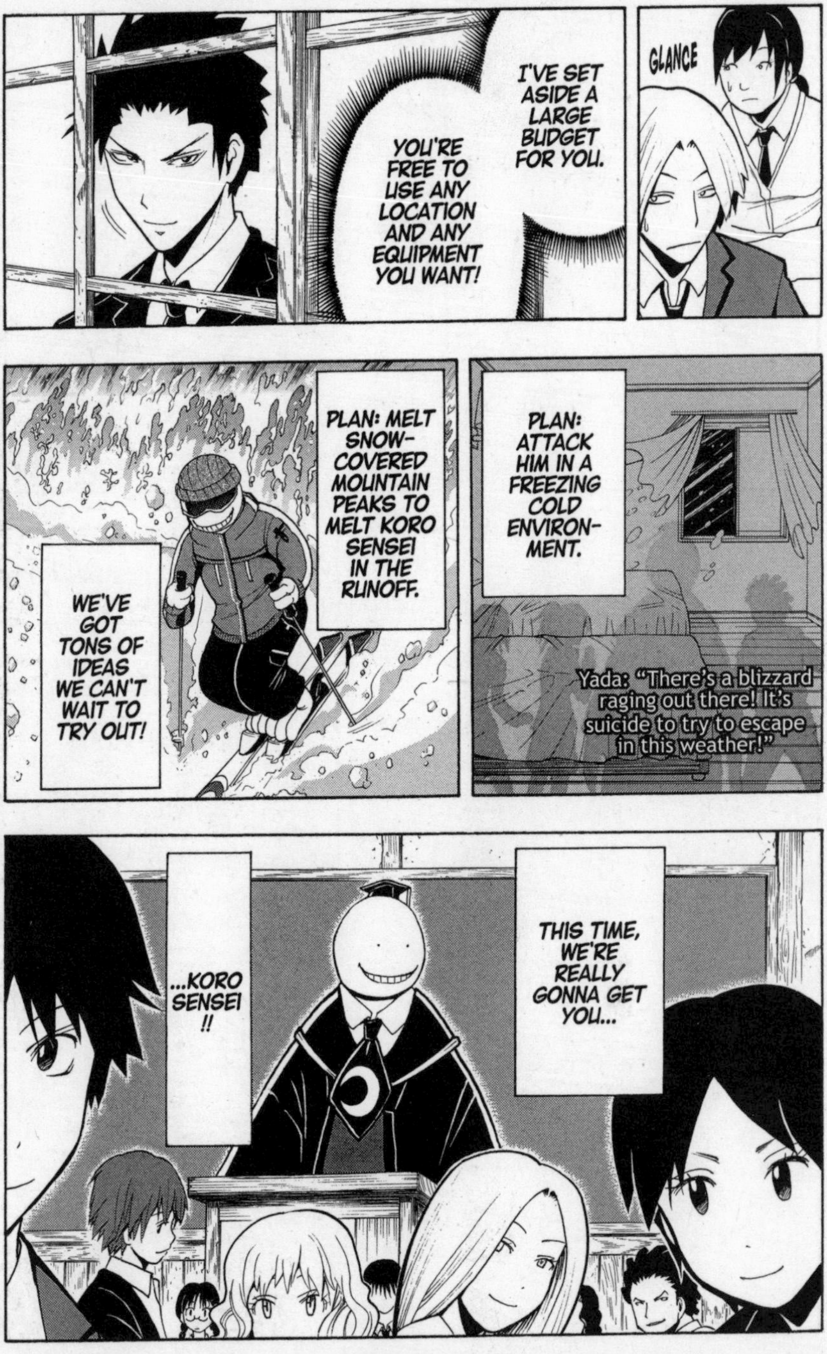
GLANCE
I'VE SET ASIDE A LARGE BUDGET FOR YOU.
YOU'RE FREE TO USE ANY LOCATION AND ANY EQUIPMENT YOU WANT!
PLAN: ATTACK HIM IN A FREEZING COLD ENVIRON-MENT.
Yada: "There's a blizzard raging out there! It's suicide to try to escape in this weather!"
PLAN: MELT SNOW-COVERED MOUNTAIN PEAKS TO MELT KORO SENSEI IN THE RUNOFF.
WE'VE GOT TONS OF IDEAS WE CAN'T WAIT TO TRY OUT!
THIS TIME, WE'RE REALLY GONNA GET YOU...
...KORO SENSEI !!

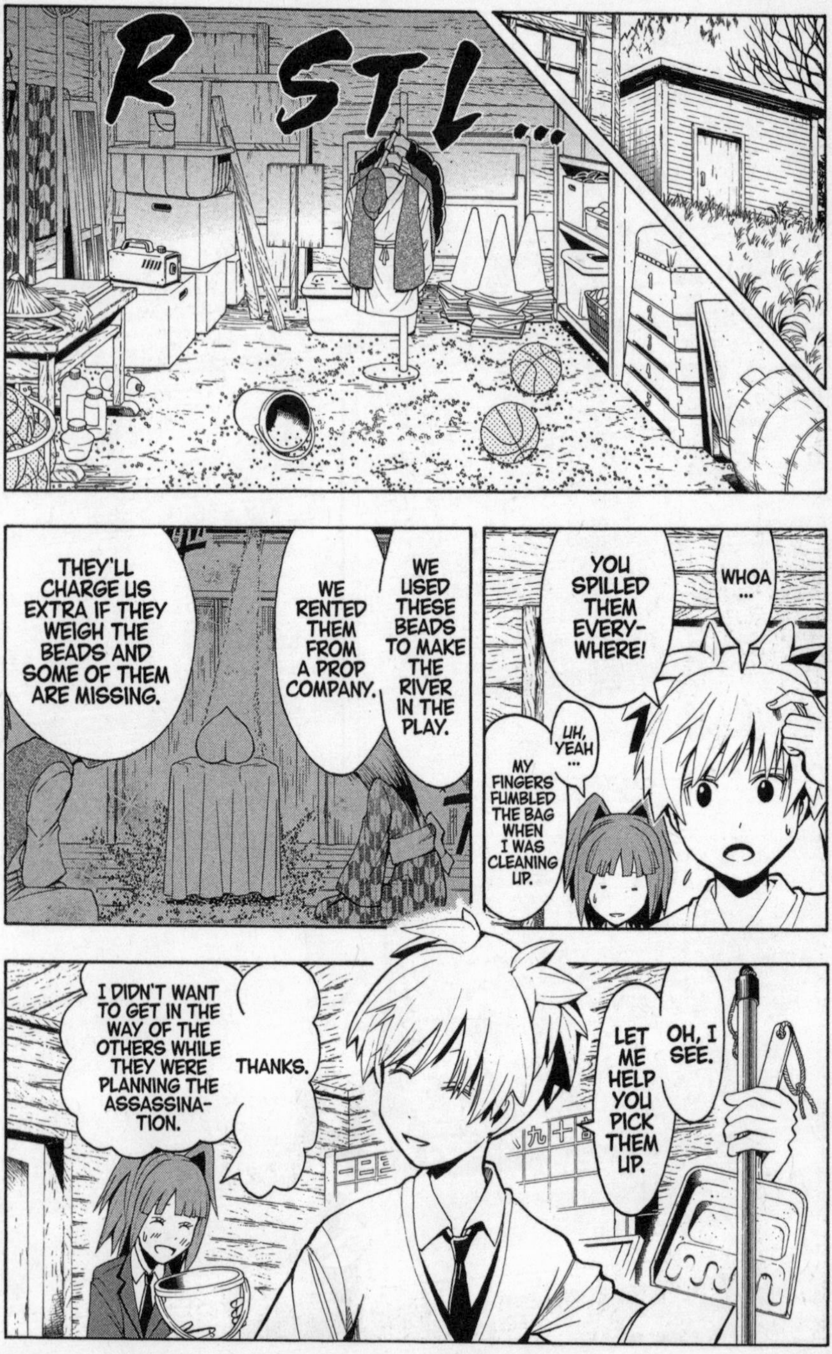
RSTL...
WHOA ...
YOU SPILLED THEM EVERY-WHERE!
UH, YEAH ...
MY FINGERS FUMBLED THE BAG WHEN I WAS CLEANING UP.
WE USED THESE BEADS TO MAKE THE RIVER IN THE PLAY.
WE RENTED THEM FROM A PROP COMPANY.
THEY'LL CHARGE US EXTRA IF THEY WEIGH THE BEADS AND SOME OF THEM ARE MISSING.
OH, I SEE.
LET ME HELP YOU PICK THEM UP.
THANKS.
I DIDN'T WANT TO GET IN THE WAY OF THE OTHERS WHILE THEY WERE PLANNING THE ASSASSINATION.

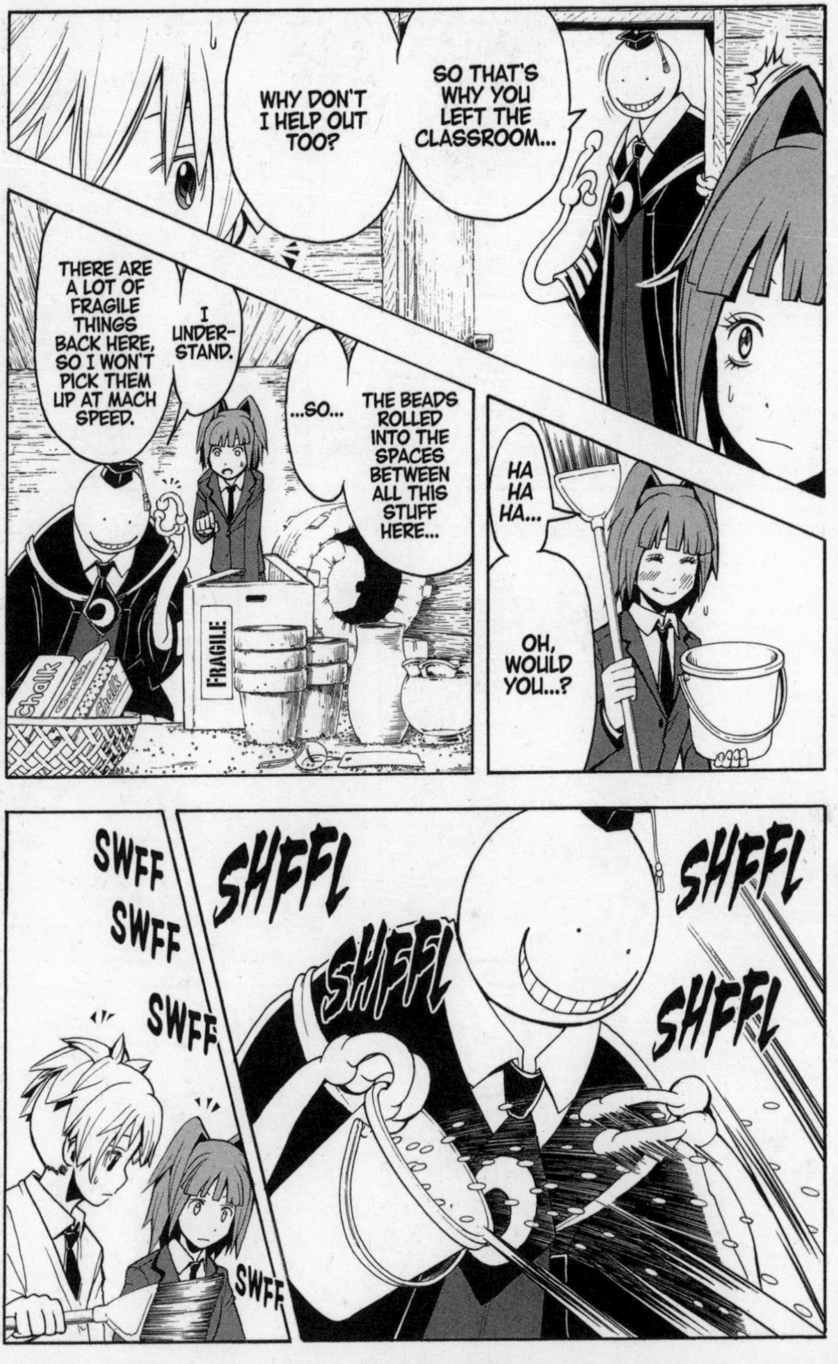
SO THAT'S WHY YOU LEFT THE CLASSROOM...
WHY DON'T I HELP OUT TOO?
HA HA HA...
OH, WOULD YOU...?
THE BEADS ROLLED INTO THE SPACES BETWEEN ALL THIS STUFF HERE...
...SO...
I UNDER-STAND.
THERE ARE A LOT OF FRAGILE THINGS BACK HERE, SO I WON'T PICK THEM UP AT MACH SPEED.
FRAGILE
chalk
SHFFL
SHFFL
SHFFL
SHFFL
SWFF
SWFF
SWFF
SWFF

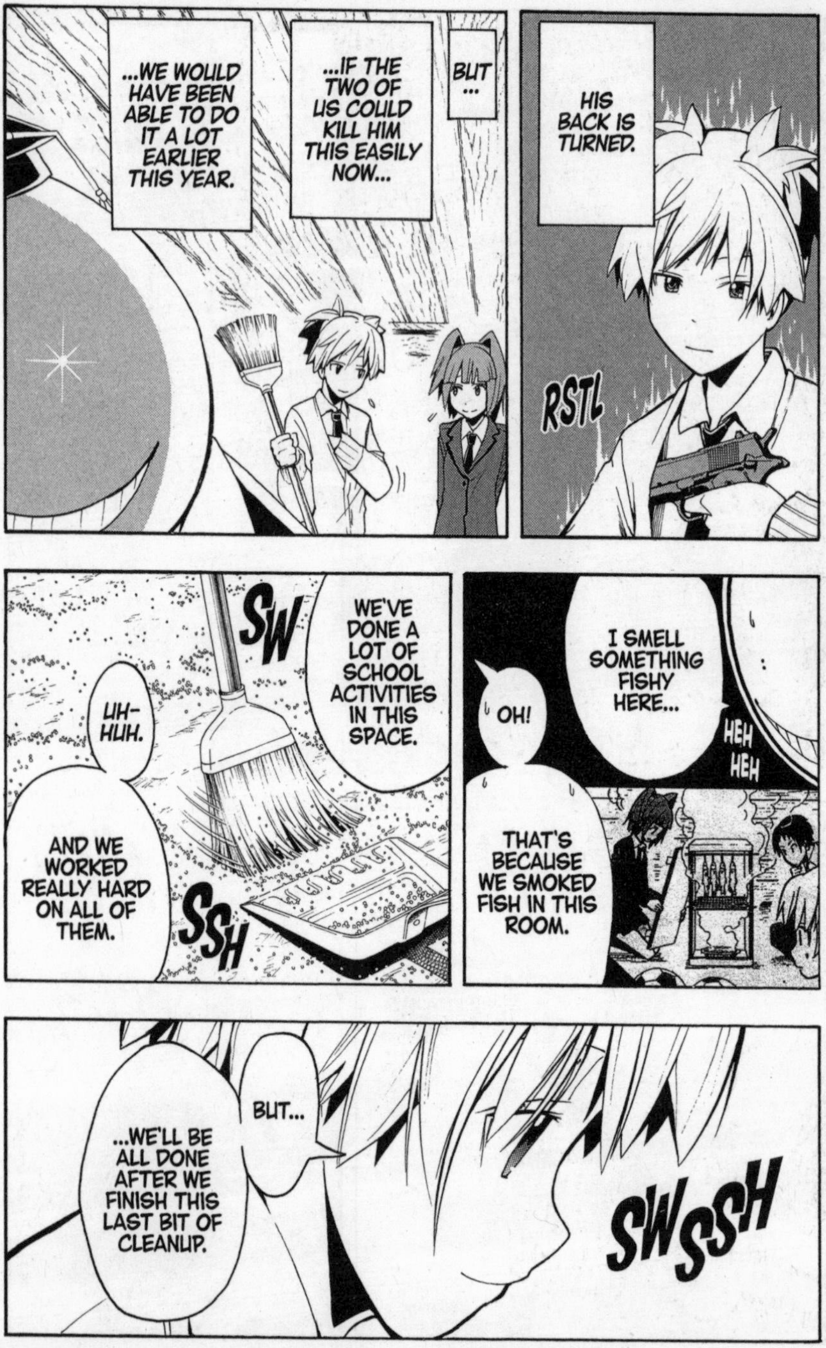
HIS BACK IS TURNED.
RSTL
BUT...
...IF THE TWO OF US COULD KILL HIM THIS EASILY NOW...
...WE WOULD HAVE BEEN ABLE TO DO IT A LOT EARLIER THIS YEAR.
I SMELL SOMETHING FISHY HERE...
HEH HEH
OH!
THAT'S BECAUSE WE SMOKED FISH IN THIS ROOM.
SW
WE'VE DONE A LOT OF SCHOOL ACTIVITIES IN THIS SPACE.
UH-HUH.
AND WE WORKED REALLY HARD ON ALL OF THEM.
SSH
BUT...
...WE'LL BE ALL DONE AFTER WE FINISH THIS LAST BIT OF CLEANUP.
SWSSH

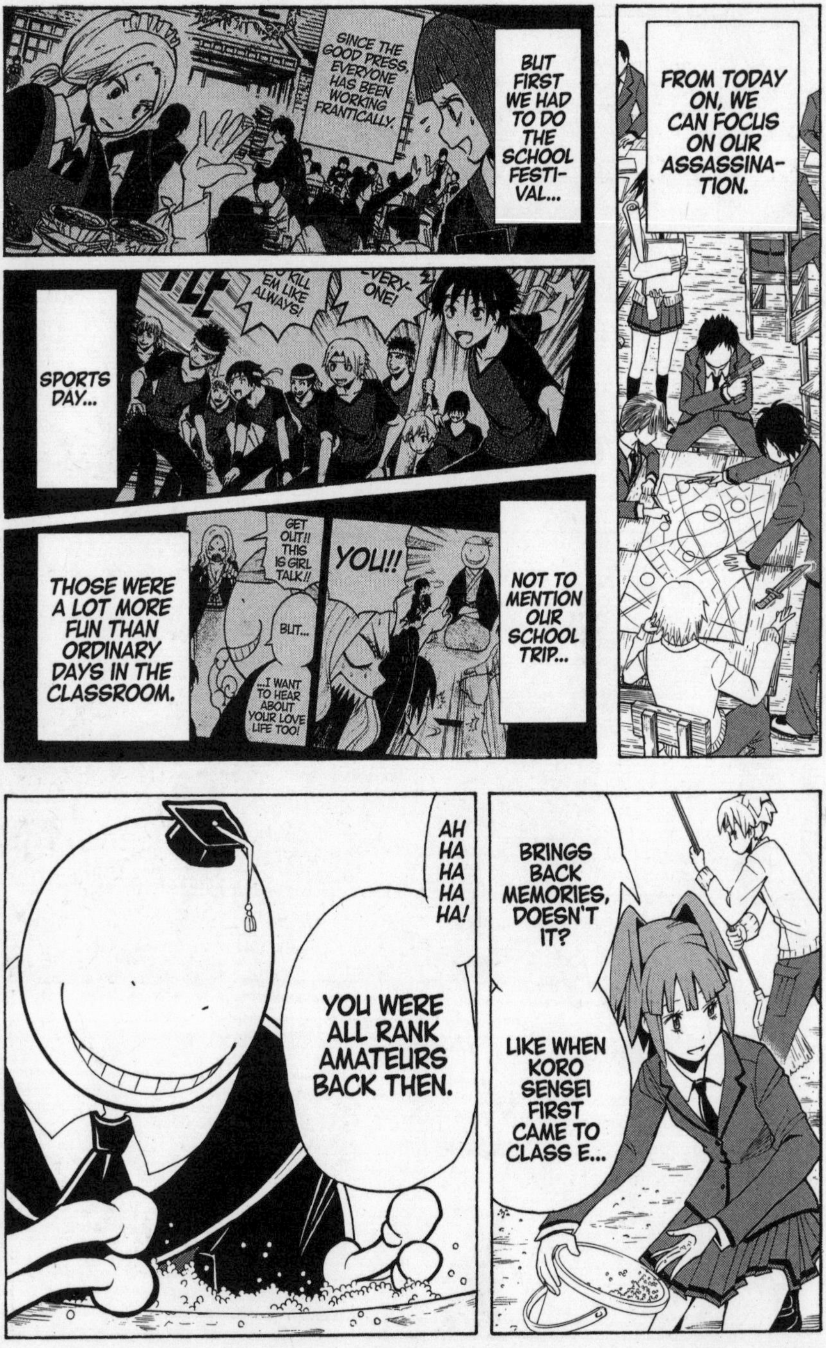
FROM TODAY ON, WE CAN FOCUS ON OUR ASSASSINATION.
BUT FIRST WE HAD TO DO THE SCHOOL FESTIVAL...
SINCE THE GOOD PRESS, EVERYONE HAS BEEN WORKING FRANTICALLY.
EVERYONE!
KILL 'EM LIKE ALWAYS!
SPORTS DAY...
NOT TO MENTION OUR SCHOOL TRIP...
YOU!!
GET OUT!! THIS IS GIRL TALK!!
BUT...
...I WANT TO HEAR ABOUT YOUR LOVE LIFE TOO!
THOSE WERE A LOT MORE FUN THAN ORDINARY DAYS IN THE CLASSROOM.
BRINGS BACK MEMORIES, DOESN'T IT?
LIKE WHEN KORO SENSEI FIRST CAME TO CLASS E...
AH HA HA HA HA!
YOU WERE ALL RANK AMATEURS BACK THEN.

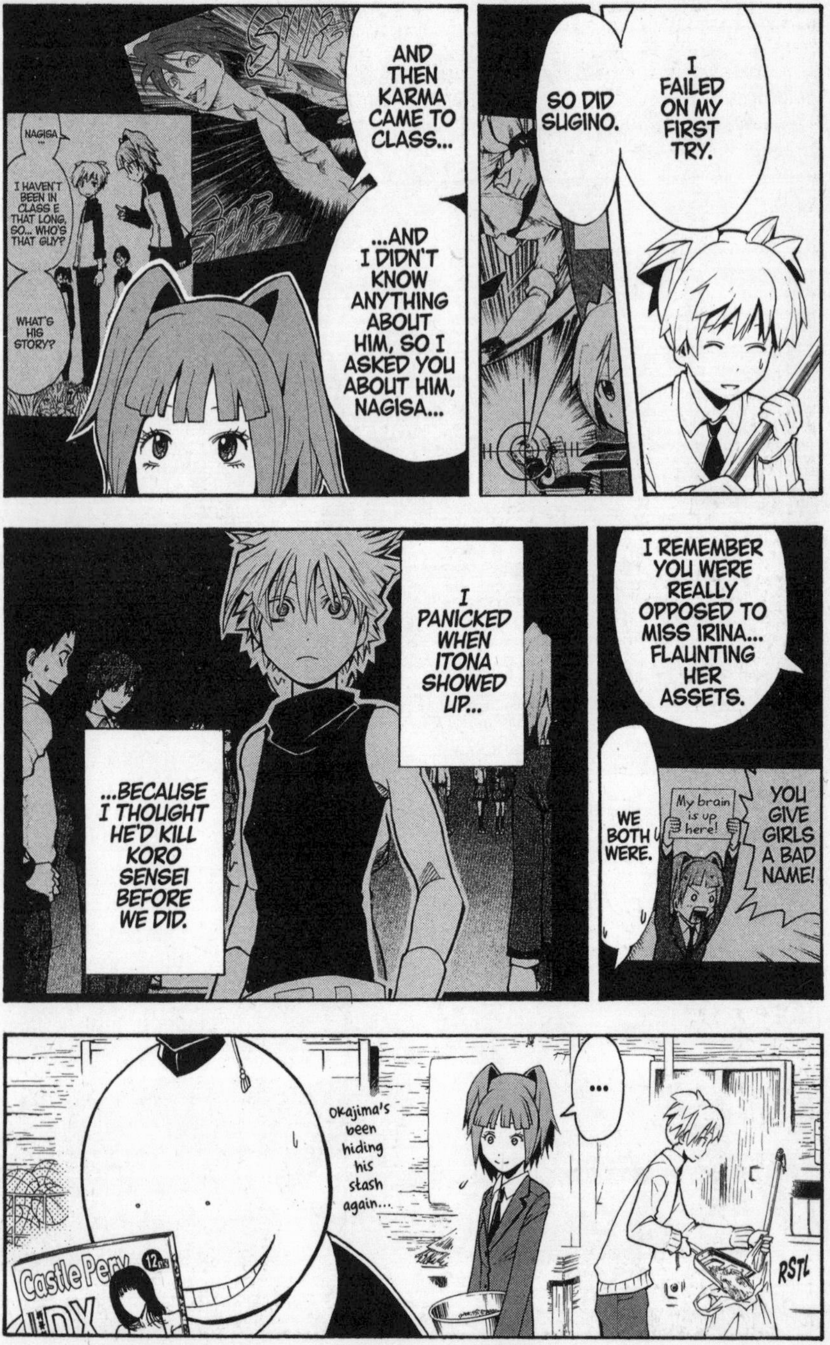
I FAILED ON MY FIRST TRY.
SO DID SUGINO.
AND THEN KARMA CAME TO CLASS...
...AND I DIDN'T KNOW ANYTHING ABOUT HIM, SO I ASKED YOU ABOUT HIM, NAGISA...
NAGISA...
I HAVEN'T BEEN IN CLASS E THAT LONG, SO... WHO'S THAT GUY?
WHAT'S HIS STORY?
I REMEMBER YOU WERE REALLY OPPOSED TO MISS IRINA... FLAUNTING HER ASSETS.
YOU GIVE GIRLS A BAD NAME!
My brain is up here!
WE BOTH WERE.
I PANICKED WHEN ITONA SHOWED UP...
...BECAUSE I THOUGHT HE'D KILL KORO SENSEI BEFORE WE DID.
...
RSTL
Okajima's been hiding his stash again...
Castle Perv DX

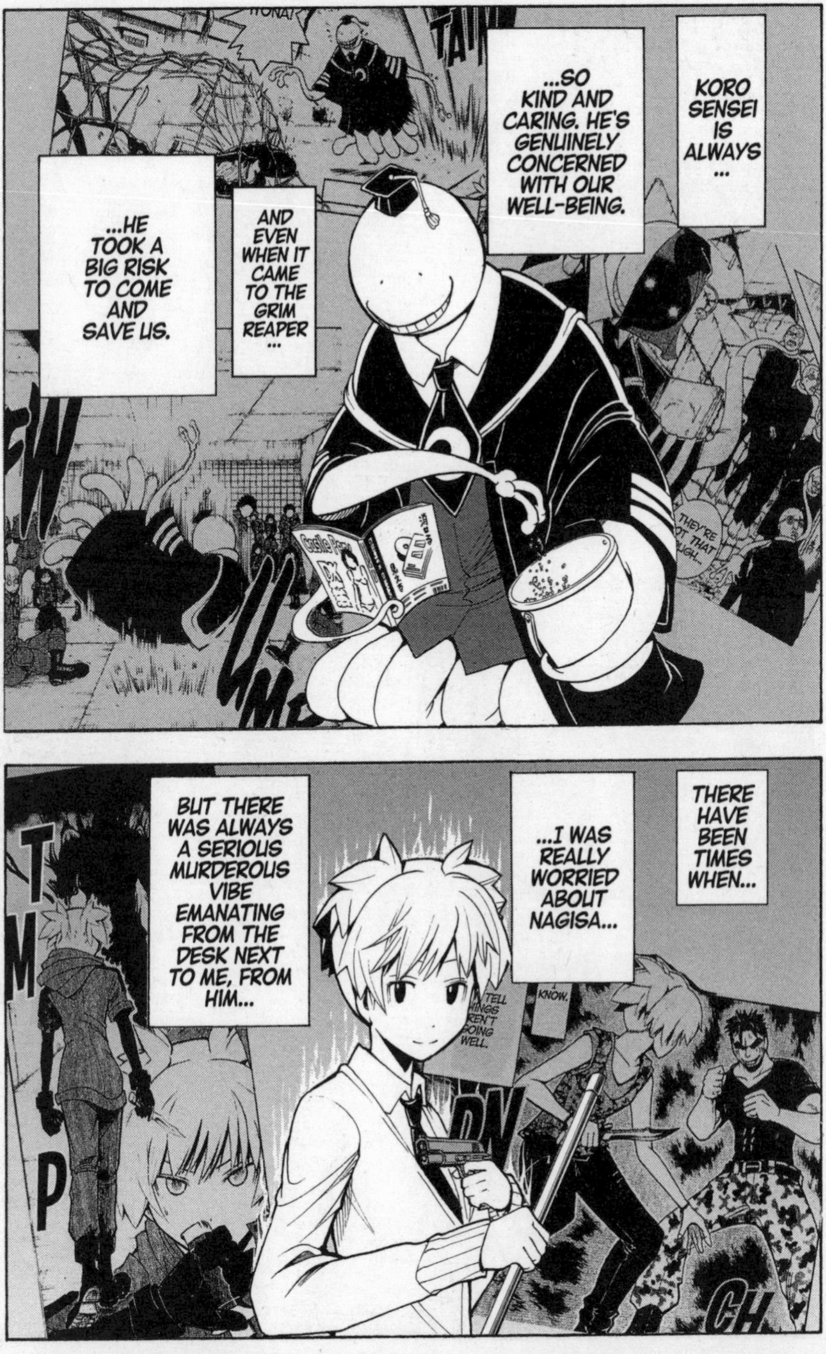
KORO SENSEI IS ALWAYS ...
...SO KIND AND CARING. HE'S GENUINELY CONCERNED WITH OUR WELL-BEING.
AND EVEN WHEN IT CAME TO THE GRIM REAPER ...
...HE TOOK A BIG RISK TO COME AND SAVE US.
THERE HAVE BEEN TIMES WHEN...
...I WAS REALLY WORRIED ABOUT NAGISA...
I KNOW.
BUT THERE WAS ALWAYS A SERIOUS MURDEROUS VIBE EMANATING FROM THE DESK NEXT TO ME, FROM HIM...

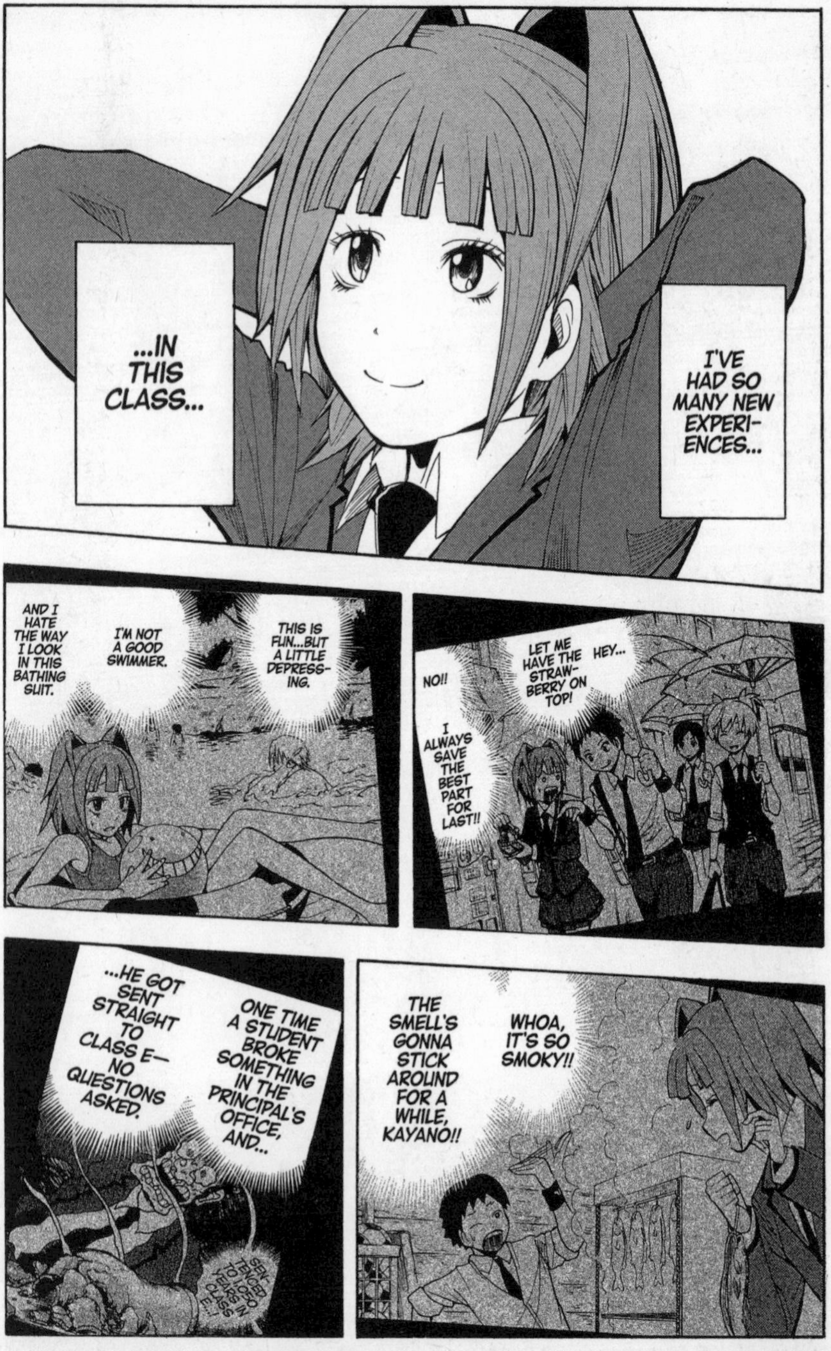
I'VE HAD SO MANY NEW EXPERIENCES...
...IN THIS CLASS...
HEY...
LET ME HAVE THE STRAWBERRY ON TOP!
NO!!
I ALWAYS SAVE THE BEST PART FOR LAST!!
THIS IS FUN...BUT A LITTLE DEPRESSING.
I'M NOT A GOOD SWIMMER.
AND I HATE THE WAY I LOOK IN THIS BATHING SUIT.
WHOA, IT'S SO SMOKY!!
THE SMELL'S GONNA STICK AROUND FOR A WHILE, KAYANO!!
ONE TIME A STUDENT BROKE SOMETHING IN THE PRINCIPAL'S OFFICE, AND...
...HE GOT SENT STRAIGHT TO CLASS E—NO QUESTIONS ASKED.
SENTENCED TO 1,050 YEARS IN CLASS E...

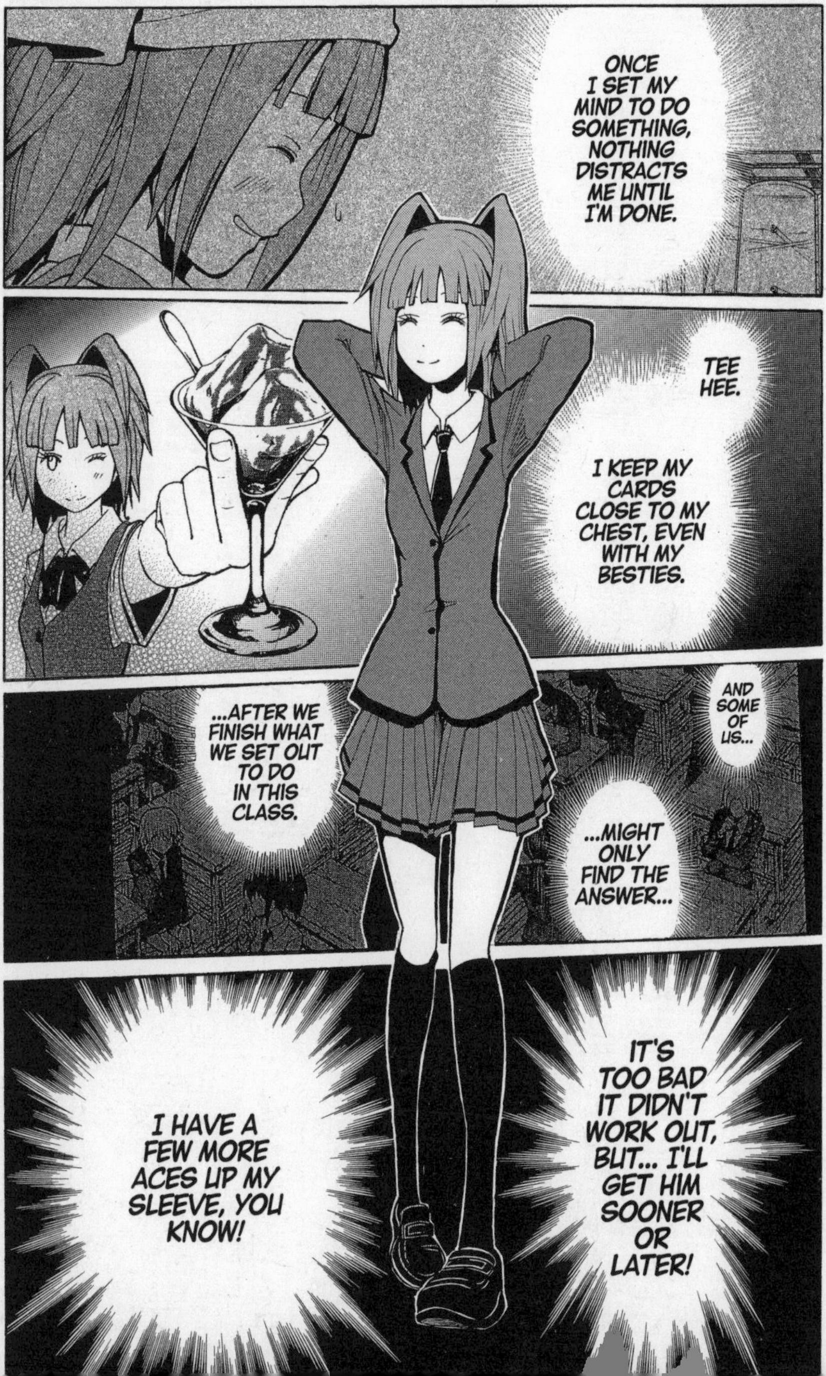
ONCE I SET MY MIND TO DO SOMETHING, NOTHING DISTRACTS ME UNTIL I'M DONE.
TEE HEE.
I KEEP MY CARDS CLOSE TO MY CHEST, EVEN WITH MY BESTIES.
AND SOME OF US...
...MIGHT ONLY FIND THE ANSWER...
...AFTER WE FINISH WHAT WE SET OUT TO DO IN THIS CLASS.
IT'S TOO BAD IT DIDN'T WORK OUT, BUT... I'LL GET HIM SOONER OR LATER!
I HAVE A FEW MORE ACES UP MY SLEEVE, YOU KNOW!

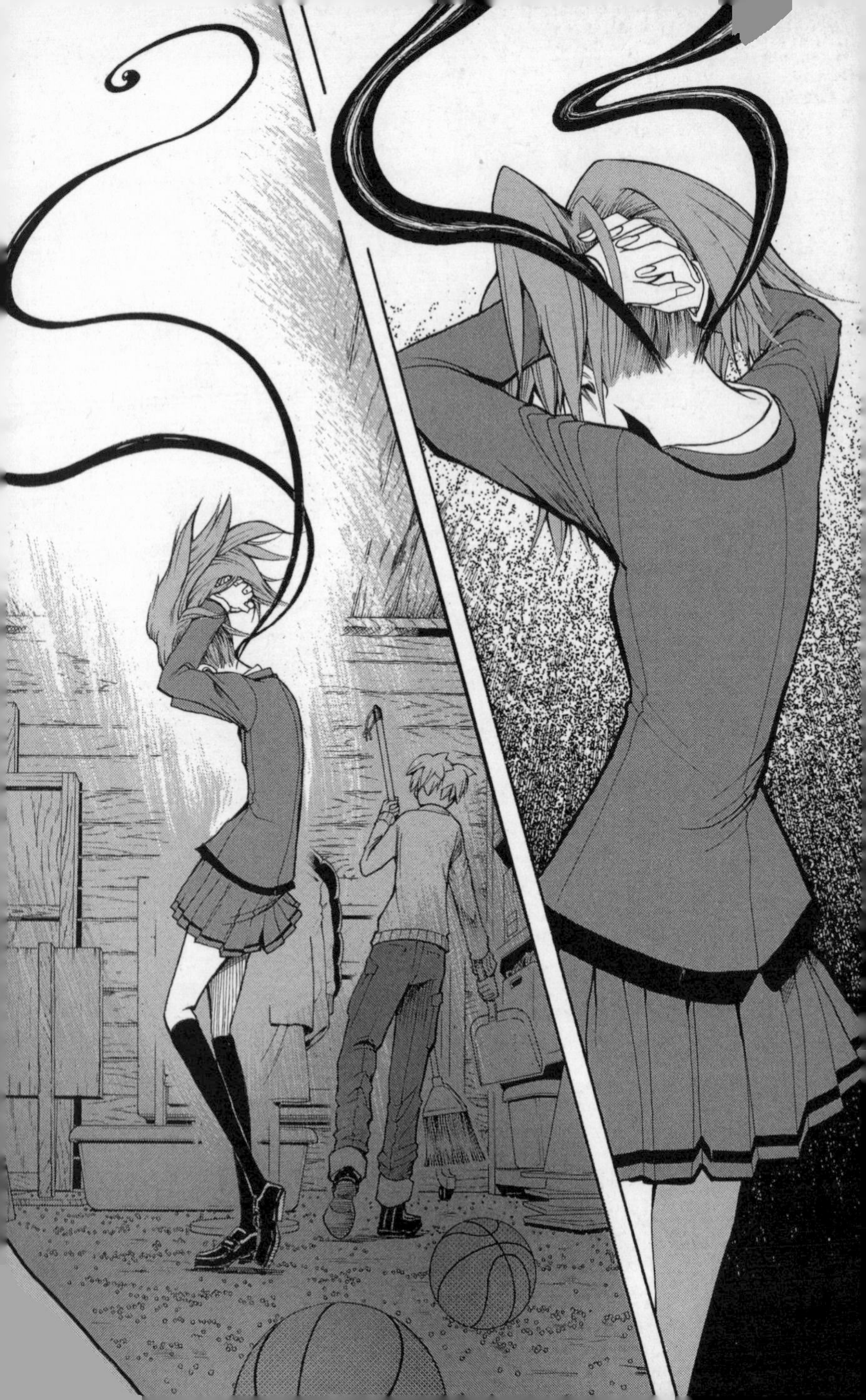

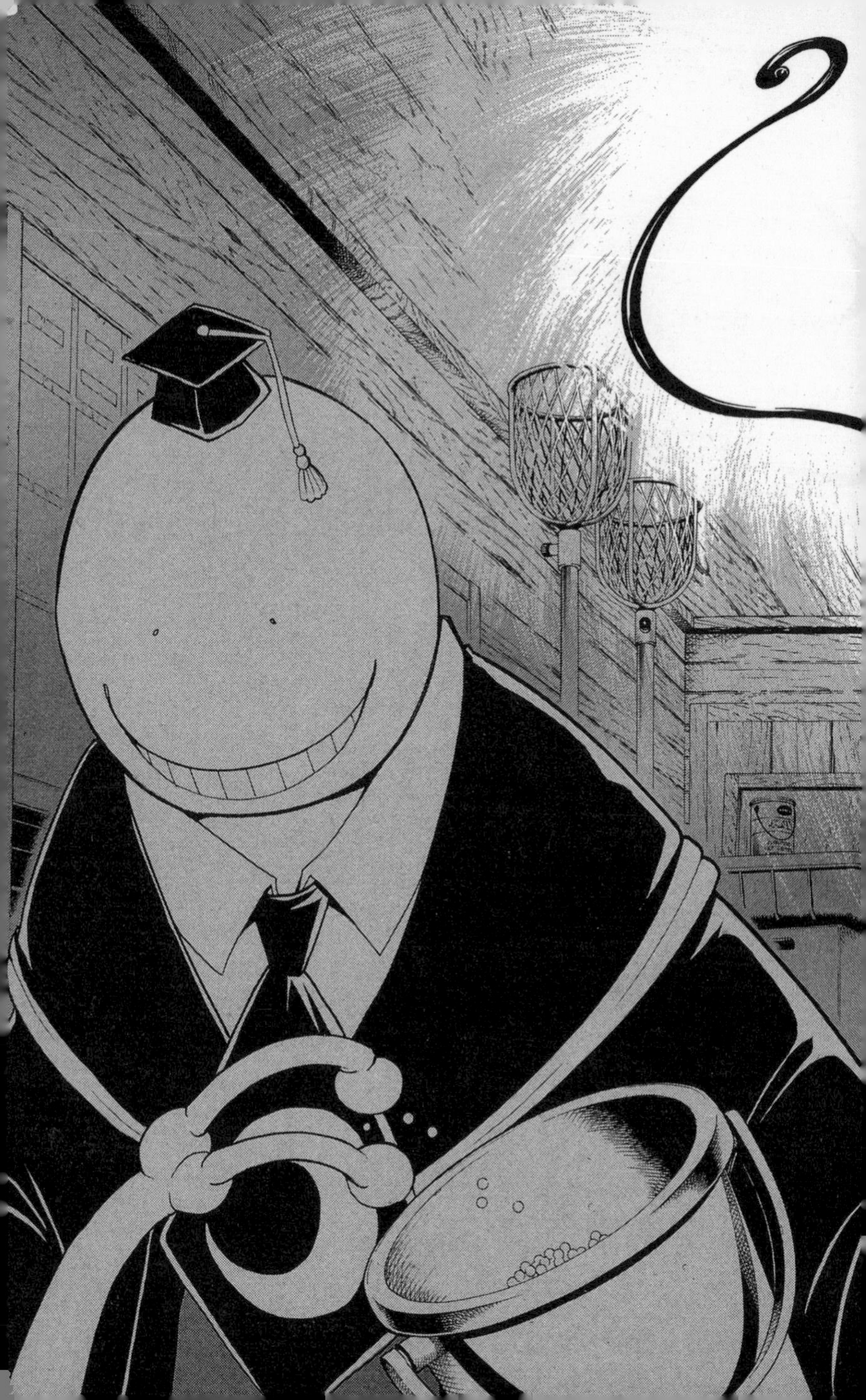

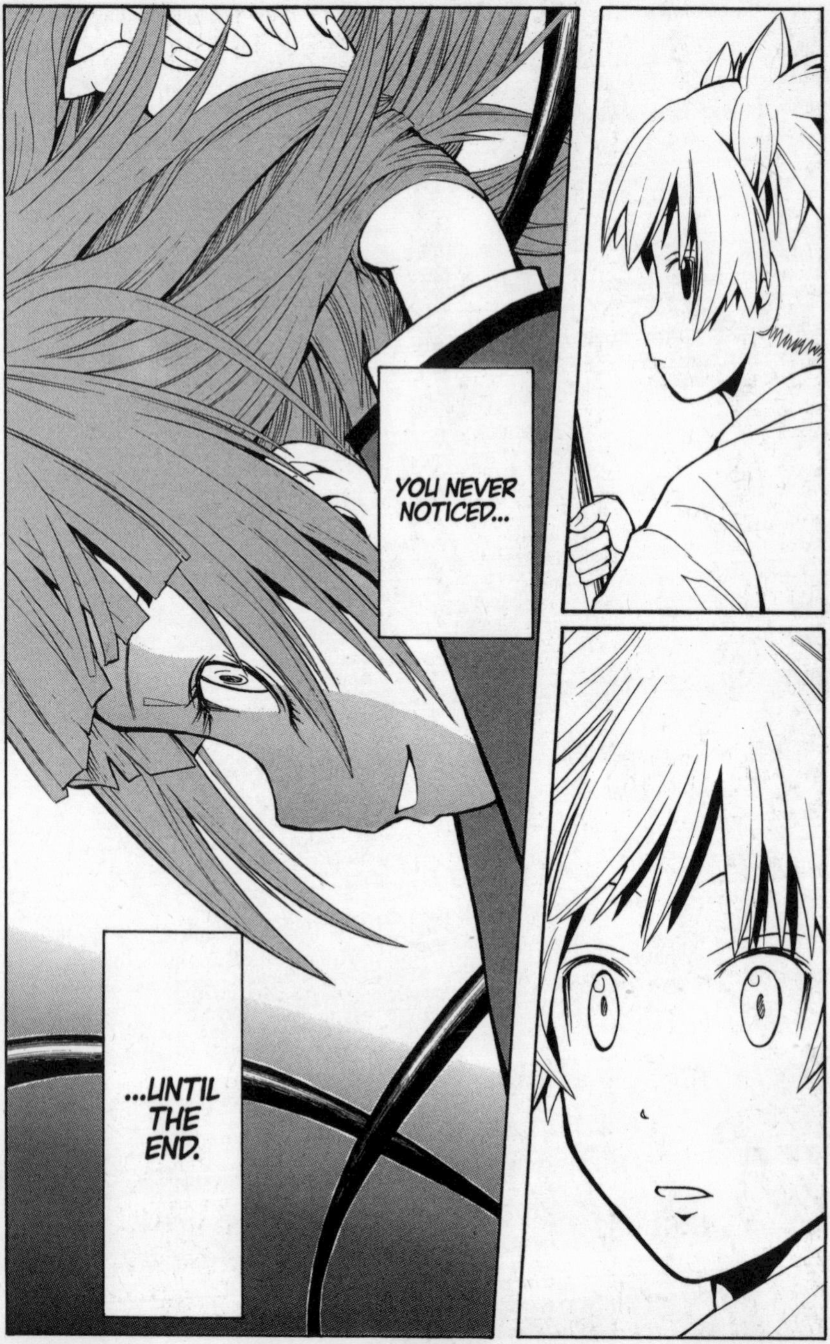
YOU NEVER NOTICED...
...UNTIL THE END.

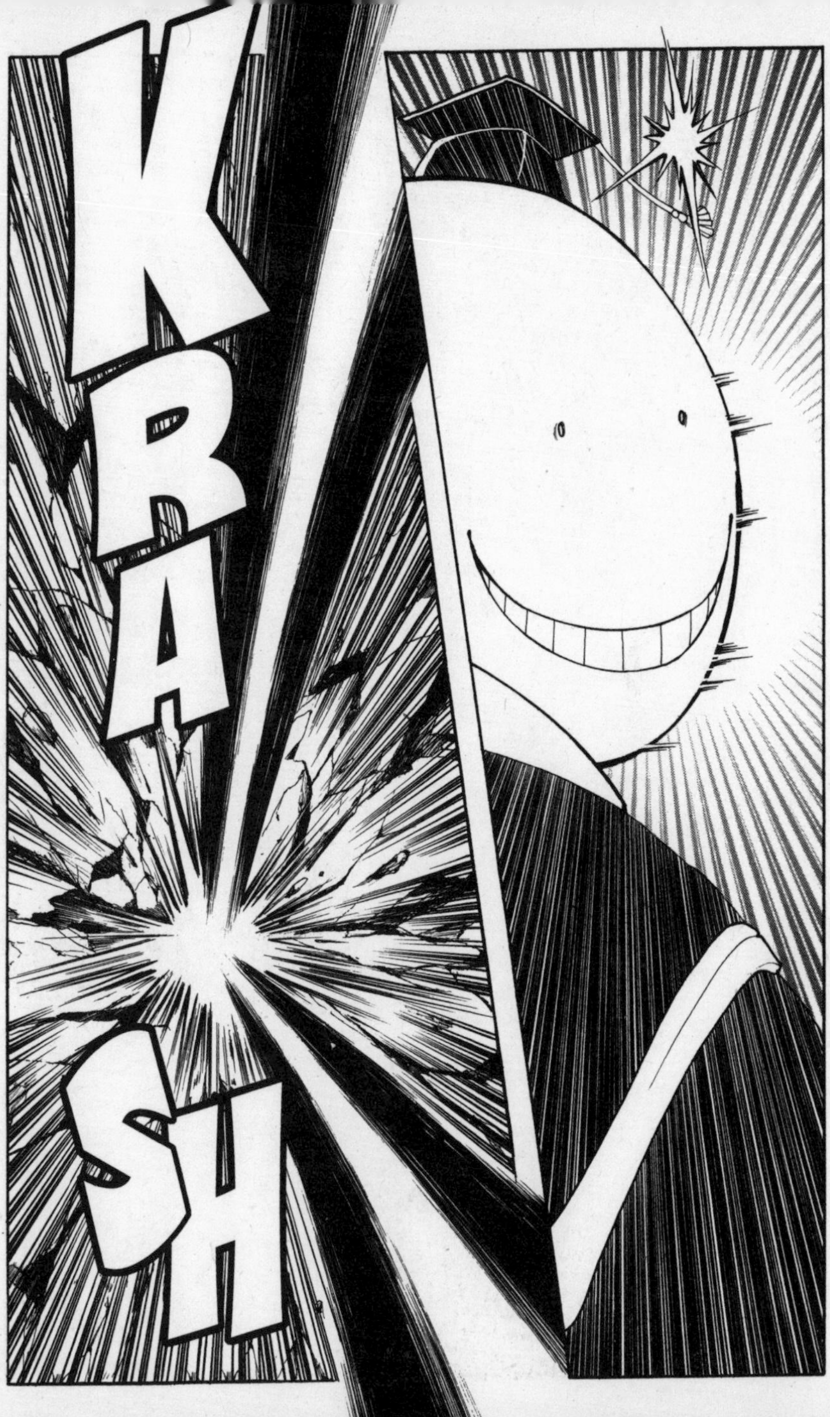
KRASH

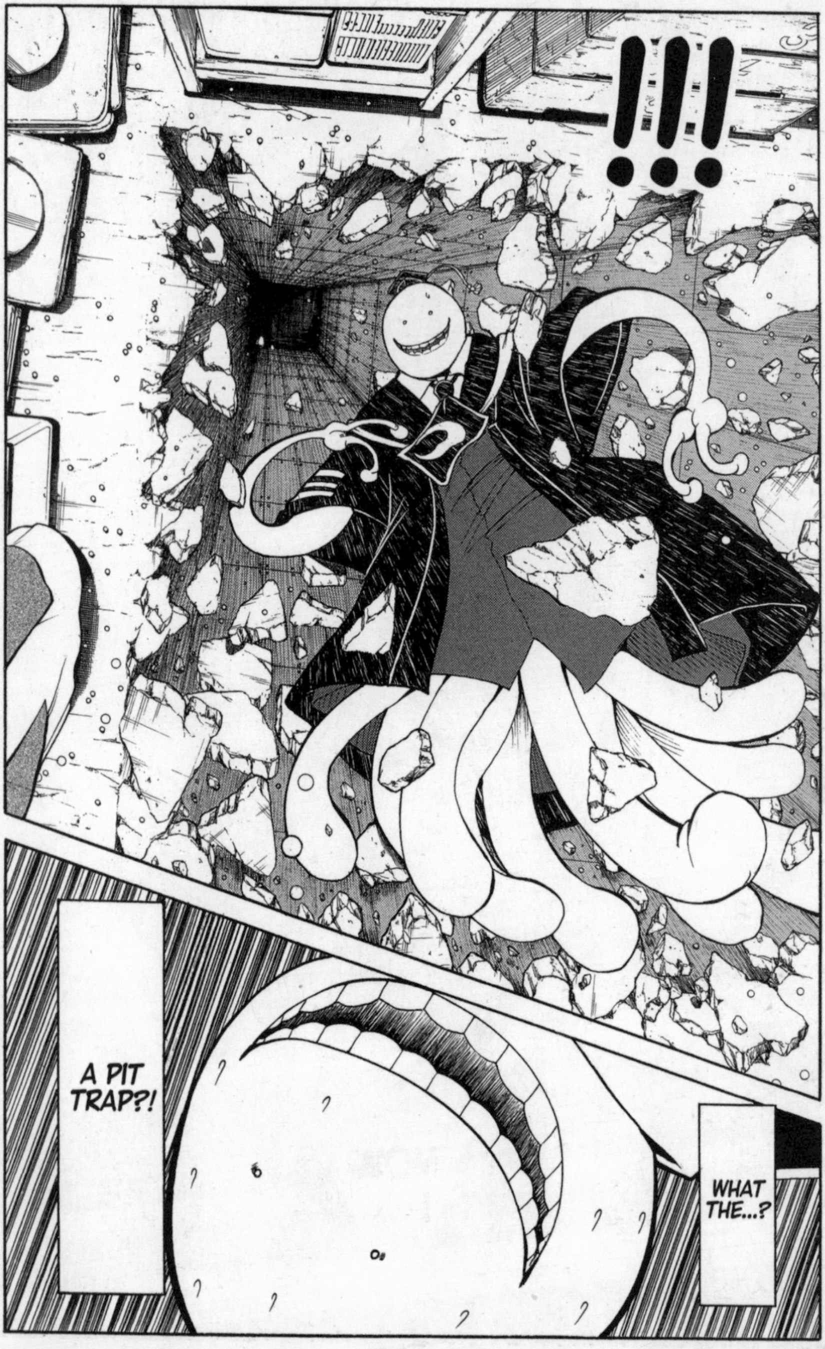
!!!
WHAT THE...?
A PIT TRAP?!

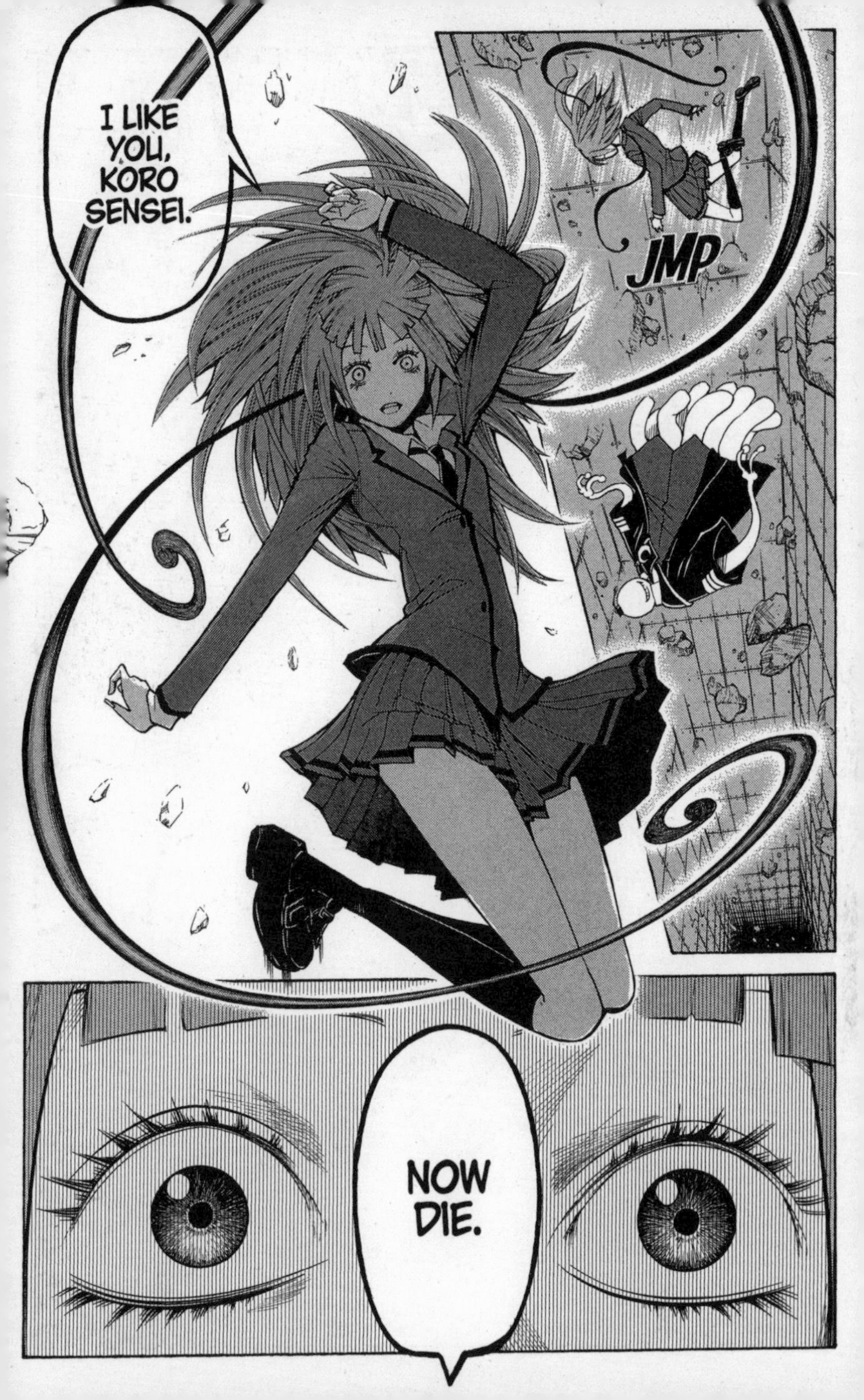
I LIKE YOU, KORO SENSEI.
JMP
NOW DIE.

Class 129 True Identity Time

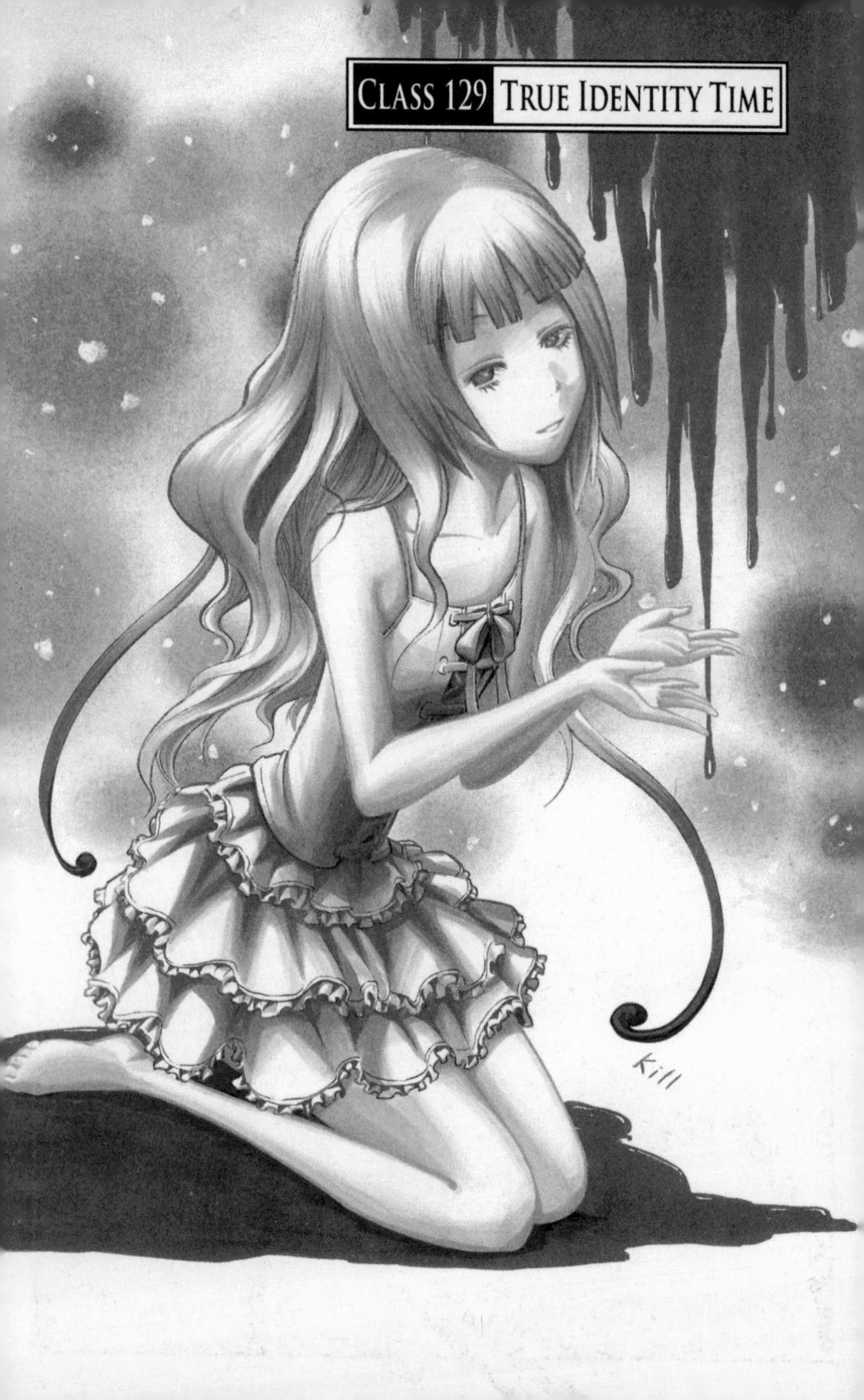
Kill

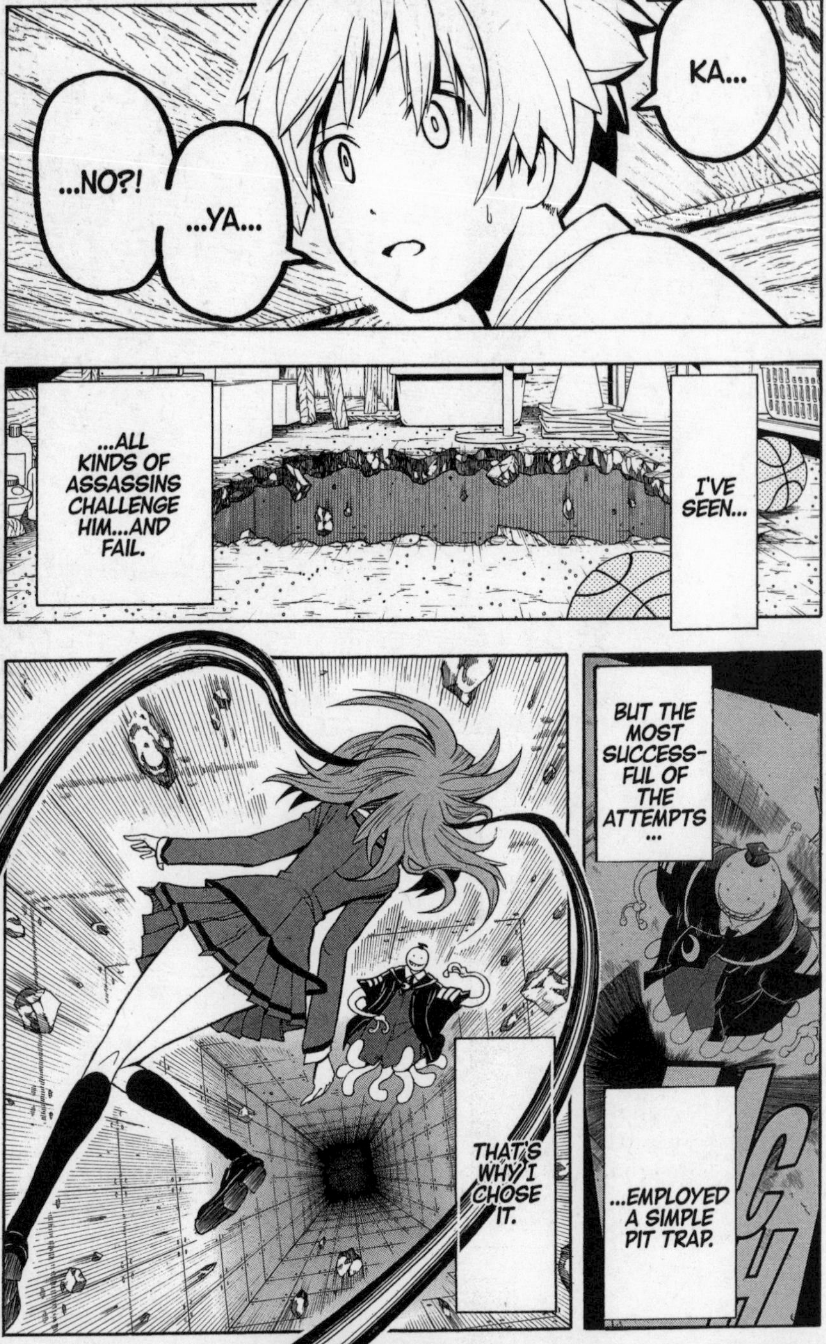
KA...
...YA...
...NO?!
I'VE SEEN...
...ALL KINDS OF ASSASSINS CHALLENGE HIM...AND FAIL.
BUT THE MOST SUCCESS-FUL OF THE ATTEMPTS...
...EMPLOYED A SIMPLE PIT TRAP.
THAT'S WHY I CHOSE IT.

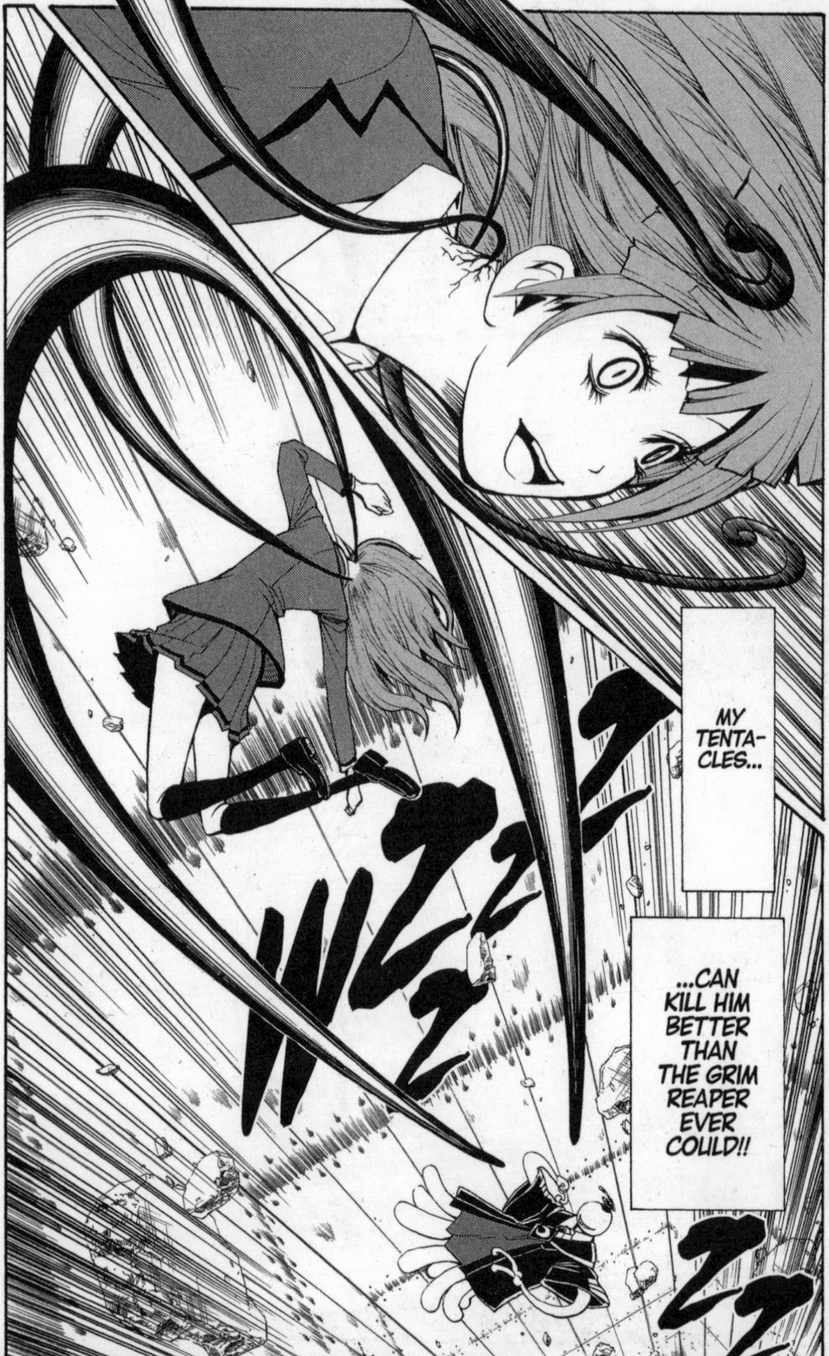

MY TENTA-CLES...
...CAN KILL HIM BETTER THAN THE GRIM REAPER EVER COULD!!

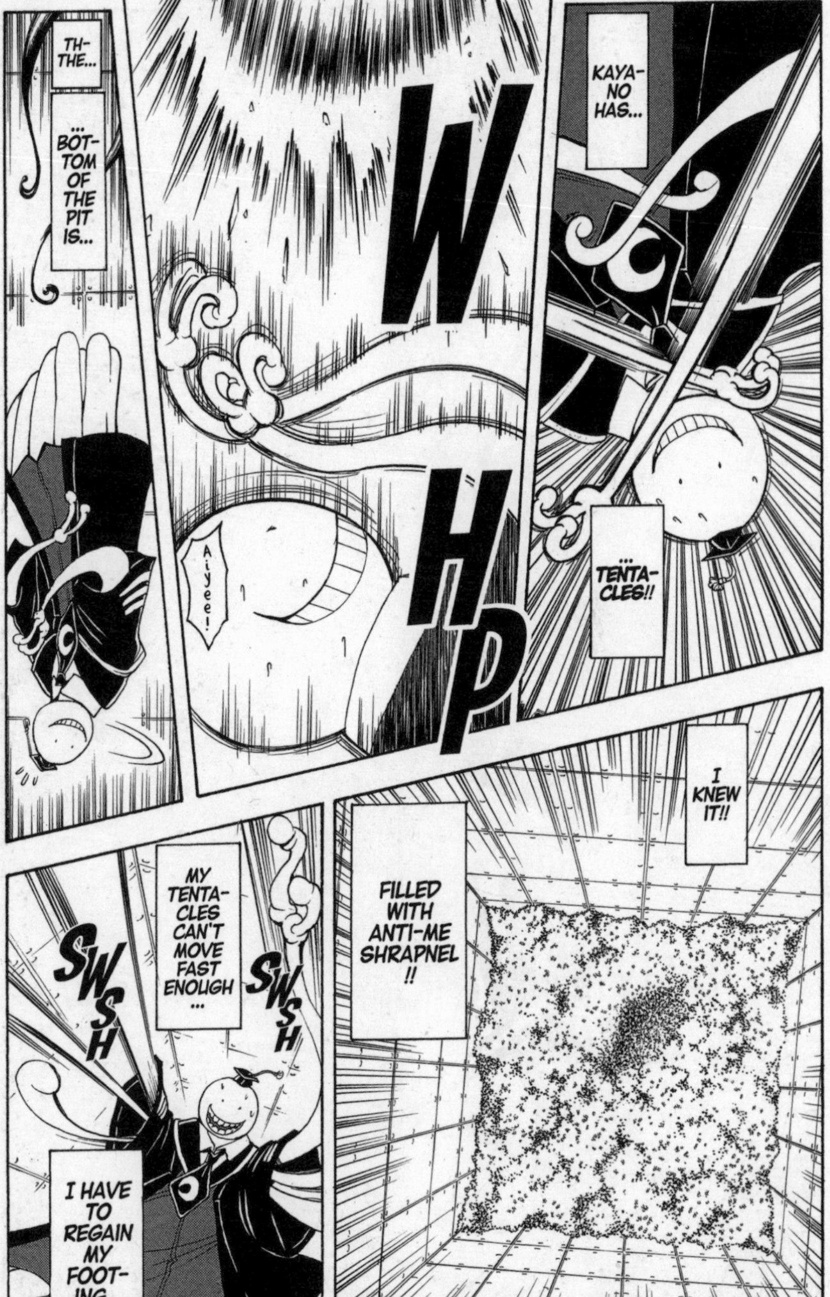
KAYA-NO HAS...
... TENTA-CLES!!
WHIP
Aiyee!
TH-THE...
... BOT-TOM OF THE PIT IS...
I KNEW IT!!
FILLED WITH ANTI-ME SHRAPNEL!!
MY TENTA-CLES CAN'T MOVE FAST ENOUGH...
SWSH
SWSH
I HAVE TO REGAIN MY FOOT-ING...

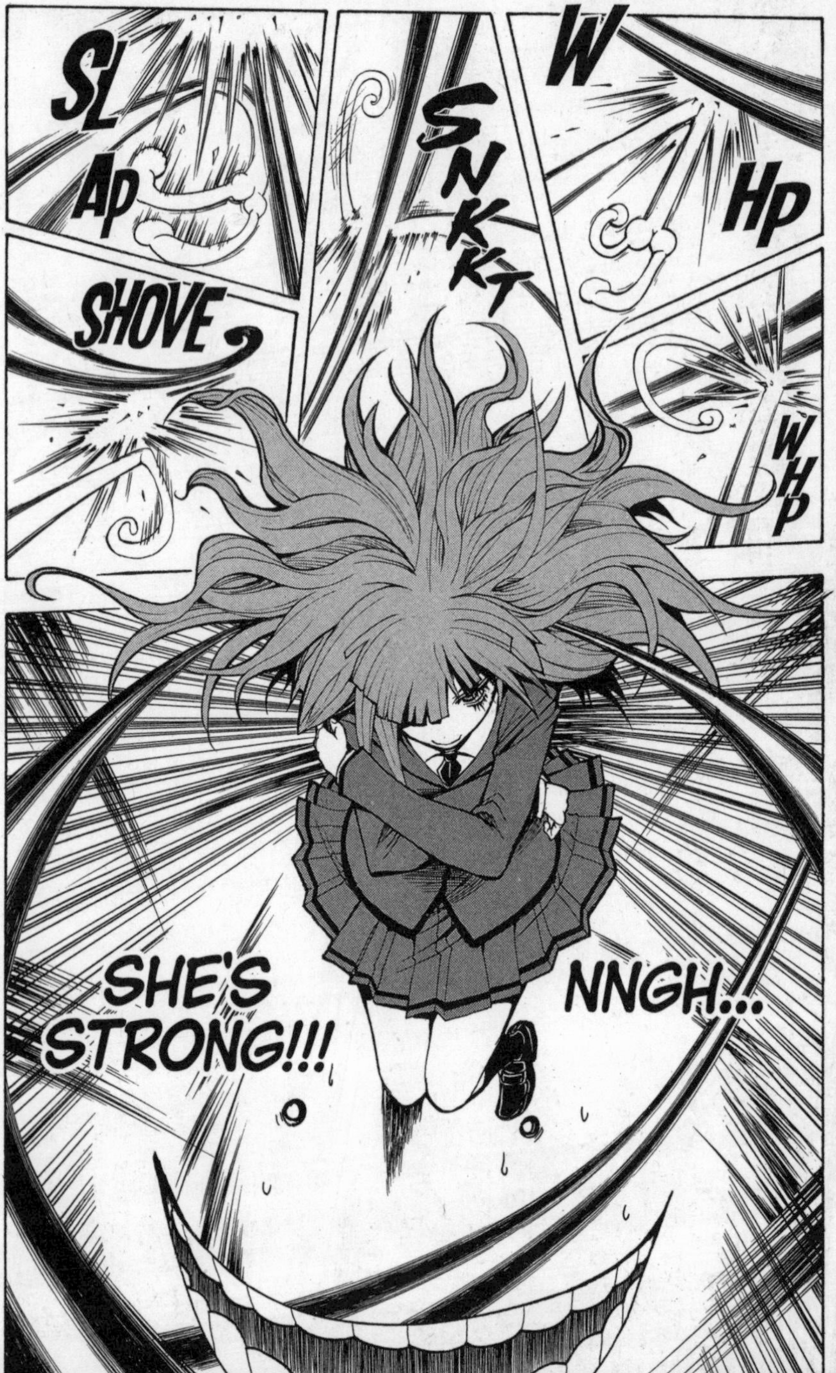
WHP
WHP
SNKKT
SLAP
SHOVE
NNGH...
SHE'S STRONG!!!

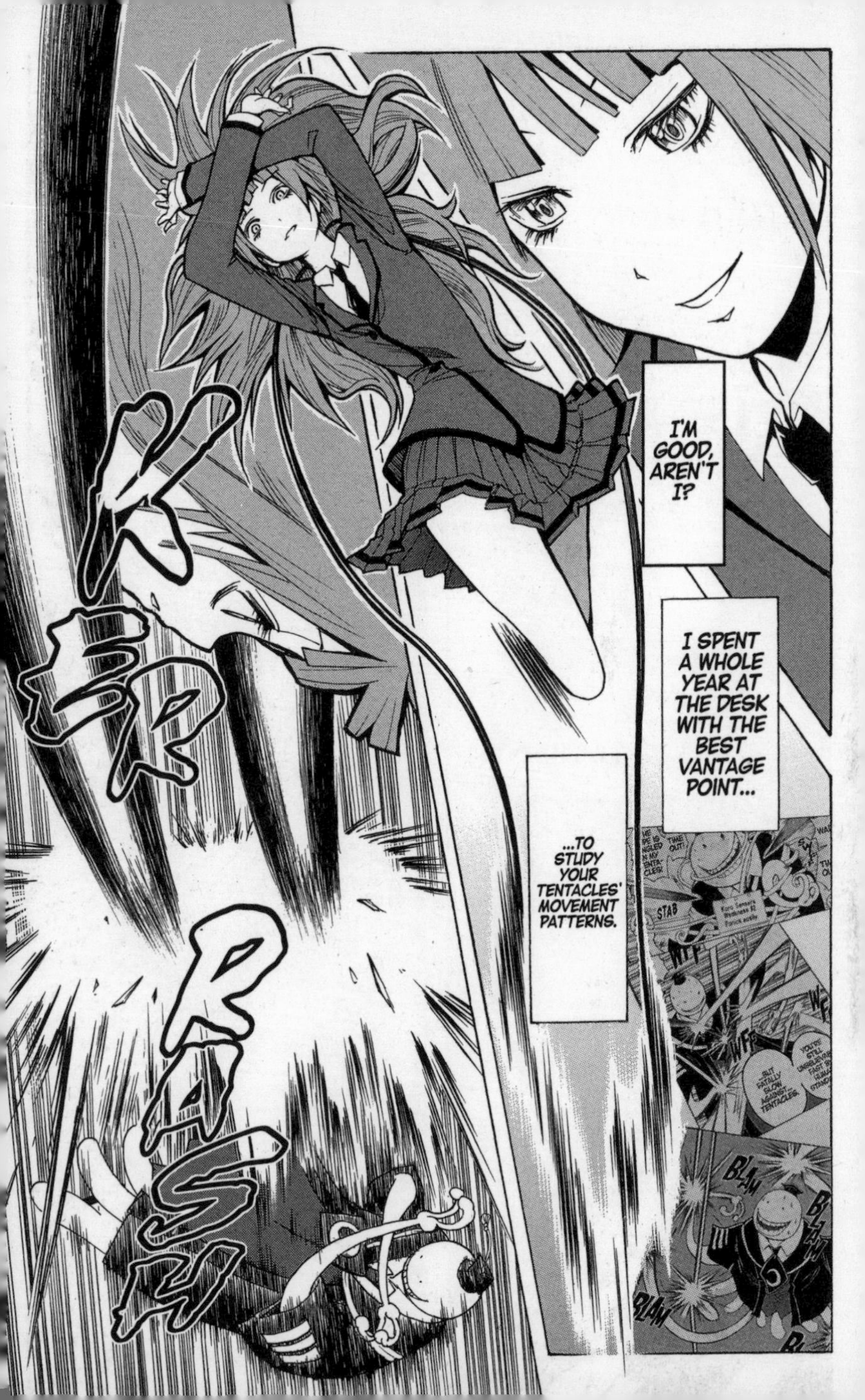
I'M GOOD, AREN'T I?
I SPENT A WHOLE YEAR AT THE DESK WITH THE BEST VANTAGE POINT...
...TO STUDY YOUR TENTACLES' MOVEMENT PATTERNS.
BLAM
BLAM
BLAM

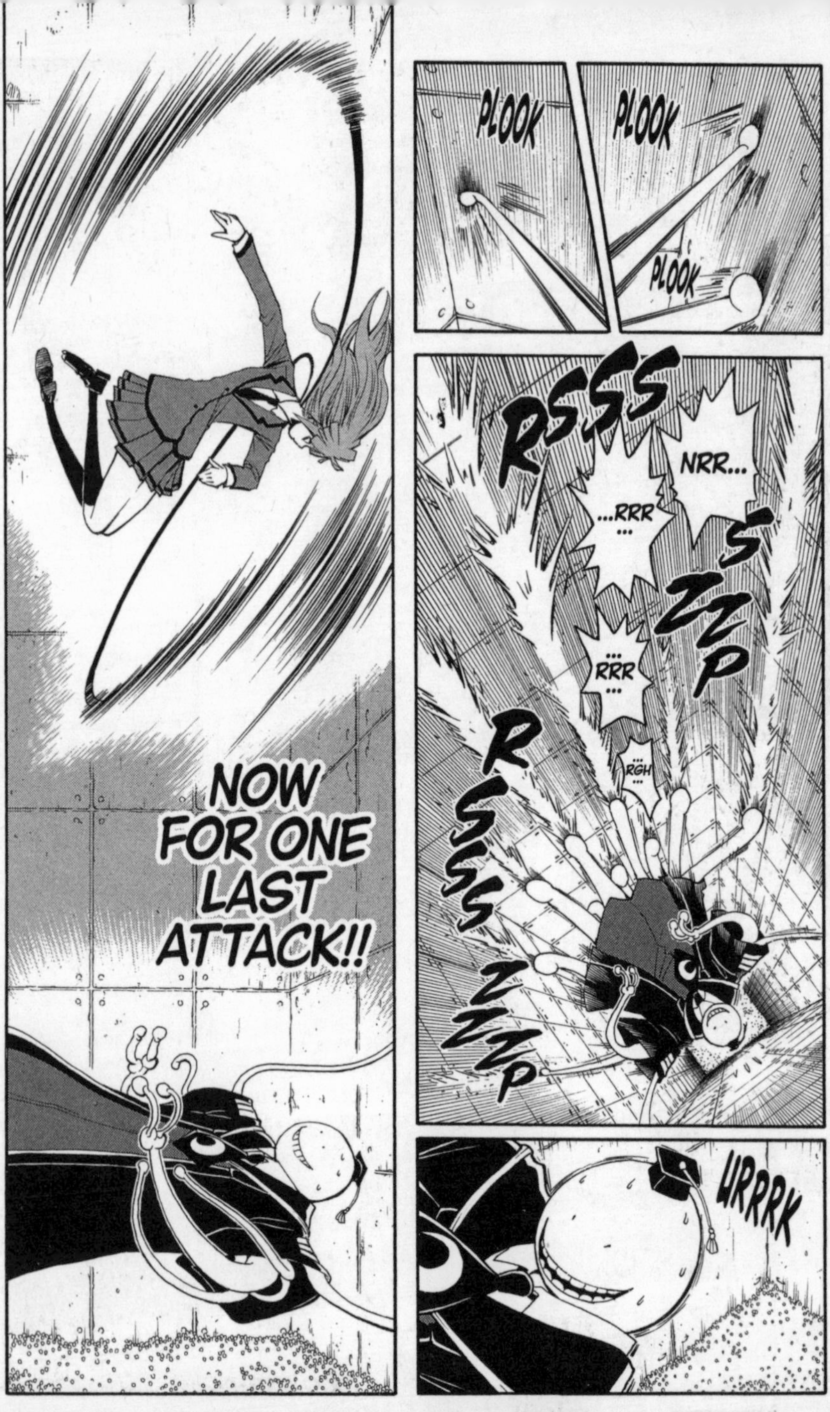

PLOOK
PLOOK
PLOOK
NRR...
RSSSS
SZZZP
...RRR...
...RRR...
...RGH...
RSSSSZZZP
URRRK
NOW FOR ONE LAST ATTACK!!

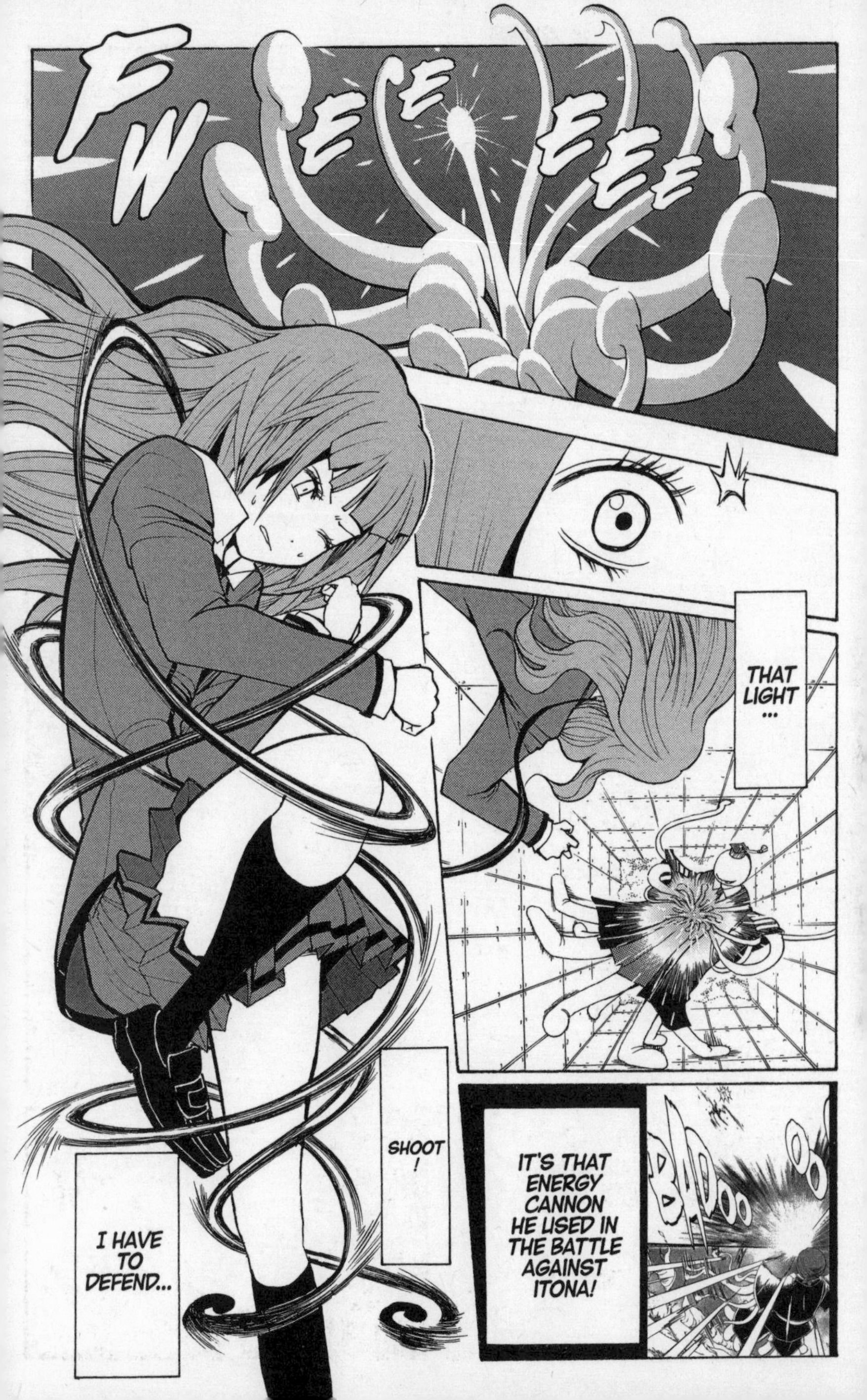
FWEEEEEEE
THAT LIGHT...
BADOOO
IT'S THAT ENERGY CANNON HE USED IN THE BATTLE AGAINST ITONA!
SHOOT!
I HAVE TO DEFEND...

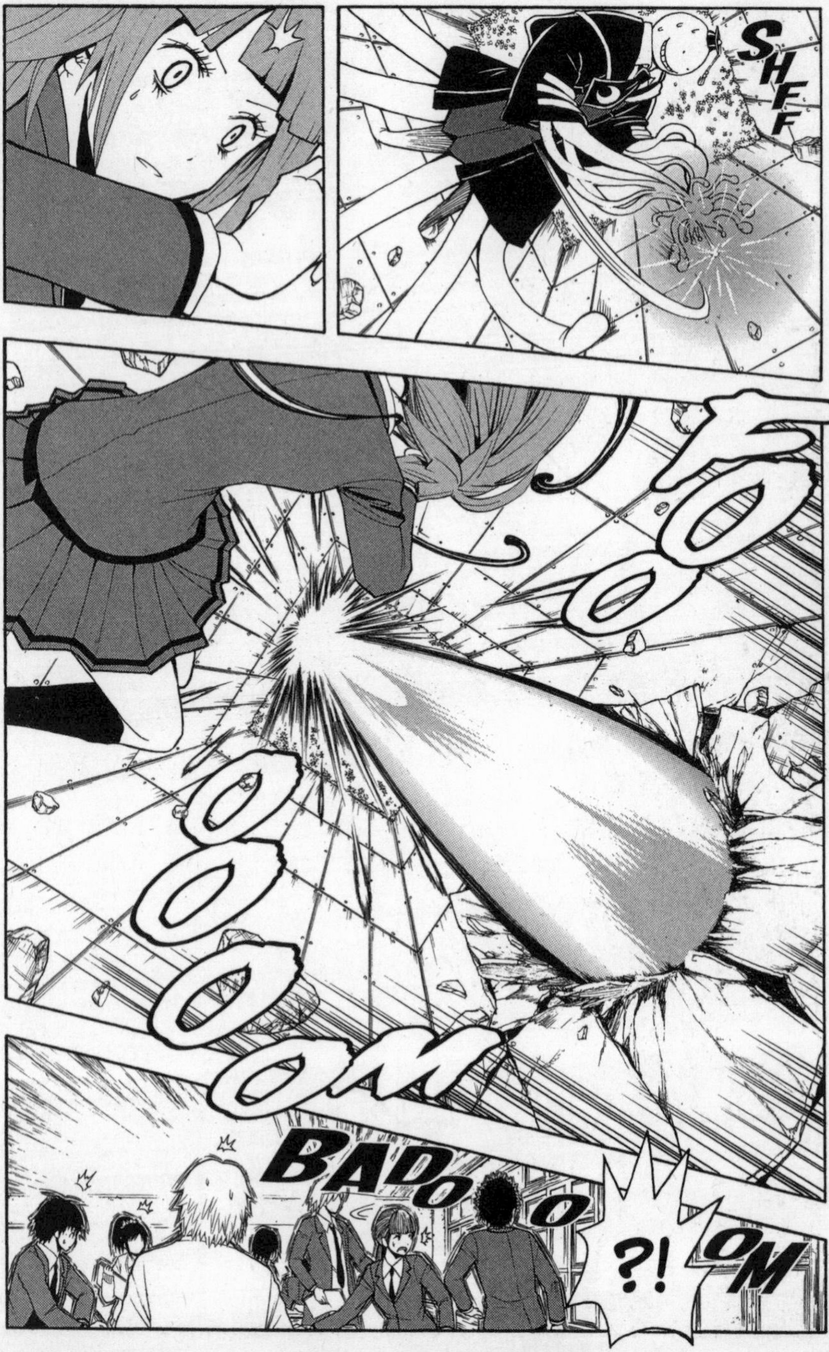
SHFF
BOOOOOOOM
BADOOOM
?!

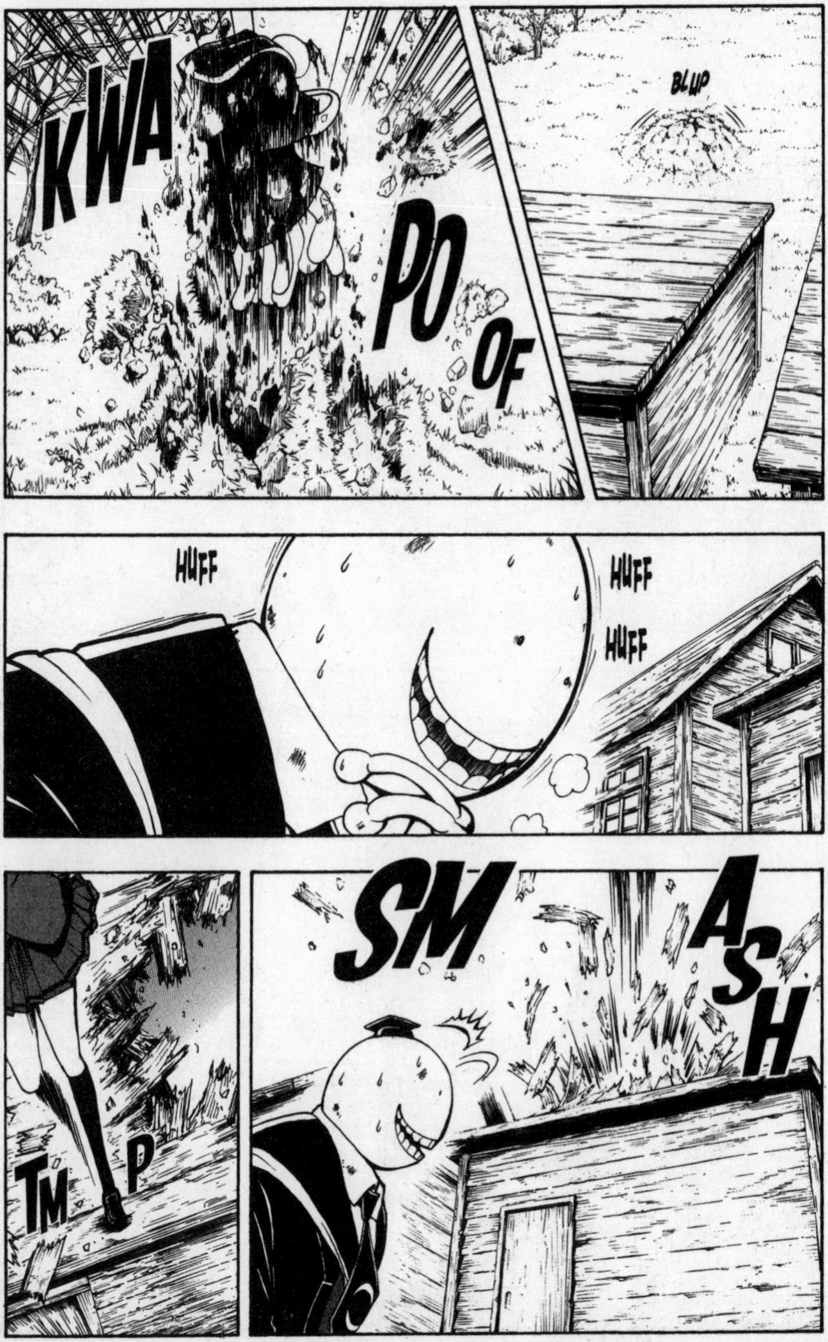
BLUP
KWA
POOF
HUFF
HUFF
HUFF
SMASH
TMP

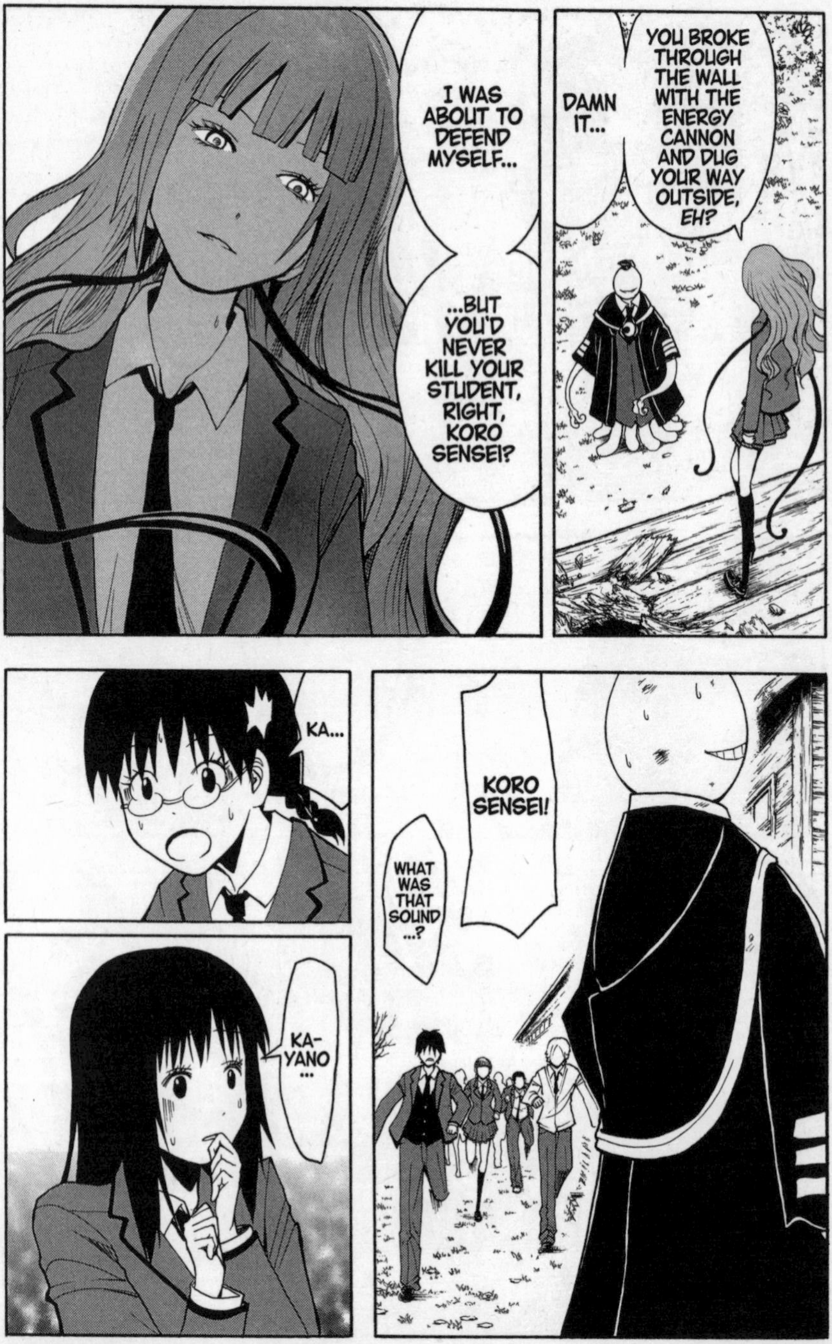
YOU BROKE THROUGH THE WALL WITH THE ENERGY CANNON AND DUG YOUR WAY OUTSIDE, EH?
DAMN IT...
I WAS ABOUT TO DEFEND MYSELF...
...BUT YOU'D NEVER KILL YOUR STUDENT, RIGHT, KORO SENSEI?
KORO SENSEI!
WHAT WAS THAT SOUND ...?
KA...
KA-YANO ...

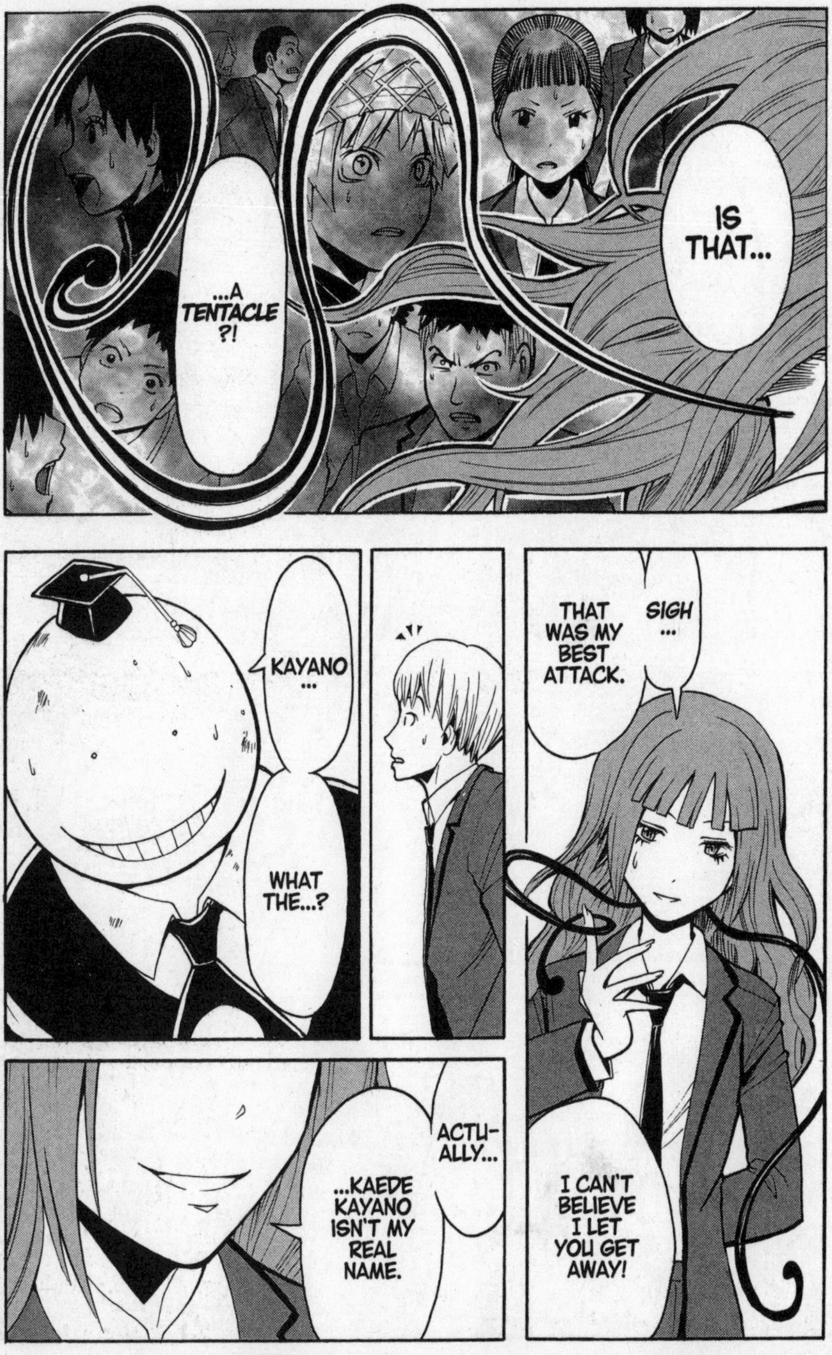
IS THAT...
...A TENTACLE?!
SIGH...
THAT WAS MY BEST ATTACK.
I CAN'T BELIEVE I LET YOU GET AWAY!
KAYANO...
WHAT THE...?
ACTU-ALLY...
...KAEDE KAYANO ISN'T MY REAL NAME.

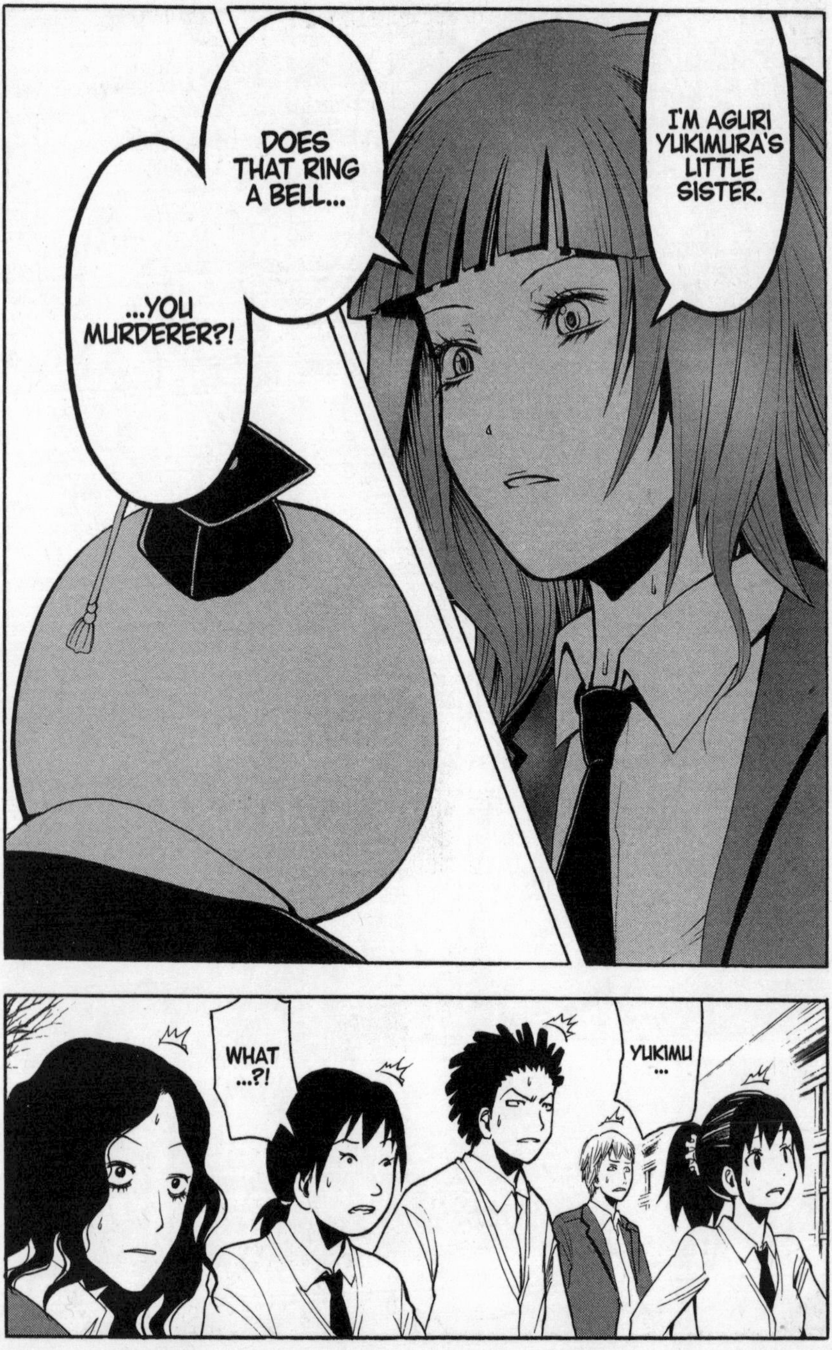
I'M AGURI YUKIMURA'S LITTLE SISTER.
DOES THAT RING A BELL...
...YOU MURDERER?!
YUKIMU ...
WHAT ...?!

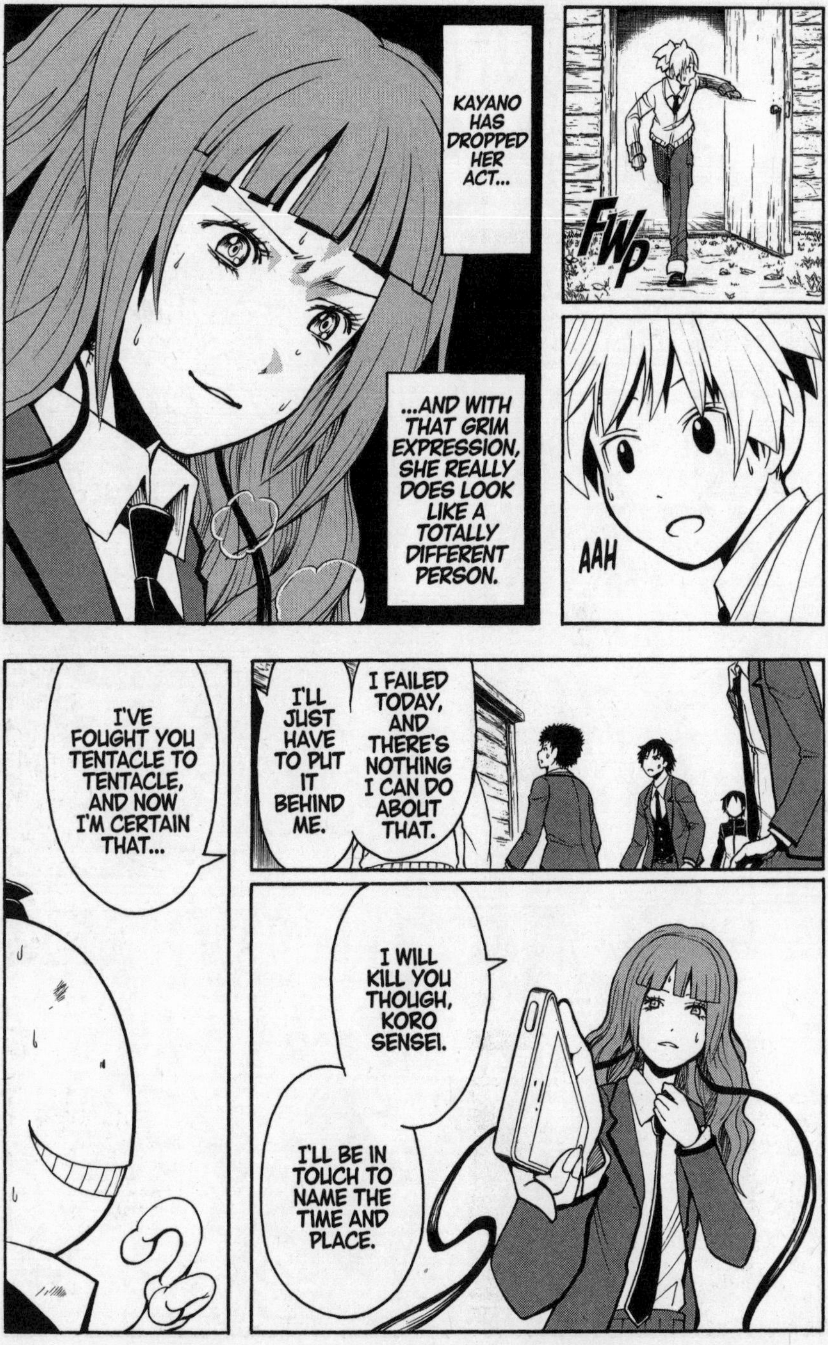
FWP
AAH
KAYANO HAS DROPPED HER ACT...
...AND WITH THAT GRIM EXPRESSION, SHE REALLY DOES LOOK LIKE A TOTALLY DIFFERENT PERSON.
I FAILED TODAY, AND THERE'S NOTHING I CAN DO ABOUT THAT.
I'LL JUST HAVE TO PUT IT BEHIND ME.
I WILL KILL YOU THOUGH, KORO SENSEI.
I'LL BE IN TOUCH TO NAME THE TIME AND PLACE.
I'VE FOUGHT YOU TENTACLE TO TENTACLE, AND NOW I'M CERTAIN THAT...

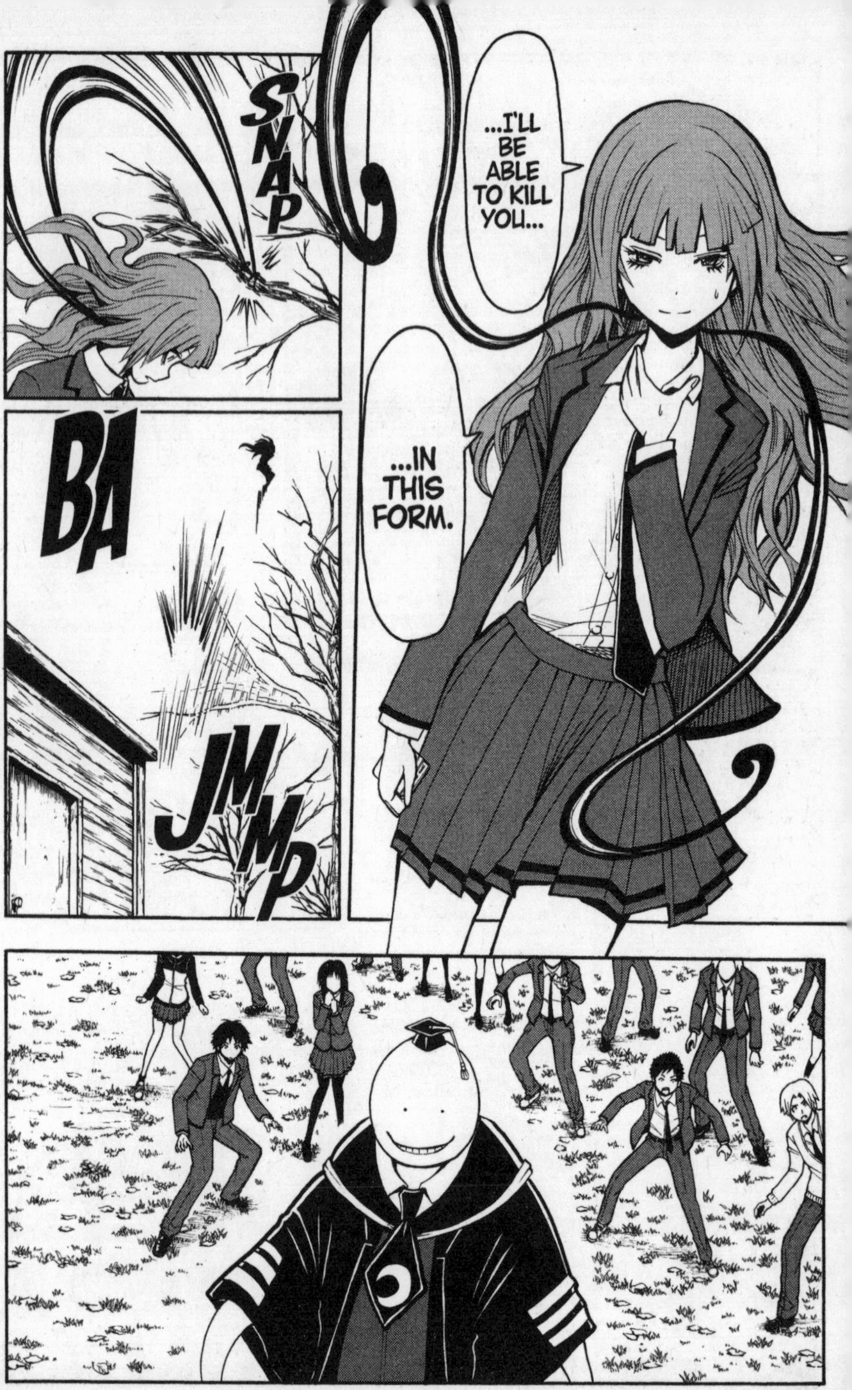
...I'LL BE ABLE TO KILL YOU...
...IN THIS FORM.
SNAP
BA
JMMP

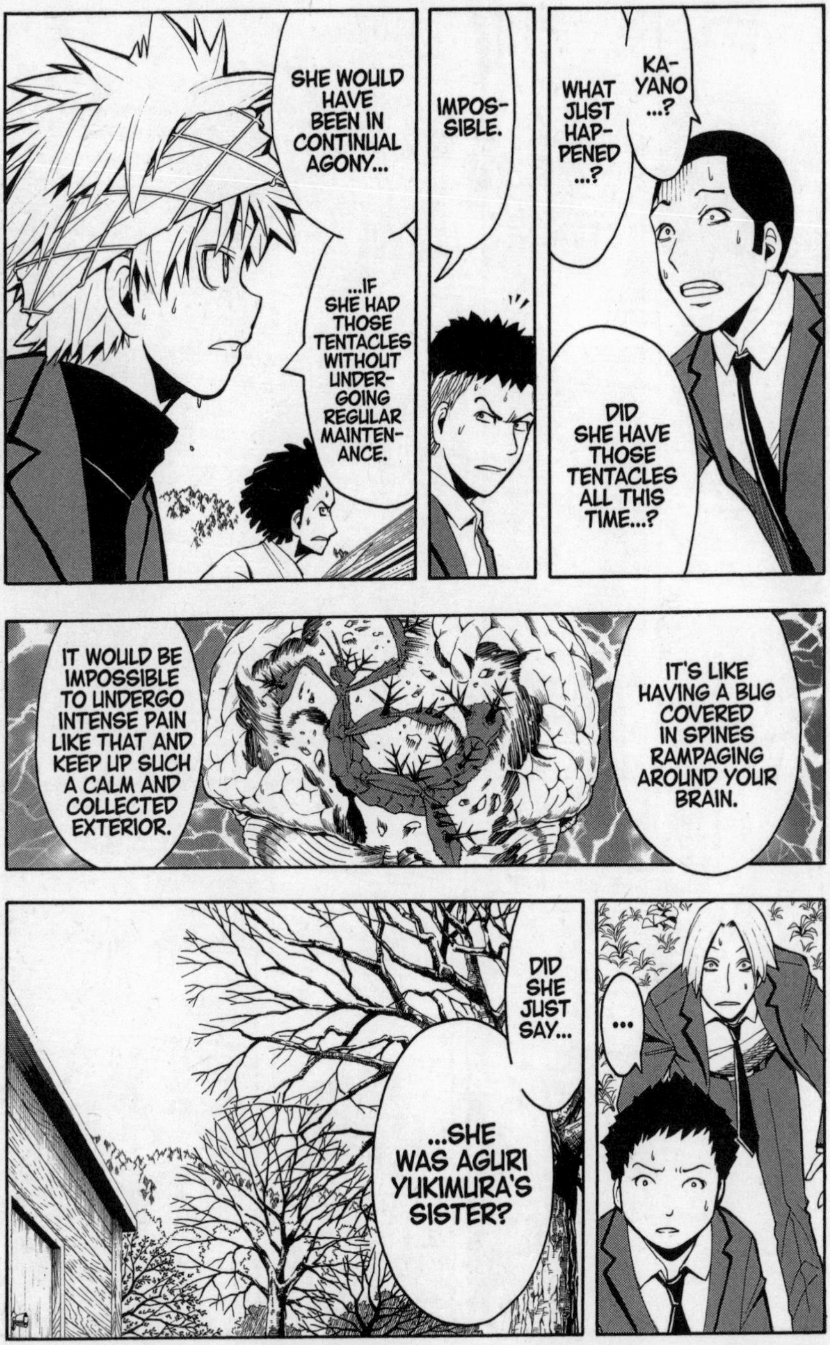
KAYANO ...?
WHAT JUST HAPPENED ...?
DID SHE HAVE THOSE TENTACLES ALL THIS TIME...?
IMPOSSIBLE.
SHE WOULD HAVE BEEN IN CONTINUAL AGONY...
...IF SHE HAD THOSE TENTACLES WITHOUT UNDERGOING REGULAR MAINTENANCE.
IT'S LIKE HAVING A BUG COVERED IN SPINES RAMPAGING AROUND YOUR BRAIN.
IT WOULD BE IMPOSSIBLE TO UNDERGO INTENSE PAIN LIKE THAT AND KEEP UP SUCH A CALM AND COLLECTED EXTERIOR.
...
DID SHE JUST SAY...
...SHE WAS AGURI YUKIMURA'S SISTER?

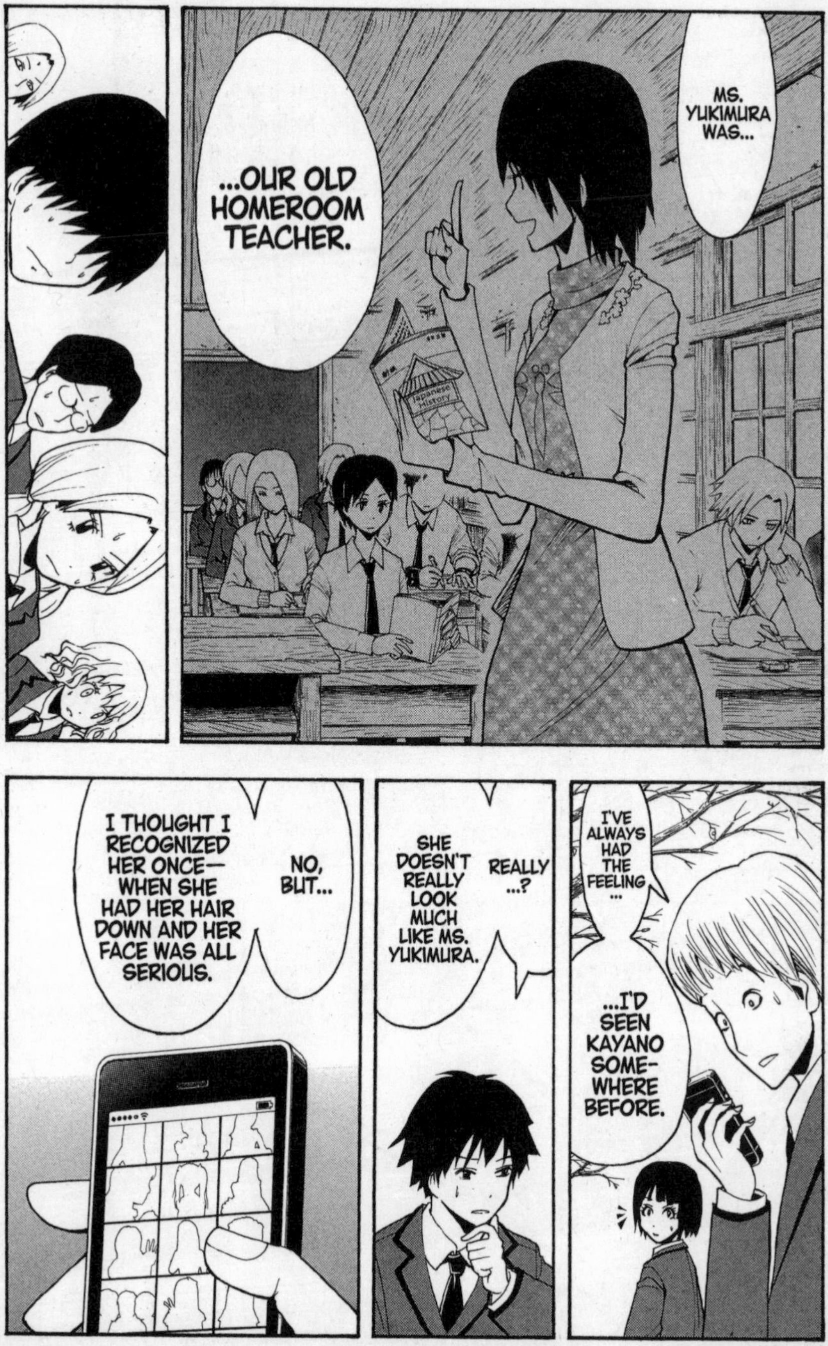
MS. YUKIMURA WAS...
...OUR OLD HOMEROOM TEACHER.
Japanese History
I'VE ALWAYS HAD THE FEELING...
...I'D SEEN KAYANO SOME-WHERE BEFORE.
REALLY ...?
SHE DOESN'T REALLY LOOK MUCH LIKE MS. YUKIMURA.
NO, BUT...
I THOUGHT I RECOGNIZED HER ONCE—WHEN SHE HAD HER HAIR DOWN AND HER FACE WAS ALL SERIOUS.

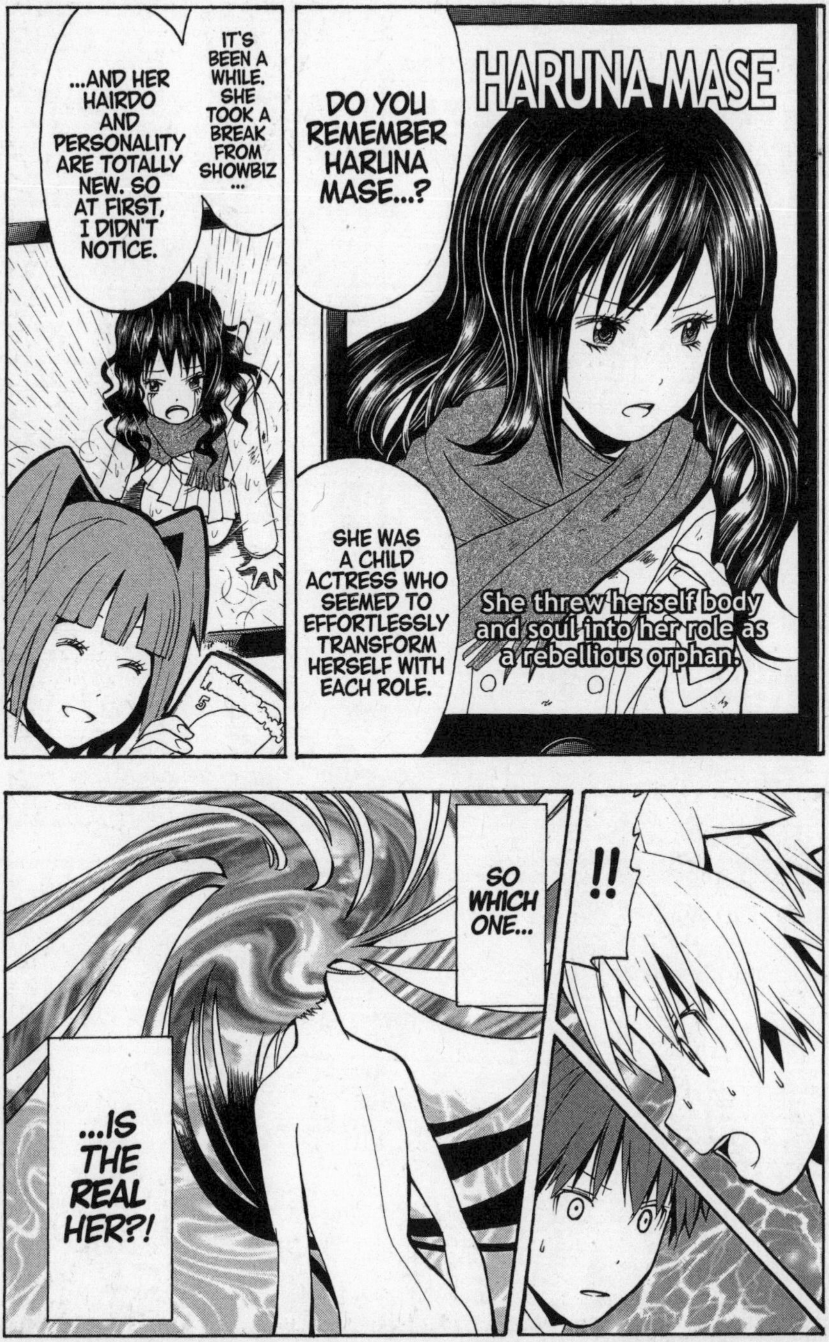
DO YOU REMEMBER HARUNA MASE...?
HARUNA MASE
SHE WAS A CHILD ACTRESS WHO SEEMED TO EFFORTLESSLY TRANSFORM HERSELF WITH EACH ROLE.
She threw herself body and soul into her role as a rebellious orphan.
IT'S BEEN A WHILE. SHE TOOK A BREAK FROM SHOWBIZ ...
...AND HER HAIRDO AND PERSONALITY ARE TOTALLY NEW. SO AT FIRST, I DIDN'T NOTICE.
!!
SO WHICH ONE...
...IS THE REAL HER?!

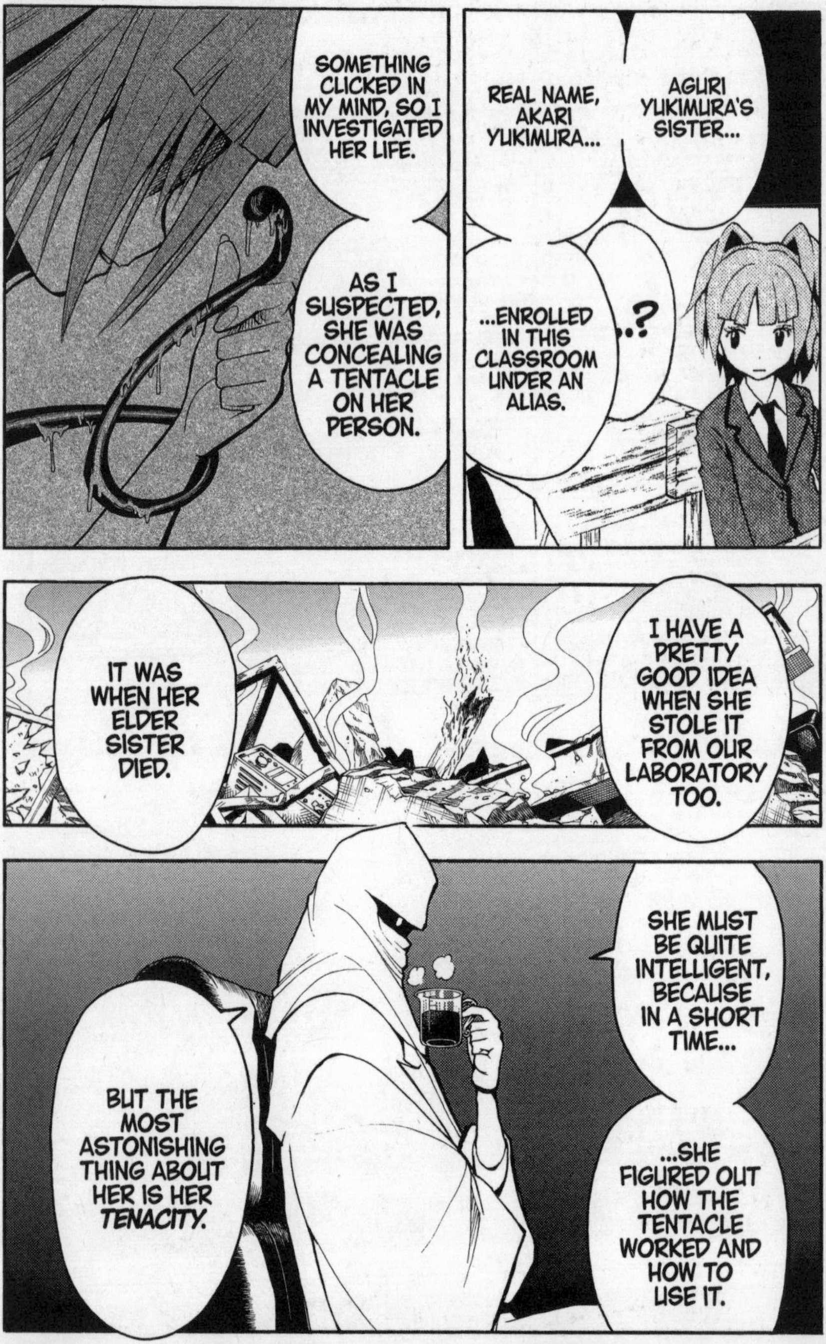

AGURI YUKIMURA'S SISTER...
REAL NAME, AKARI YUKIMURA...
..?
...ENROLLED IN THIS CLASSROOM UNDER AN ALIAS.
SOMETHING CLICKED IN MY MIND, SO I INVESTIGATED HER LIFE.
AS I SUSPECTED, SHE WAS CONCEALING A TENTACLE ON HER PERSON.
I HAVE A PRETTY GOOD IDEA WHEN SHE STOLE IT FROM OUR LABORATORY TOO.
IT WAS WHEN HER ELDER SISTER DIED.
SHE MUST BE QUITE INTELLIGENT, BECAUSE IN A SHORT TIME...
...SHE FIGURED OUT HOW THE TENTACLE WORKED AND HOW TO USE IT.
BUT THE MOST ASTONISHING THING ABOUT HER IS HER *TENACITY*.

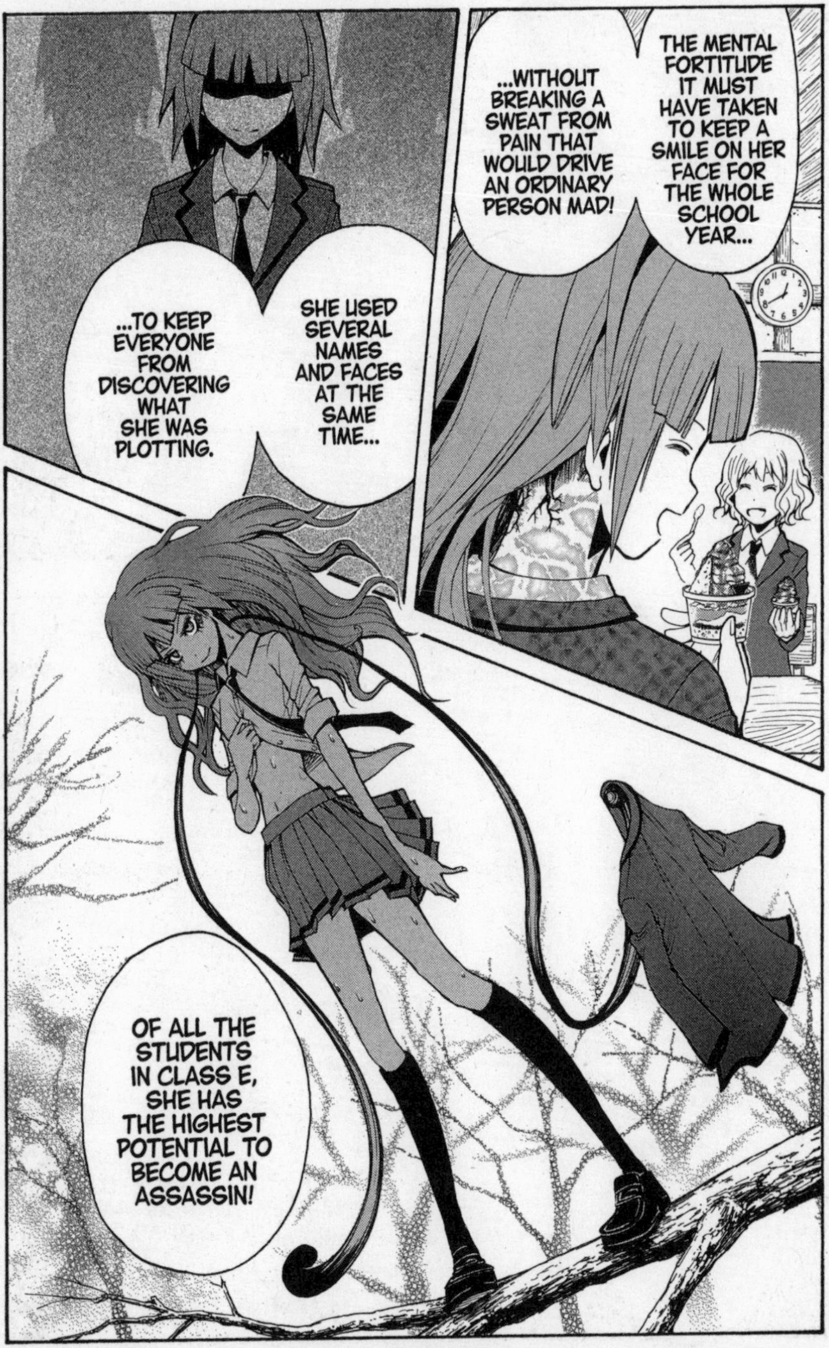
THE MENTAL FORTITUDE IT MUST HAVE TAKEN TO KEEP A SMILE ON HER FACE FOR THE WHOLE SCHOOL YEAR...
...WITHOUT BREAKING A SWEAT FROM PAIN THAT WOULD DRIVE AN ORDINARY PERSON MAD!
SHE USED SEVERAL NAMES AND FACES AT THE SAME TIME...
...TO KEEP EVERYONE FROM DISCOVERING WHAT SHE WAS PLOTTING.
OF ALL THE STUDENTS IN CLASS E, SHE HAS THE HIGHEST POTENTIAL TO BECOME AN ASSASSIN!

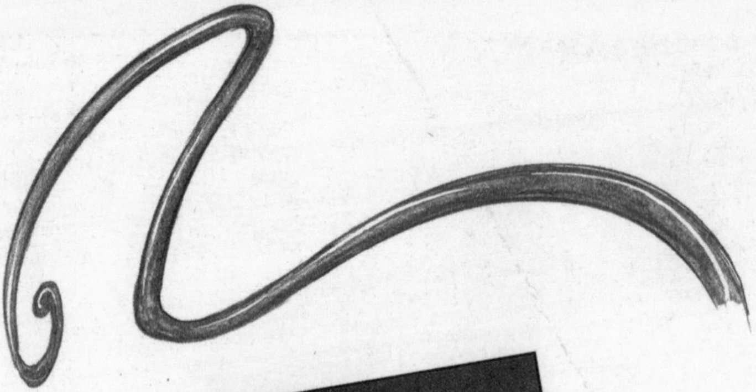

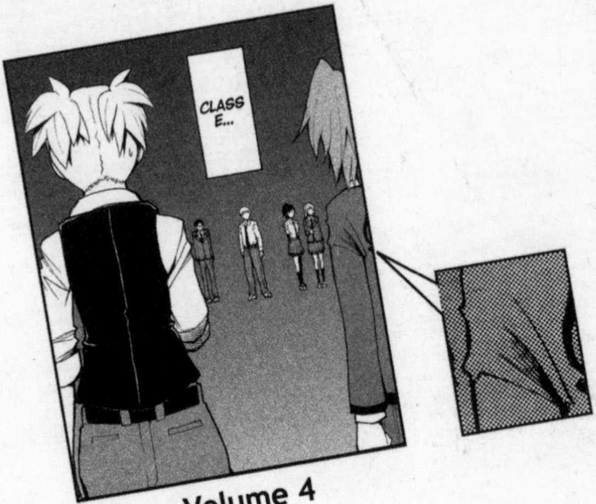
CLASS E...

Volume 4

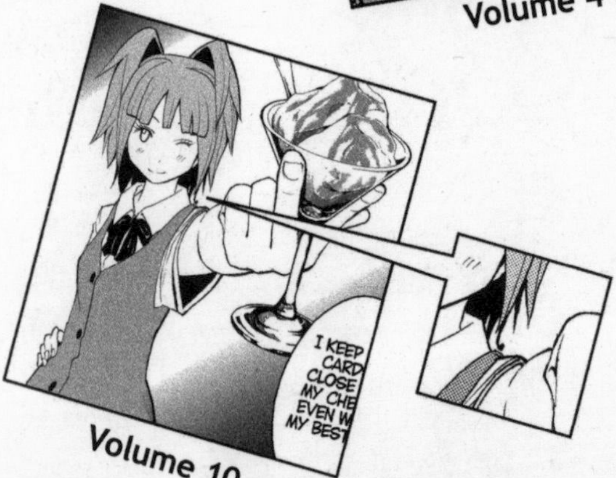
I KEEP
CARD
CLOSE
MY CHE
EVEN W
MY BEST

Volume 10

There are several other scenes where you can see it, although I myself have forgotten how many times I've drawn it... I hope you enjoy searching for it if you have the time...

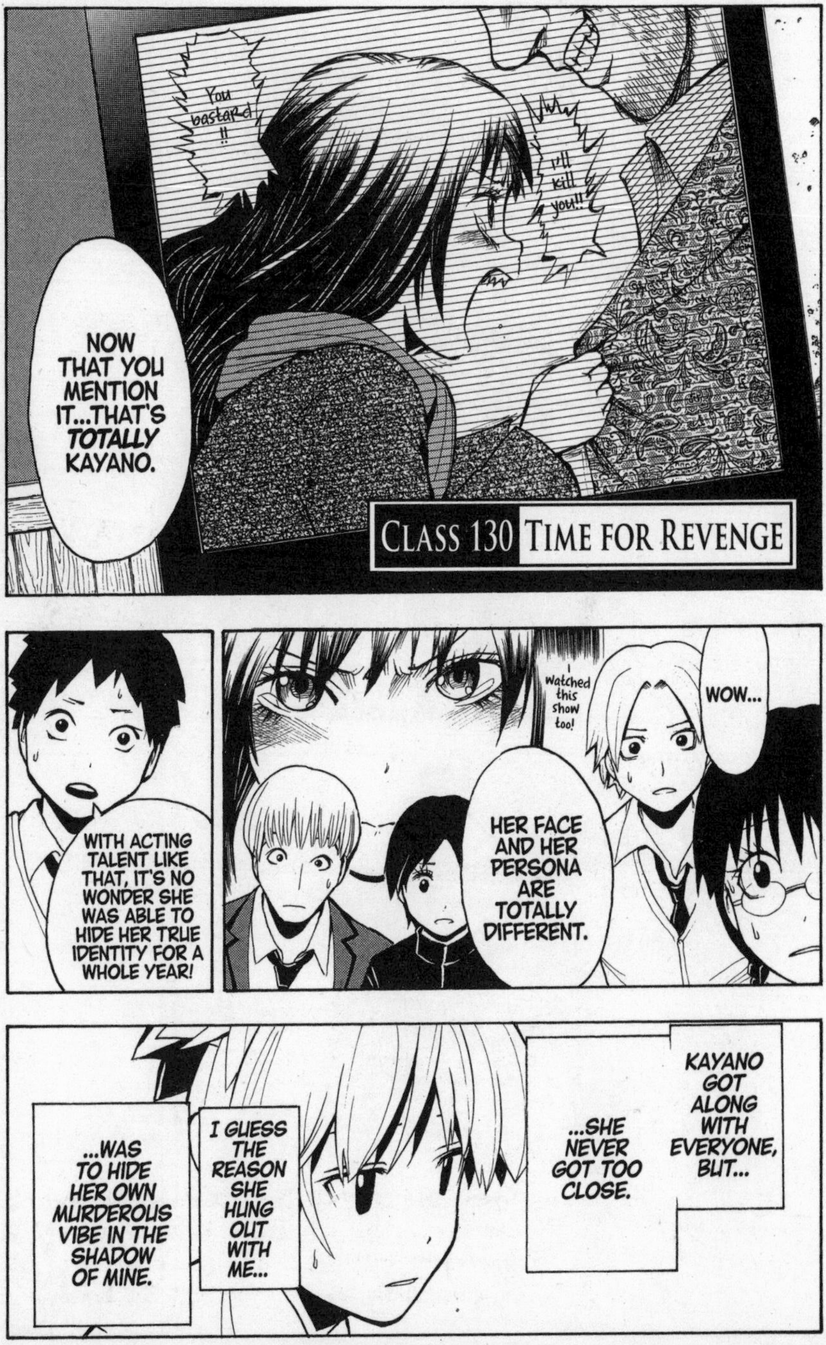
I'll kill you!!
You bastard!!
NOW THAT YOU MENTION IT...THAT'S *TOTALLY* KAYANO.
CLASS 130 TIME FOR REVENGE
WOW...
I watched this show too!
HER FACE AND HER PERSONA ARE TOTALLY DIFFERENT.
WITH ACTING TALENT LIKE THAT, IT'S NO WONDER SHE WAS ABLE TO HIDE HER TRUE IDENTITY FOR A WHOLE YEAR!
KAYANO GOT ALONG WITH EVERYONE, BUT...
...SHE NEVER GOT TOO CLOSE.
I GUESS THE REASON SHE HUNG OUT WITH ME...
...WAS TO HIDE HER OWN MURDEROUS VIBE IN THE SHADOW OF MINE.

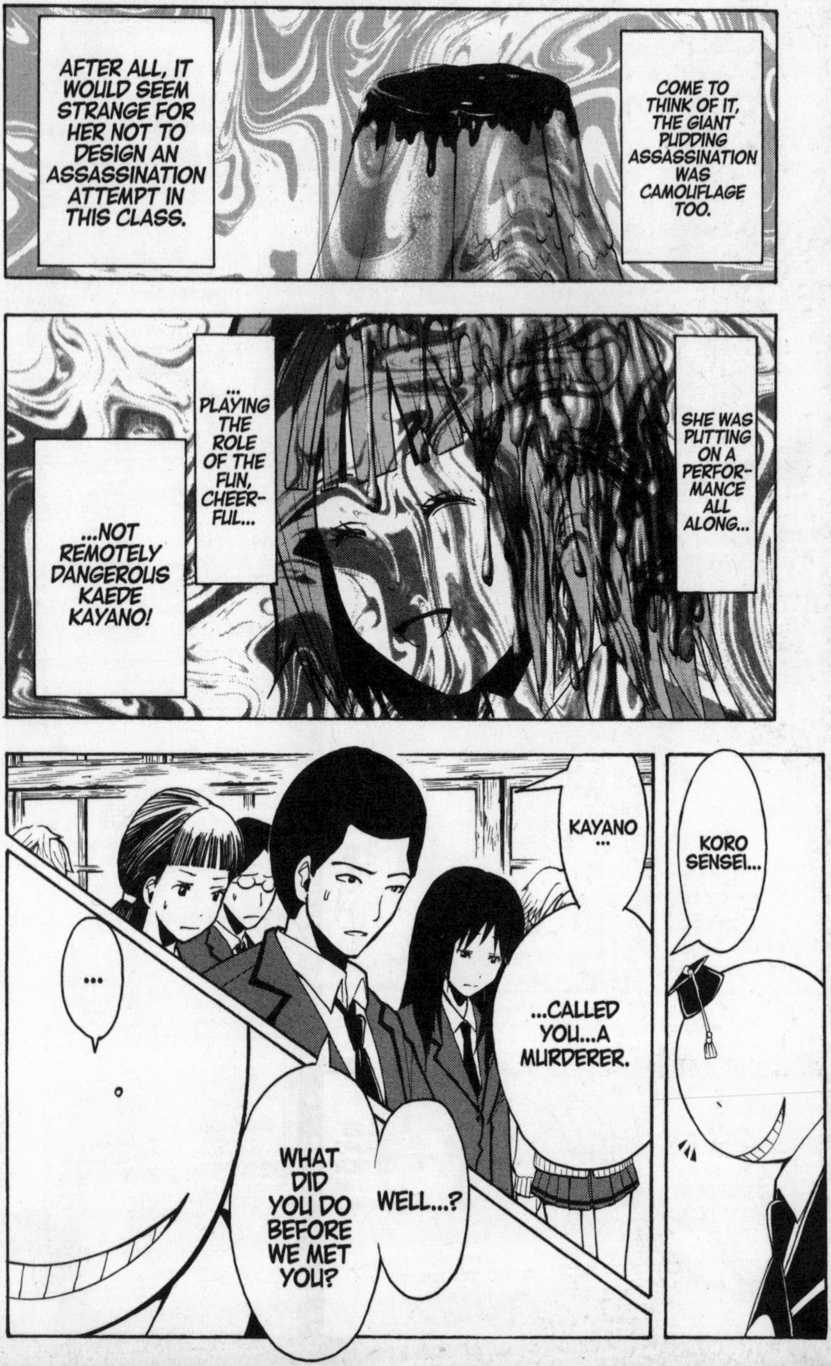
COME TO THINK OF IT, THE GIANT PUDDING ASSASSINATION WAS CAMOUFLAGE TOO.
AFTER ALL, IT WOULD SEEM STRANGE FOR HER NOT TO DESIGN AN ASSASSINATION ATTEMPT IN THIS CLASS.
SHE WAS PUTTING ON A PERFORMANCE ALL ALONG...
...PLAYING THE ROLE OF THE FUN, CHEERFUL...
...NOT REMOTELY DANGEROUS KAEDE KAYANO!
KORO SENSEI...
KAYANO ...
...CALLED YOU...A MURDERER.
WELL...?
WHAT DID YOU DO BEFORE WE MET YOU?
...

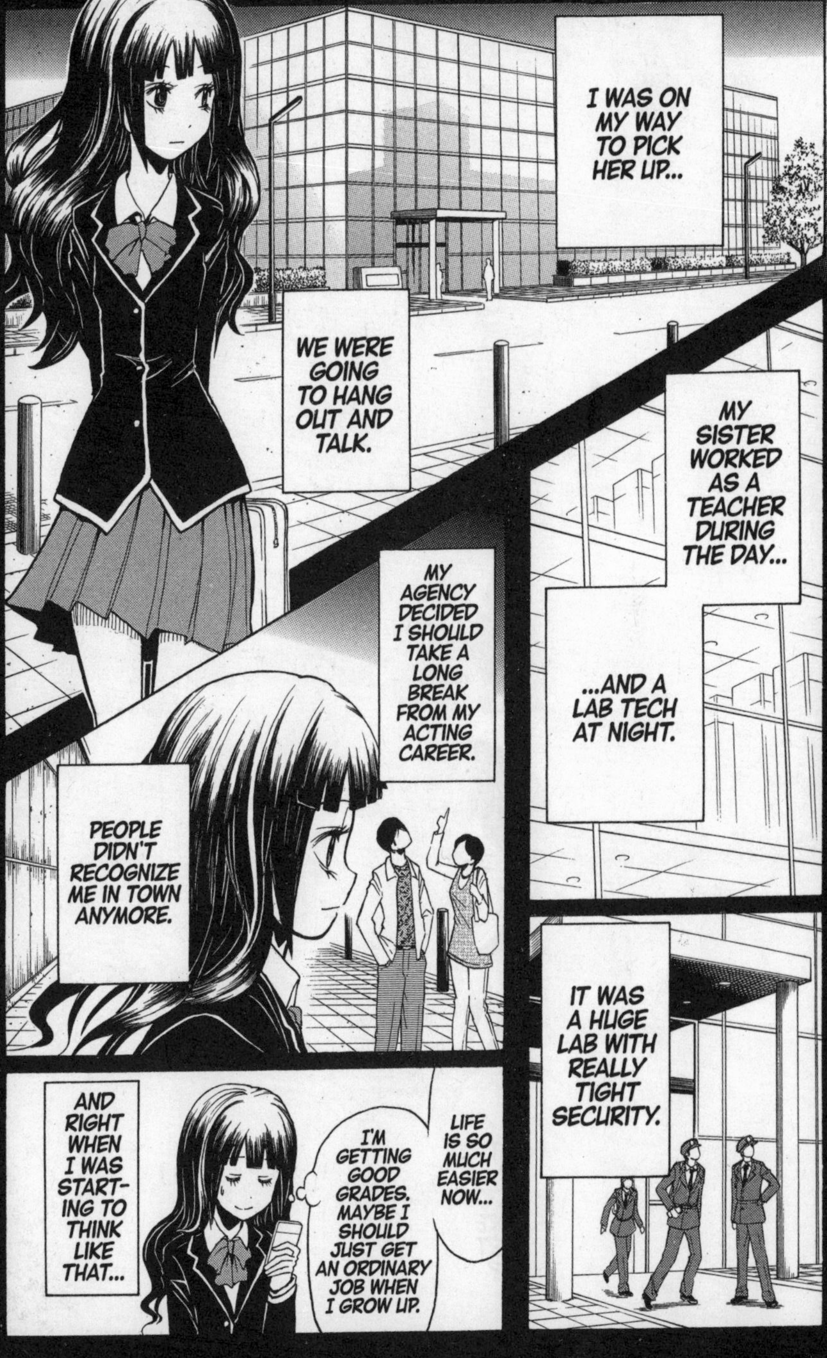
I WAS ON MY WAY TO PICK HER UP...
WE WERE GOING TO HANG OUT AND TALK.
MY SISTER WORKED AS A TEACHER DURING THE DAY...
...AND A LAB TECH AT NIGHT.
IT WAS A HUGE LAB WITH REALLY TIGHT SECURITY.
MY AGENCY DECIDED I SHOULD TAKE A LONG BREAK FROM MY ACTING CAREER.
PEOPLE DIDN'T RECOGNIZE ME IN TOWN ANYMORE.
LIFE IS SO MUCH EASIER NOW...
I'M GETTING GOOD GRADES. MAYBE I SHOULD JUST GET AN ORDINARY JOB WHEN I GROW UP.
AND RIGHT WHEN I WAS START-ING TO THINK LIKE THAT...

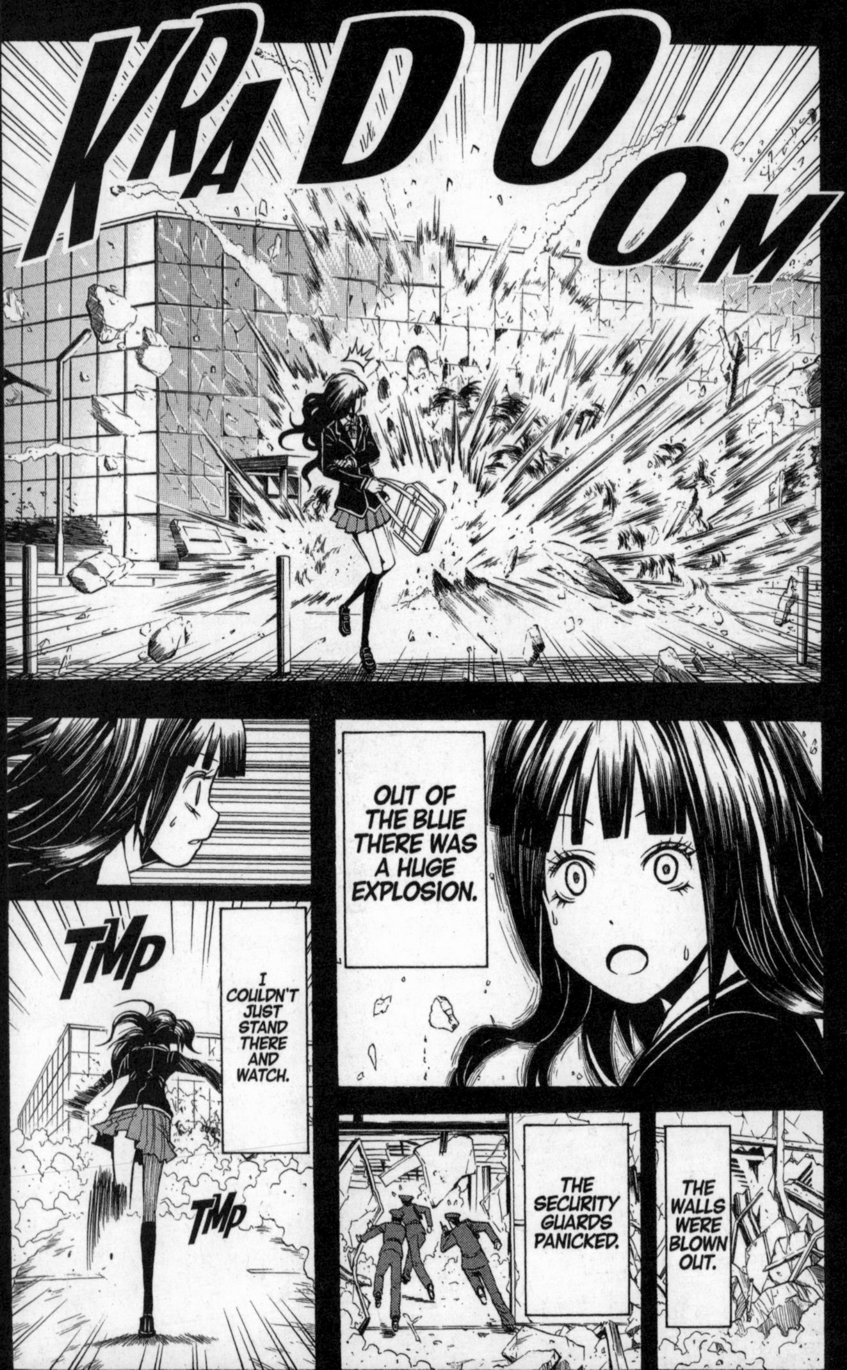
KRADOOM
OUT OF THE BLUE THERE WAS A HUGE EXPLOSION.
THE WALLS WERE BLOWN OUT.
THE SECURITY GUARDS PANICKED.
TMP
I COULDN'T JUST STAND THERE AND WATCH.
TMP

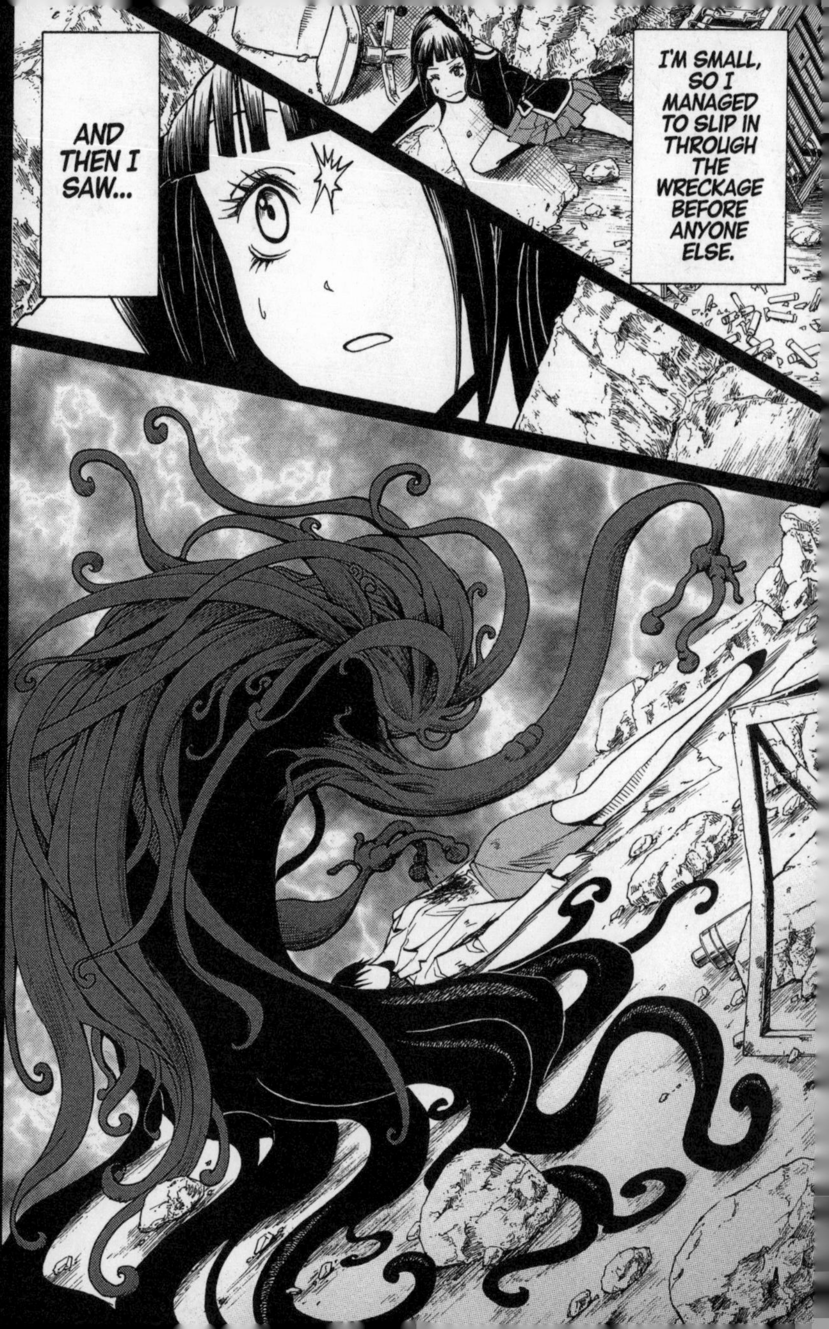
I'M SMALL, SO I MANAGED TO SLIP IN THROUGH THE WRECKAGE BEFORE ANYONE ELSE.
AND THEN I SAW...

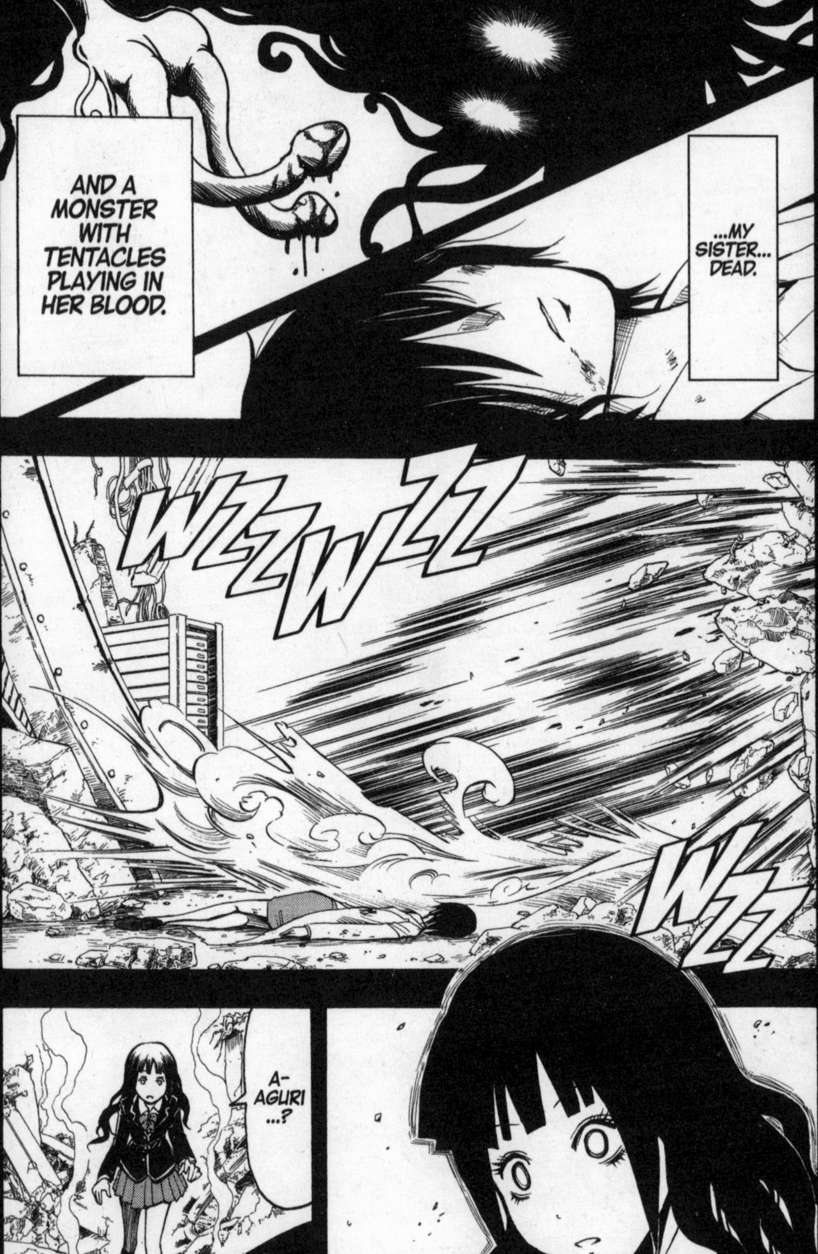
...MY SISTER... DEAD.
AND A MONSTER WITH TENTACLES PLAYING IN HER BLOOD.
WZZWZZ
WZZ
A-AGURI ...?

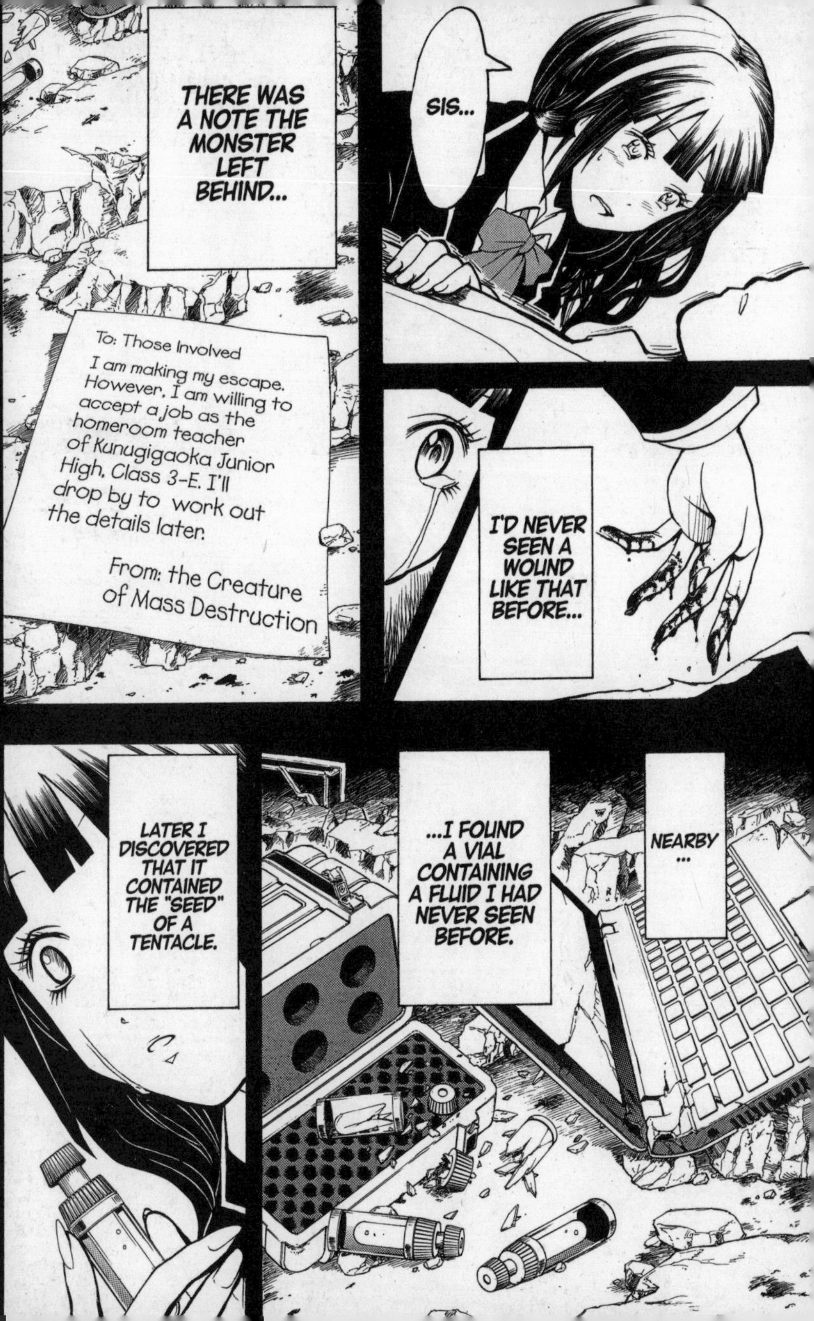
SIS...
I'D NEVER SEEN A WOUND LIKE THAT BEFORE...
THERE WAS A NOTE THE MONSTER LEFT BEHIND...
To: Those Involved
I am making my escape. However, I am willing to accept a job as the homeroom teacher of Kunugigaoka Junior High, Class 3-E. I'll drop by to work out the details later.
From: the Creature of Mass Destruction
NEARBY...
...I FOUND A VIAL CONTAINING A FLUID I HAD NEVER SEEN BEFORE.
LATER I DISCOVERED THAT IT CONTAINED THE "SEED" OF A TENTACLE.

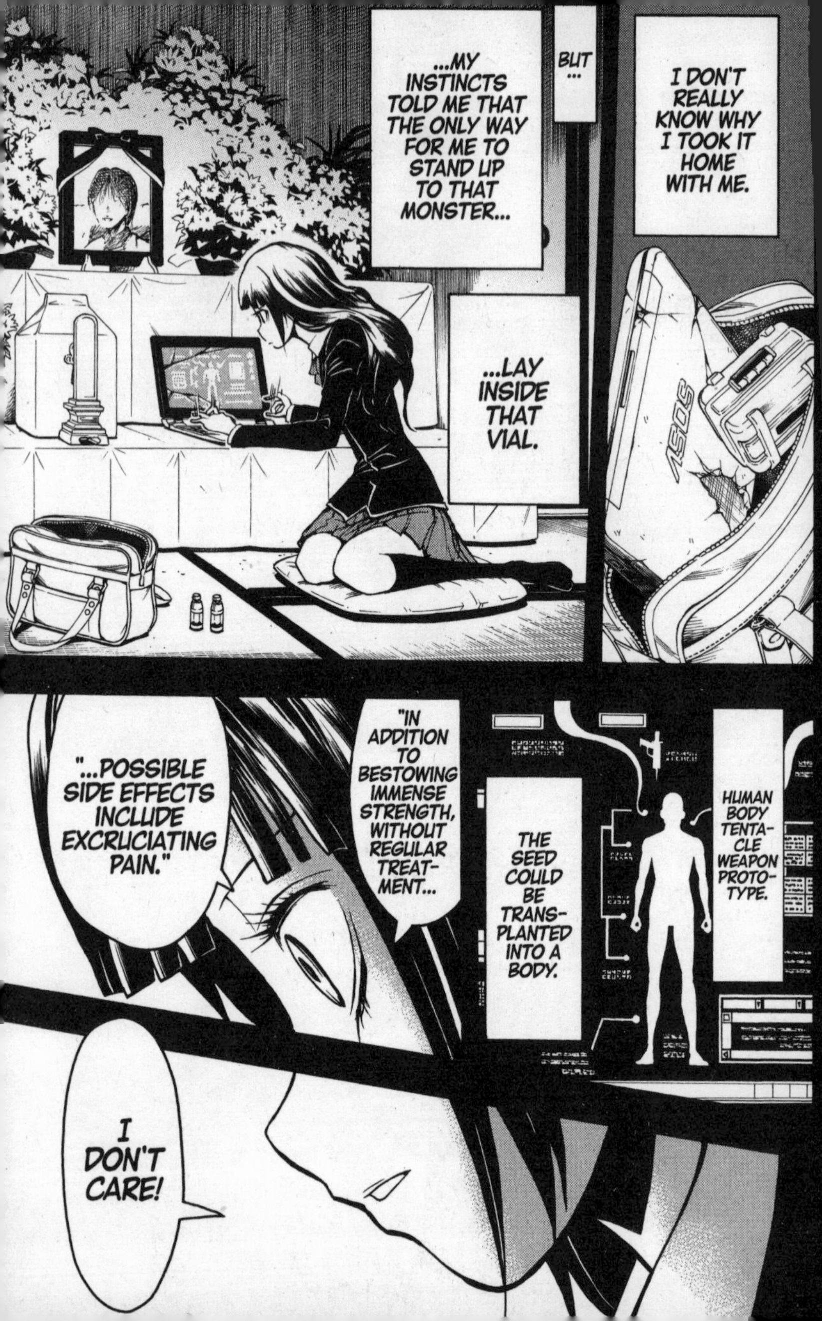
I DON'T REALLY KNOW WHY I TOOK IT HOME WITH ME.
SOS1
BUT...
...MY INSTINCTS TOLD ME THAT THE ONLY WAY FOR ME TO STAND UP TO THAT MONSTER...
...LAY INSIDE THAT VIAL.
HUMAN BODY TENTACLE WEAPON PROTOTYPE.
THE SEED COULD BE TRANSPLANTED INTO A BODY.
"IN ADDITION TO BESTOWING IMMENSE STRENGTH, WITHOUT REGULAR TREATMENT...
"...POSSIBLE SIDE EFFECTS INCLUDE EXCRUCIATING PAIN."
I DON'T CARE!

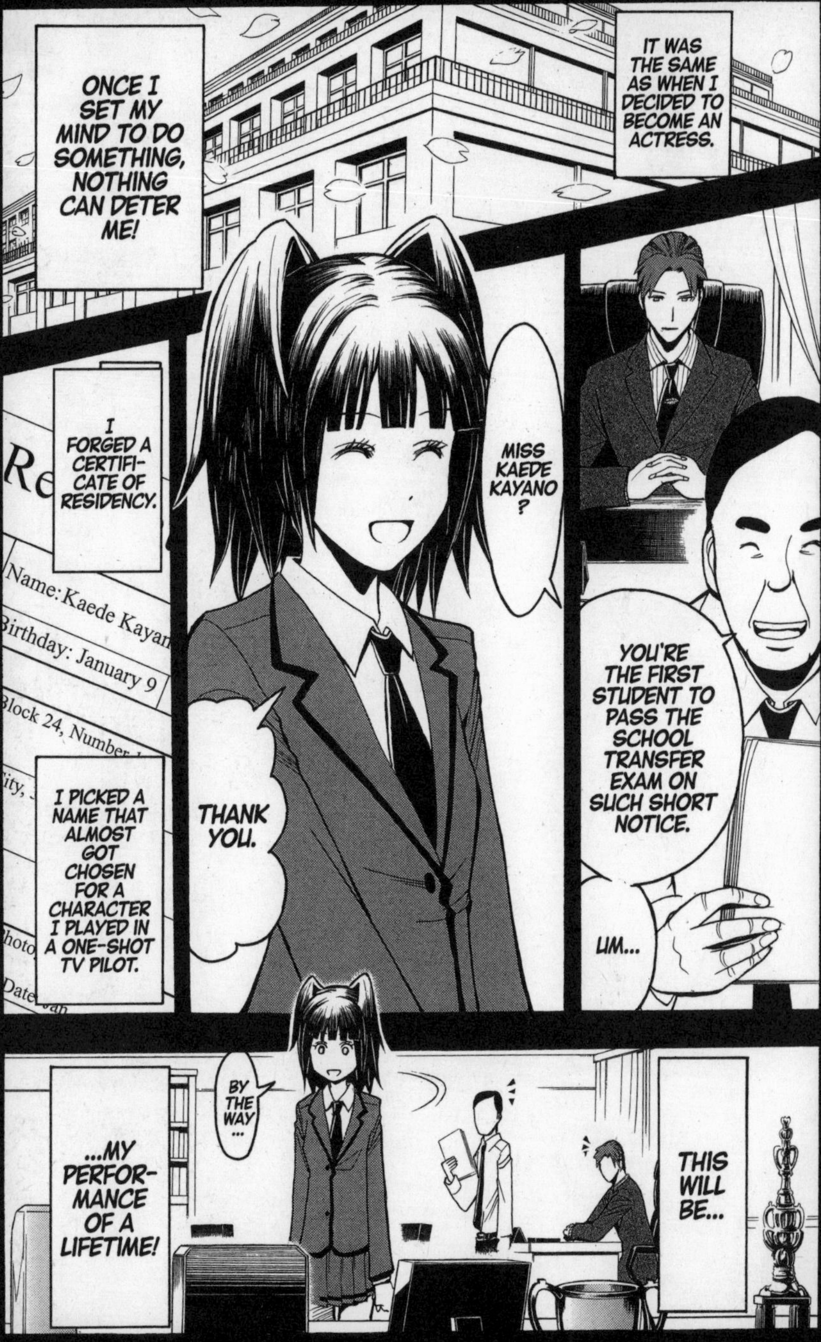
IT WAS THE SAME AS WHEN I DECIDED TO BECOME AN ACTRESS.
ONCE I SET MY MIND TO DO SOMETHING, NOTHING CAN DETER ME!
YOU'RE THE FIRST STUDENT TO PASS THE SCHOOL TRANSFER EXAM ON SUCH SHORT NOTICE.
UM...
MISS KAEDE KAYANO?
THANK YOU.
I FORGED A CERTIFICATE OF RESIDENCY.
Birthday: January 9
I PICKED A NAME THAT ALMOST GOT CHOSEN FOR A CHARACTER I PLAYED IN A ONE-SHOT TV PILOT.
THIS WILL BE...
BY THE WAY...
...MY PERFORMANCE OF A LIFETIME!

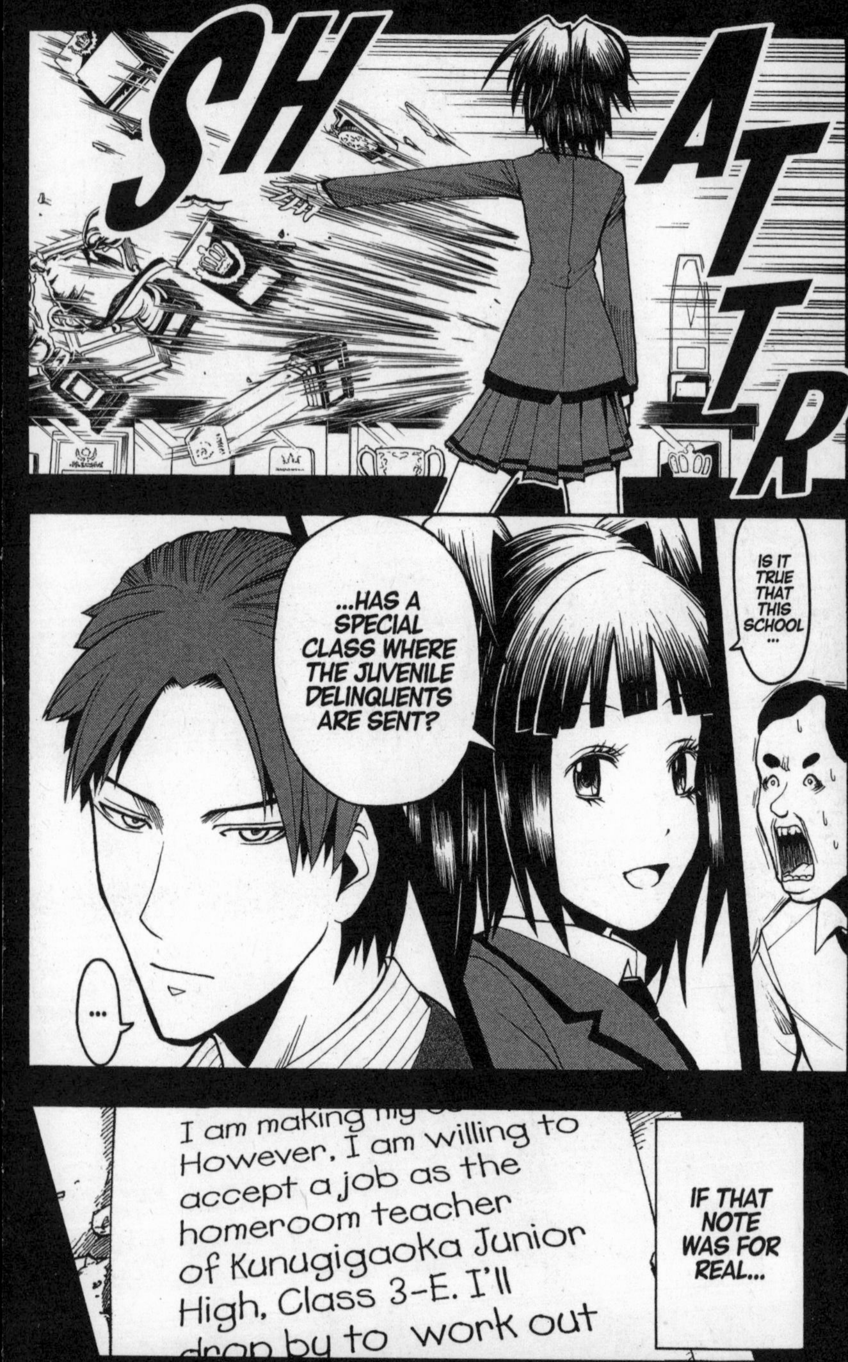
SHATR
IS IT TRUE THAT THIS SCHOOL...
...HAS A SPECIAL CLASS WHERE THE JUVENILE DELINQUENTS ARE SENT?
...
IF THAT NOTE WAS FOR REAL...
I am making
However, I am willing to
accept a job as the
homeroom teacher
of Kunugigaoka Junior
High, Class 3-E. I'll
drop by to work out

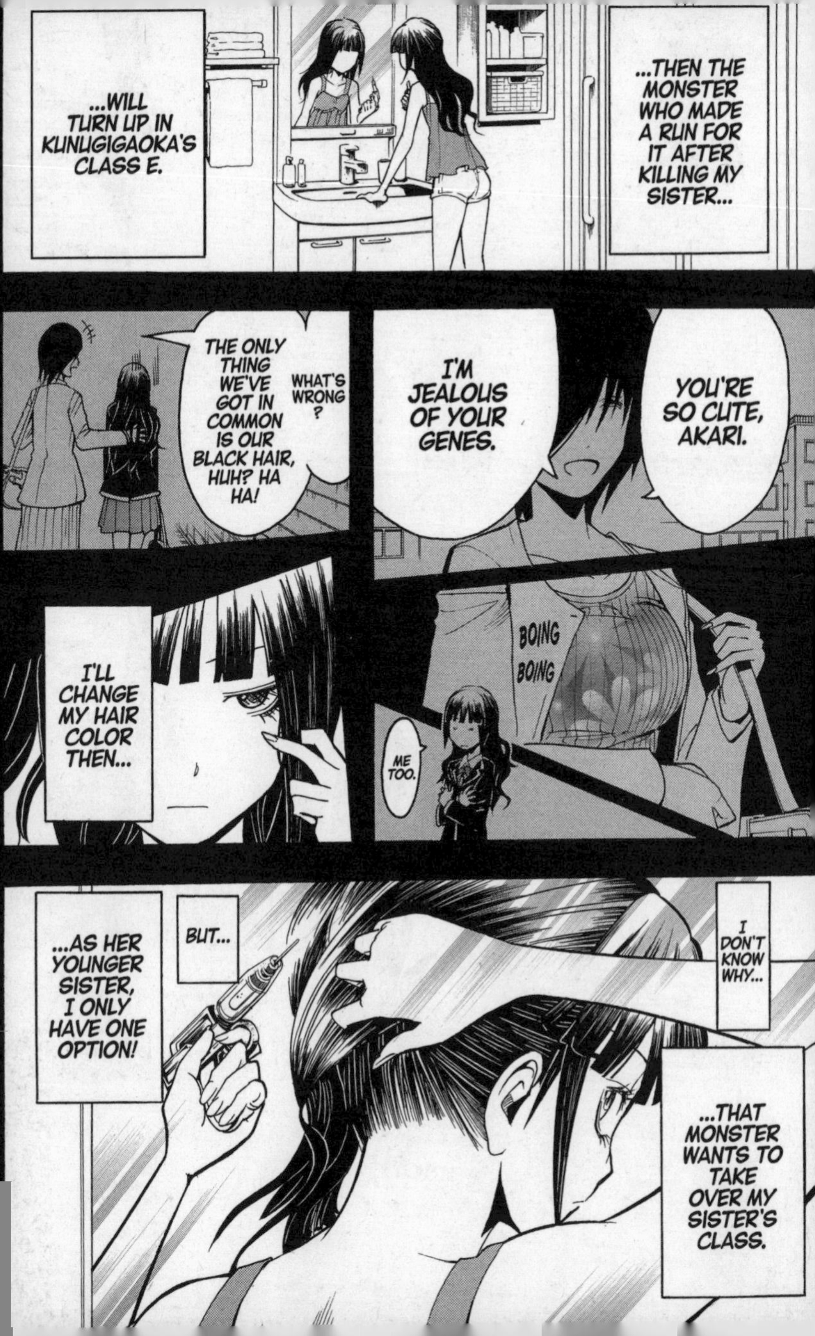
...THEN THE MONSTER WHO MADE A RUN FOR IT AFTER KILLING MY SISTER...
...WILL TURN UP IN KUNUGIGAOKA'S CLASS E.
YOU'RE SO CUTE, AKARI.
I'M JEALOUS OF YOUR GENES.
WHAT'S WRONG?
THE ONLY THING WE'VE GOT IN COMMON IS OUR BLACK HAIR, HUH? HA HA!
BOING
BOING
ME TOO.
I'LL CHANGE MY HAIR COLOR THEN...
I DON'T KNOW WHY...
...THAT MONSTER WANTS TO TAKE OVER MY SISTER'S CLASS.
BUT...
...AS HER YOUNGER SISTER, I ONLY HAVE ONE OPTION!

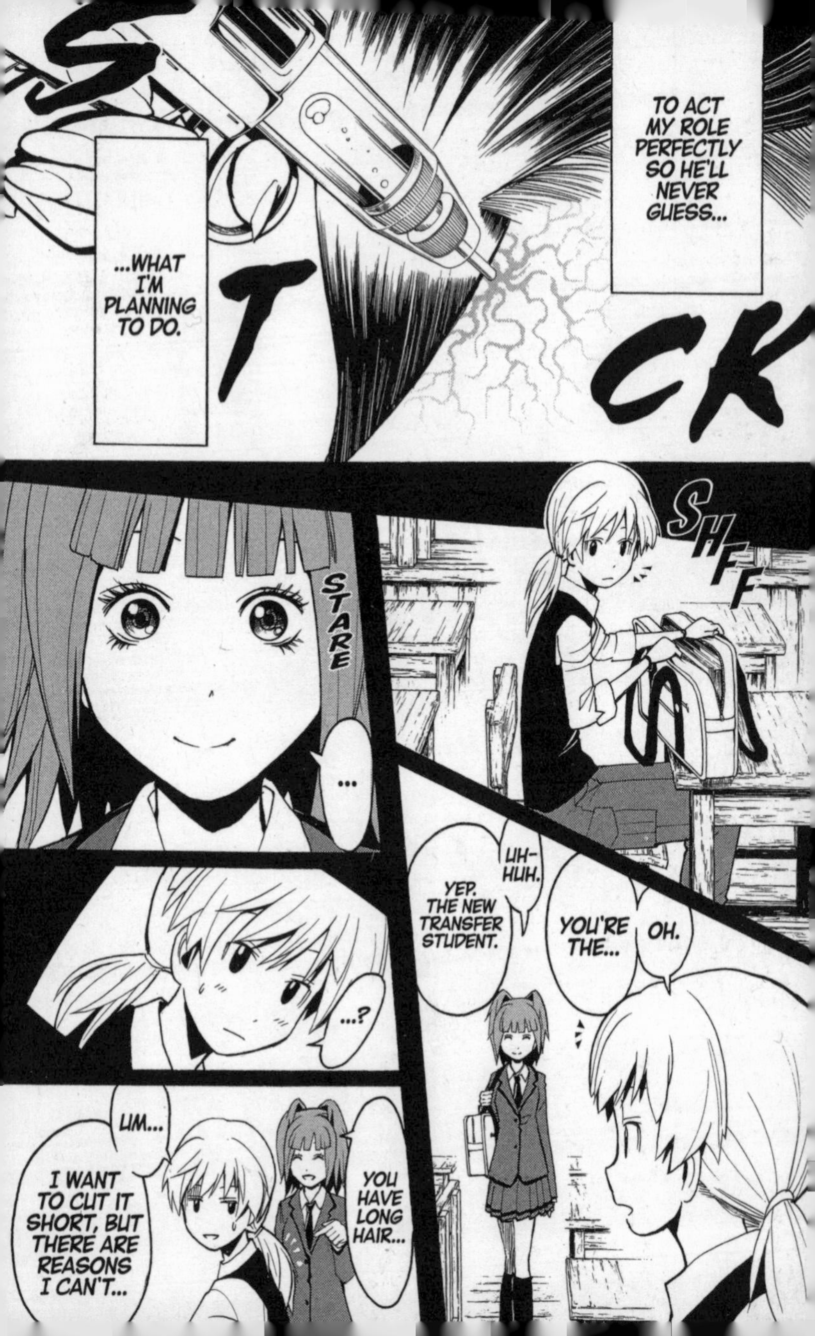
TO ACT MY ROLE PERFECTLY SO HE'LL NEVER GUESS...
...WHAT I'M PLANNING TO DO.
S T CK
SHFF
STARE
...
OH.
YOU'RE THE...
UH-HUH.
YEP. THE NEW TRANSFER STUDENT.
...?
YOU HAVE LONG HAIR...
UM...
I WANT TO CUT IT SHORT, BUT THERE ARE REASONS I CAN'T...

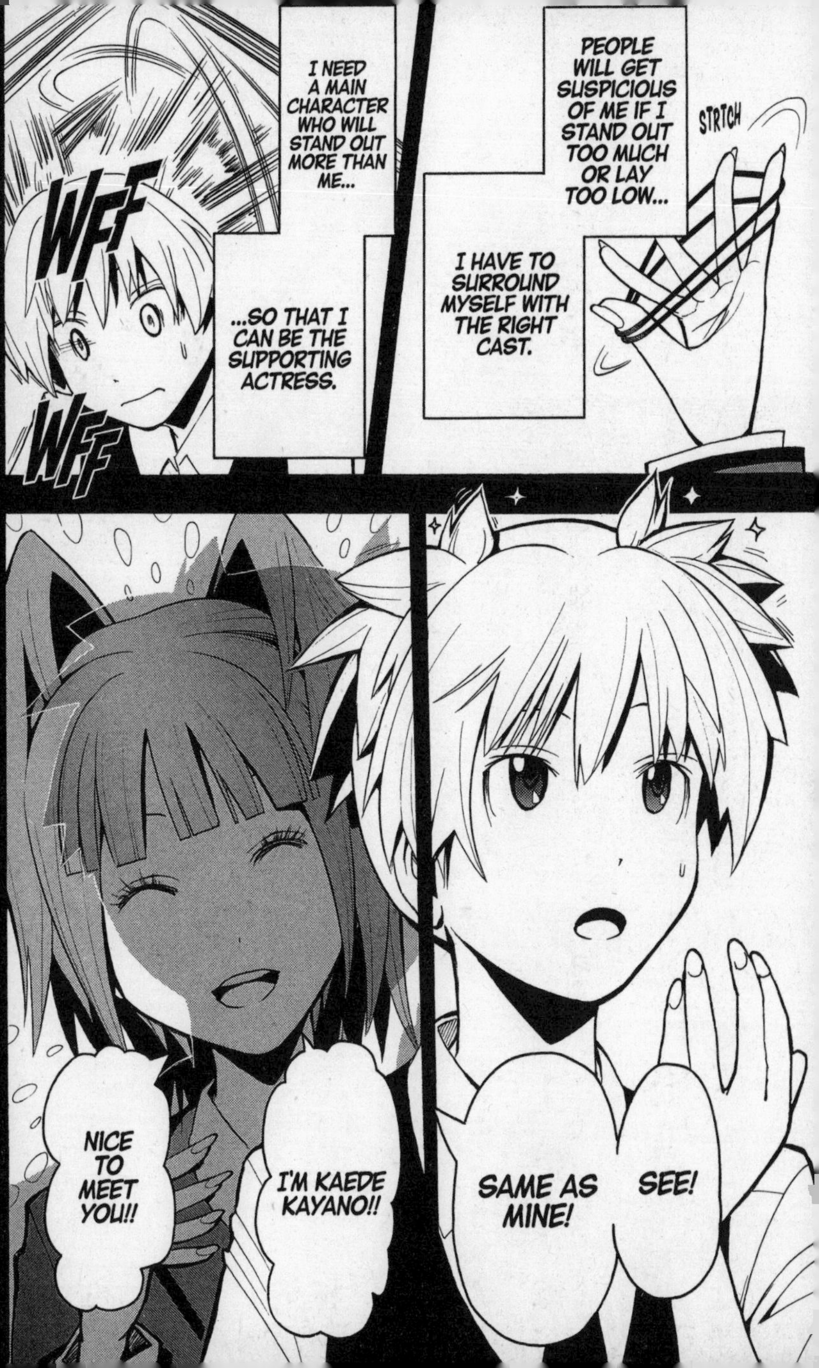
PEOPLE WILL GET SUSPICIOUS OF ME IF I STAND OUT TOO MUCH OR LAY TOO LOW...
STRTCH
I HAVE TO SURROUND MYSELF WITH THE RIGHT CAST.
I NEED A MAIN CHARACTER WHO WILL STAND OUT MORE THAN ME...
...SO THAT I CAN BE THE SUPPORTING ACTRESS.
WFF
WFF
SEE!
SAME AS MINE!
I'M KAEDE KAYANO!!
NICE TO MEET YOU!!

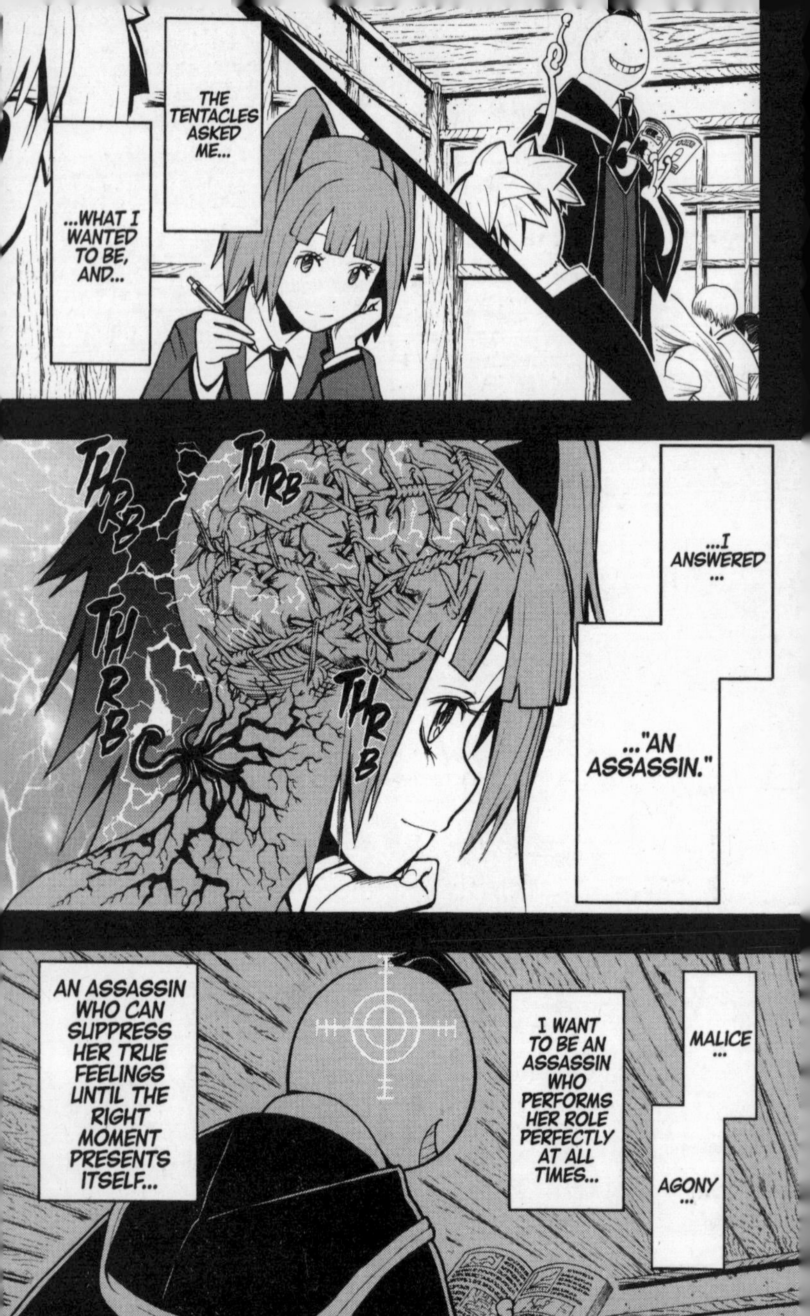
THE TENTACLES ASKED ME...
...WHAT I WANTED TO BE, AND...
...I ANSWERED...
..."AN ASSASSIN."
THRB
THRB
THRB
THRB
MALICE...
AGONY...
I WANT TO BE AN ASSASSIN WHO PERFORMS HER ROLE PERFECTLY AT ALL TIMES...
AN ASSASSIN WHO CAN SUPPRESS HER TRUE FEELINGS UNTIL THE RIGHT MOMENT PRESENTS ITSELF...

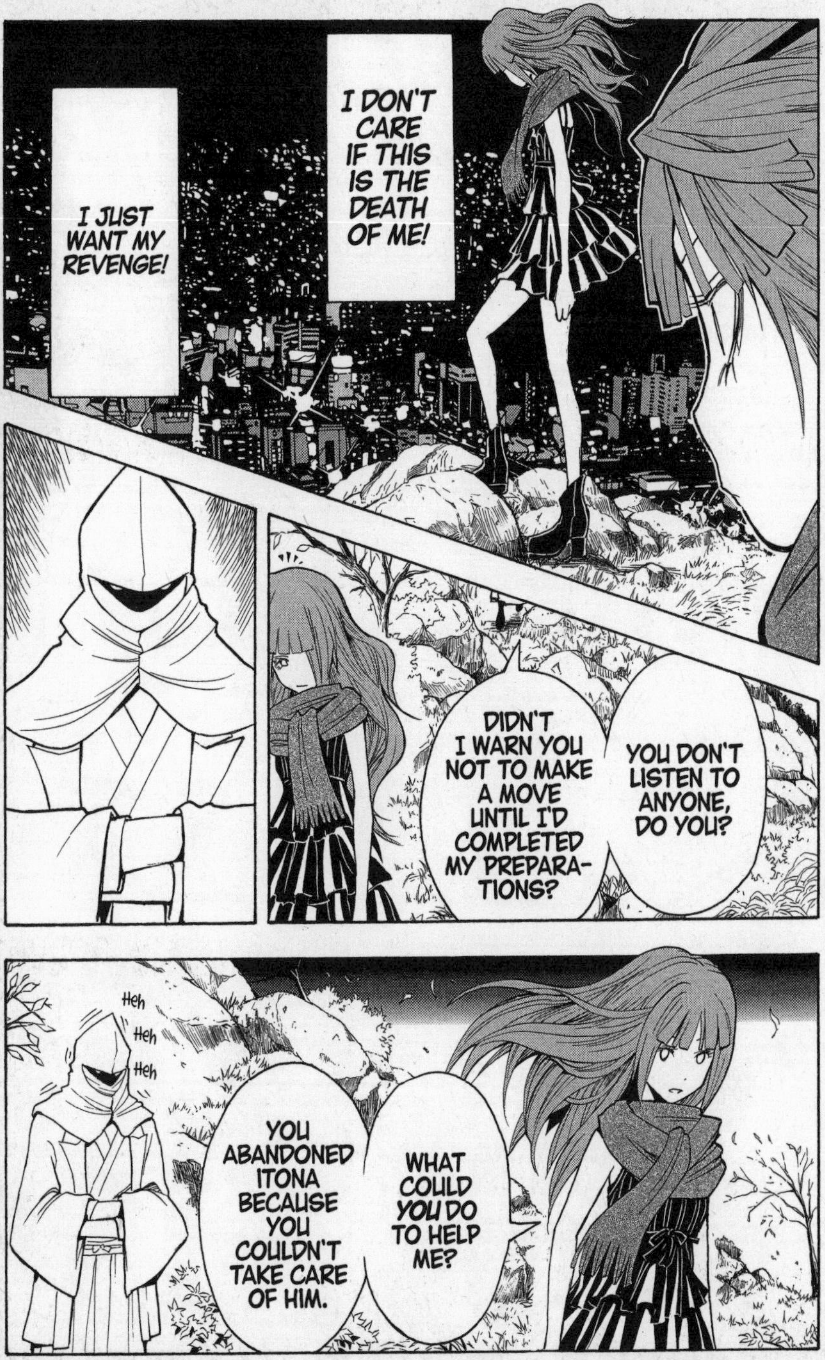
I DON'T CARE IF THIS IS THE DEATH OF ME!
I JUST WANT MY REVENGE!
YOU DON'T LISTEN TO ANYONE, DO YOU?
DIDN'T I WARN YOU NOT TO MAKE A MOVE UNTIL I'D COMPLETED MY PREPARA-TIONS?
Heh Heh Heh
WHAT COULD YOU DO TO HELP ME?
YOU ABANDONED ITONA BECAUSE YOU COULDN'T TAKE CARE OF HIM.

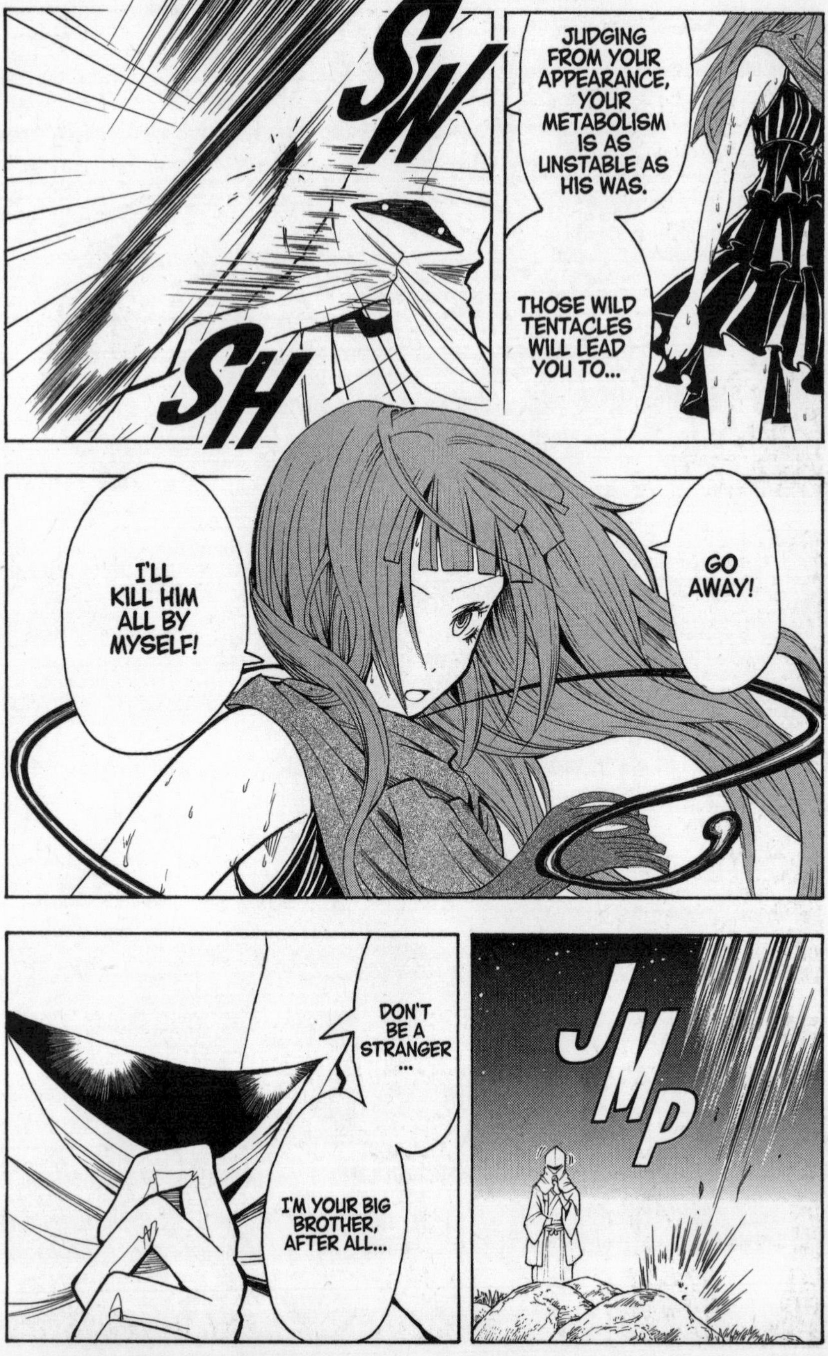
JUDGING FROM YOUR APPEARANCE, YOUR METABOLISM IS AS UNSTABLE AS HIS WAS.
THOSE WILD TENTACLES WILL LEAD YOU TO...
SW
SH
GO AWAY!
I'LL KILL HIM ALL BY MYSELF!
JMP
DON'T BE A STRANGER ...
I'M YOUR BIG BROTHER, AFTER ALL...

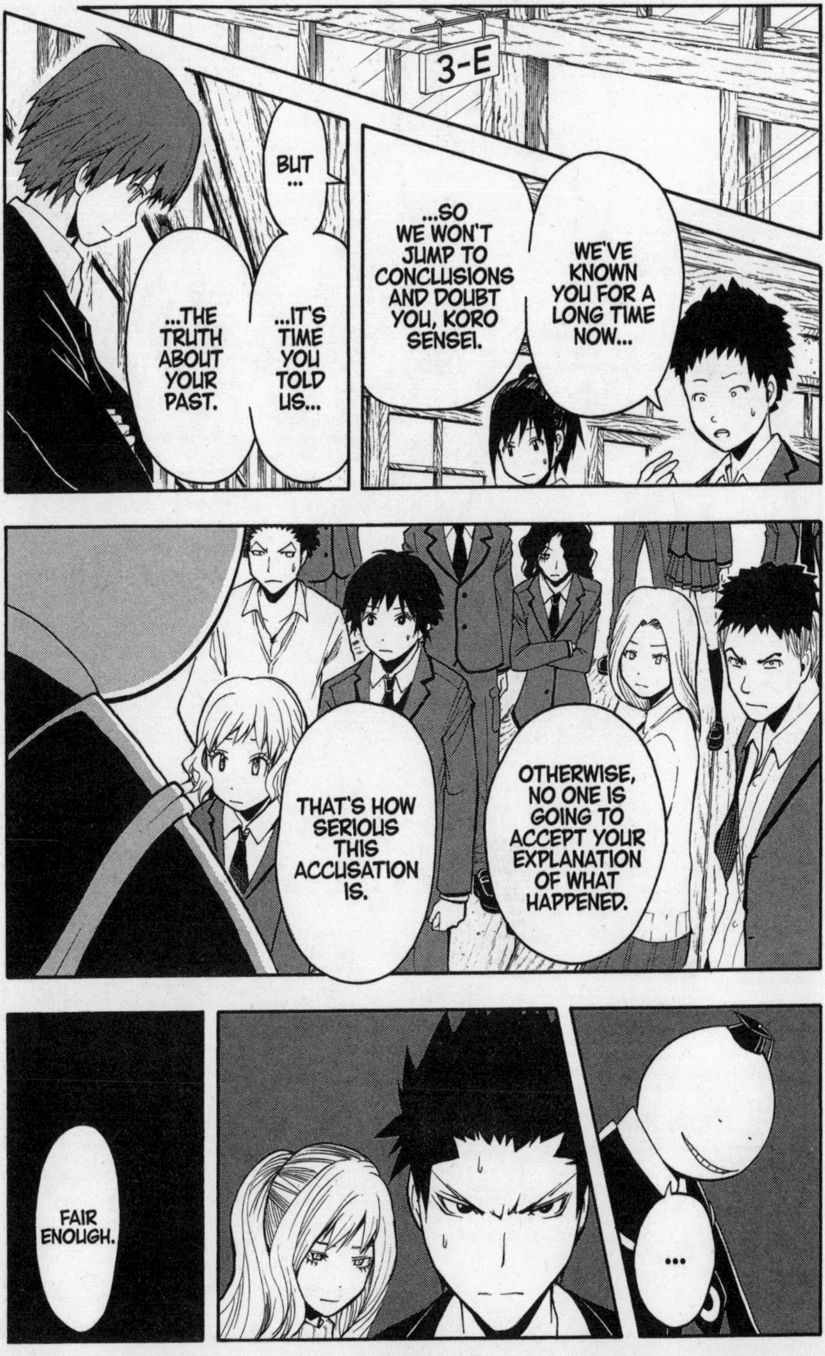
3-E
WE'VE KNOWN YOU FOR A LONG TIME NOW...
...SO WE WON'T JUMP TO CONCLUSIONS AND DOUBT YOU, KORO SENSEI.
BUT ...
...IT'S TIME YOU TOLD US...
...THE TRUTH ABOUT YOUR PAST.
OTHERWISE, NO ONE IS GOING TO ACCEPT YOUR EXPLANATION OF WHAT HAPPENED.
THAT'S HOW SERIOUS THIS ACCUSATION IS.
...
FAIR ENOUGH.

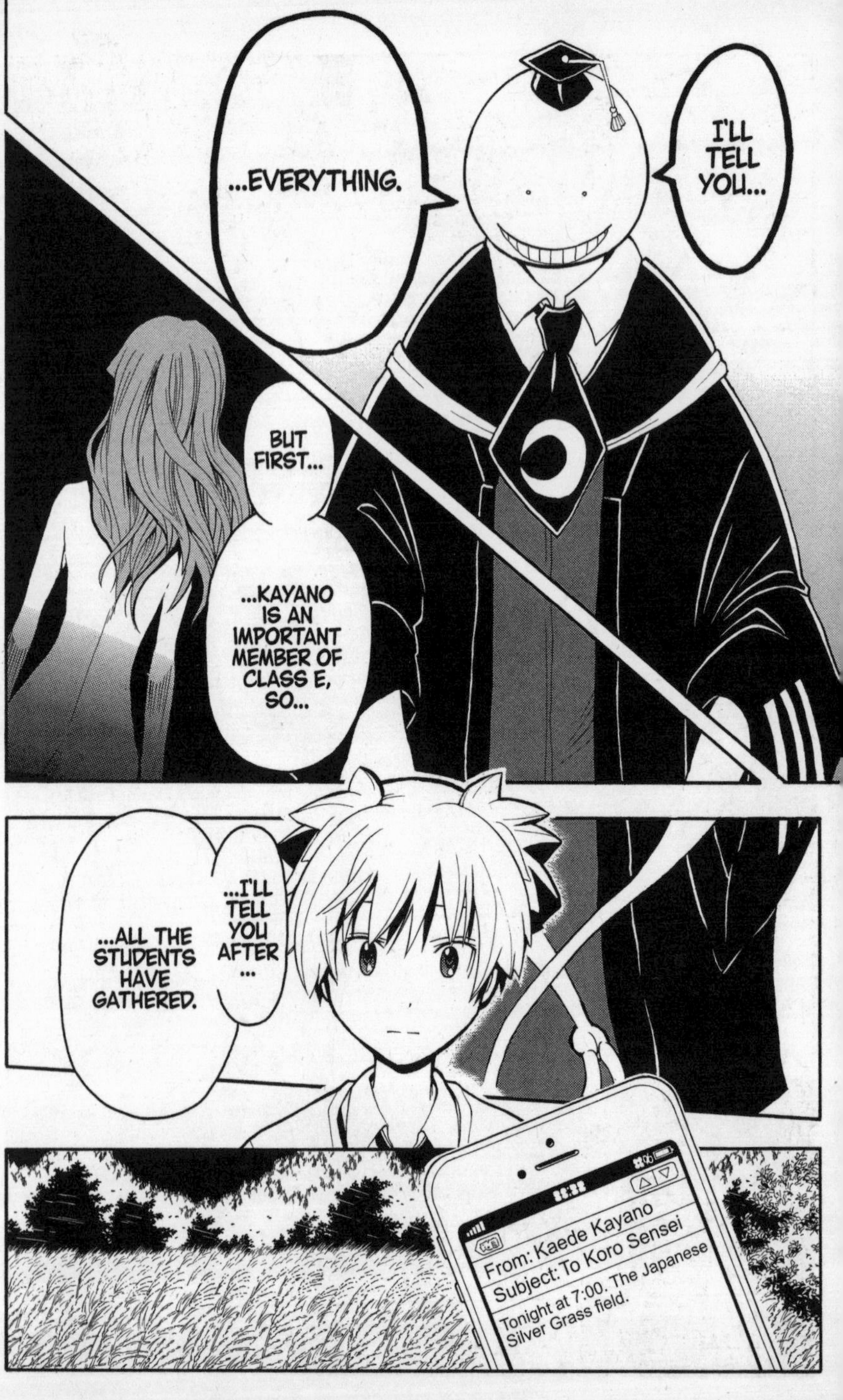
I'LL TELL YOU...
...EVERYTHING.
BUT FIRST...
...KAYANO IS AN IMPORTANT MEMBER OF CLASS E, SO...
...I'LL TELL YOU AFTER...
...ALL THE STUDENTS HAVE GATHERED.
From: Kaede Kayano
Subject: To Koro Sensei
Tonight at 7:00. The Japanese Silver Grass field.

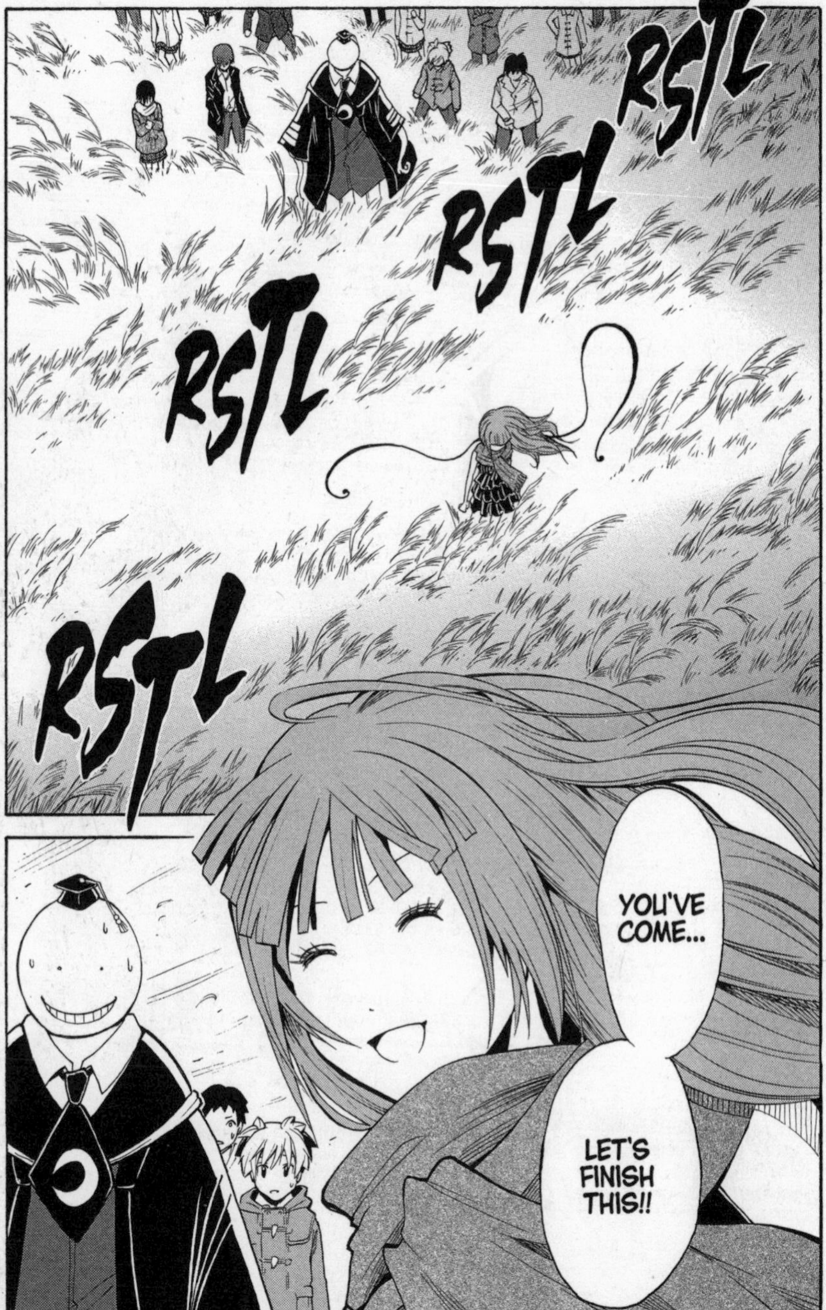
RSTL
RSTL
RSTL
RSTL
YOU'VE COME...
LET'S FINISH THIS!!

Results and changes observed in the recipient after the transplant of the Human Body Tentacle Weapon Prototype

1: Acute Pain

Combining the human body and a genetically different life-form causes extreme organ rejection. The transplant recipient will experience pain on a daily basis. It requires a massive amount of energy to stabilize the recipient and prevent rejection.

2: Decline in Performance

The bonding with the recipient's neurons initiates a decline in the precision of neurotransmissions, resulting in a 10% to 30% decline in mental and physical performance. Therefore, the recipient must either receive further body modification or use their tentacles to compensate for the decline in physical performance if they are to be used for battles on warfare.

3: Mental Instability

Because the tentacles are linked directly to the recipient's neurons, in some cases the excessive tentacle energy will overstimulate the brain. This overstimulation can trigger bouts of rage which can physically damage the recipient and are extremely dangerous to both the recipient and others.

4: Metabolic Instability

The recipient's body temperature is frequently observed to rise while the recipient simultaneously experiences a chill in the thoracic region. This is probably attributable to the fact that the organ, which is equivalent to the heart of the Perfect Tentacle Creature, did not originate inside the body of the transplant recipient. The chill is merely a sensory abnormality, but the rise in temperature may have negative ramifications for the body and mind of the recipient if it continues for a prolonged period of time.

5: Aversion to Water

Due to osmotic pressure, the movement of the tentacle is dulled when it comes in contact with water; thus recipients tend to instinctively avoid it. However, water merely destabilizes the balance of the tentacles, and no serious repercussions are currently known to occur.

6: Change in Eating Habits

There is a tendency for recipients to develop a sweet tooth. This is thought to result from the recipient requiring a large amount of energy to maintain a connection with the tentacles; however, no serious repercussions are known to occur from this condition either.

7: Major Obsession with Certain Body Parts

The recipient will develop a strong obsession with soft-tissue parts of the human body. It is presumed that the tentacle feels a strong sense of fellowship with these body parts because of their similar consistency. However, this preoccupation could be linked to number 3, so some caution is recommended in this regard.

CLASS 131 | TIME FOR CORROSION

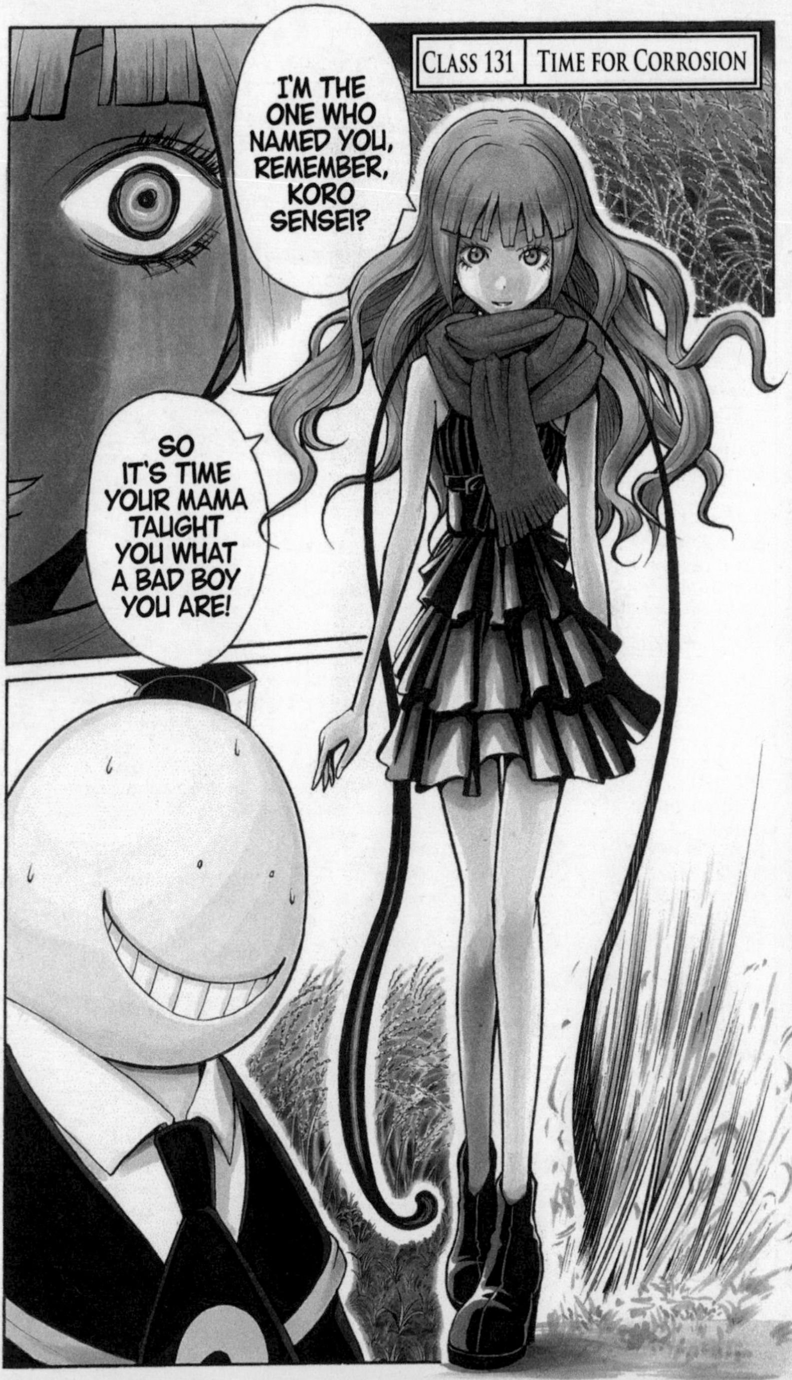
I'M THE ONE WHO NAMED YOU, REMEMBER, KORO SENSEI?
SO IT'S TIME YOUR MAMA TAUGHT YOU WHAT A BAD BOY YOU ARE!

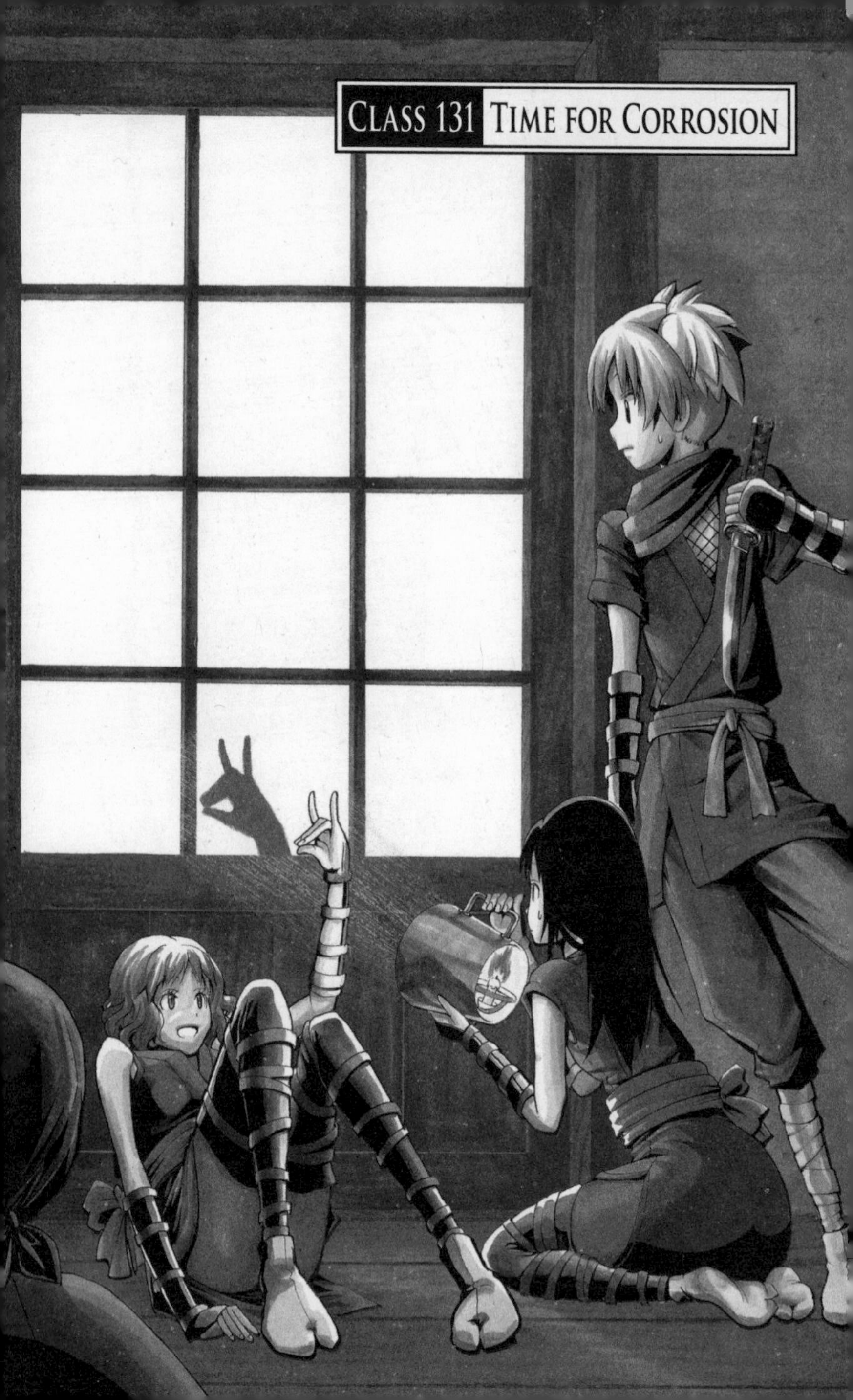
CLASS 131 TIME FOR CORROSION

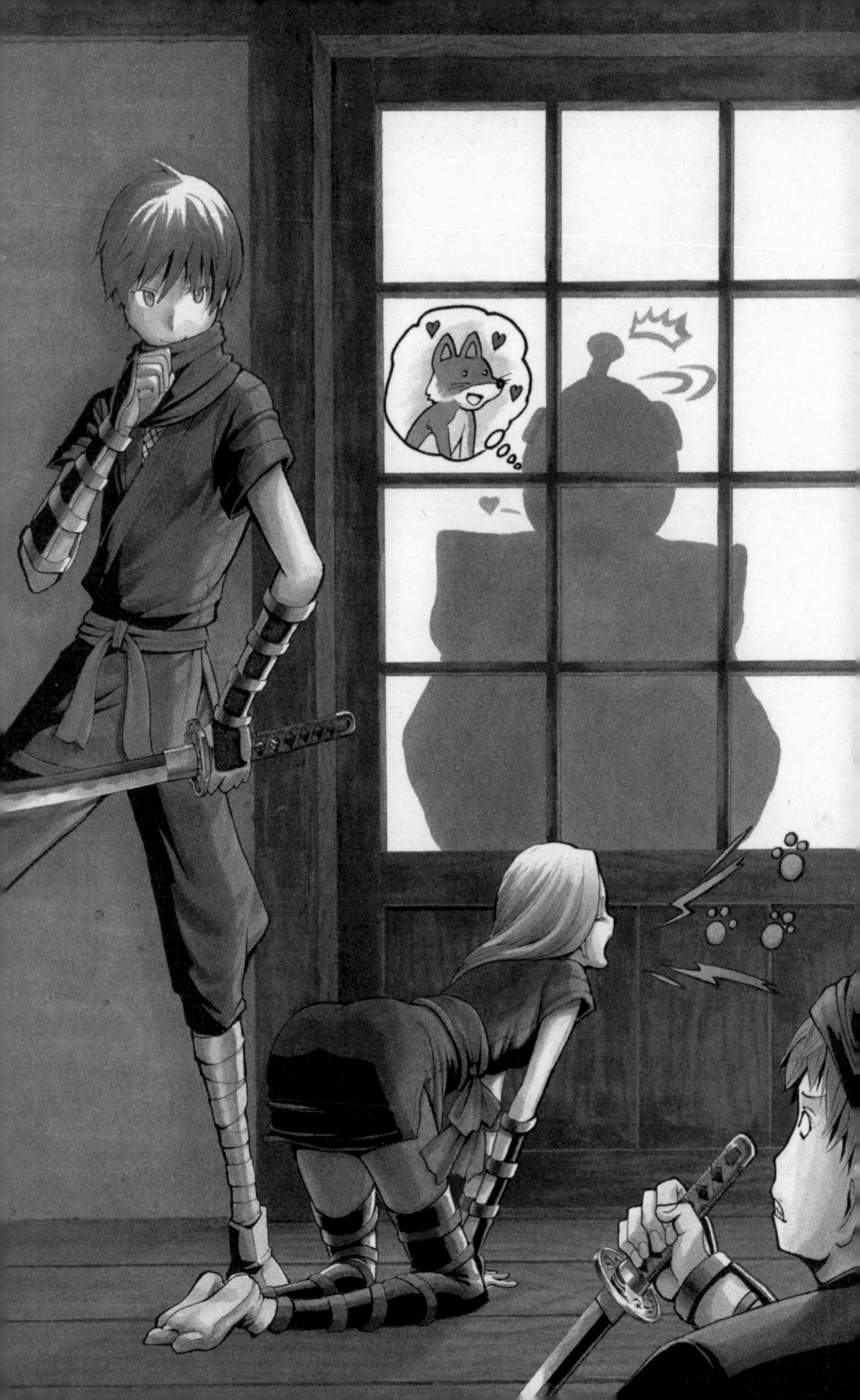

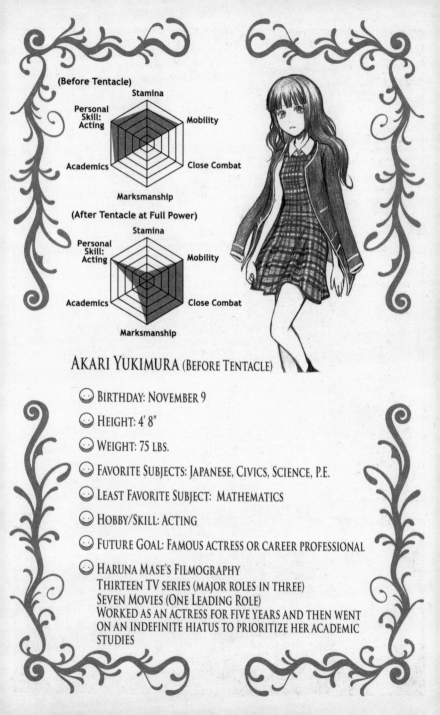

(Before Tentacle)

Radar chart axes: Stamina, Mobility, Close Combat, Marksmanship, Academics, Personal Skill: Acting

(After Tentacle at Full Power)

Radar chart axes: Stamina, Mobility, Close Combat, Marksmanship, Academics, Personal Skill: Acting

AKARI YUKIMURA (BEFORE TENTACLE)

🙂 BIRTHDAY: NOVEMBER 9

🙂 HEIGHT: 4' 8"

🙂 WEIGHT: 75 LBS.

🙂 FAVORITE SUBJECTS: JAPANESE, CIVICS, SCIENCE, P.E.

🙂 LEAST FAVORITE SUBJECT: MATHEMATICS

🙂 HOBBY/SKILL: ACTING

🙂 FUTURE GOAL: FAMOUS ACTRESS OR CAREER PROFESSIONAL

🙂 HARUNA MASE'S FILMOGRAPHY
THIRTEEN TV SERIES (MAJOR ROLES IN THREE)
SEVEN MOVIES (ONE LEADING ROLE)
WORKED AS AN ACTRESS FOR FIVE YEARS AND THEN WENT
ON AN INDEFINITE HIATUS TO PRIORITIZE HER ACADEMIC
STUDIES

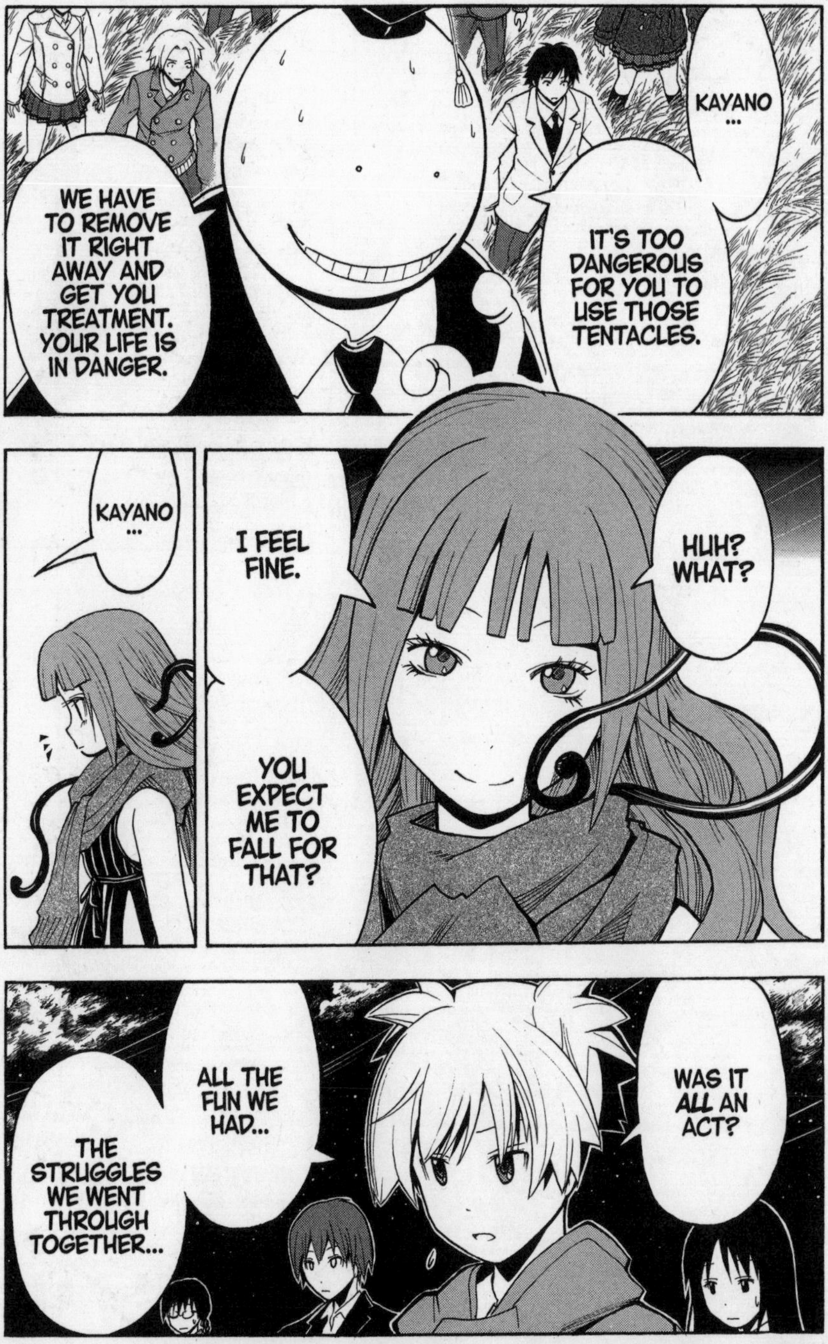
KAYANO...
IT'S TOO DANGEROUS FOR YOU TO USE THOSE TENTACLES.
WE HAVE TO REMOVE IT RIGHT AWAY AND GET YOU TREATMENT. YOUR LIFE IS IN DANGER.
HUH? WHAT?
I FEEL FINE.
YOU EXPECT ME TO FALL FOR THAT?
KAYANO...
WAS IT ALL AN ACT?
ALL THE FUN WE HAD...
THE STRUGGLES WE WENT THROUGH TOGETHER...

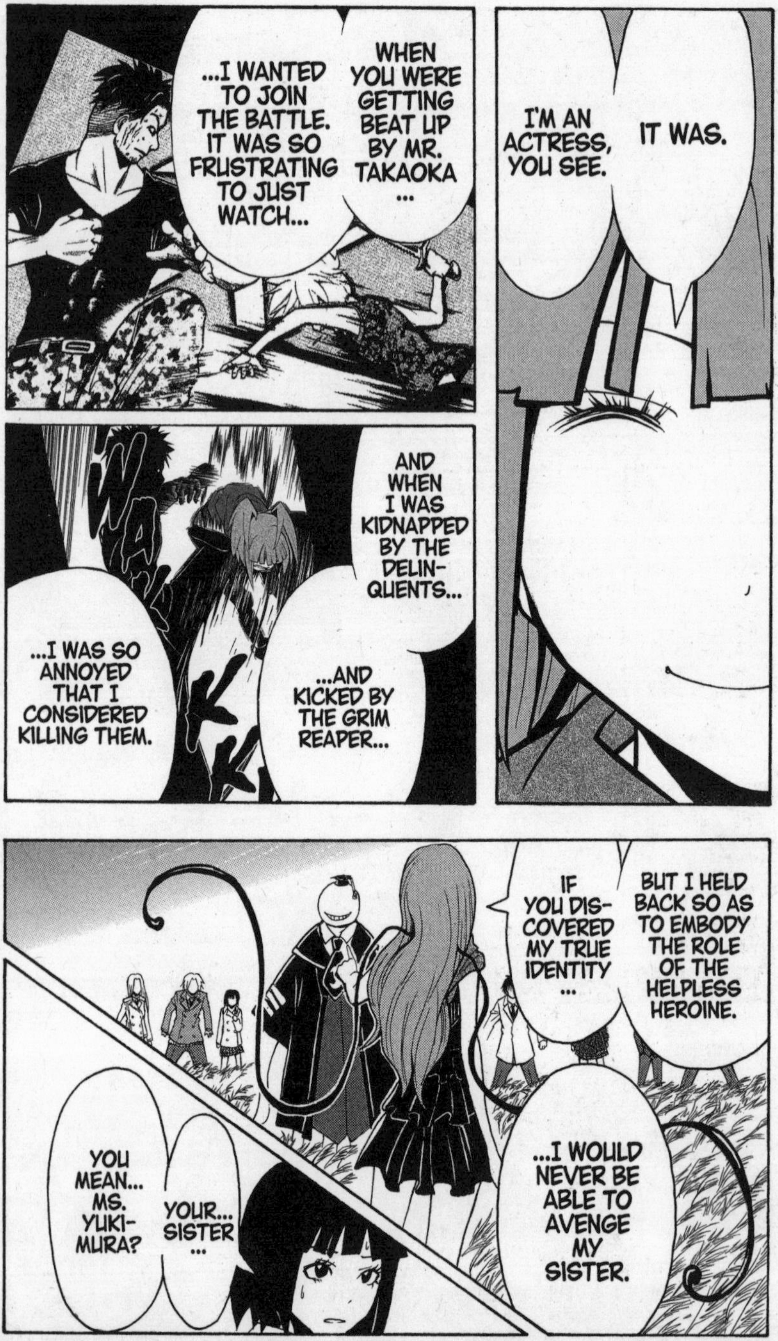
IT WAS.
I'M AN ACTRESS, YOU SEE.
WHEN YOU WERE GETTING BEAT UP BY MR. TAKAOKA...
...I WANTED TO JOIN THE BATTLE. IT WAS SO FRUSTRATING TO JUST WATCH...
AND WHEN I WAS KIDNAPPED BY THE DELINQUENTS...
...AND KICKED BY THE GRIM REAPER...
...I WAS SO ANNOYED THAT I CONSIDERED KILLING THEM.
BUT I HELD BACK SO AS TO EMBODY THE ROLE OF THE HELPLESS HEROINE.
IF YOU DISCOVERED MY TRUE IDENTITY...
...I WOULD NEVER BE ABLE TO AVENGE MY SISTER.
YOUR... SISTER...
YOU MEAN... MS. YUKIMURA?

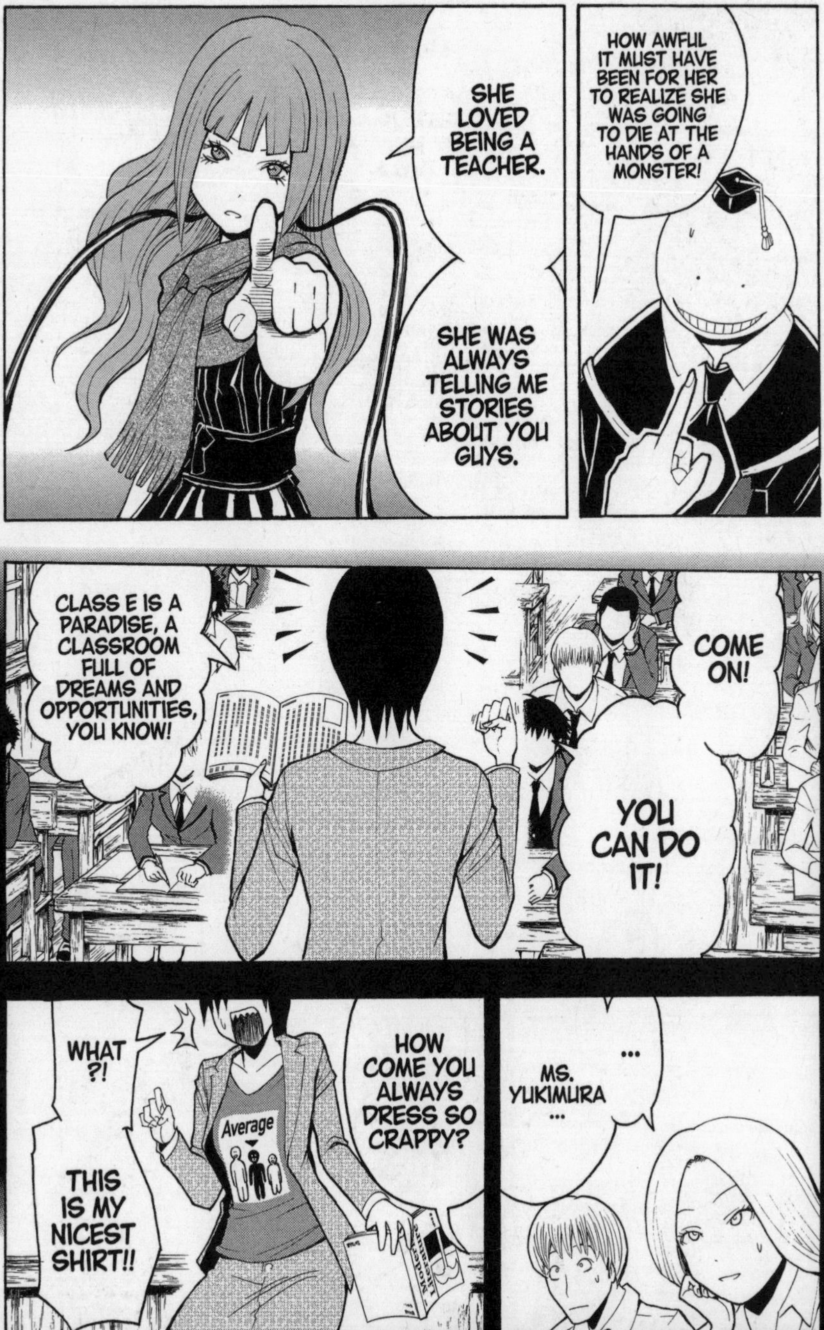
HOW AWFUL IT MUST HAVE BEEN FOR HER TO REALIZE SHE WAS GOING TO DIE AT THE HANDS OF A MONSTER!
SHE LOVED BEING A TEACHER.
SHE WAS ALWAYS TELLING ME STORIES ABOUT YOU GUYS.
COME ON!
YOU CAN DO IT!
CLASS E IS A PARADISE, A CLASSROOM FULL OF DREAMS AND OPPORTUNITIES, YOU KNOW!
...
MS. YUKIMURA...
HOW COME YOU ALWAYS DRESS SO CRAPPY?
WHAT?!
THIS IS MY NICEST SHIRT!!
Average

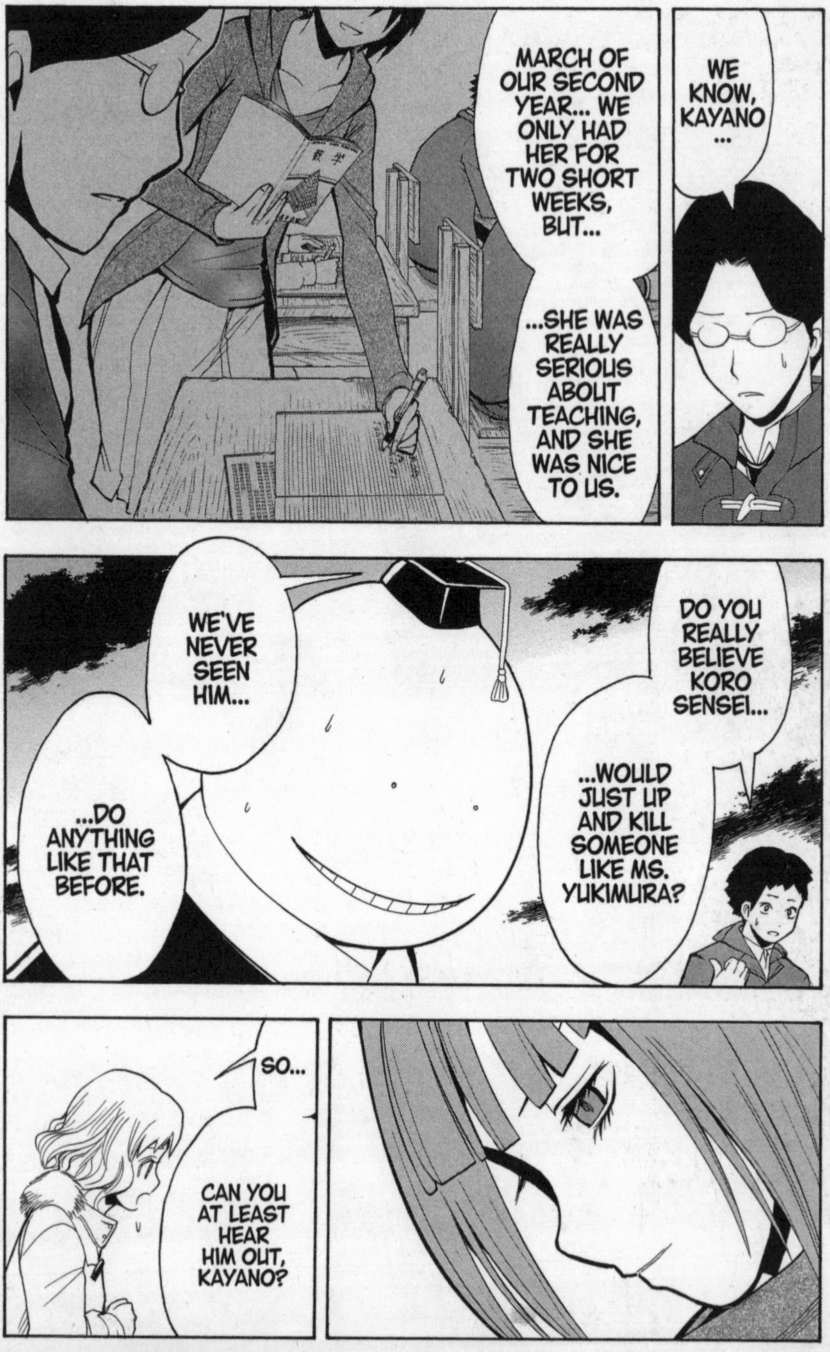
WE KNOW, KAYANO...
MARCH OF OUR SECOND YEAR... WE ONLY HAD HER FOR TWO SHORT WEEKS, BUT...
...SHE WAS REALLY SERIOUS ABOUT TEACHING, AND SHE WAS NICE TO US.
DO YOU REALLY BELIEVE KORO SENSEI...
...WOULD JUST UP AND KILL SOMEONE LIKE MS. YUKIMURA?
WE'VE NEVER SEEN HIM...
...DO ANYTHING LIKE THAT BEFORE.
SO...
CAN YOU AT LEAST HEAR HIM OUT, KAYANO?

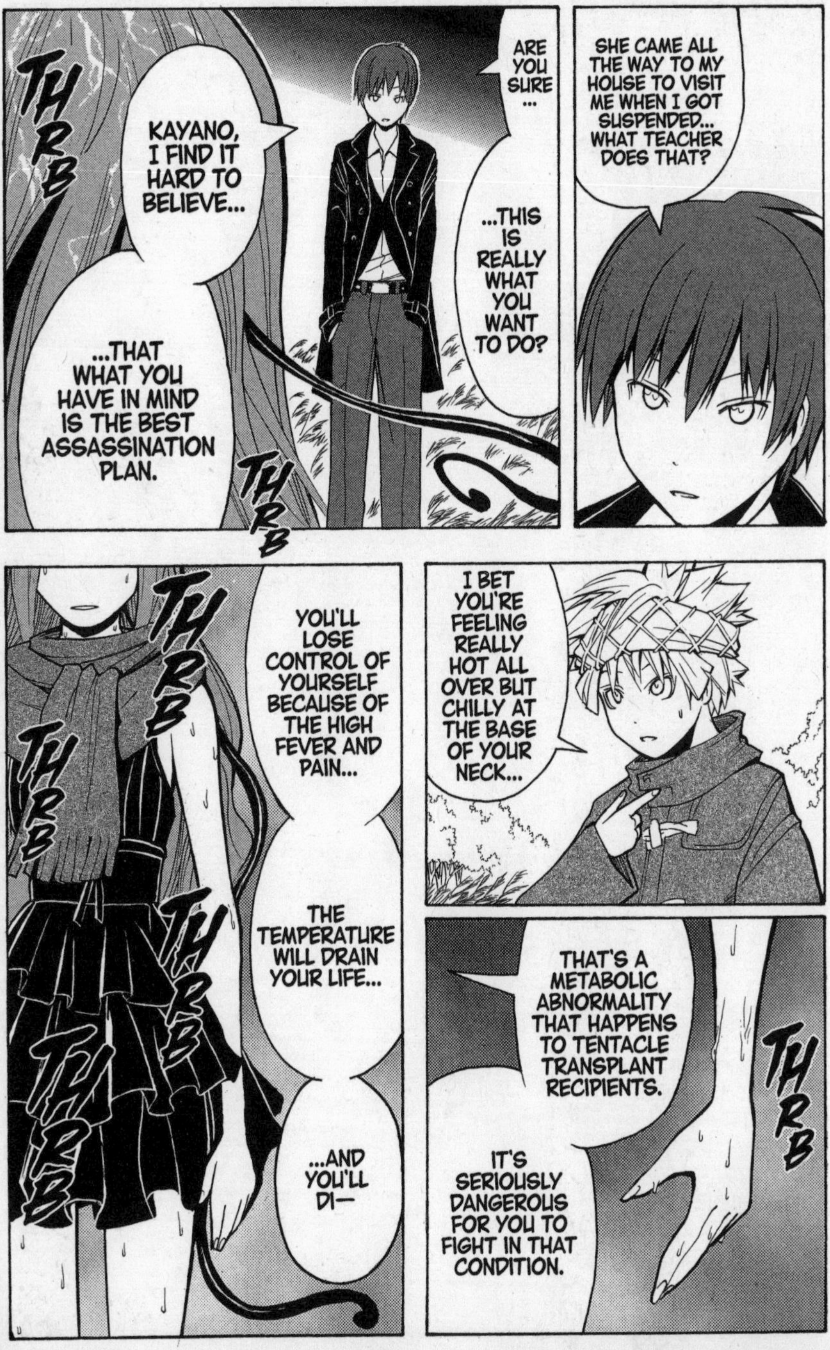
SHE CAME ALL THE WAY TO MY HOUSE TO VISIT ME WHEN I GOT SUSPENDED... WHAT TEACHER DOES THAT?
ARE YOU SURE ...
...THIS IS REALLY WHAT YOU WANT TO DO?
KAYANO, I FIND IT HARD TO BELIEVE...
...THAT WHAT YOU HAVE IN MIND IS THE BEST ASSASSINATION PLAN.
THRB
THRB
I BET YOU'RE FEELING REALLY HOT ALL OVER BUT CHILLY AT THE BASE OF YOUR NECK...
THAT'S A METABOLIC ABNORMALITY THAT HAPPENS TO TENTACLE TRANSPLANT RECIPIENTS.
IT'S SERIOUSLY DANGEROUS FOR YOU TO FIGHT IN THAT CONDITION.
THRB
YOU'LL LOSE CONTROL OF YOURSELF BECAUSE OF THE HIGH FEVER AND PAIN...
THE TEMPERATURE WILL DRAIN YOUR LIFE...
...AND YOU'LL DI—
THRB
THRB
THRB
THRB

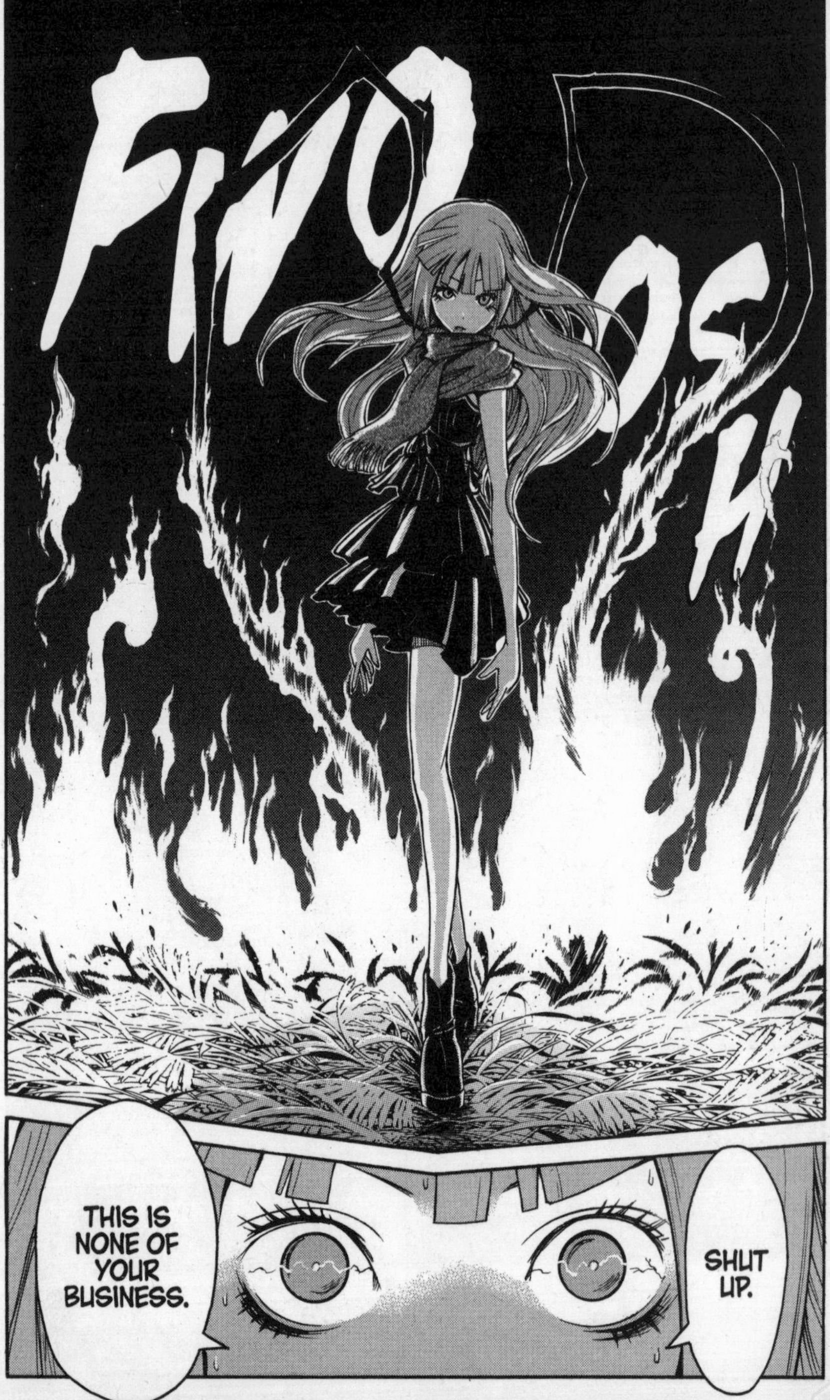
FWOOSH
SHUT UP.
THIS IS NONE OF YOUR BUSINESS.

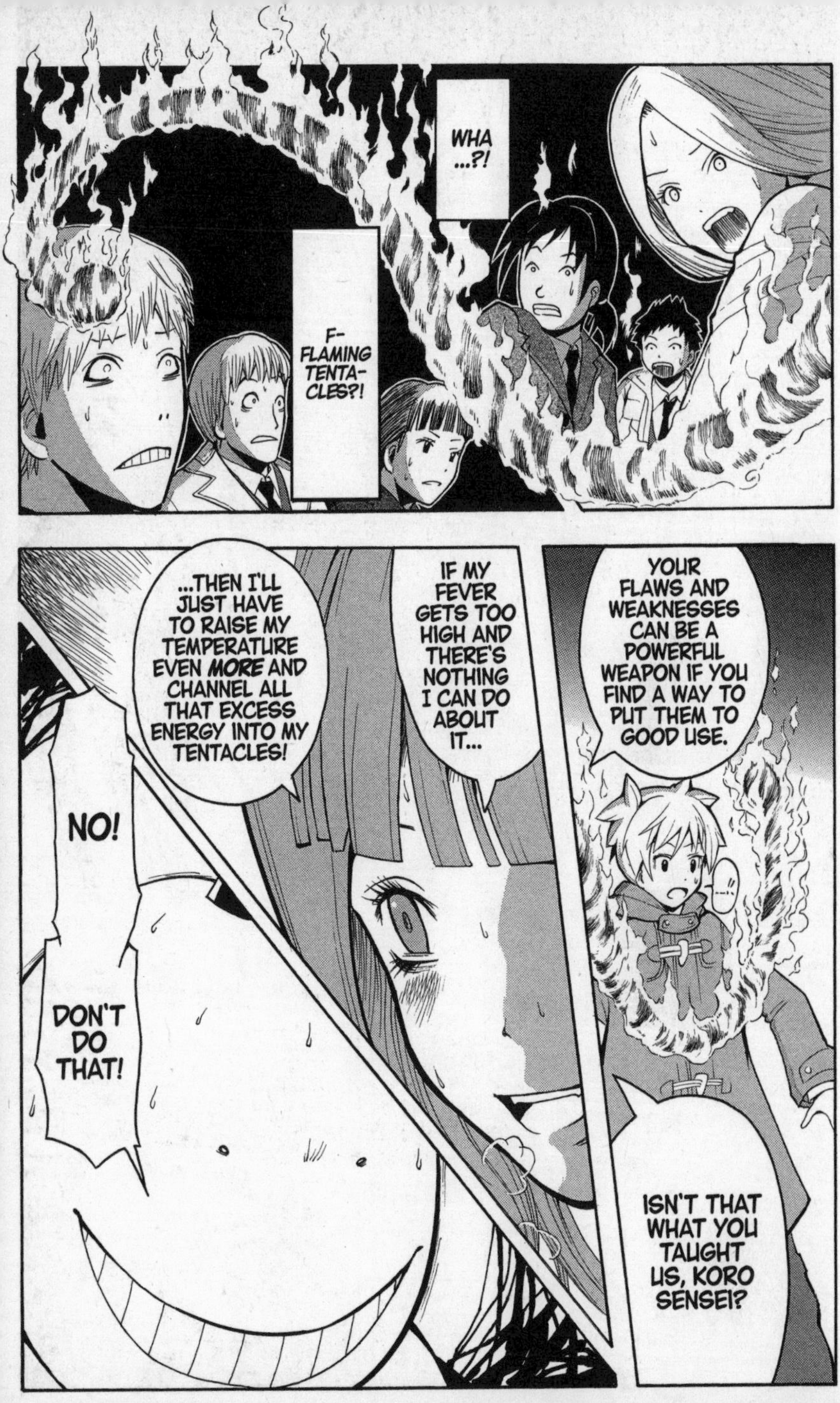
WHA ...?!
F-FLAMING TENTA-CLES?!
YOUR FLAWS AND WEAKNESSES CAN BE A POWERFUL WEAPON IF YOU FIND A WAY TO PUT THEM TO GOOD USE.
...!
ISN'T THAT WHAT YOU TAUGHT US, KORO SENSEI?
IF MY FEVER GETS TOO HIGH AND THERE'S NOTHING I CAN DO ABOUT IT...
...THEN I'LL JUST HAVE TO RAISE MY TEMPERATURE EVEN MORE AND CHANNEL ALL THAT EXCESS ENERGY INTO MY TENTACLES!
NO!
DON'T DO THAT!

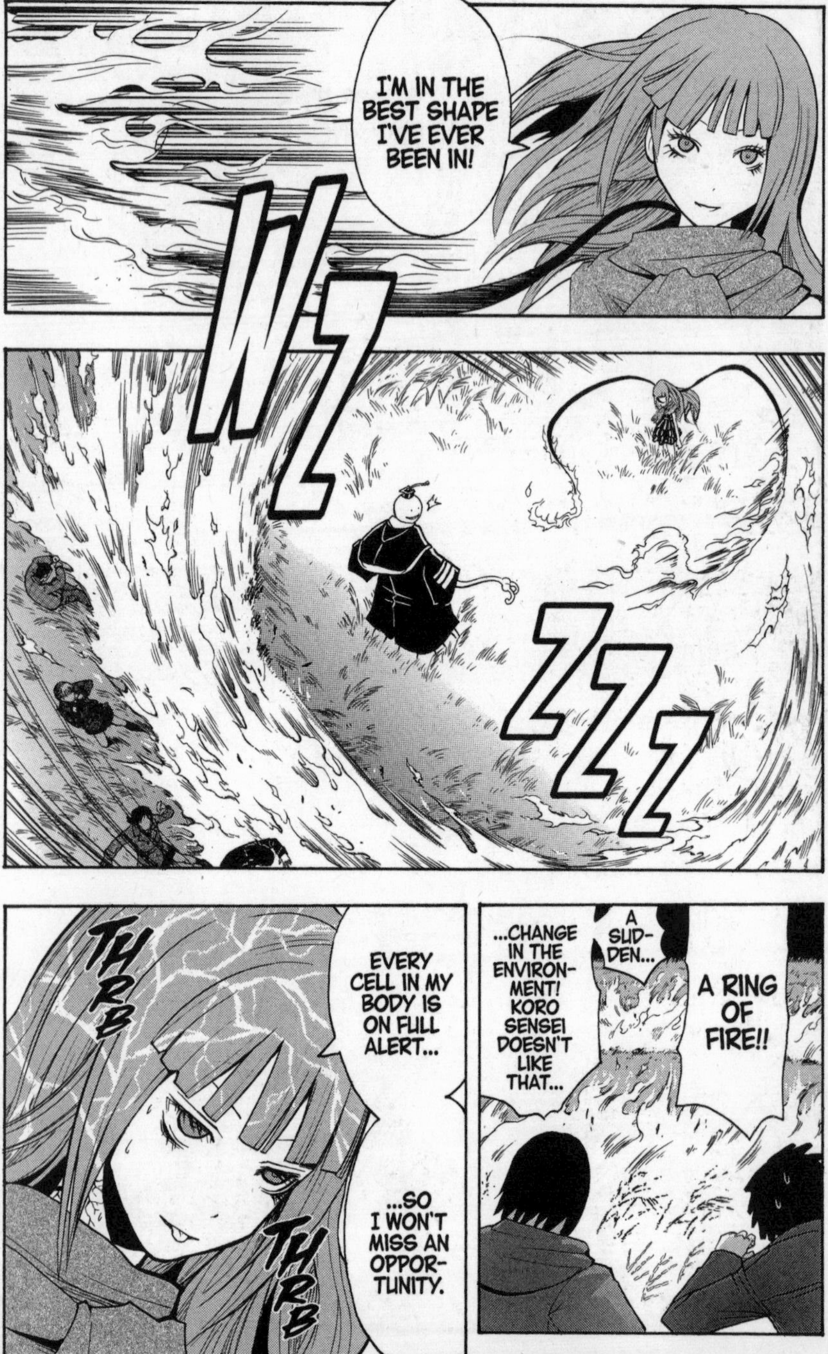
I'M IN THE BEST SHAPE I'VE EVER BEEN IN!
WZ
ZZZ
A SUDDEN...
...CHANGE IN THE ENVIRONMENT! KORO SENSEI DOESN'T LIKE THAT...
A RING OF FIRE!!
THRB
EVERY CELL IN MY BODY IS ON FULL ALERT...
...SO I WON'T MISS AN OPPORTUNITY.
THRB

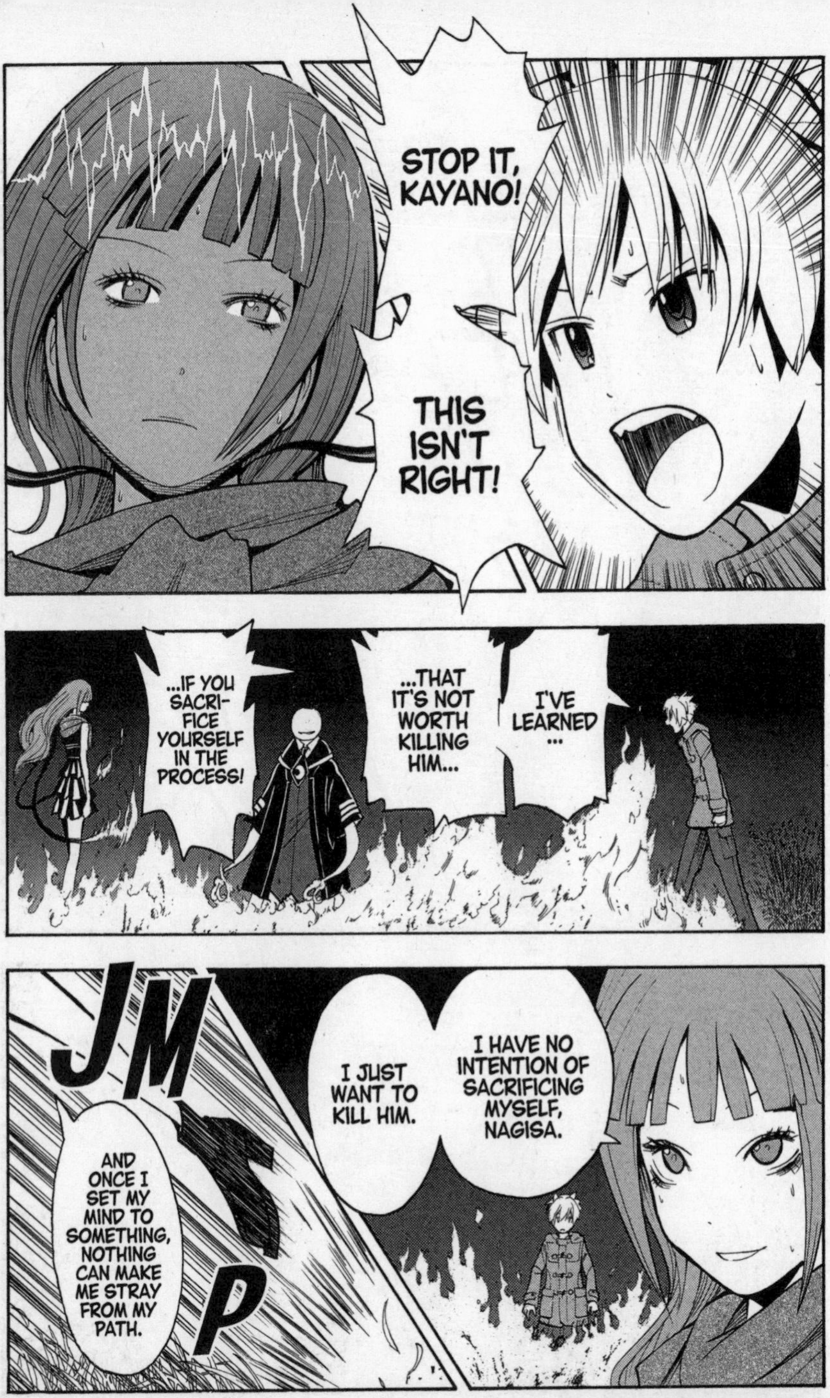
STOP IT, KAYANO!
THIS ISN'T RIGHT!
I'VE LEARNED ...
...THAT IT'S NOT WORTH KILLING HIM...
...IF YOU SACRIFICE YOURSELF IN THE PROCESS!
I HAVE NO INTENTION OF SACRIFICING MYSELF, NAGISA.
I JUST WANT TO KILL HIM.
AND ONCE I SET MY MIND TO SOMETHING, NOTHING CAN MAKE ME STRAY FROM MY PATH.
JMP

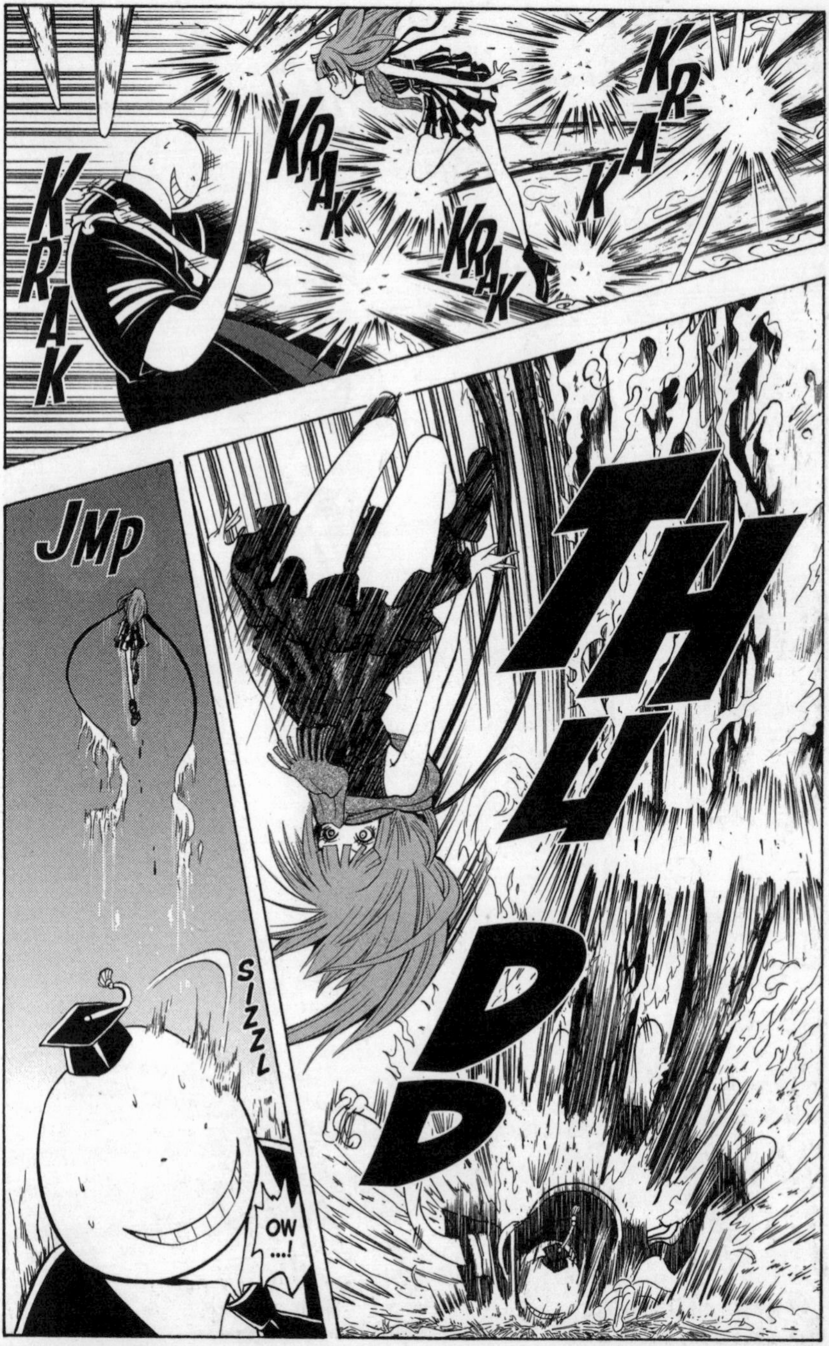
KRAK
KRAK
KRAK
KRAK
THUDD
JMP
SIZZL
OW ...!

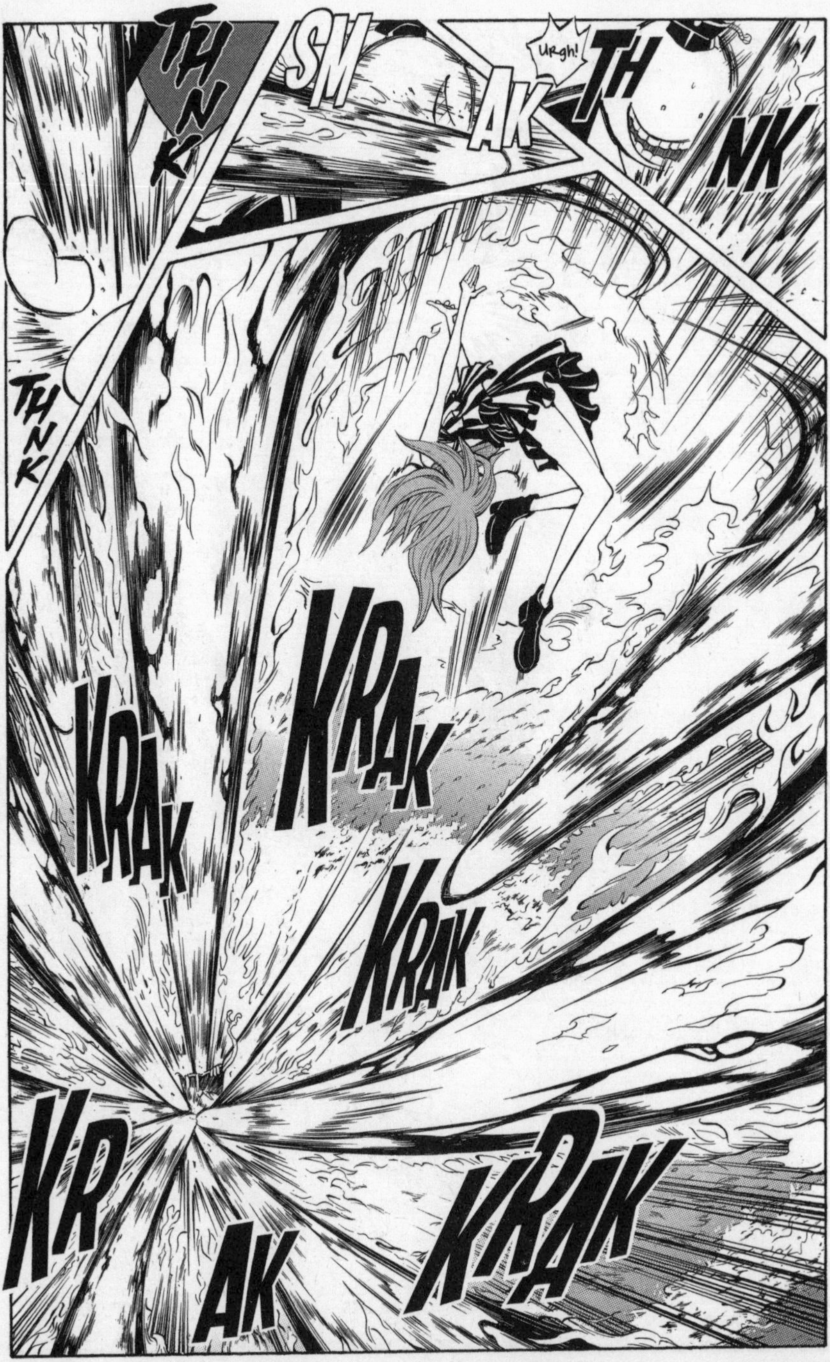
Urgh!
THNK
SMAK
THNK
THNK
KRAK
KRAK
KRAK
KRAK
KRAK

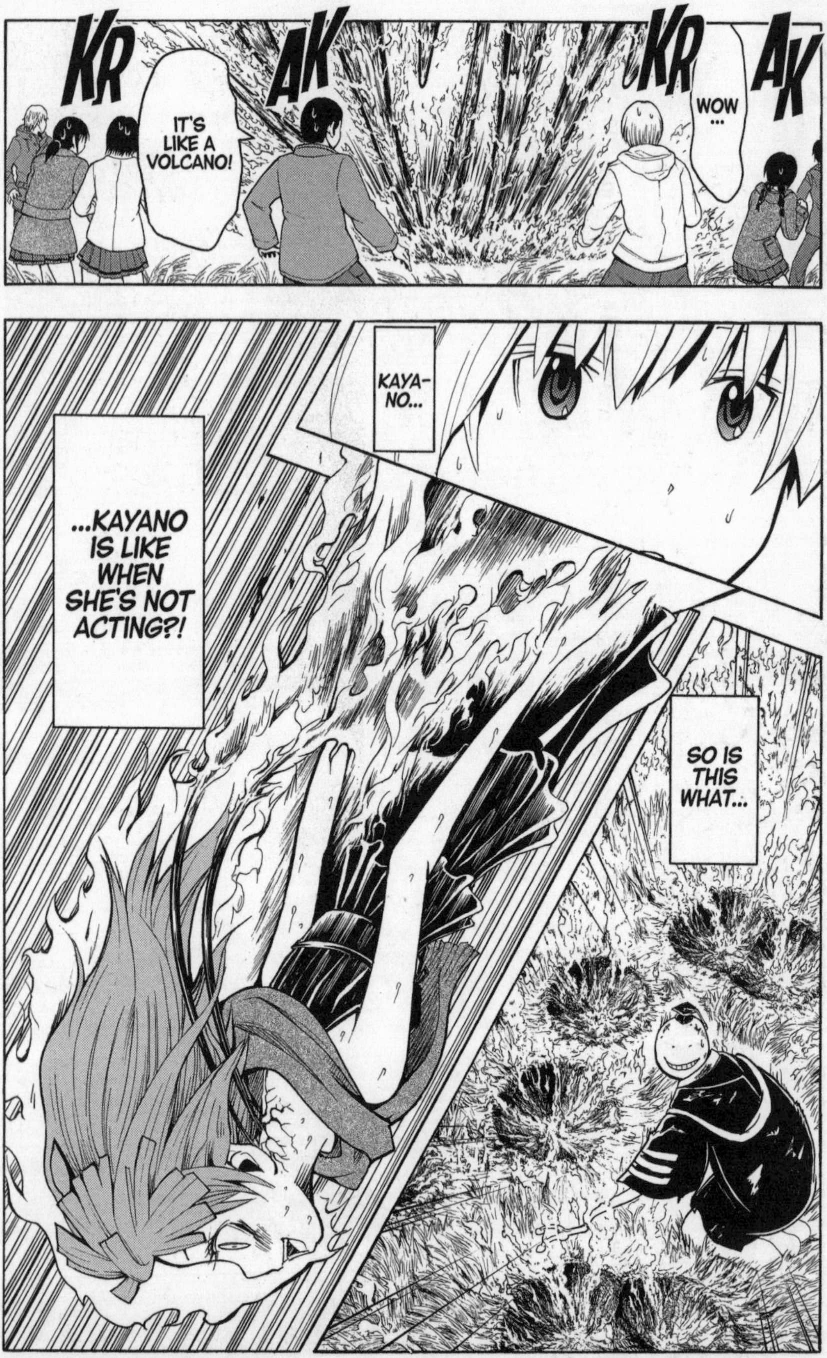
KRAK
WOW ...
KRAK
IT'S LIKE A VOLCANO!
KAYA-NO...
SO IS THIS WHAT...
...KAYANO IS LIKE WHEN SHE'S NOT ACTING?!

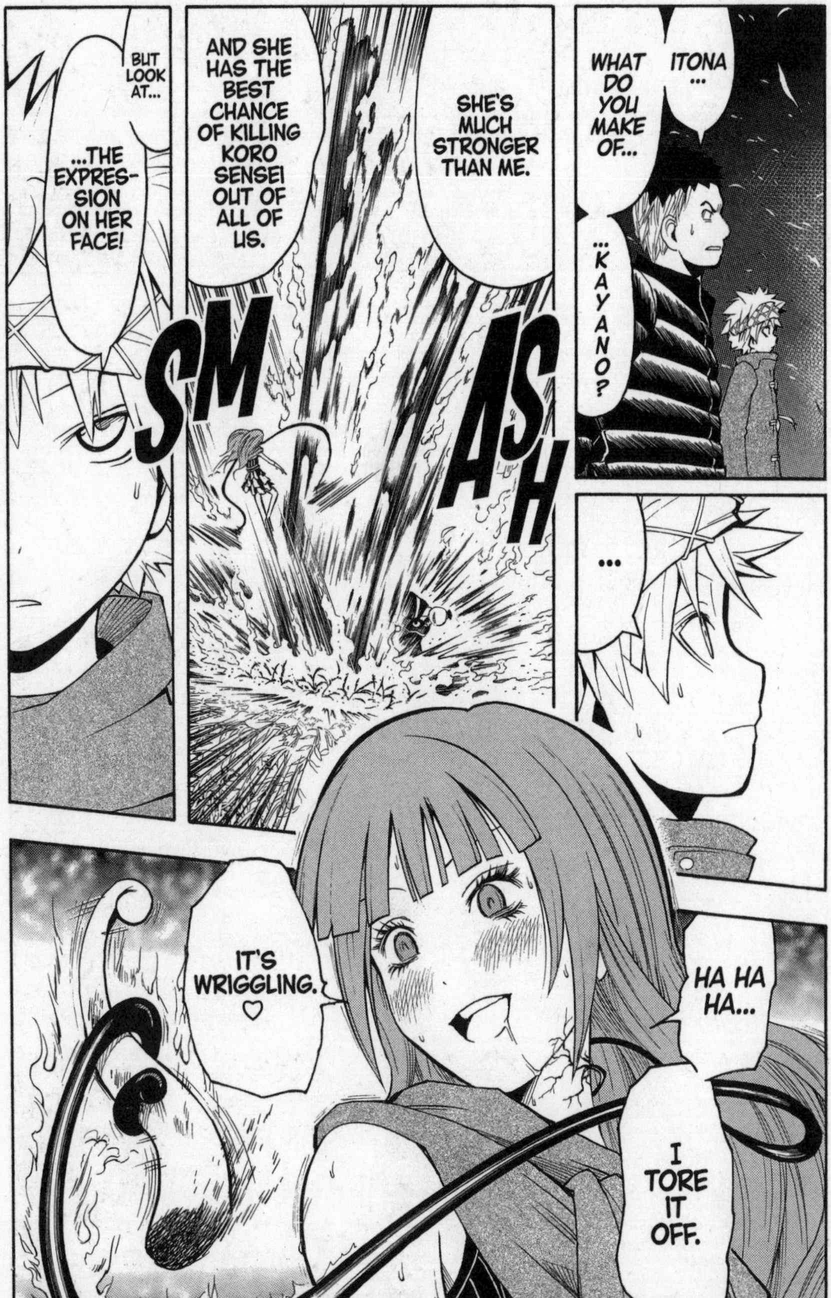
ITONA...
WHAT DO YOU MAKE OF...
...KAYANO?
...
SHE'S MUCH STRONGER THAN ME.
AND SHE HAS THE BEST CHANCE OF KILLING KORO SENSEI OUT OF ALL OF US.
SMASH
BUT LOOK AT...
...THE EXPRESSION ON HER FACE!
HA HA HA...
I TORE IT OFF.
IT'S WRIGGLING. ♡

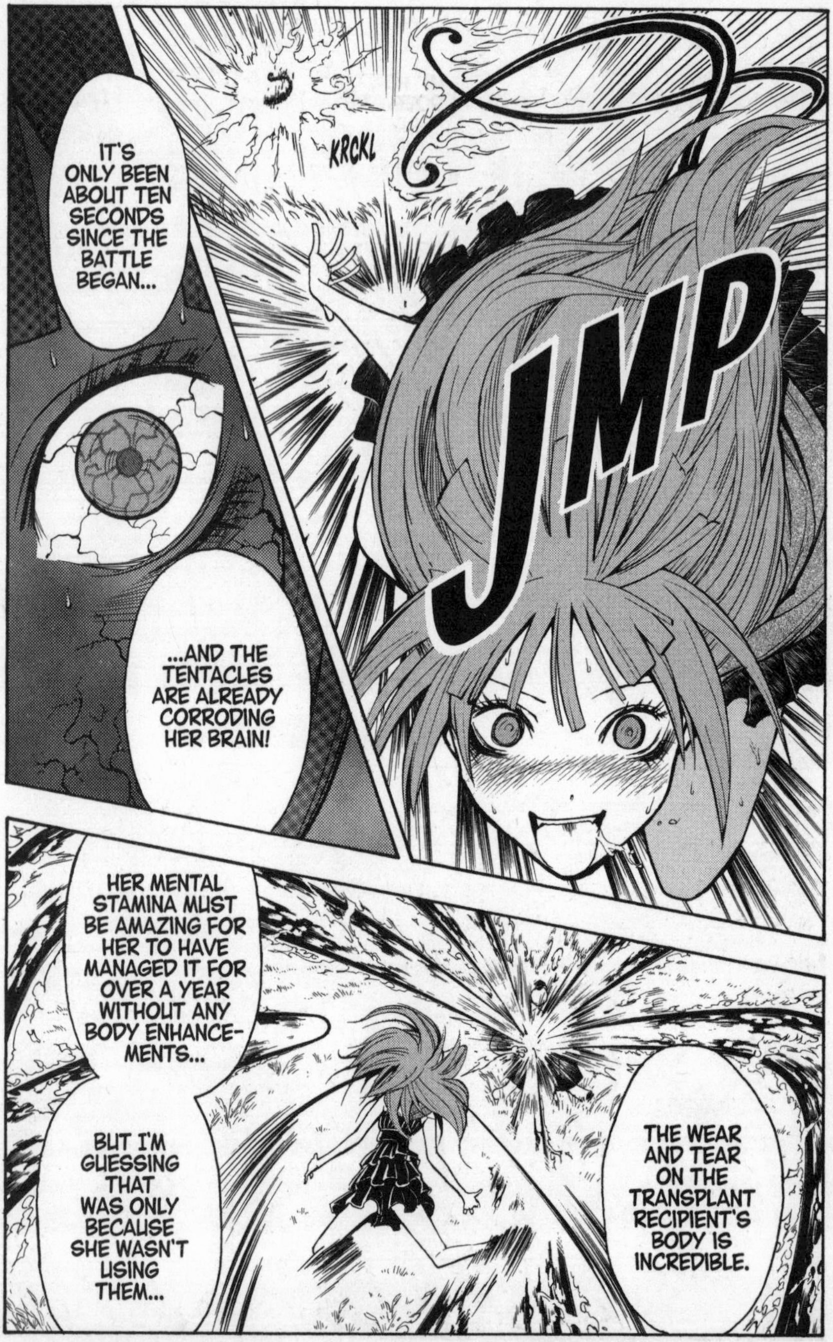
KRCKL
JMP
IT'S ONLY BEEN ABOUT TEN SECONDS SINCE THE BATTLE BEGAN...
...AND THE TENTACLES ARE ALREADY CORRODING HER BRAIN!
HER MENTAL STAMINA MUST BE AMAZING FOR HER TO HAVE MANAGED IT FOR OVER A YEAR WITHOUT ANY BODY ENHANCE-MENTS...
BUT I'M GUESSING THAT WAS ONLY BECAUSE SHE WASN'T USING THEM...
THE WEAR AND TEAR ON THE TRANSPLANT RECIPIENT'S BODY IS INCREDIBLE.

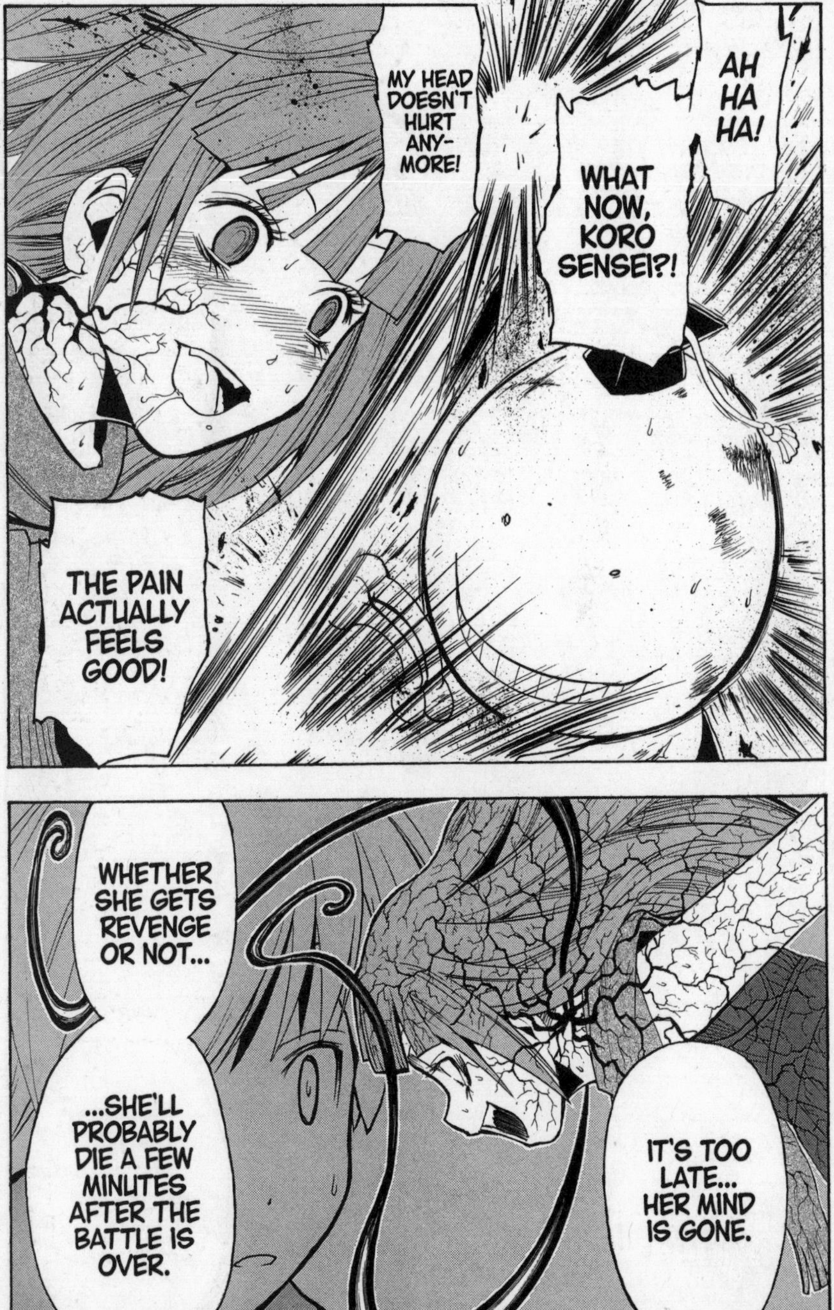
AH HA HA!
WHAT NOW, KORO SENSEI?!
MY HEAD DOESN'T HURT ANY-MORE!
THE PAIN ACTUALLY FEELS GOOD!
IT'S TOO LATE... HER MIND IS GONE.
WHETHER SHE GETS REVENGE OR NOT...
...SHE'LL PROBABLY DIE A FEW MINUTES AFTER THE BATTLE IS OVER.

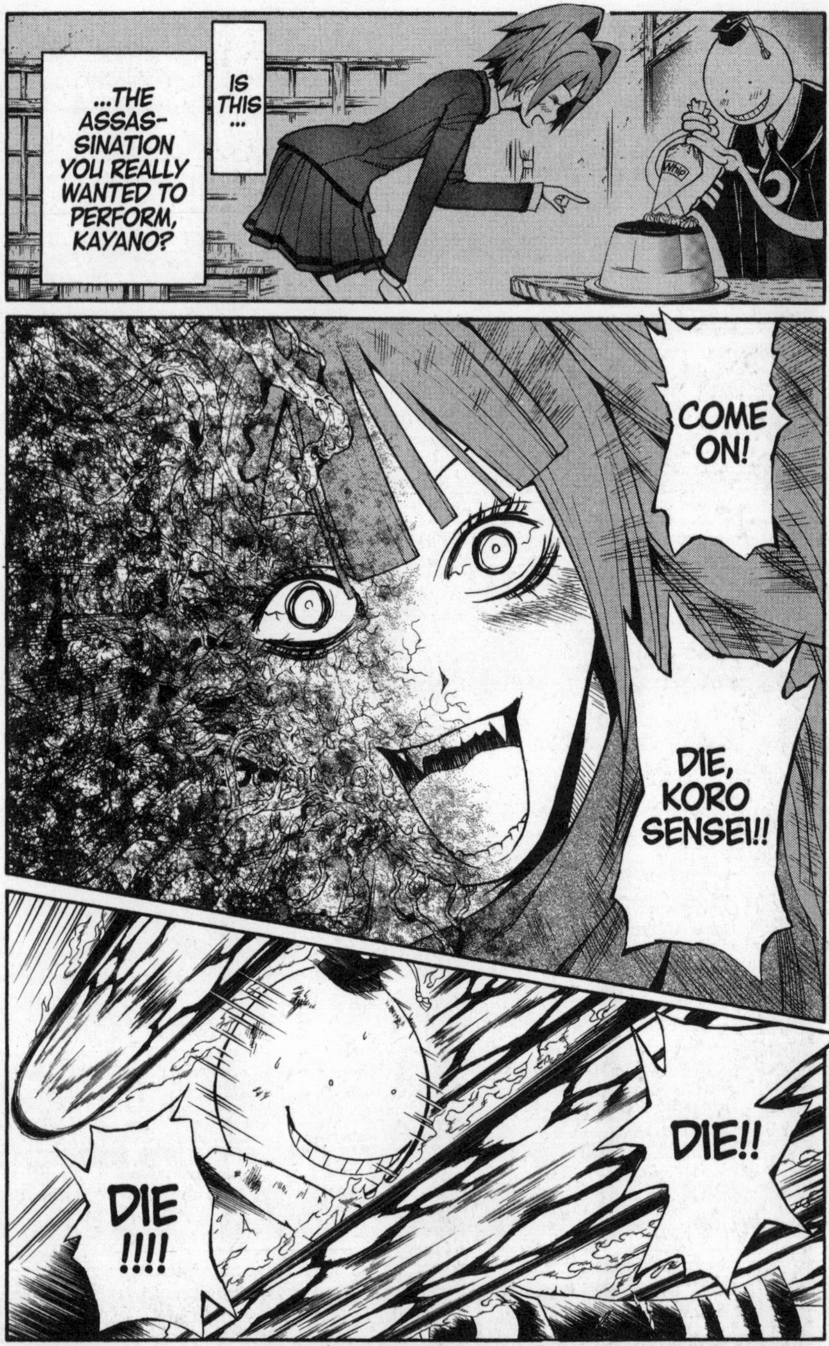
IS THIS...
...THE ASSASSINATION YOU REALLY WANTED TO PERFORM, KAYANO?
COME ON!
DIE, KORO SENSEI!!
DIE!!
DIE!!!!

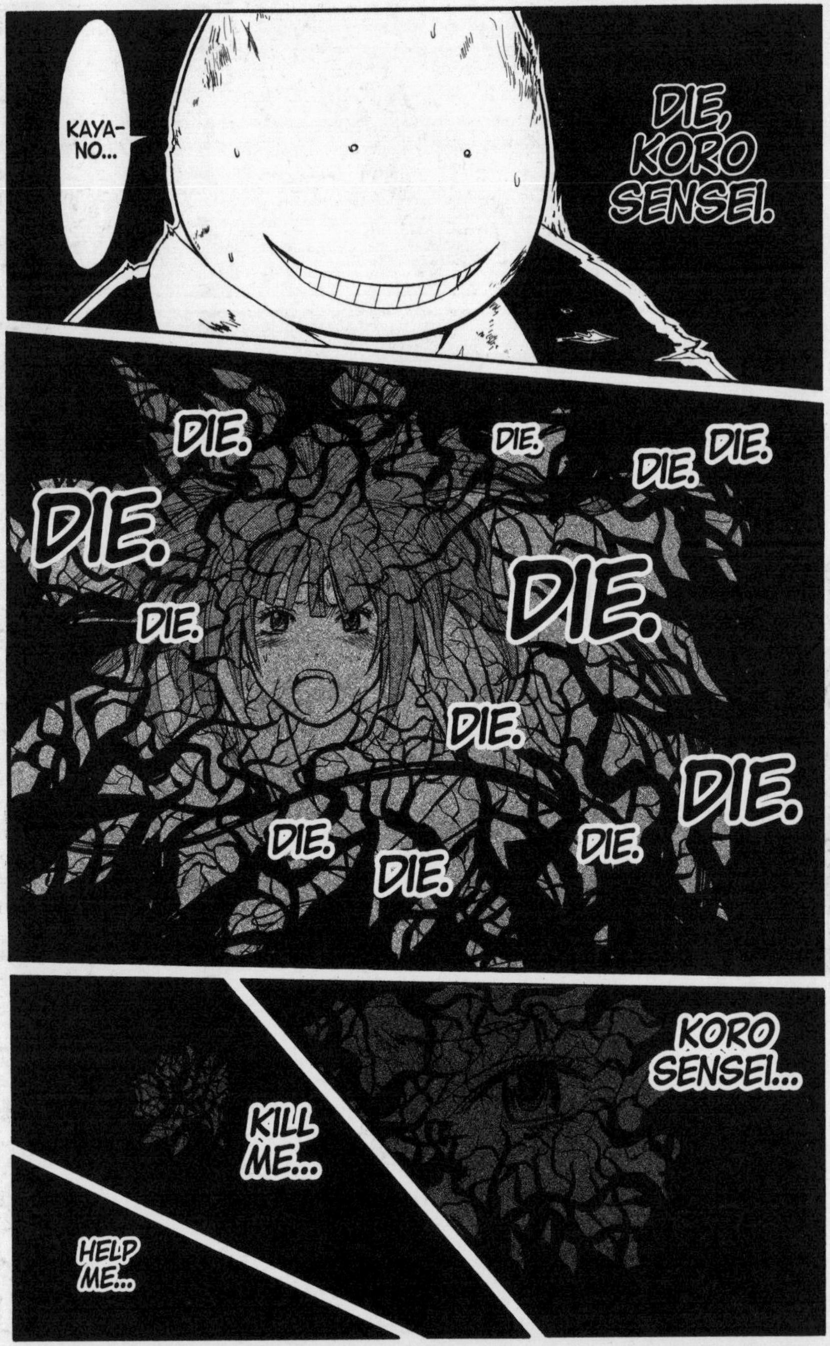
DIE, KORO SENSEI.
KAYA-NO...
DIE.
DIE.
DIE.
DIE.
DIE.
DIE.
DIE.
DIE.
DIE.
DIE.
DIE.
DIE.
KORO SENSEI...
KILL ME...
HELP ME...

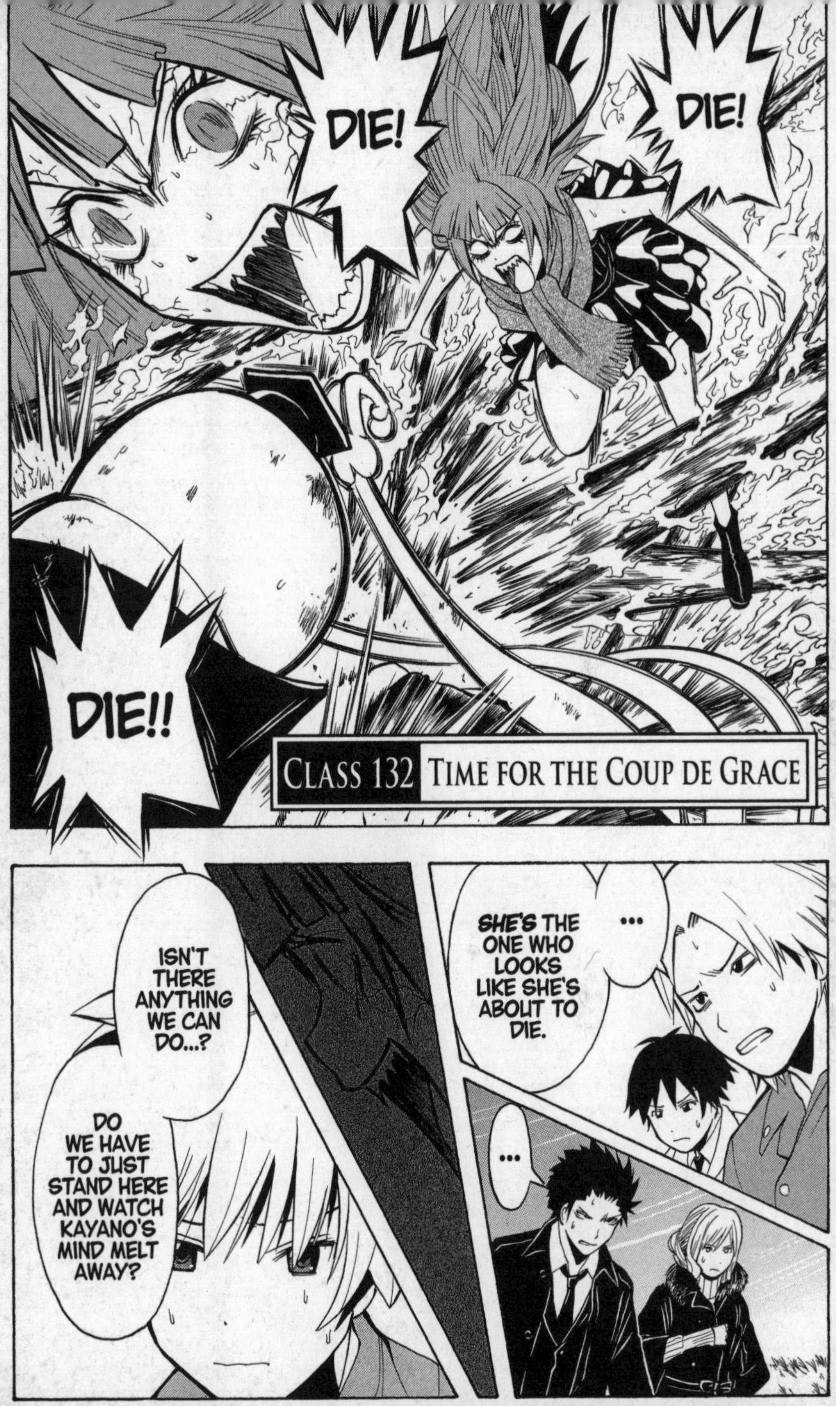
DIE!
DIE!
DIE!!
CLASS 132 TIME FOR THE COUP DE GRACE
...
SHE'S THE ONE WHO LOOKS LIKE SHE'S ABOUT TO DIE.
...
ISN'T THERE ANYTHING WE CAN DO...?
DO WE HAVE TO JUST STAND HERE AND WATCH KAYANO'S MIND MELT AWAY?

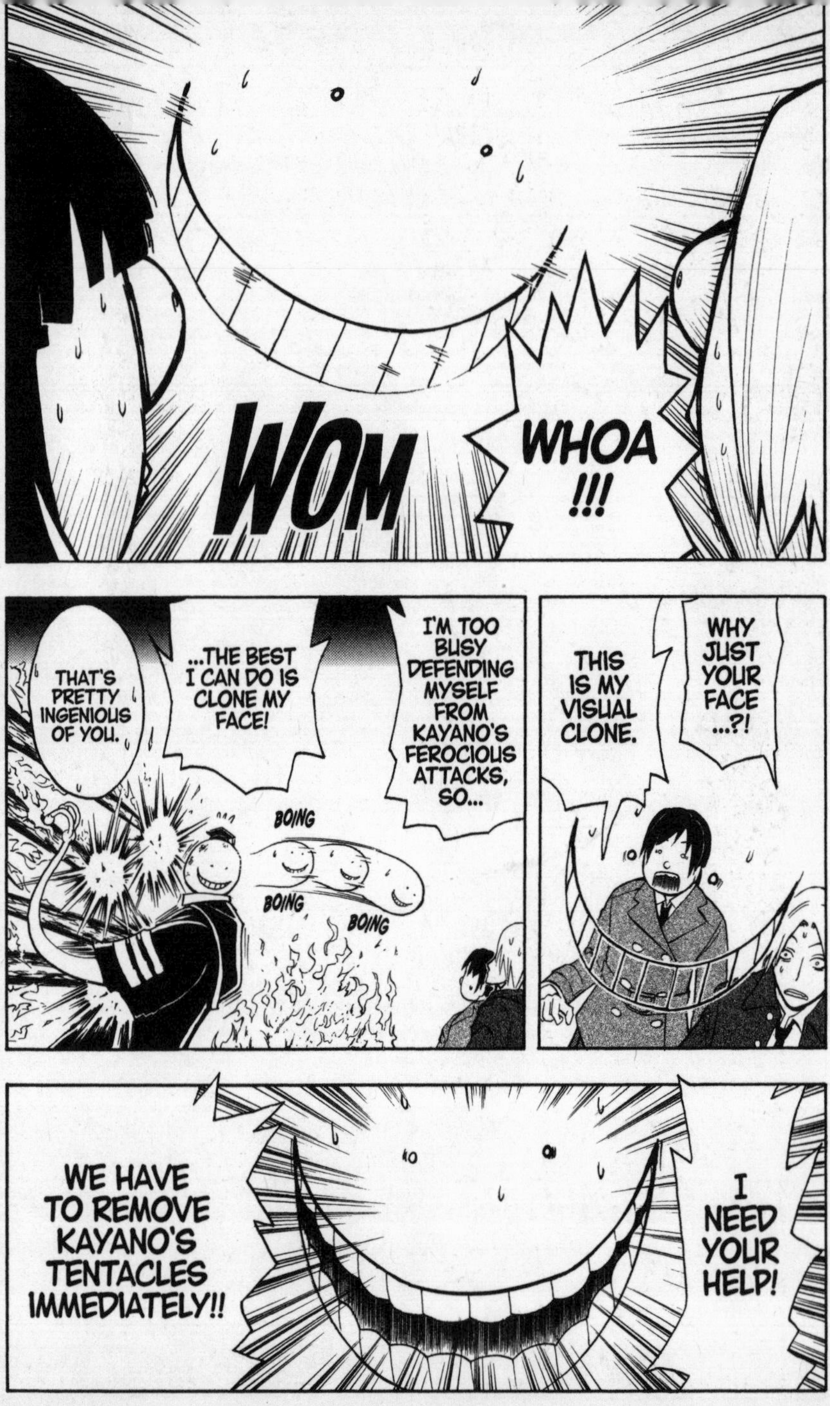
WHOA !!!
WOM
WHY JUST YOUR FACE ...?!
THIS IS MY VISUAL CLONE.
I'M TOO BUSY DEFENDING MYSELF FROM KAYANO'S FEROCIOUS ATTACKS, SO...
...THE BEST I CAN DO IS CLONE MY FACE!
BOING
BOING
BOING
THAT'S PRETTY INGENIOUS OF YOU.
I NEED YOUR HELP!
WE HAVE TO REMOVE KAYANO'S TENTACLES IMMEDIATELY!!

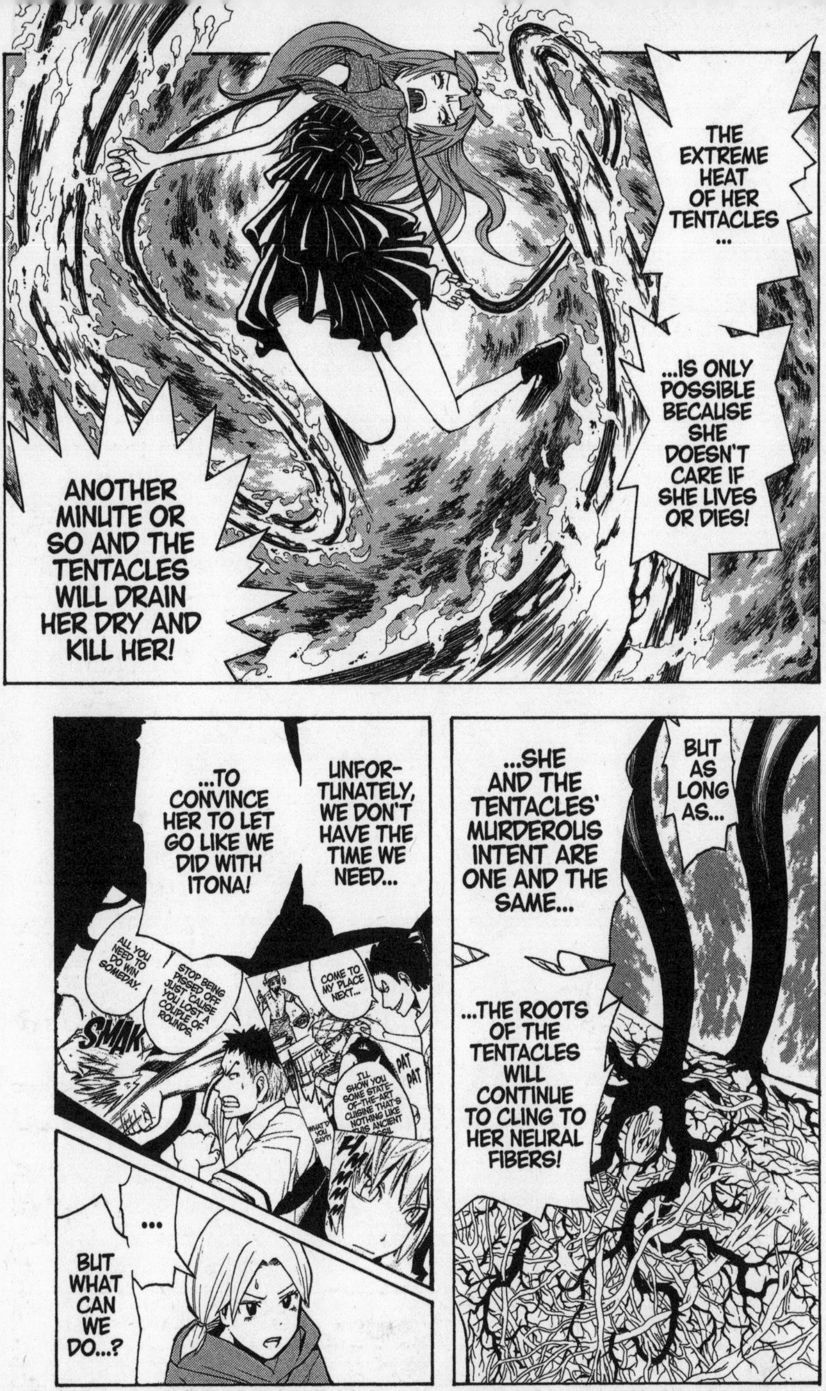
THE EXTREME HEAT OF HER TENTACLES...
...IS ONLY POSSIBLE BECAUSE SHE DOESN'T CARE IF SHE LIVES OR DIES!
ANOTHER MINUTE OR SO AND THE TENTACLES WILL DRAIN HER DRY AND KILL HER!
BUT AS LONG AS...
...SHE AND THE TENTACLES' MURDEROUS INTENT ARE ONE AND THE SAME...
...THE ROOTS OF THE TENTACLES WILL CONTINUE TO CLING TO HER NEURAL FIBERS!
UNFORTUNATELY, WE DON'T HAVE THE TIME WE NEED...
...TO CONVINCE HER TO LET GO LIKE WE DID WITH ITONA!
COME TO MY PLACE NEXT...
PAT PAT
I'LL SHOW YOU SOME STATE-OF-THE-ART CUISINE THAT'S NOTHING LIKE THIS ANCIENT
WHAT'D YOU SAY?!
STOP BEING PISSED OFF JUST 'CAUSE YOU LOST A COUPLE OF ROUNDS.
ALL YOU NEED TO DO WIN SOMEDAY.
SMAK
...
BUT WHAT CAN WE DO...?

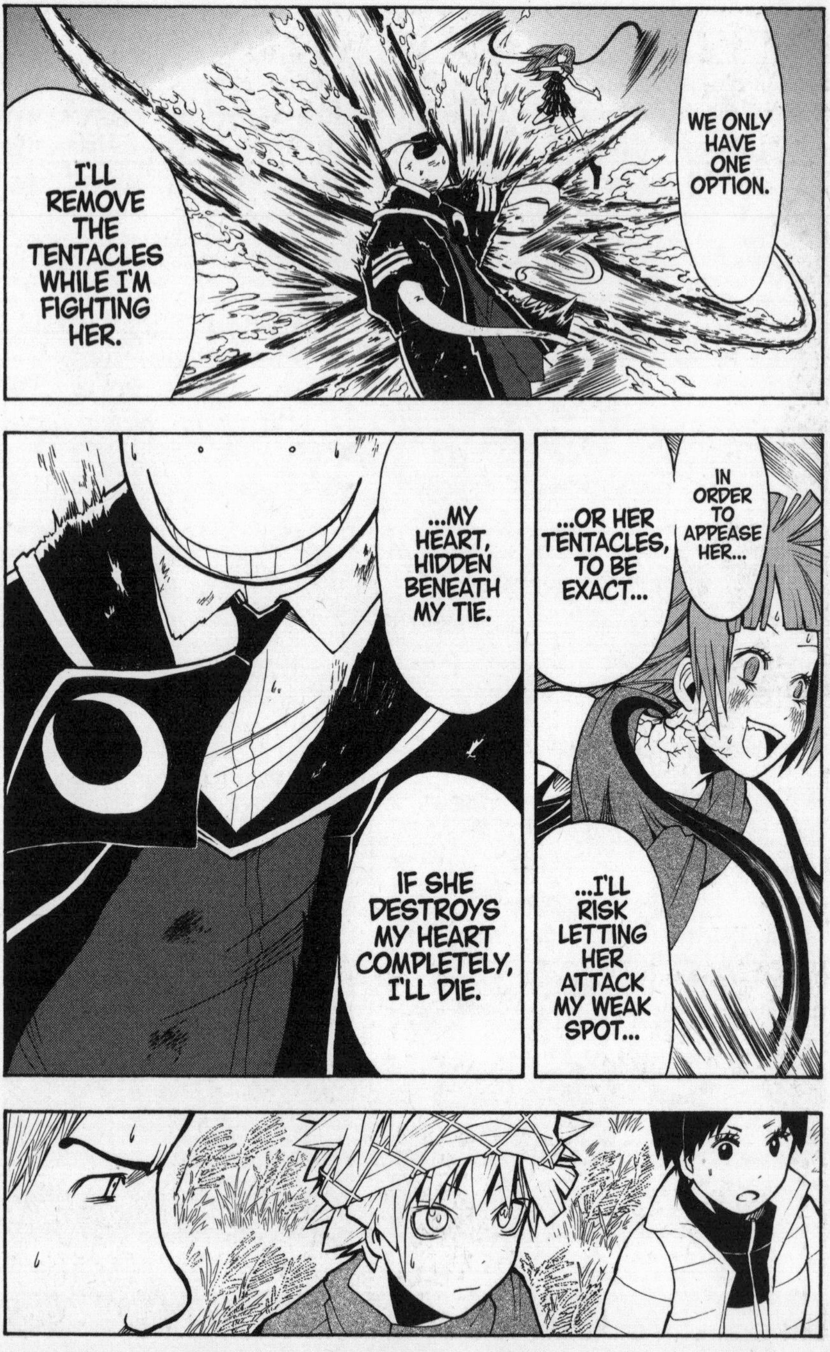
WE ONLY HAVE ONE OPTION.
I'LL REMOVE THE TENTACLES WHILE I'M FIGHTING HER.
IN ORDER TO APPEASE HER...
...OR HER TENTACLES, TO BE EXACT...
...I'LL RISK LETTING HER ATTACK MY WEAK SPOT...
...MY HEART, HIDDEN BENEATH MY TIE.
IF SHE DESTROYS MY HEART COMPLETELY, I'LL DIE.

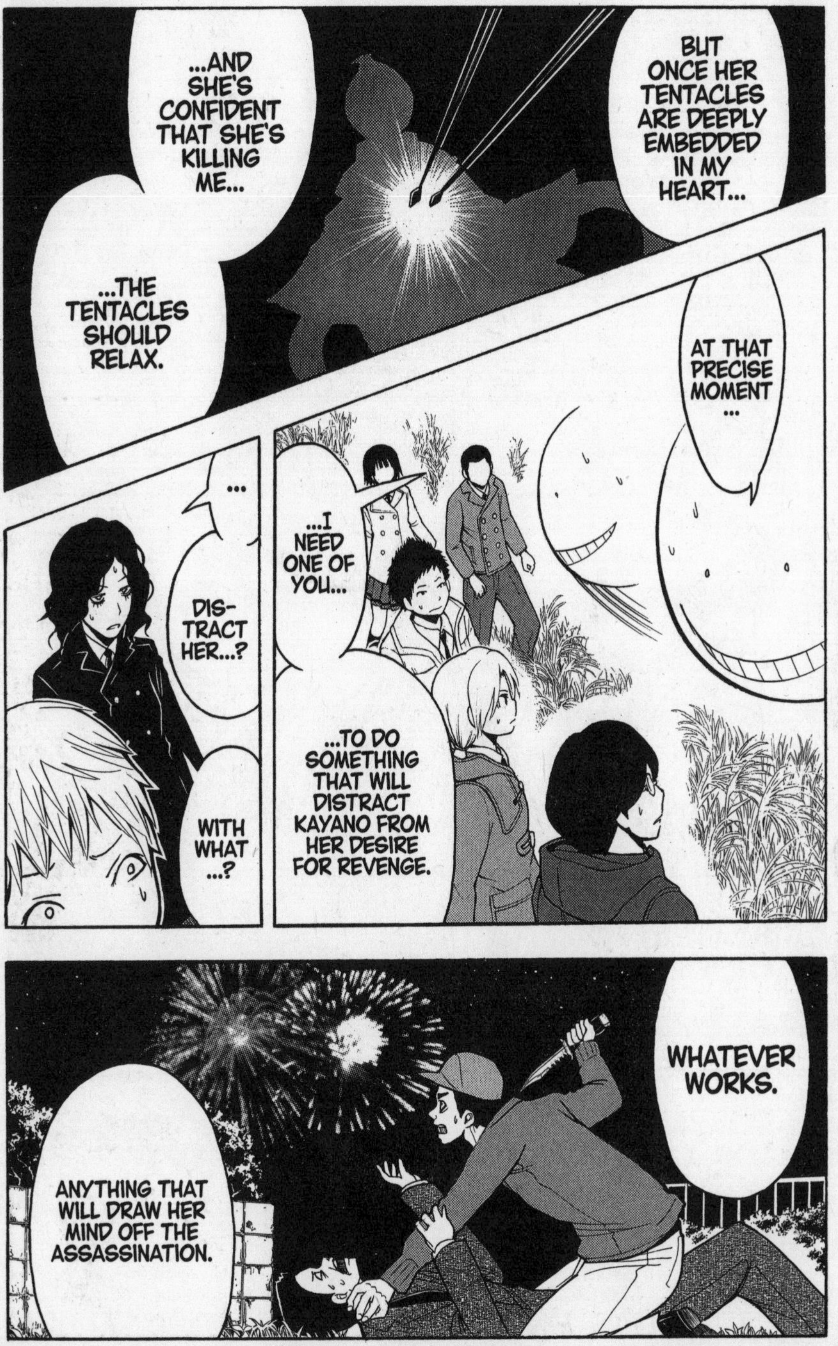
BUT ONCE HER TENTACLES ARE DEEPLY EMBEDDED IN MY HEART...
...AND SHE'S CONFIDENT THAT SHE'S KILLING ME...
...THE TENTACLES SHOULD RELAX.
AT THAT PRECISE MOMENT ...
...I NEED ONE OF YOU...
...TO DO SOMETHING THAT WILL DISTRACT KAYANO FROM HER DESIRE FOR REVENGE.
...
DIS-TRACT HER...?
WITH WHAT ...?
WHATEVER WORKS.
ANYTHING THAT WILL DRAW HER MIND OFF THE ASSASSINATION.

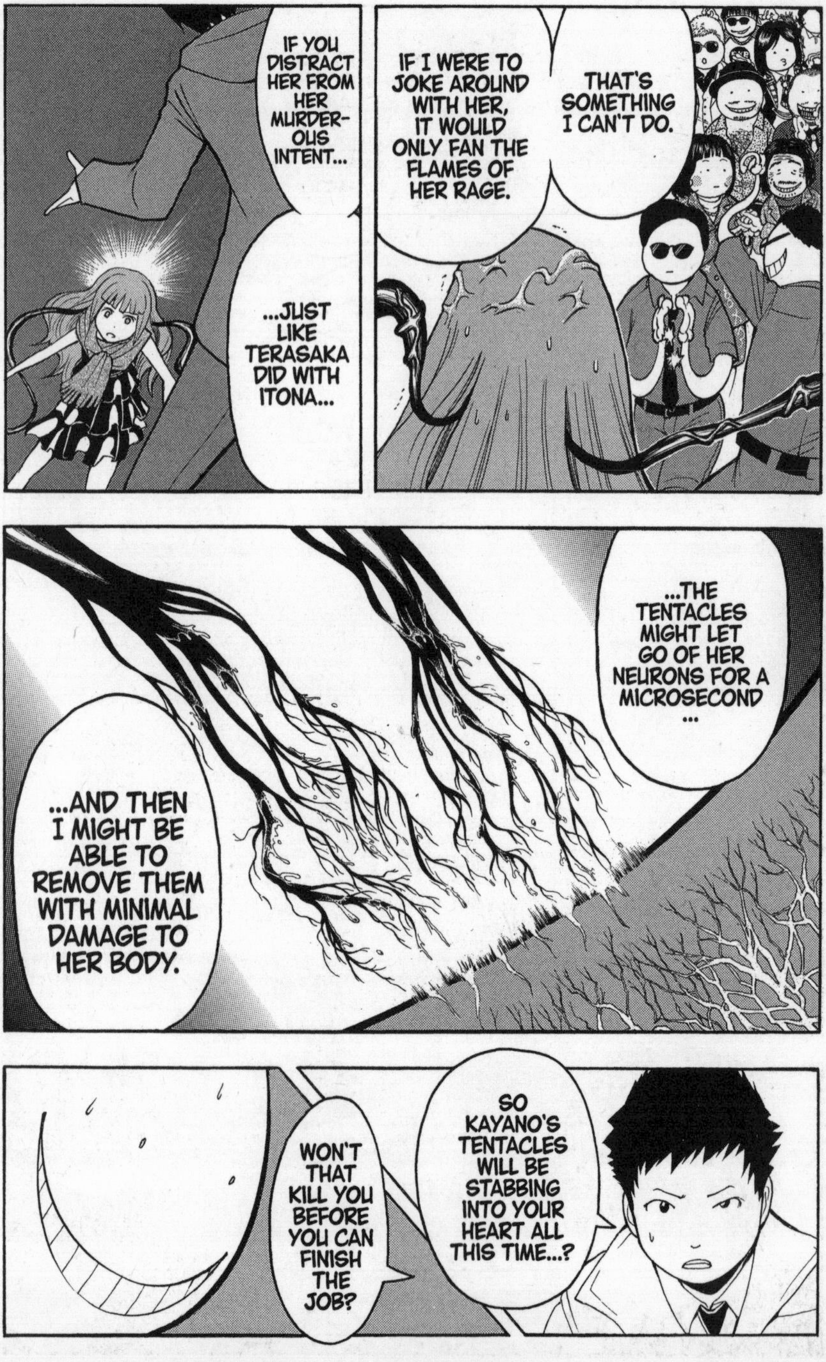
THAT'S SOMETHING I CAN'T DO.
IF I WERE TO JOKE AROUND WITH HER, IT WOULD ONLY FAN THE FLAMES OF HER RAGE.
IF YOU DISTRACT HER FROM HER MURDER-OUS INTENT...
...JUST LIKE TERASAKA DID WITH ITONA...
...THE TENTACLES MIGHT LET GO OF HER NEURONS FOR A MICROSECOND...
...AND THEN I MIGHT BE ABLE TO REMOVE THEM WITH MINIMAL DAMAGE TO HER BODY.
SO KAYANO'S TENTACLES WILL BE STABBING INTO YOUR HEART ALL THIS TIME...?
WON'T THAT KILL YOU BEFORE YOU CAN FINISH THE JOB?

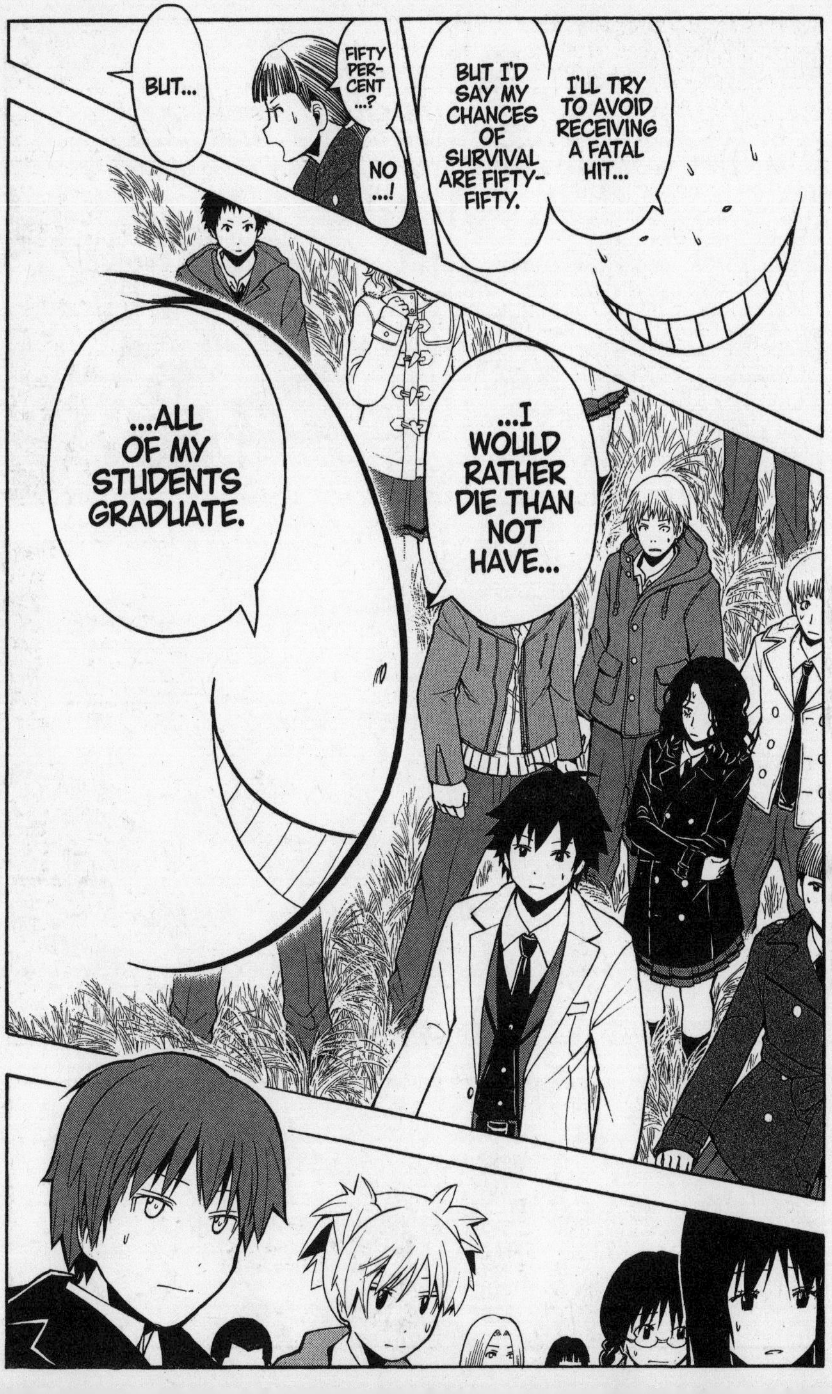
I'LL TRY TO AVOID RECEIVING A FATAL HIT...
BUT I'D SAY MY CHANCES OF SURVIVAL ARE FIFTY-FIFTY.
FIFTY PER-CENT ...?
NO ...!
BUT...
...I WOULD RATHER DIE THAN NOT HAVE...
...ALL OF MY STUDENTS GRADUATE.

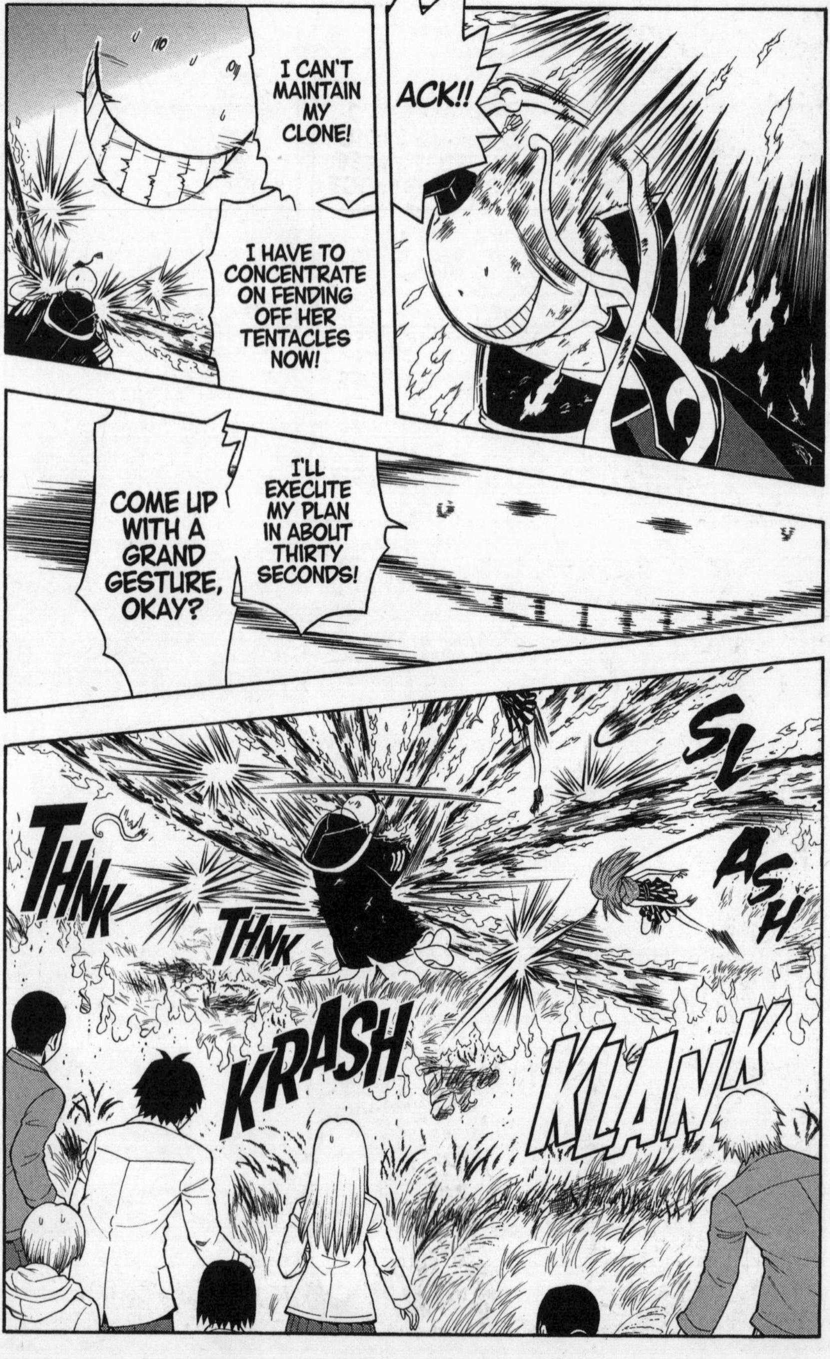
ACK!!
I CAN'T MAINTAIN MY CLONE!
I HAVE TO CONCENTRATE ON FENDING OFF HER TENTACLES NOW!
I'LL EXECUTE MY PLAN IN ABOUT THIRTY SECONDS!
COME UP WITH A GRAND GESTURE, OKAY?
SLASH
THNK
THNK
KLANK
KRASH

HOW ARE WE GOING TO BARGE INTO THAT MELEE TO DISTRACT KAYANO?!

DOES HE WANT US TO PULL OFF SOME KIND OF PARTY STUNT OR SOMETHING?!

...CAN WE DO?

W-WHAT...

NOW?!

SHE'LL KILL ME!!

PLAY AIR GUITAR!

SHOW HER WHAT A KICK-ASS AIR GUITARIST YOU ARE!

MI-MURA...

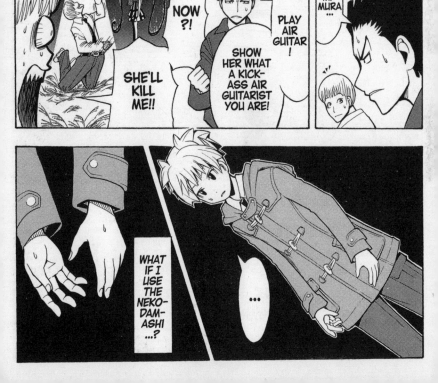

WHAT IF I USE THE NEKO-DAMASHI...?

...

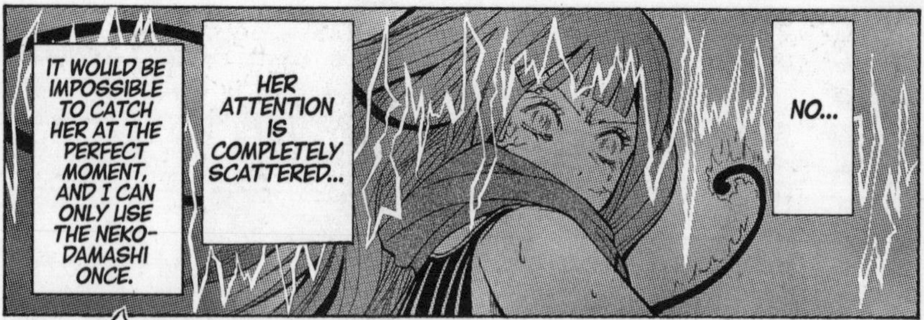
NO...
HER ATTENTION IS COMPLETELY SCATTERED...
IT WOULD BE IMPOSSIBLE TO CATCH HER AT THE PERFECT MOMENT, AND I CAN ONLY USE THE NEKO-DAMASHI ONCE.

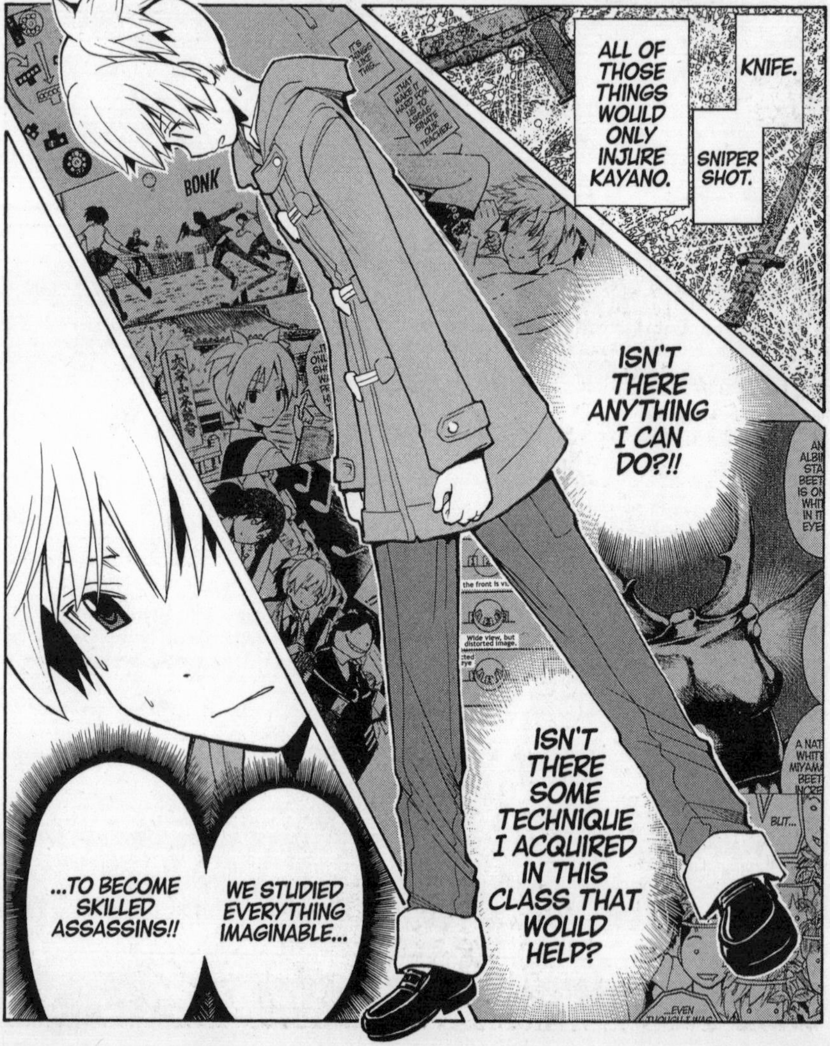
KNIFE.
SNIPER SHOT.
ALL OF THOSE THINGS WOULD ONLY INJURE KAYANO.
IT'S THINGS LIKE THIS.
...THAT MAKE IT HARD FOR US TO ASSASSINATE OUR TEACHER.
BONK
ISN'T THERE ANYTHING I CAN DO?!!
Wide view, but distorted image.
BUT...
ISN'T THERE SOME TECHNIQUE I ACQUIRED IN THIS CLASS THAT WOULD HELP?
WE STUDIED EVERYTHING IMAGINABLE...
...TO BECOME SKILLED ASSASSINS!!

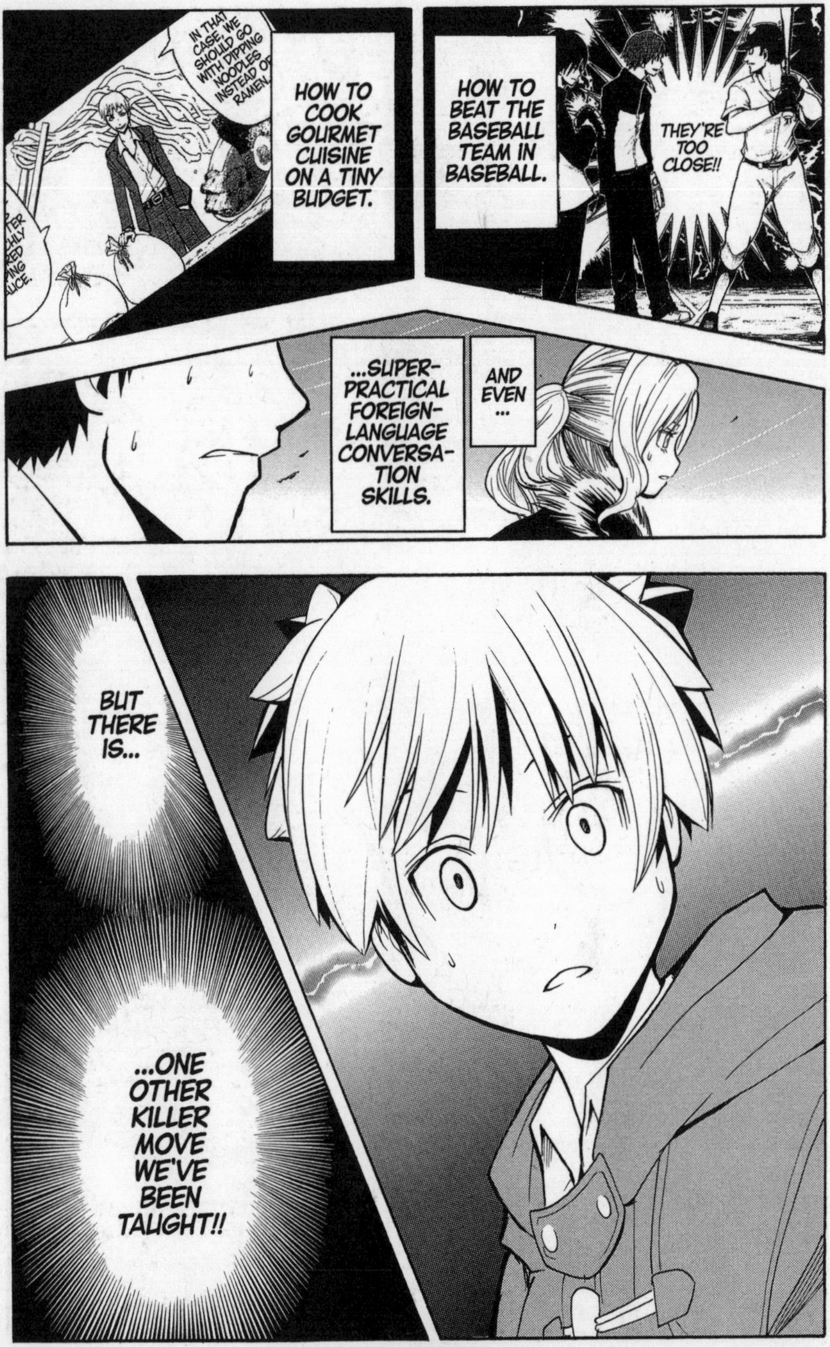
HOW TO BEAT THE BASEBALL TEAM IN BASEBALL.
THEY'RE TOO CLOSE!!
HOW TO COOK GOURMET CUISINE ON A TINY BUDGET.
IN THAT CASE, WE SHOULD GO WITH DIPPING NOODLES INSTEAD OF RAMEN.
AND EVEN...
...SUPER-PRACTICAL FOREIGN-LANGUAGE CONVERSATION SKILLS.
BUT THERE IS...
...ONE OTHER KILLER MOVE WE'VE BEEN TAUGHT!!

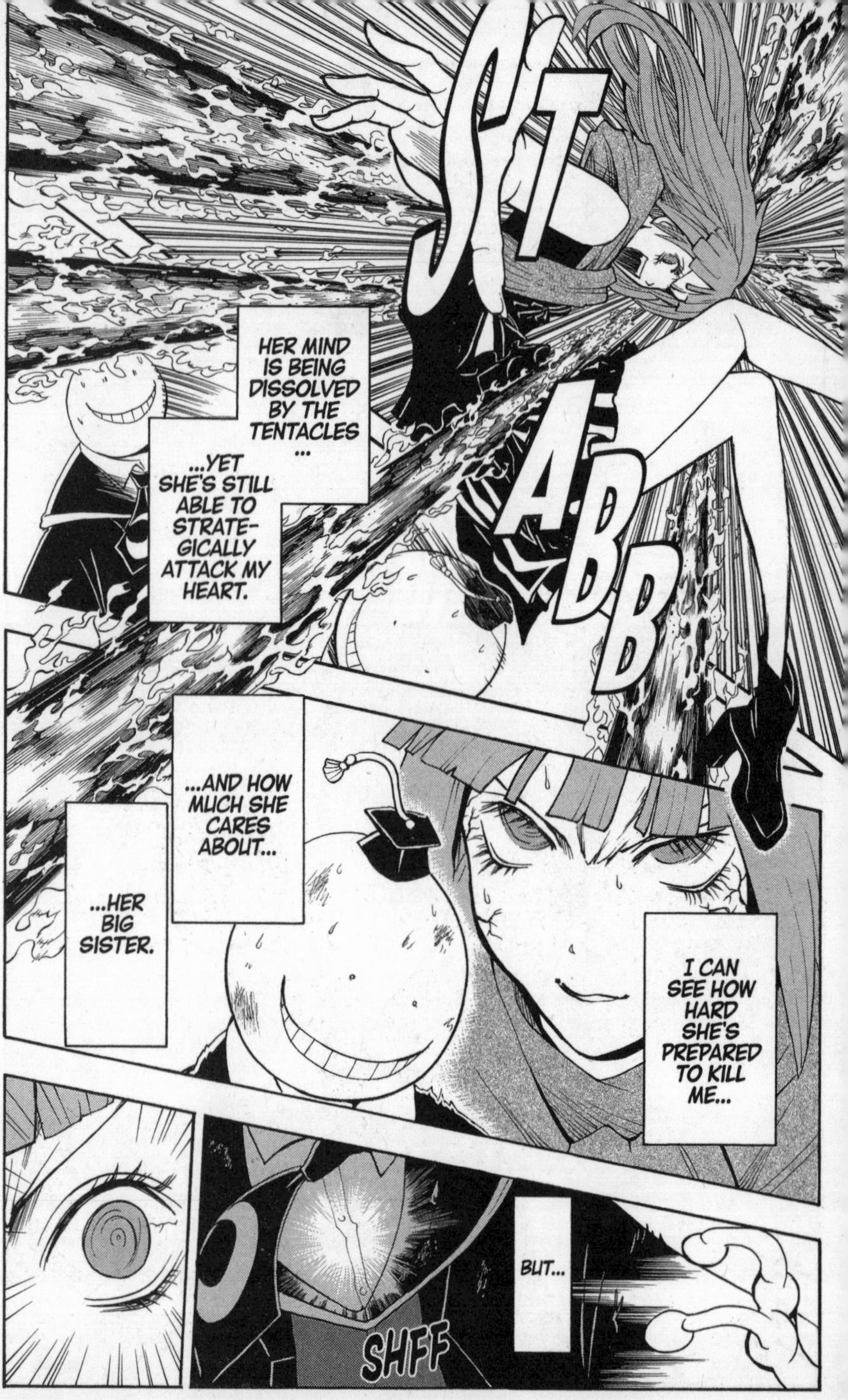
STABB
HER MIND IS BEING DISSOLVED BY THE TENTACLES ...
...YET SHE'S STILL ABLE TO STRATE-GICALLY ATTACK MY HEART.
I CAN SEE HOW HARD SHE'S PREPARED TO KILL ME...
...AND HOW MUCH SHE CARES ABOUT...
...HER BIG SISTER.
BUT...
SHFF

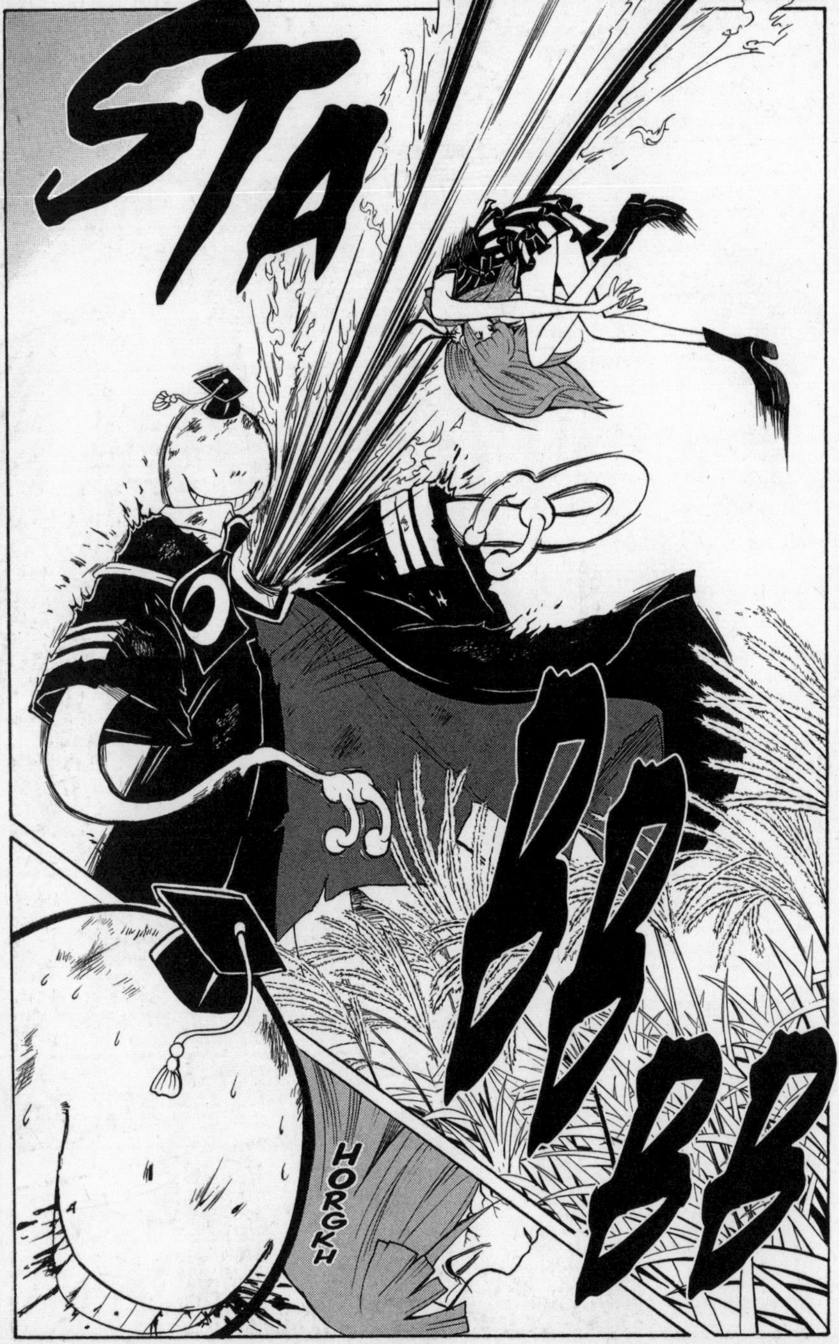
STA
BBBB
HORGKH

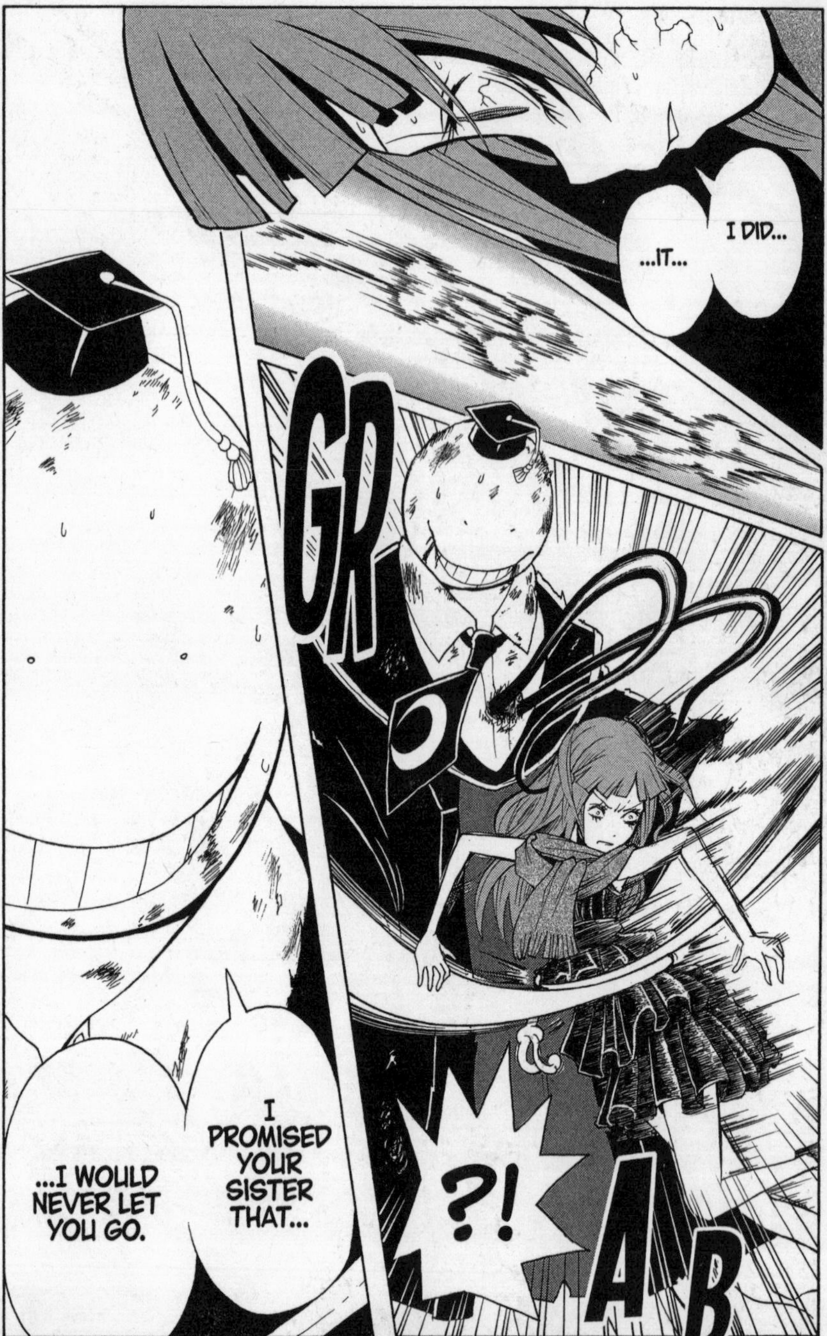
I DID...
...IT...
GR
?!
AB
I PROMISED YOUR SISTER THAT...
...I WOULD NEVER LET YOU GO.

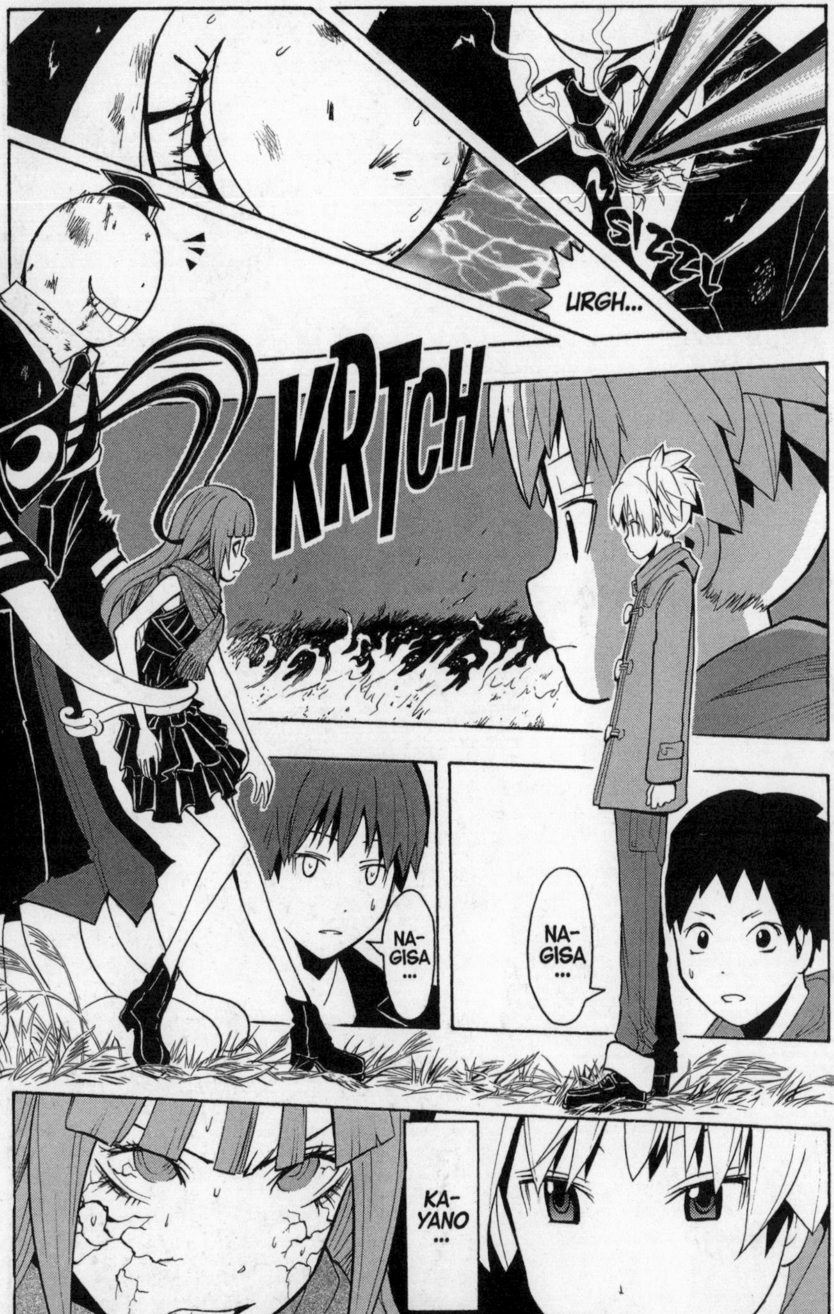
SIZZZL
URGH...
KRTCH
NA-GISA...
NA-GISA...
KA-YANO...

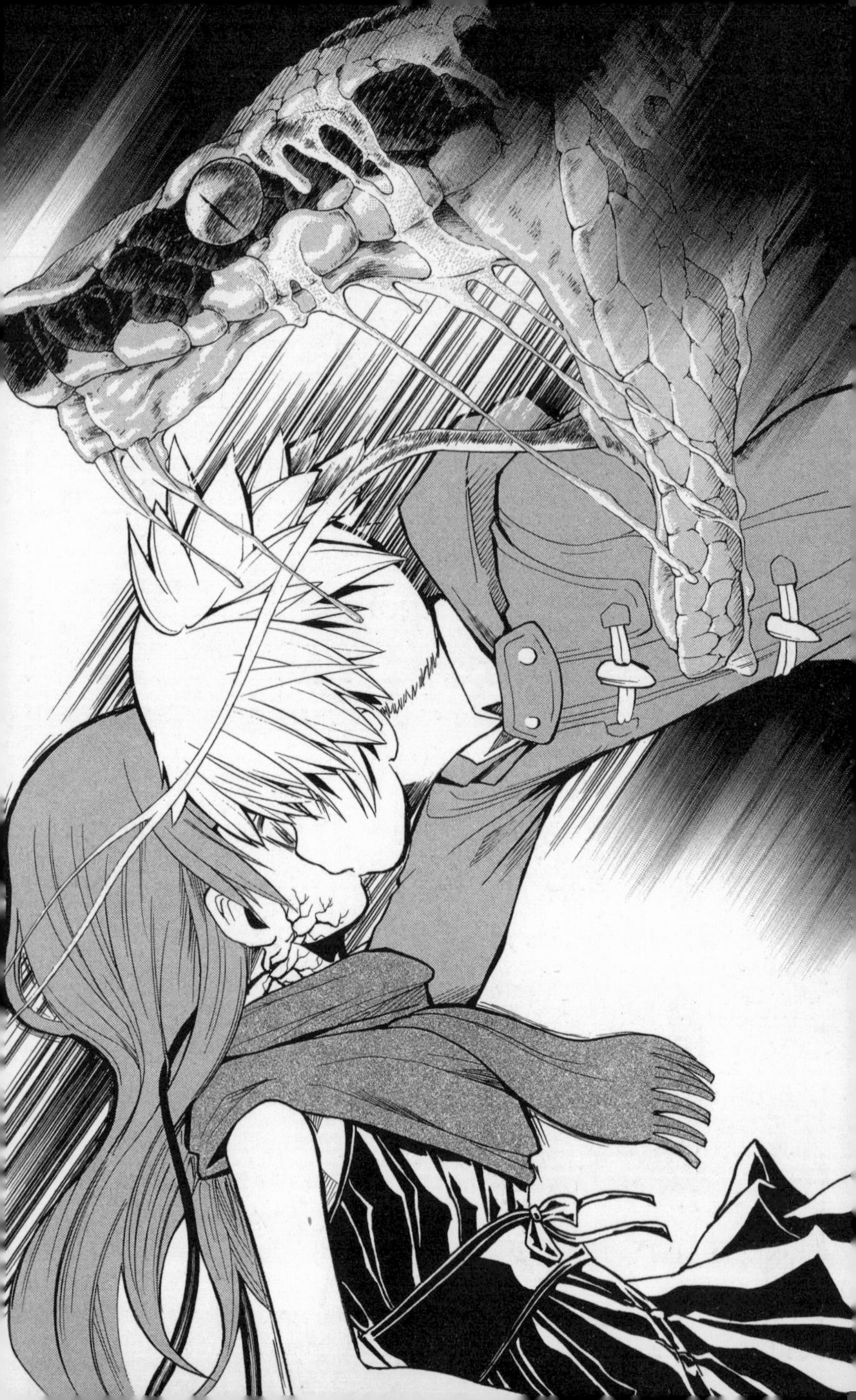

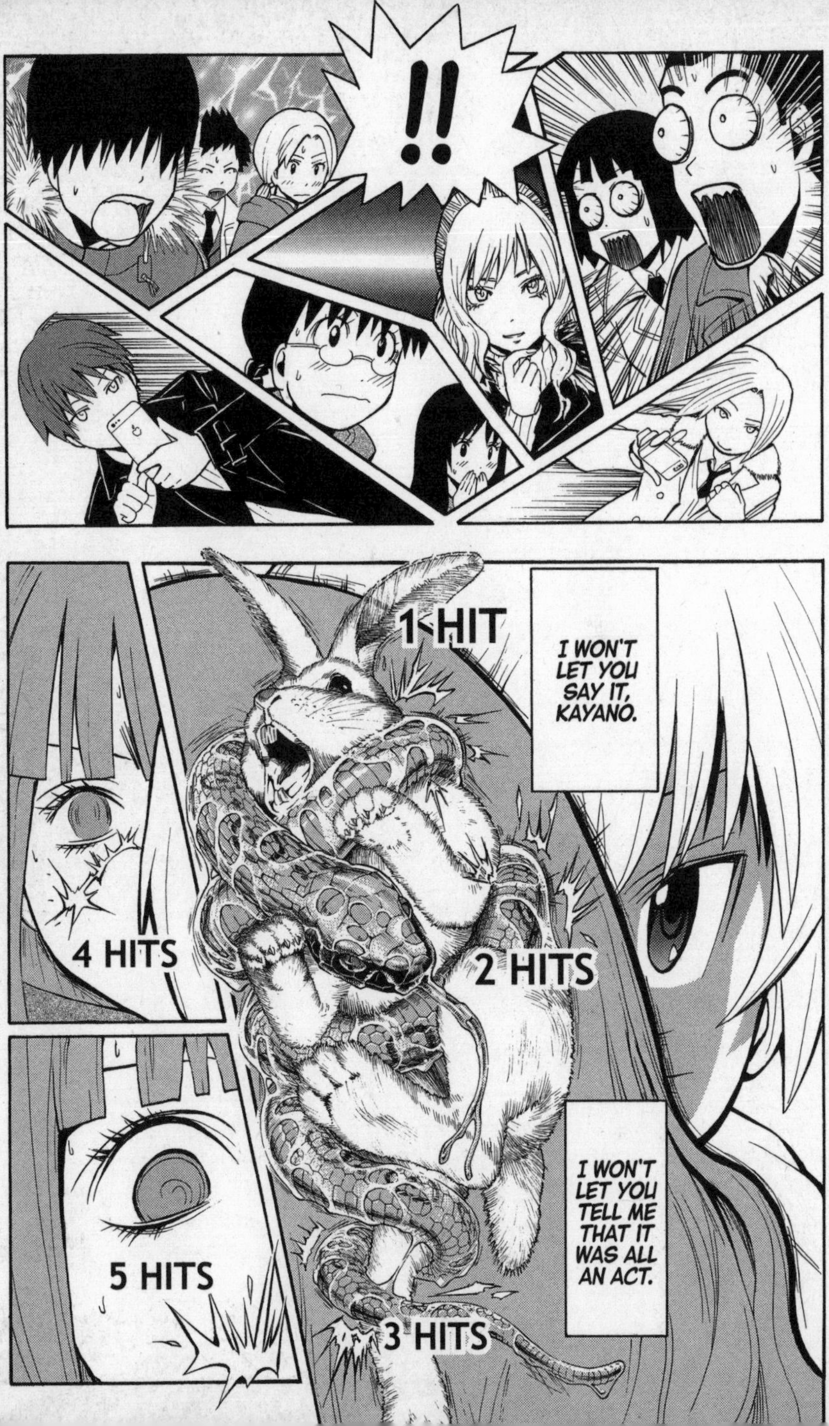
!!
I WON'T LET YOU SAY IT, KAYANO.
1 HIT
2 HITS
I WON'T LET YOU TELL ME THAT IT WAS ALL AN ACT.
3 HITS
4 HITS
5 HITS

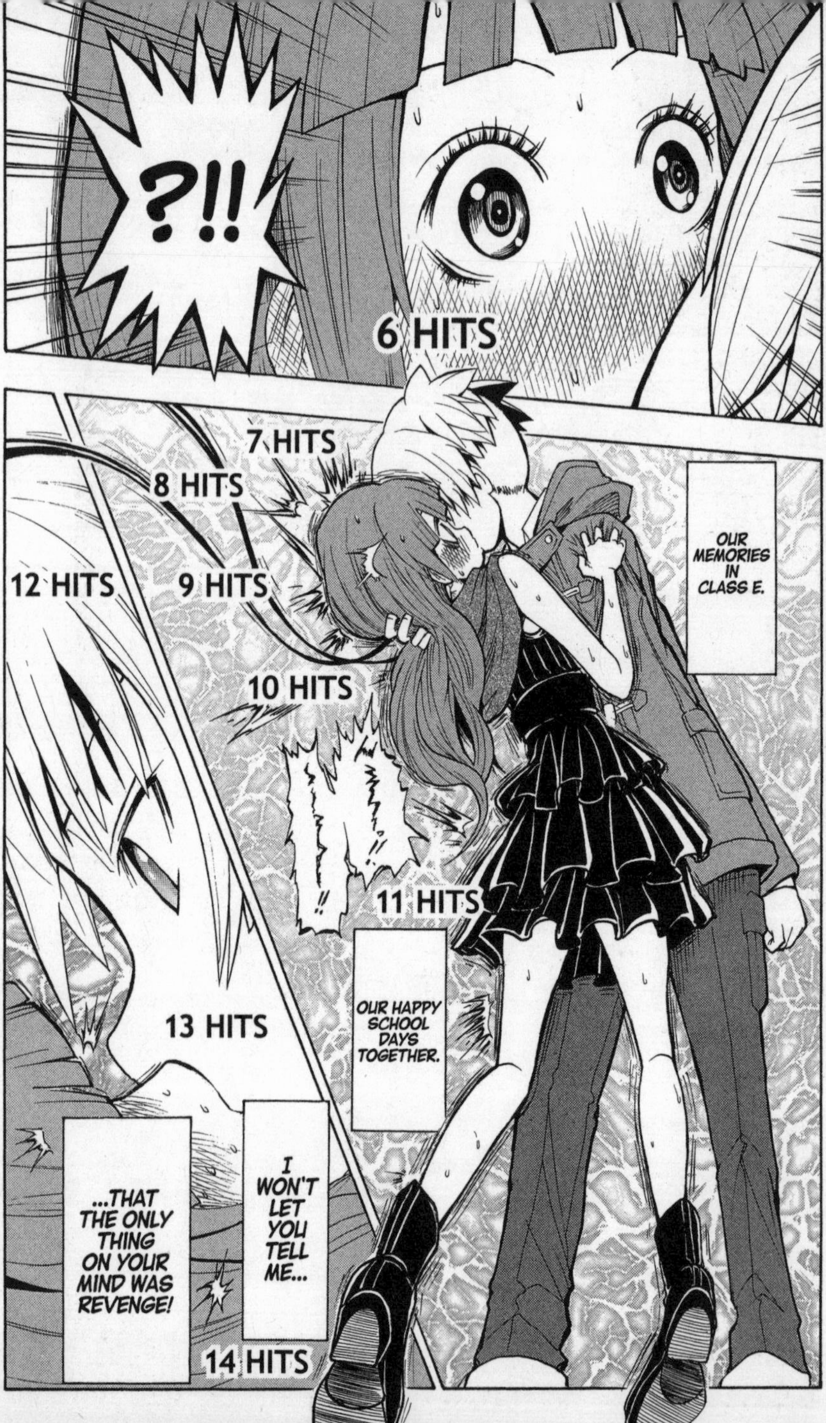
?!!
6 HITS
OUR MEMORIES IN CLASS E.
7 HITS
8 HITS
9 HITS
10 HITS
11 HITS
OUR HAPPY SCHOOL DAYS TOGETHER.
12 HITS
13 HITS
I WON'T LET YOU TELL ME...
...THAT THE ONLY THING ON YOUR MIND WAS REVENGE!
14 HITS

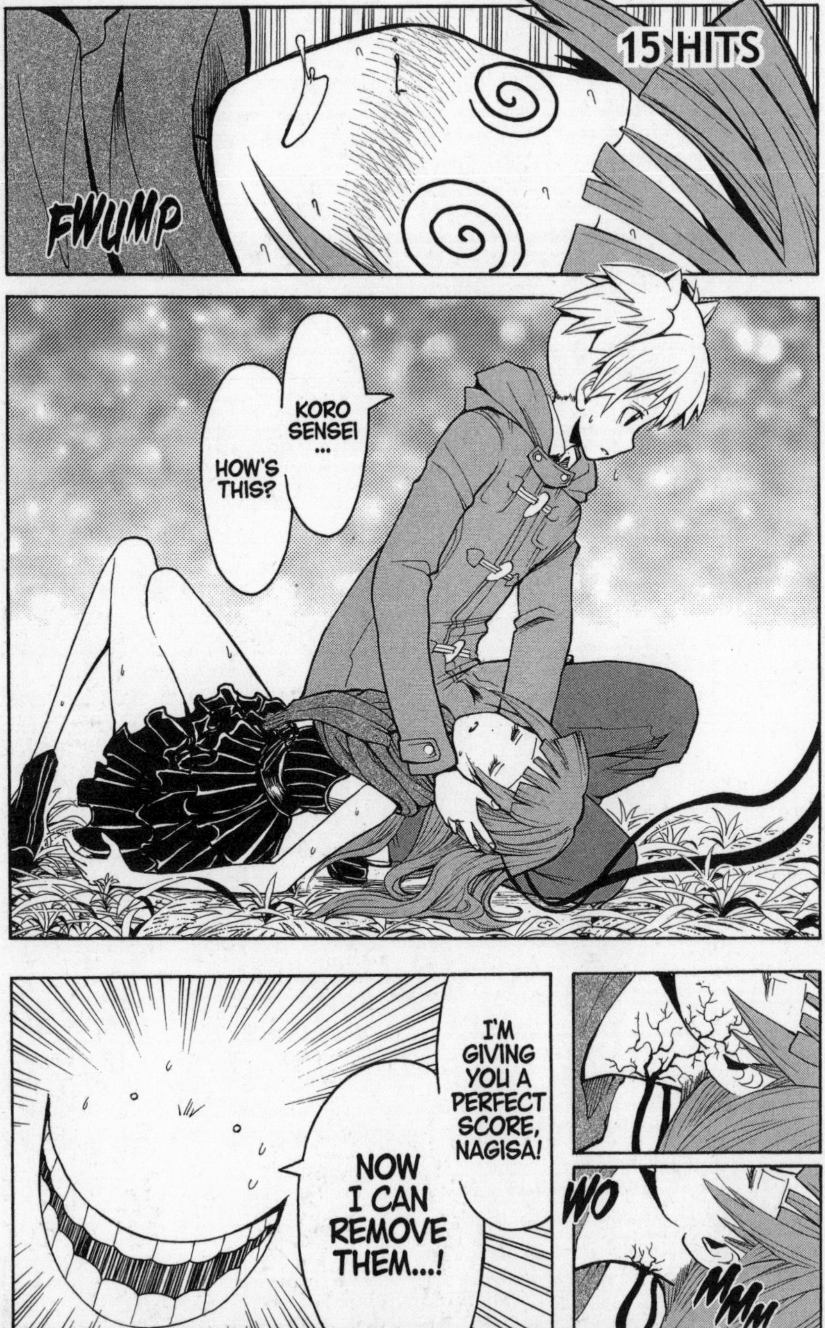
15 HITS
FWUMP
KORO SENSEI ...
HOW'S THIS?
WO
MMM
I'M GIVING YOU A PERFECT SCORE, NAGISA!
NOW I CAN REMOVE THEM...!

Class 3-E Best 5

Kissing Techniques

The kissing technique ranking of the Class E students, solely determined by Ms. Vitch from her personal experience as a cougar and an assassin.

1 Nagisa Shiota

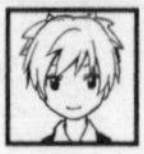

His technique is only in the upper-middle rank, but this business is all about producing results in the real world. Only those who can produce results have the right to call themselves true assassins.

2 Toka Yada

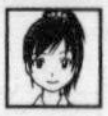

A true work of art, who I have personally nurtured. She's good at both kissing and being kissed. But she seems to have a desire to separate her technique from her practice.

3 Karma Akabane

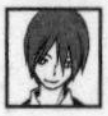

He's skilled at everything, but seems strangely familiar with this activity. There's nothing for me to improve on, which makes him boring to teach.

4 Hiroto Maehara

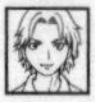

I ranked him at this level because he relies too much on tricks. He needs to prioritize creating the right atmosphere.

5 Manami Okuda

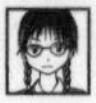

She doesn't realize it, but she has a natural genius for receiving kisses. That is, if her body wasn't so tense... But I don't think she'll ever be able to relax.

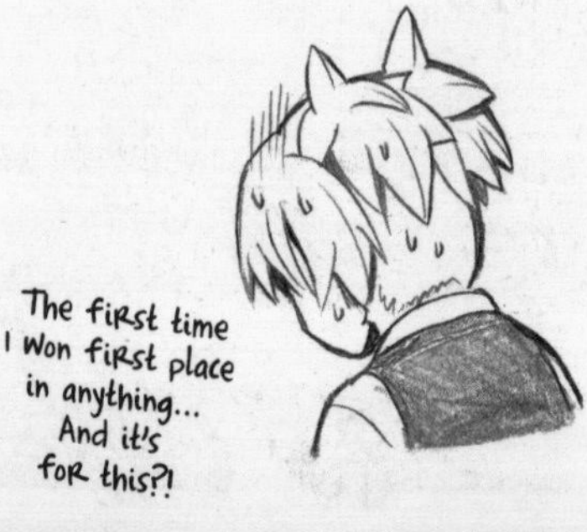
The first time I won first place in anything... And it's for this?!

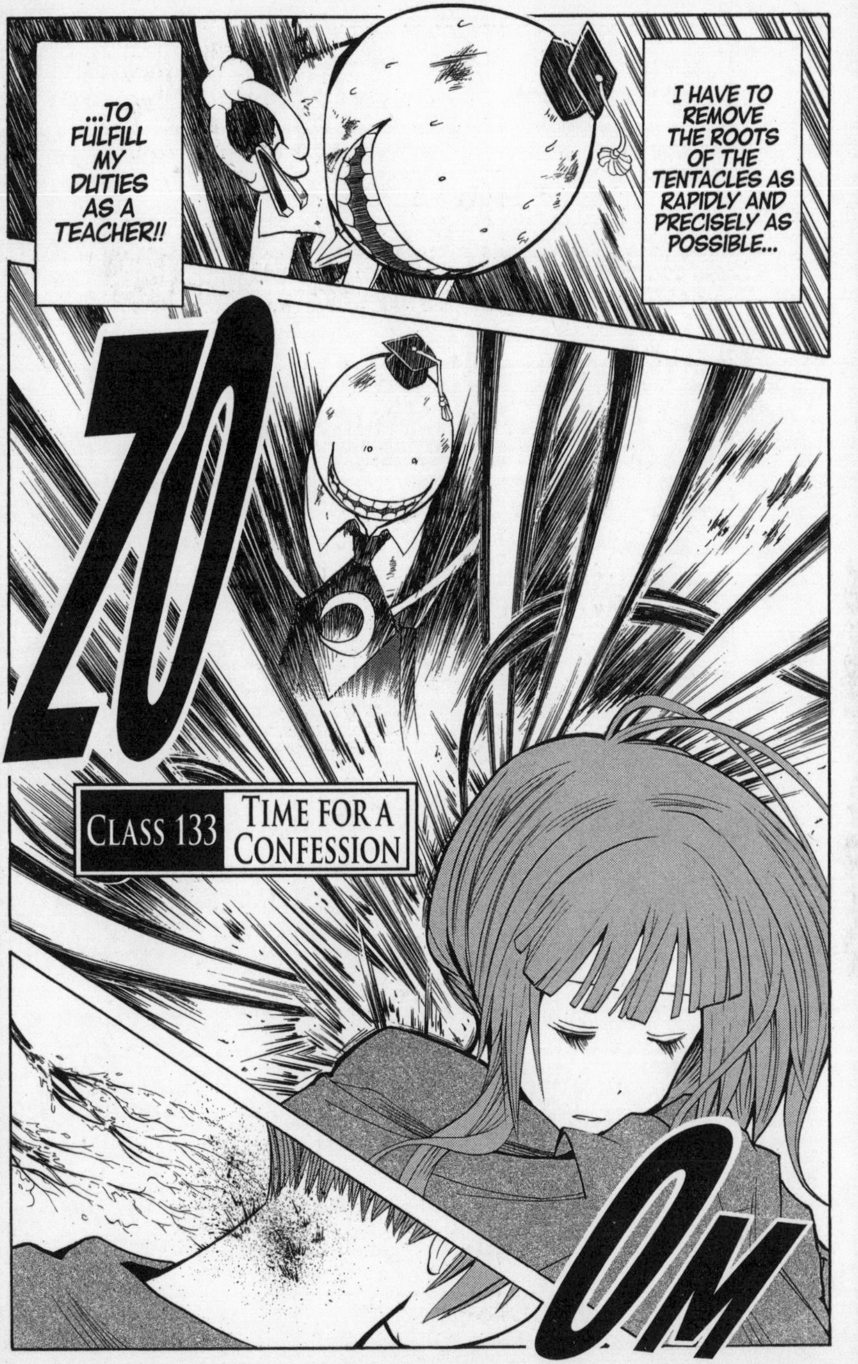
I HAVE TO REMOVE THE ROOTS OF THE TENTACLES AS RAPIDLY AND PRECISELY AS POSSIBLE...
...TO FULFILL MY DUTIES AS A TEACHER!!
ZO
CLASS 133 TIME FOR A CONFESSION
OM

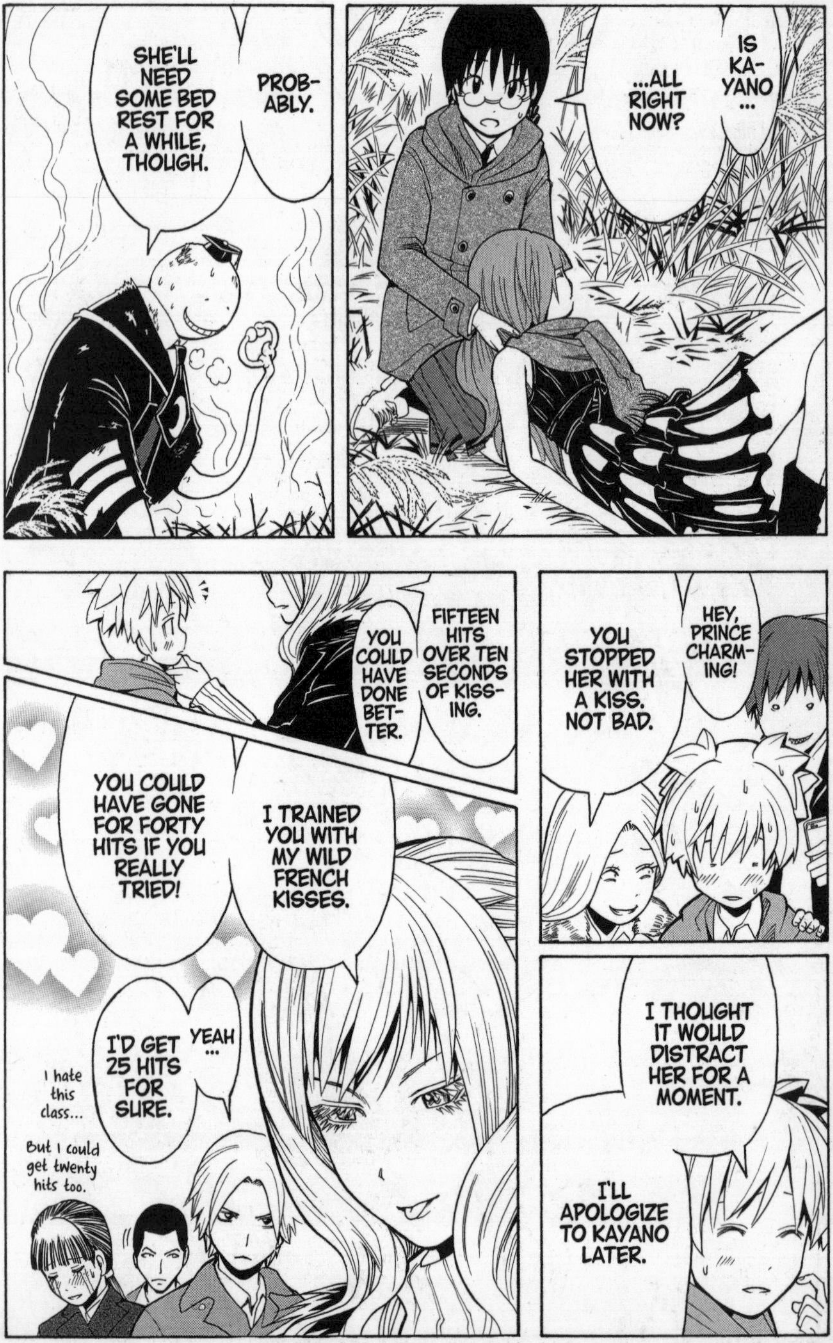
IS KA-YANO ...
...ALL RIGHT NOW?
PROB-ABLY.
SHE'LL NEED SOME BED REST FOR A WHILE, THOUGH.
HEY, PRINCE CHARMING!
YOU STOPPED HER WITH A KISS. NOT BAD.
I THOUGHT IT WOULD DISTRACT HER FOR A MOMENT.
I'LL APOLOGIZE TO KAYANO LATER.
FIFTEEN HITS OVER TEN SECONDS OF KISS-ING.
YOU COULD HAVE DONE BET-TER.
I TRAINED YOU WITH MY WILD FRENCH KISSES.
YOU COULD HAVE GONE FOR FORTY HITS IF YOU REALLY TRIED!
YEAH ...
I'D GET 25 HITS FOR SURE.
I hate this class...
But I could get twenty hits too.

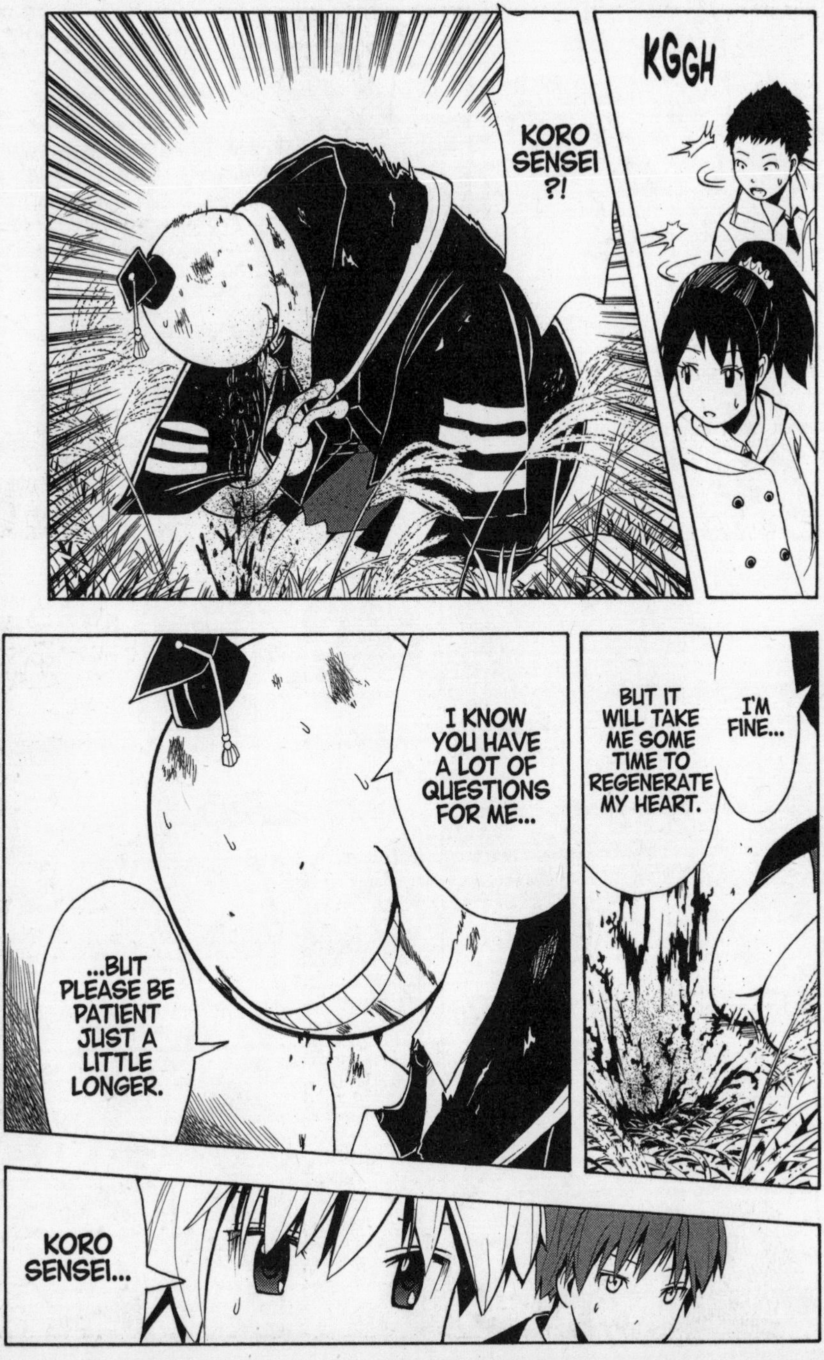
KGGH
KORO SENSEI ?!
I'M FINE...
BUT IT WILL TAKE ME SOME TIME TO REGENERATE MY HEART.
I KNOW YOU HAVE A LOT OF QUESTIONS FOR ME...
...BUT PLEASE BE PATIENT JUST A LITTLE LONGER.
KORO SENSEI...

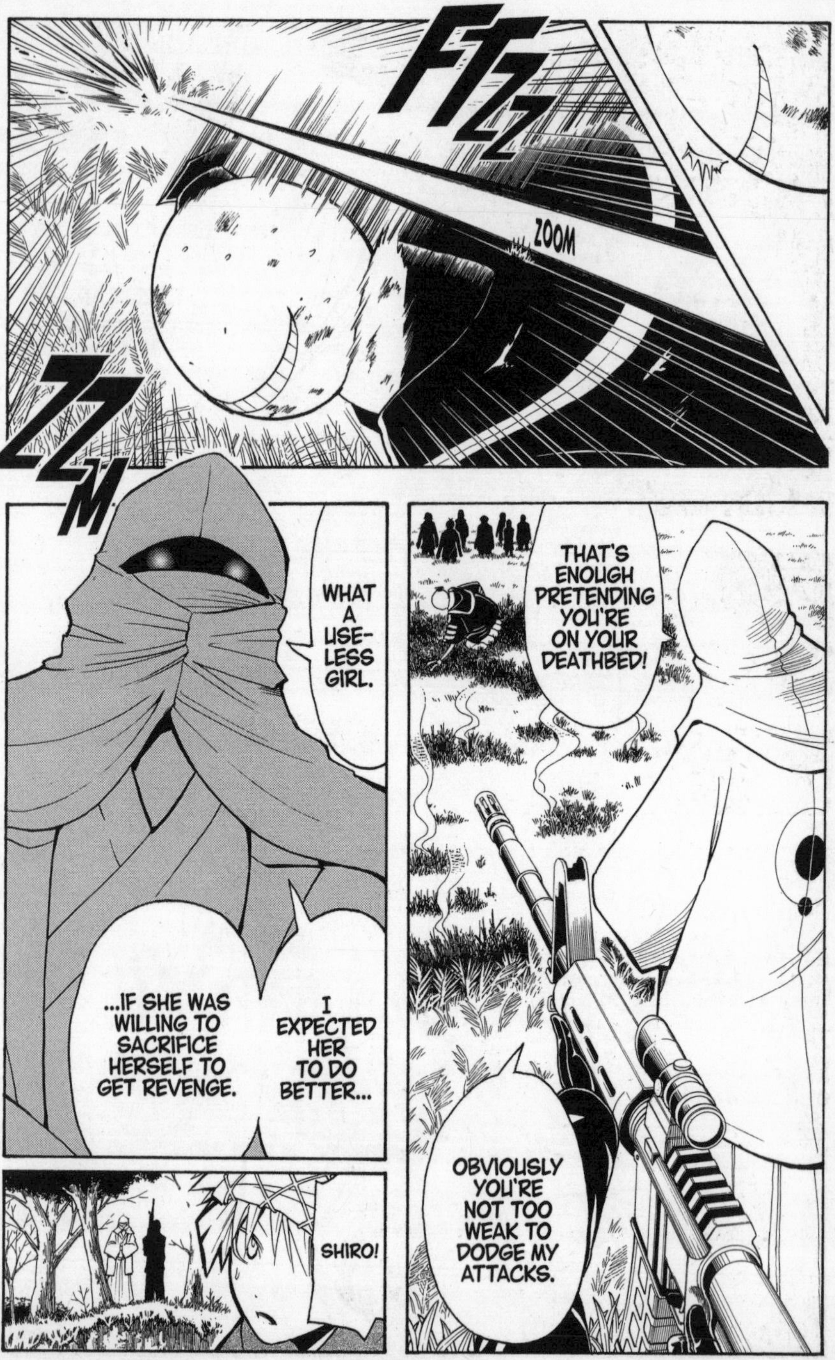
FTZZ
ZOOM
ZZM
THAT'S ENOUGH PRETENDING YOU'RE ON YOUR DEATHBED!
OBVIOUSLY YOU'RE NOT TOO WEAK TO DODGE MY ATTACKS.
WHAT A USE-LESS GIRL.
I EXPECTED HER TO DO BETTER...
...IF SHE WAS WILLING TO SACRIFICE HERSELF TO GET REVENGE.
SHIRO!

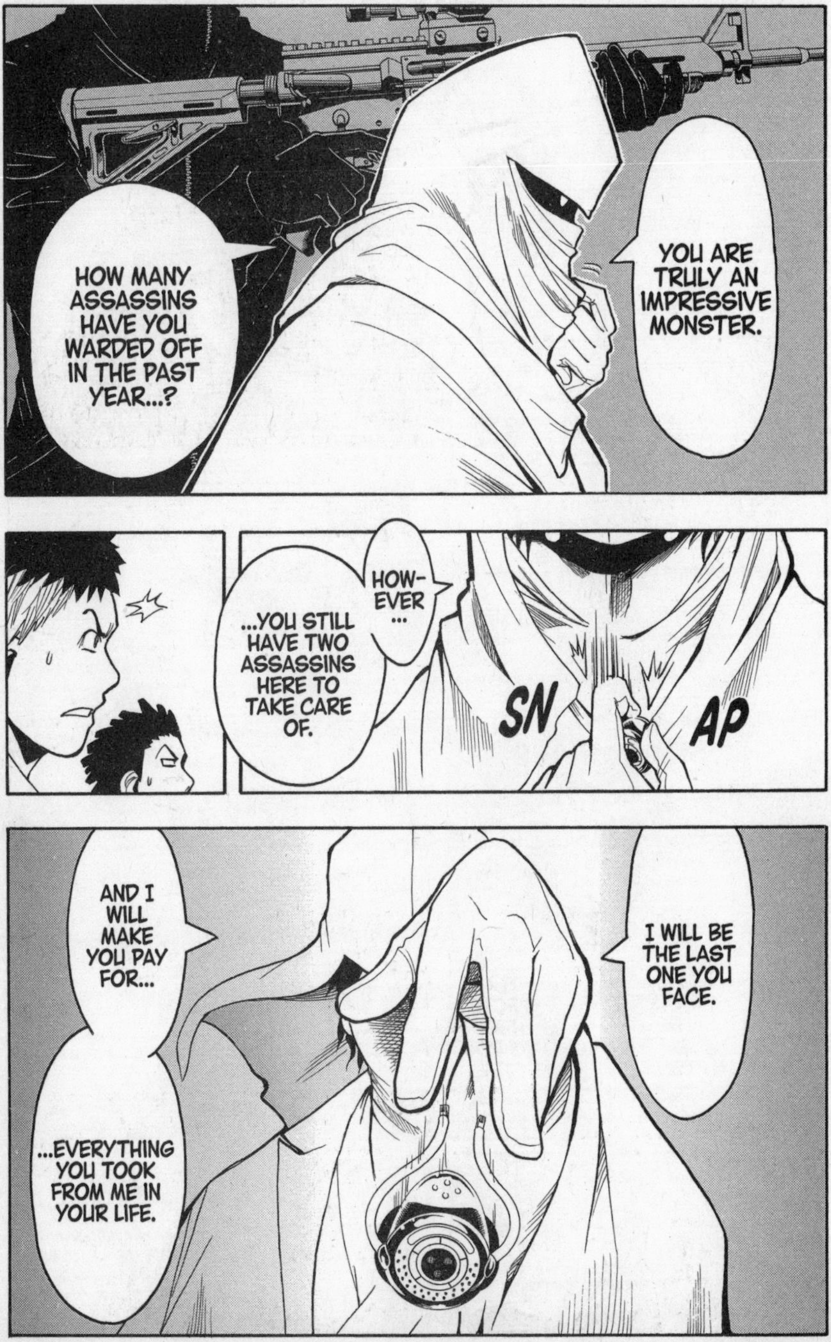
YOU ARE TRULY AN IMPRESSIVE MONSTER.
HOW MANY ASSASSINS HAVE YOU WARDED OFF IN THE PAST YEAR...?
HOW-EVER...
...YOU STILL HAVE TWO ASSASSINS HERE TO TAKE CARE OF.
SNAP
I WILL BE THE LAST ONE YOU FACE.
AND I WILL MAKE YOU PAY FOR...
...EVERYTHING YOU TOOK FROM ME IN YOUR LIFE.

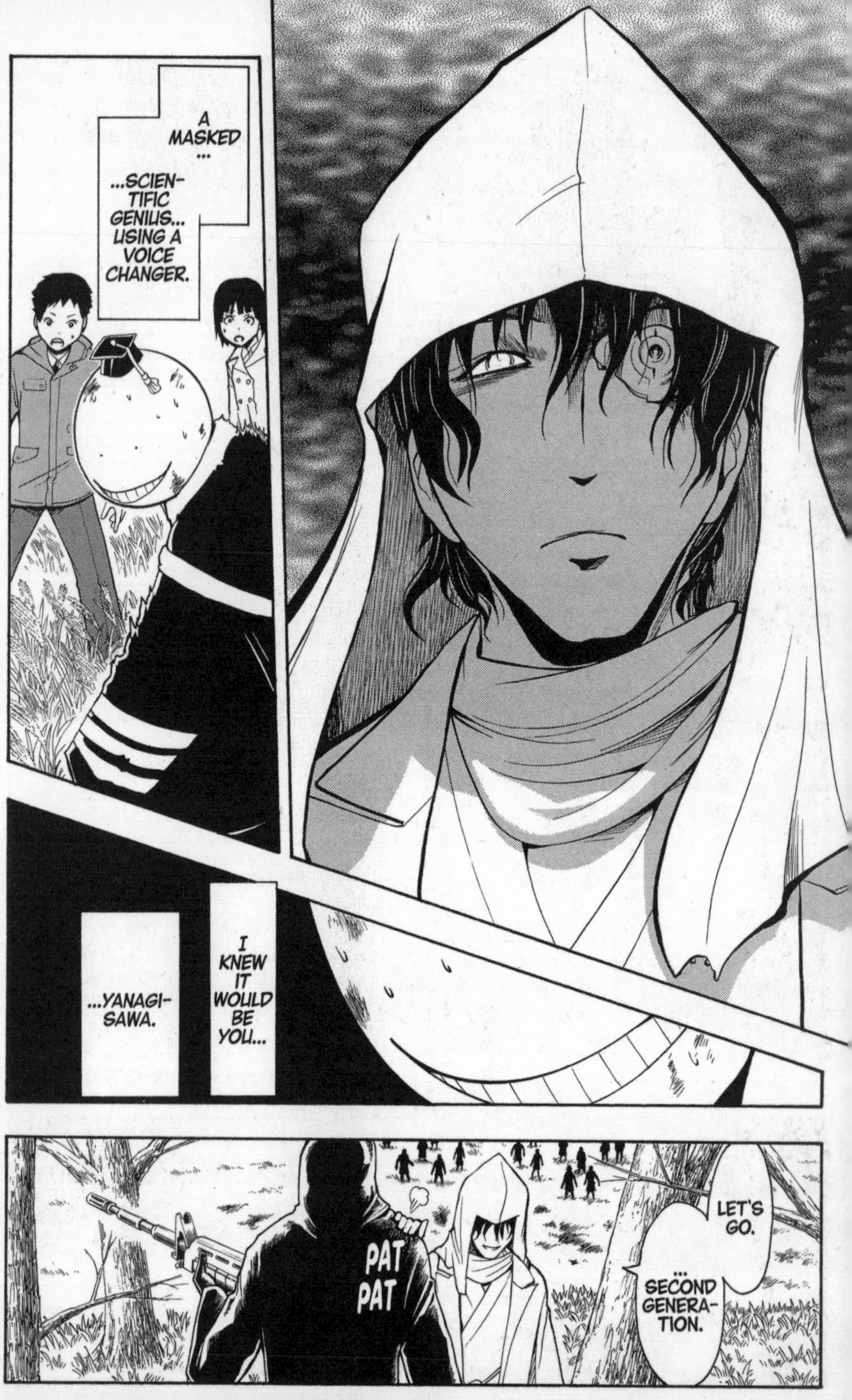
A MASKED...
...SCIENTIFIC GENIUS... USING A VOICE CHANGER.
I KNEW IT WOULD BE YOU...
...YANAGISAWA.
LET'S GO.
...SECOND GENERATION.
PAT PAT

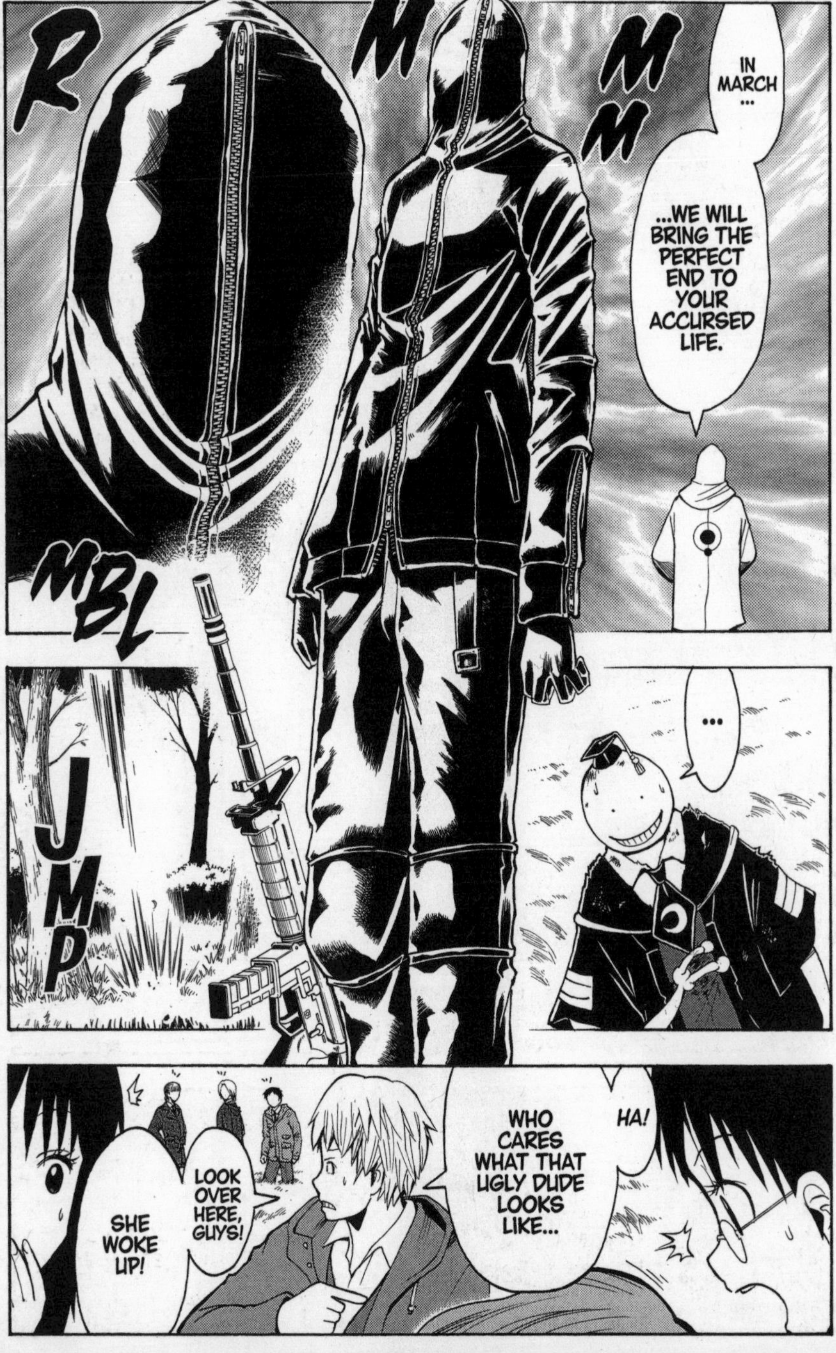

IN MARCH...
...WE WILL BRING THE PERFECT END TO YOUR ACCURSED LIFE.
RMMMMMMBL
...
JMP
HA!
WHO CARES WHAT THAT UGLY DUDE LOOKS LIKE...
LOOK OVER HERE, GUYS!
SHE WOKE UP!

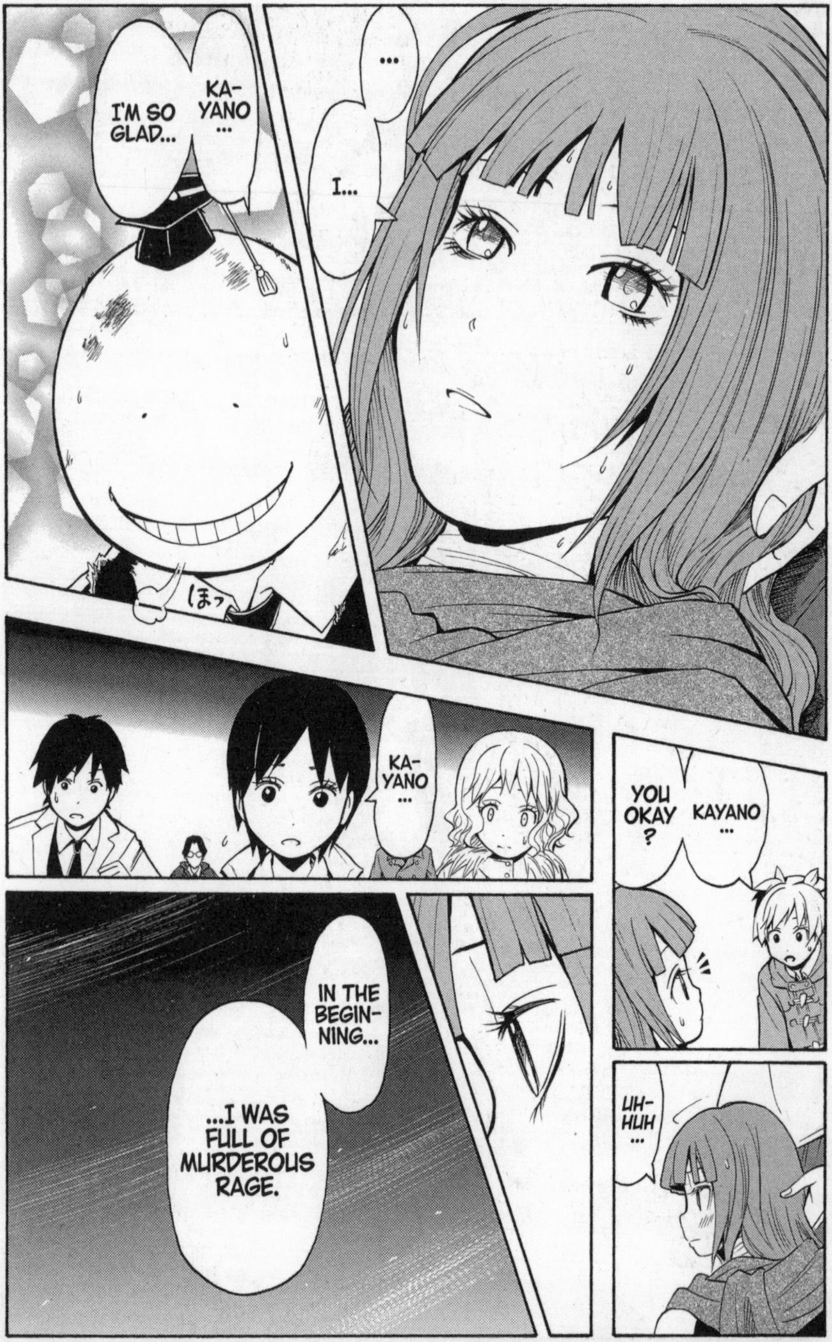
...
I...
KA-YANO...
I'M SO GLAD...
ほっ
KA-YANO...
KAYANO...
YOU OKAY?
UH-HUH...
IN THE BEGIN-NING...
...I WAS FULL OF MURDEROUS RAGE.

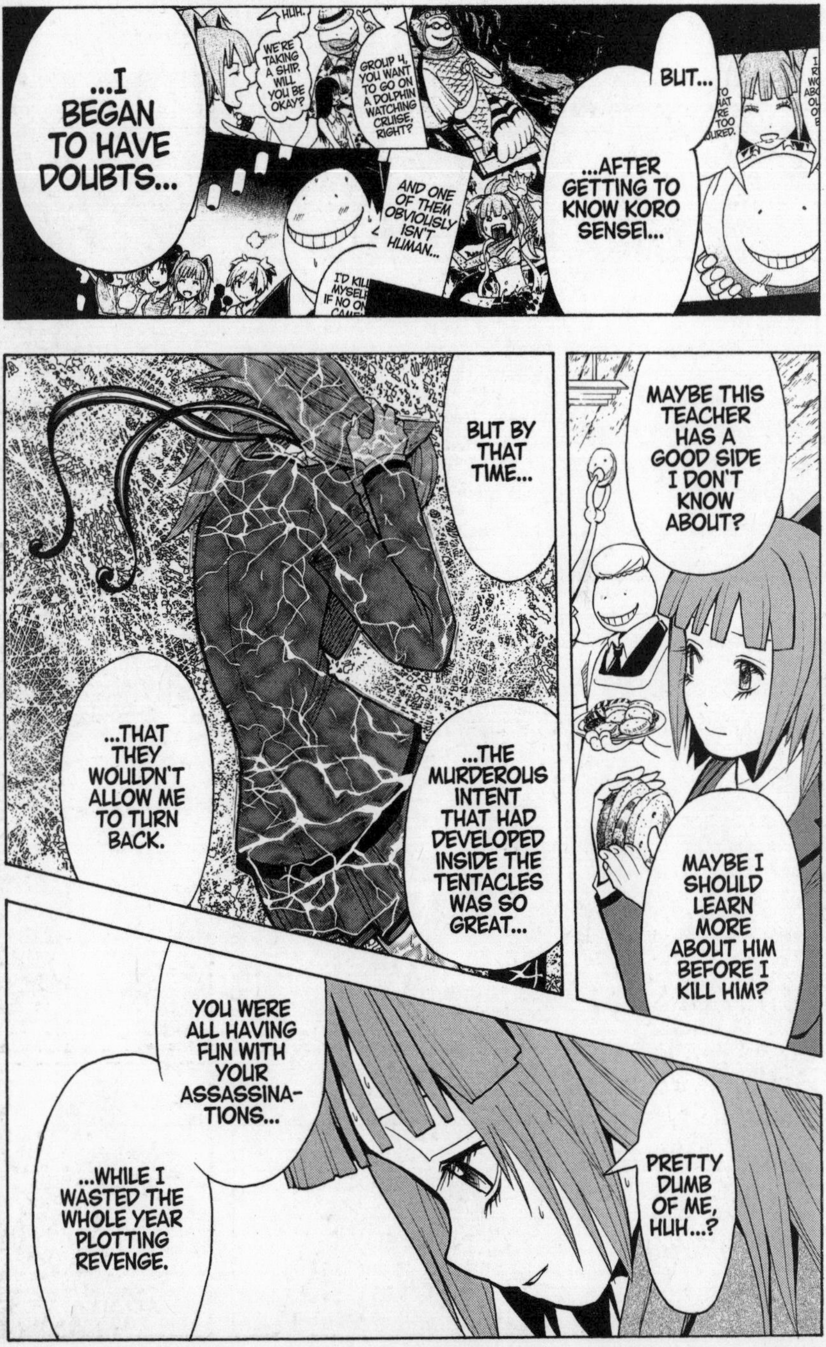
BUT...
...AFTER GETTING TO KNOW KORO SENSEI...
GROUP 4, YOU WANT TO GO ON A DOLPHIN WATCHING CRUISE, RIGHT?
HUH.
WE'RE TAKING A SHIP. WILL YOU BE OKAY?
AND ONE OF THEM OBVIOUSLY ISN'T HUMAN...
...I BEGAN TO HAVE DOUBTS...
MAYBE THIS TEACHER HAS A GOOD SIDE I DON'T KNOW ABOUT?
MAYBE I SHOULD LEARN MORE ABOUT HIM BEFORE I KILL HIM?
BUT BY THAT TIME...
...THE MURDEROUS INTENT THAT HAD DEVELOPED INSIDE THE TENTACLES WAS SO GREAT...
...THAT THEY WOULDN'T ALLOW ME TO TURN BACK.
PRETTY DUMB OF ME, HUH...?
YOU WERE ALL HAVING FUN WITH YOUR ASSASSINA-TIONS...
...WHILE I WASTED THE WHOLE YEAR PLOTTING REVENGE.

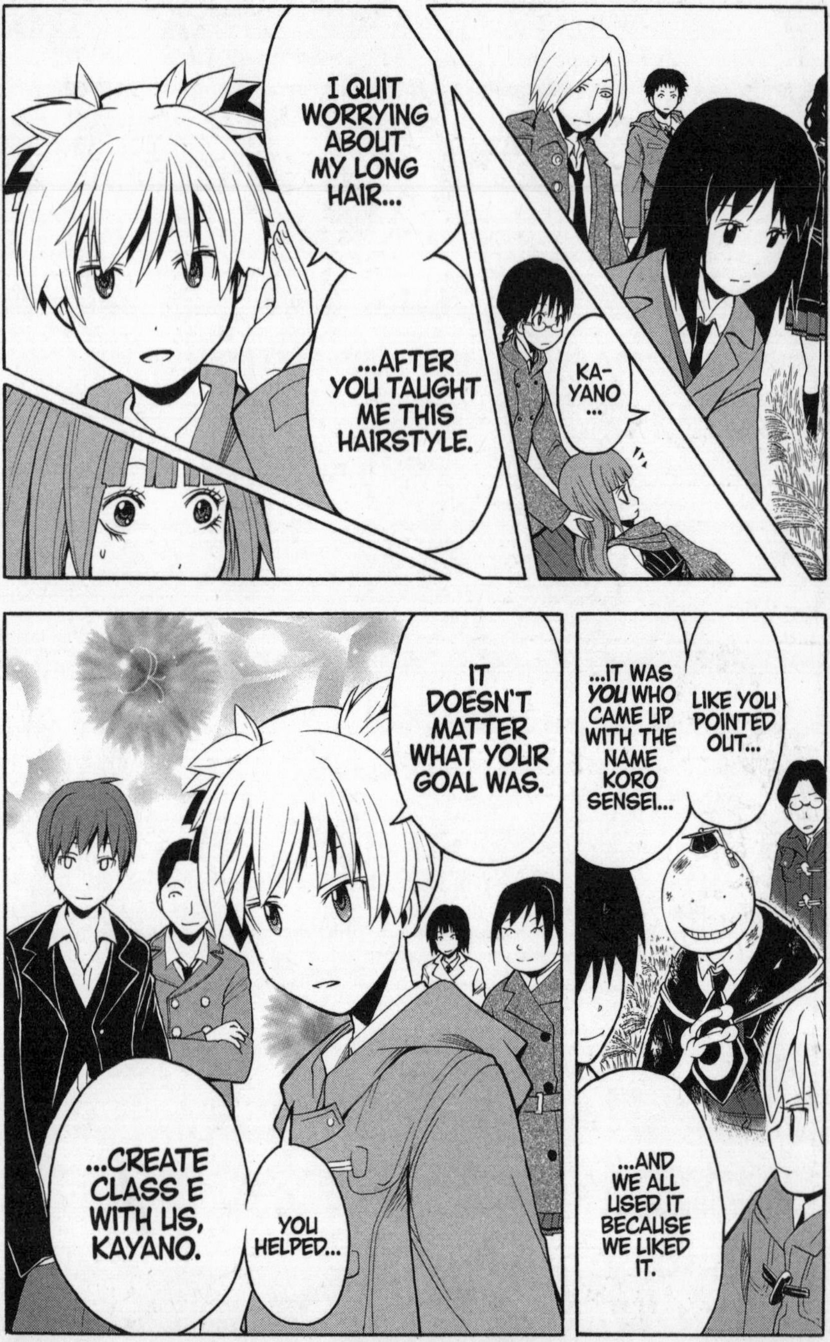
KA-YANO...
I QUIT WORRYING ABOUT MY LONG HAIR...
...AFTER YOU TAUGHT ME THIS HAIRSTYLE.
LIKE YOU POINTED OUT...
...IT WAS *YOU* WHO CAME UP WITH THE NAME KORO SENSEI...
...AND WE ALL USED IT BECAUSE WE LIKED IT.
IT DOESN'T MATTER WHAT YOUR GOAL WAS.
YOU HELPED...
...CREATE CLASS E WITH US, KAYANO.

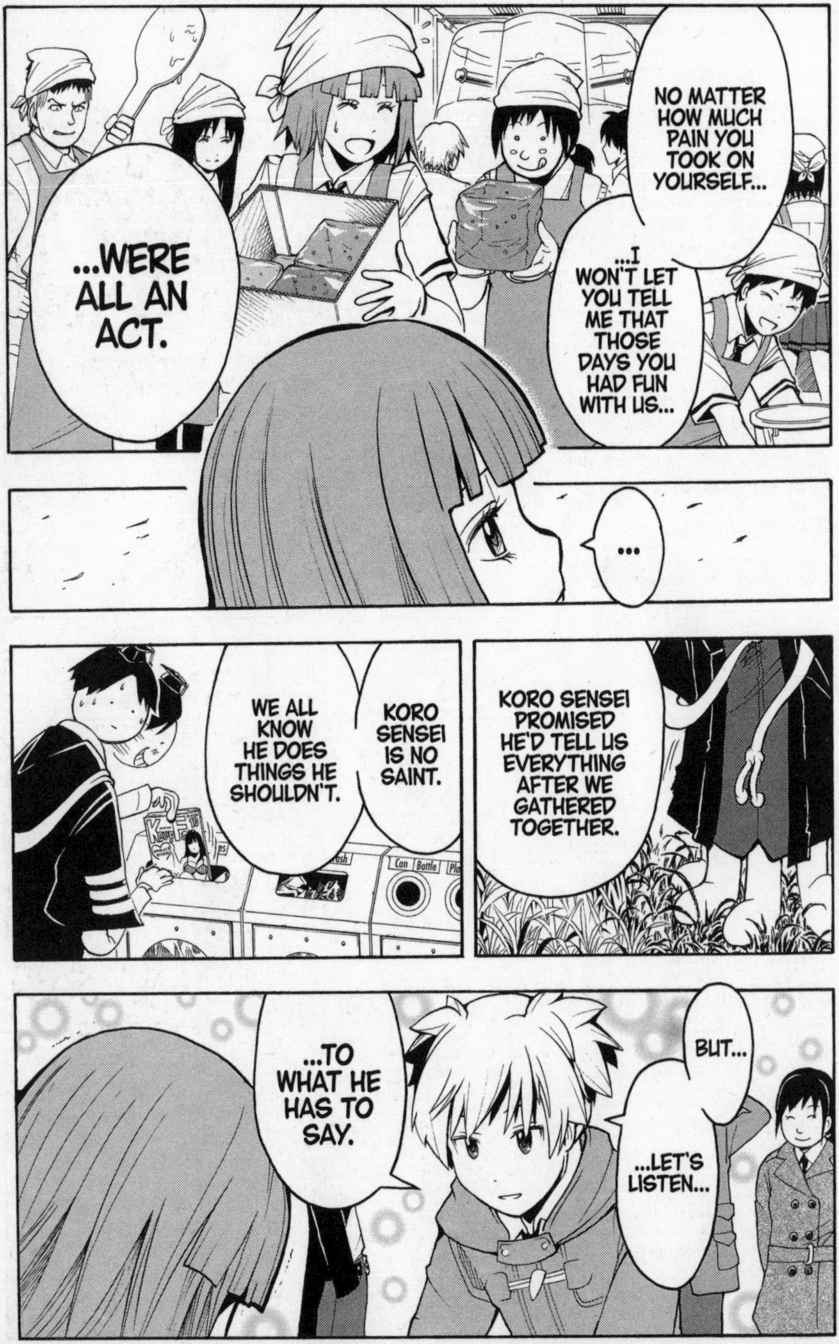
NO MATTER HOW MUCH PAIN YOU TOOK ON YOURSELF...
...I WON'T LET YOU TELL ME THAT THOSE DAYS YOU HAD FUN WITH US...
...WERE ALL AN ACT.
...
KORO SENSEI PROMISED HE'D TELL US EVERYTHING AFTER WE GATHERED TOGETHER.
KORO SENSEI IS NO SAINT.
WE ALL KNOW HE DOES THINGS HE SHOULDN'T.
Can
Bottle
BUT...
...LET'S LISTEN...
...TO WHAT HE HAS TO SAY.

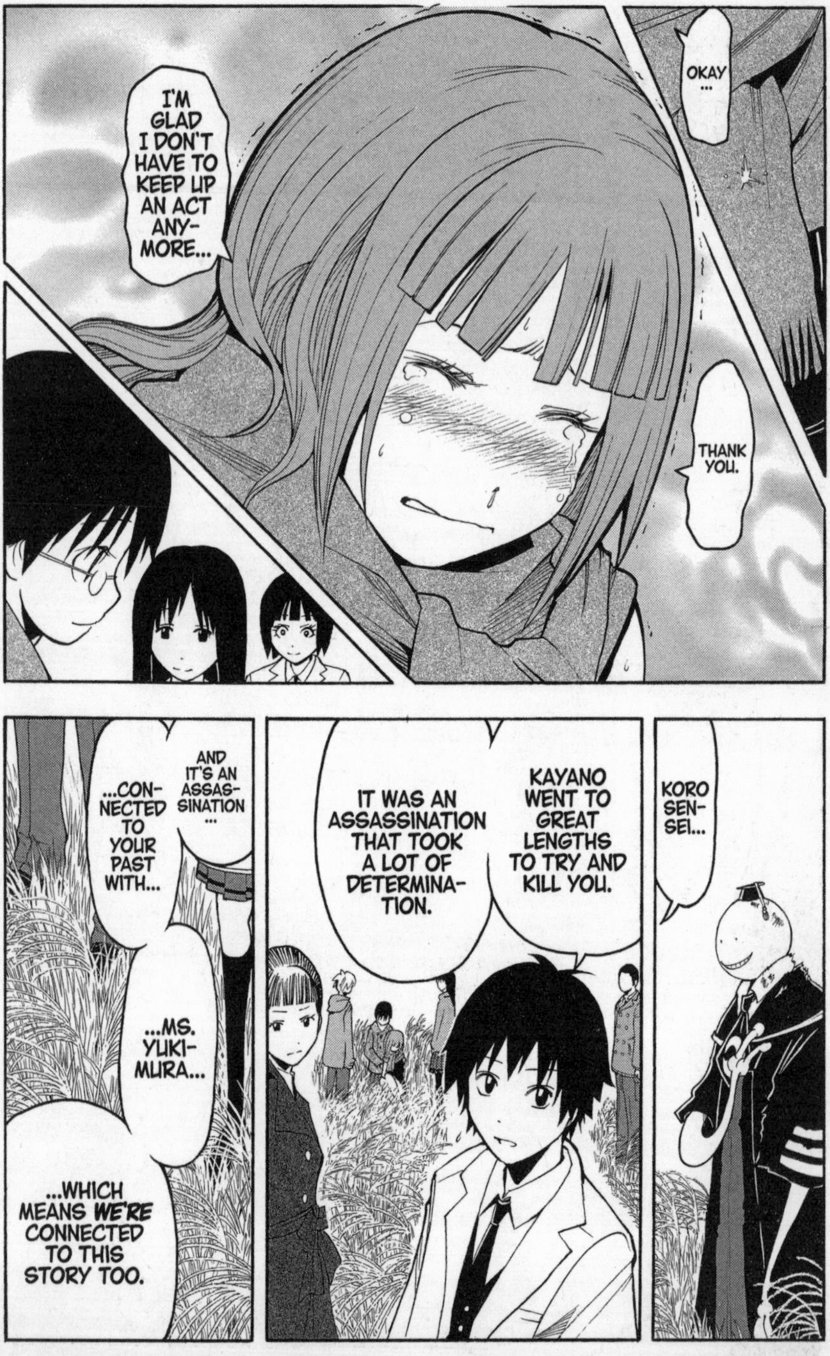
OKAY...
THANK YOU.
I'M GLAD I DON'T HAVE TO KEEP UP AN ACT ANY-MORE...
KORO SEN-SEI...
KAYANO WENT TO GREAT LENGTHS TO TRY AND KILL YOU.
IT WAS AN ASSASSINATION THAT TOOK A LOT OF DETERMINA-TION.
AND IT'S AN ASSAS-SINATION...
...CON-NECTED TO YOUR PAST WITH...
...MS. YUKI-MURA...
...WHICH MEANS **WE'RE** CONNECTED TO THIS STORY TOO.

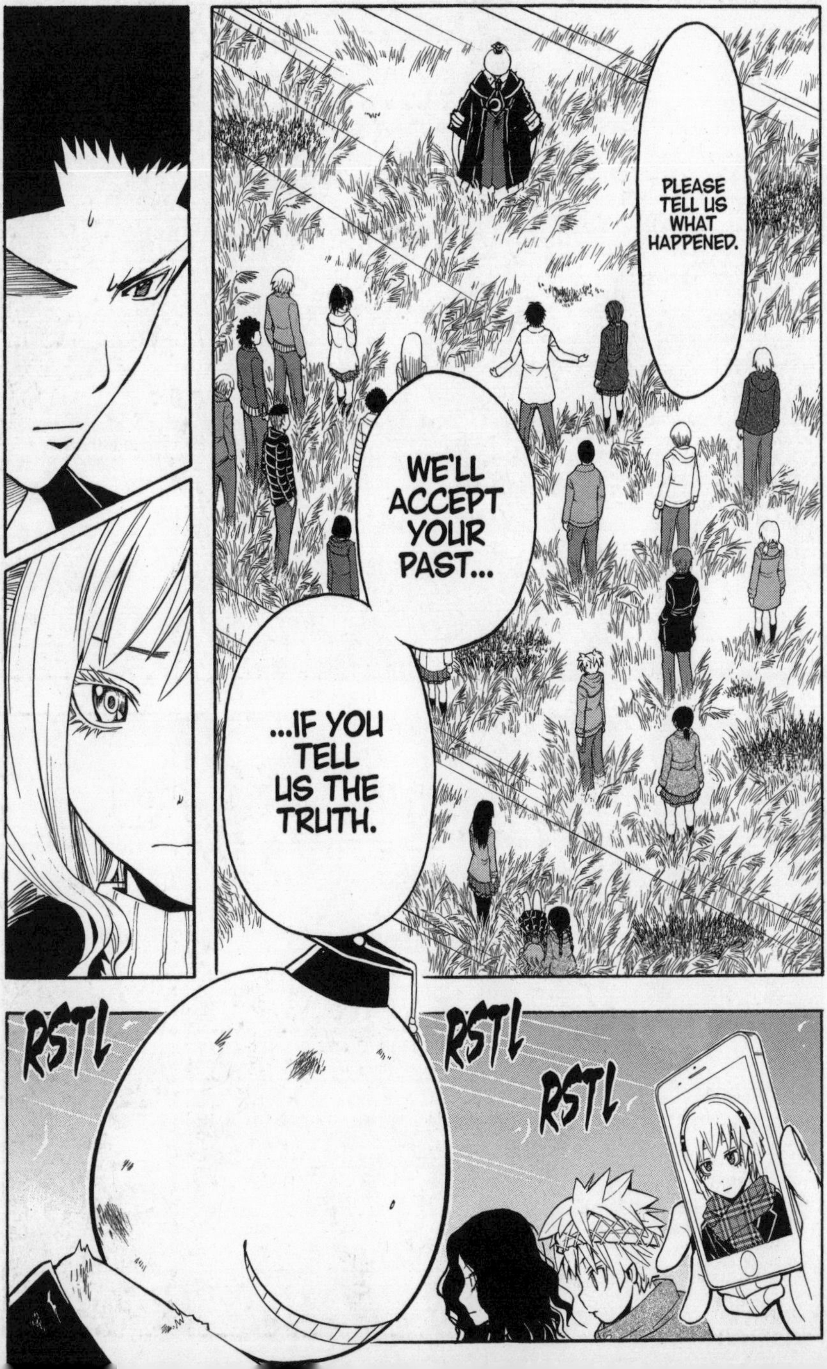
PLEASE TELL US WHAT HAPPENED.
WE'LL ACCEPT YOUR PAST...
...IF YOU TELL US THE TRUTH.
RSTL
RSTL
RSTL

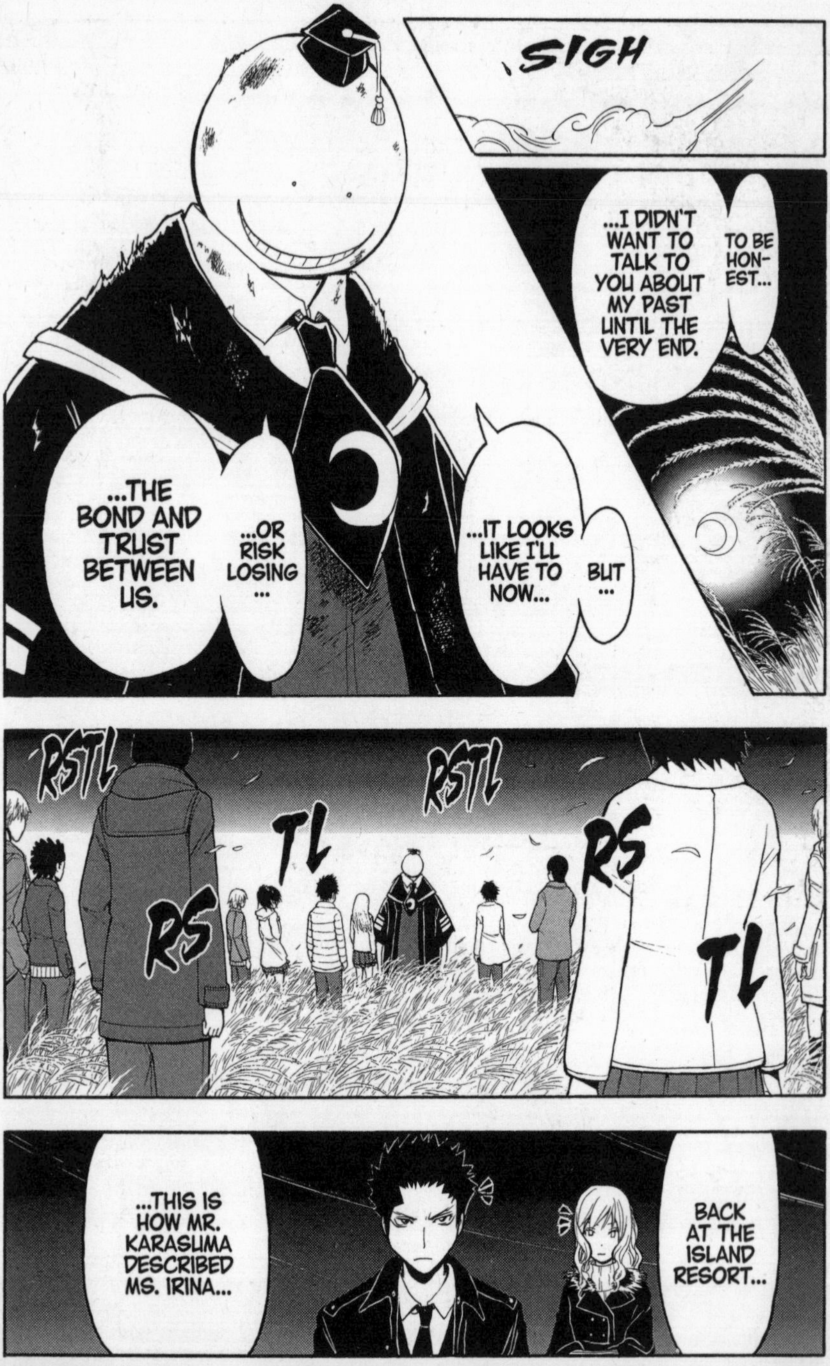
SIGH
TO BE HONEST...
...I DIDN'T WANT TO TALK TO YOU ABOUT MY PAST UNTIL THE VERY END.
BUT...
...IT LOOKS LIKE I'LL HAVE TO NOW...
...OR RISK LOSING...
...THE BOND AND TRUST BETWEEN US.
RSTL
TL
RS
RSTL
TL
RS
BACK AT THE ISLAND RESORT...
...THIS IS HOW MR. KARASUMA DESCRIBED MS. IRINA...

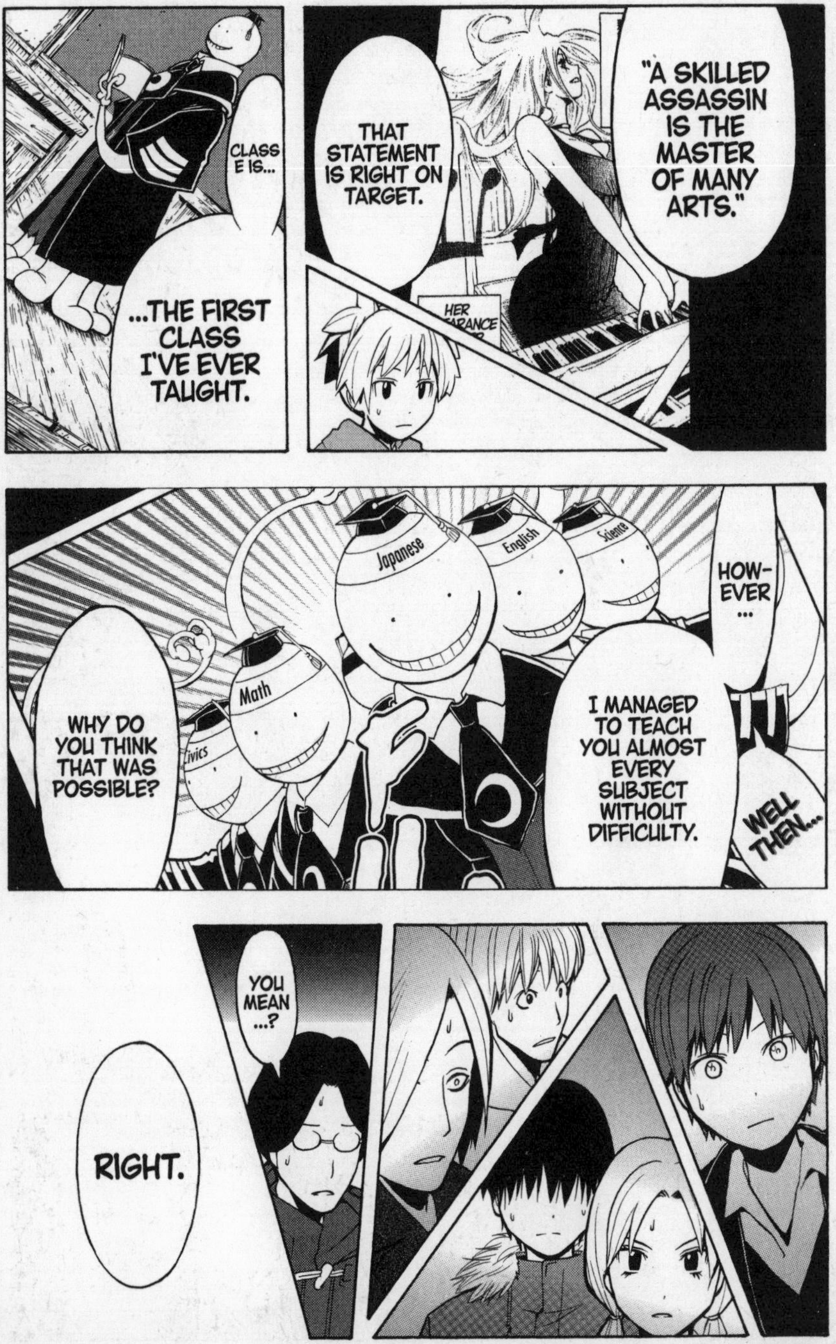
"A SKILLED ASSASSIN IS THE MASTER OF MANY ARTS."
THAT STATEMENT IS RIGHT ON TARGET.
CLASS E IS...
...THE FIRST CLASS I'VE EVER TAUGHT.
HOW-EVER...
Science
English
Japanese
Math
Civics
I MANAGED TO TEACH YOU ALMOST EVERY SUBJECT WITHOUT DIFFICULTY.
WELL THEN...
WHY DO YOU THINK THAT WAS POSSIBLE?
YOU MEAN...?
RIGHT.

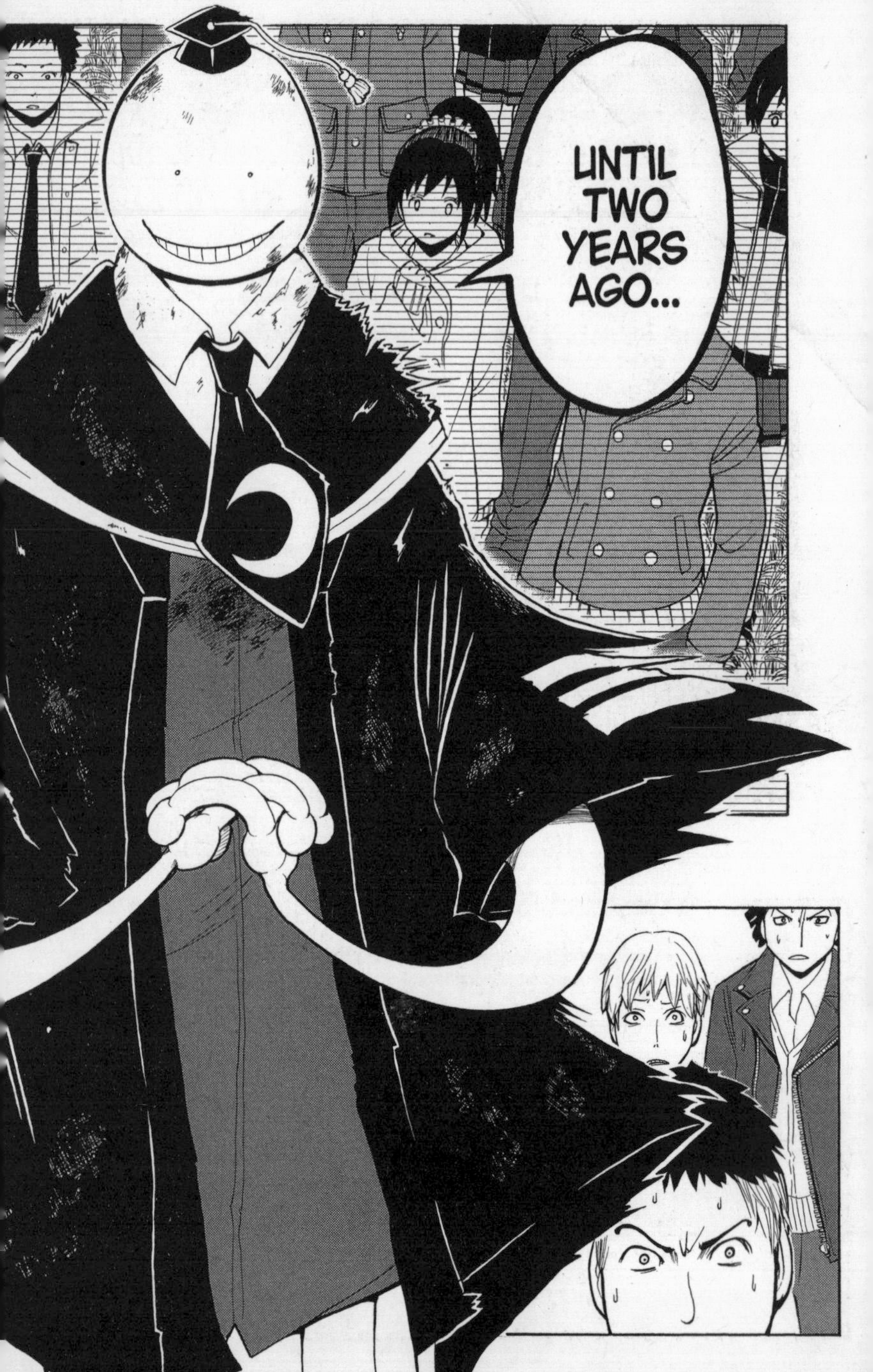
UNTIL TWO YEARS AGO...

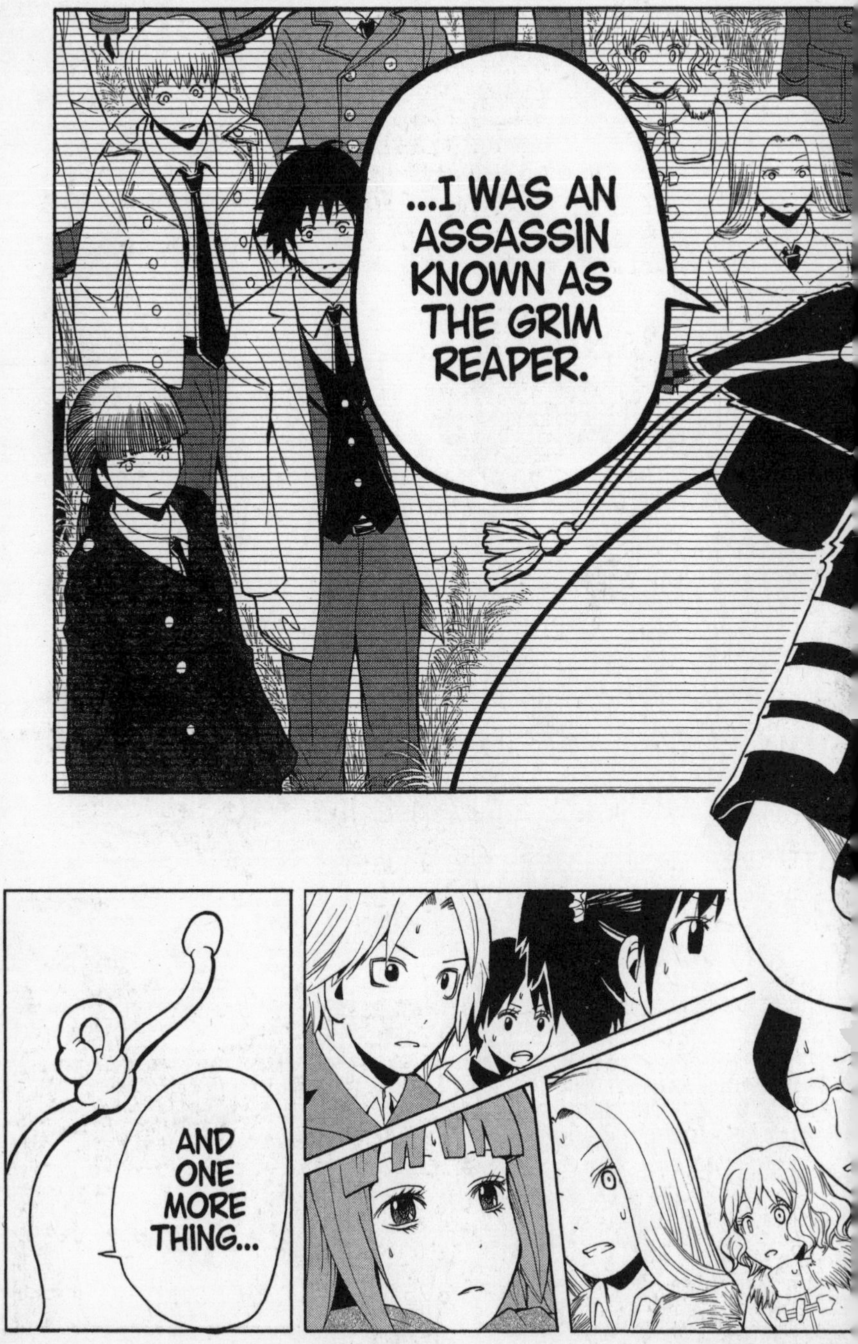
...I WAS AN ASSASSIN KNOWN AS THE GRIM REAPER.
AND ONE MORE THING...

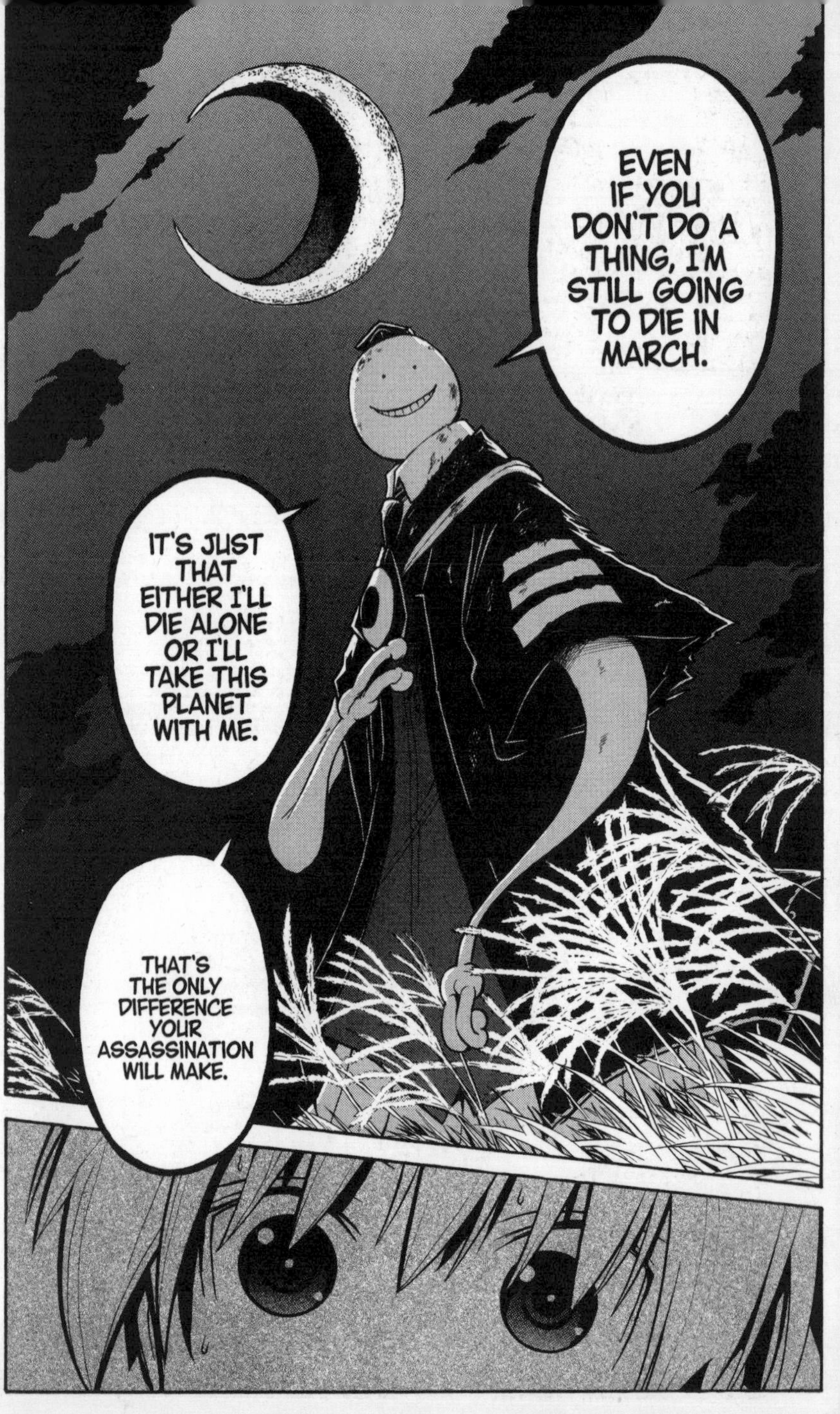
EVEN IF YOU DON'T DO A THING, I'M STILL GOING TO DIE IN MARCH.
IT'S JUST THAT EITHER I'LL DIE ALONE OR I'LL TAKE THIS PLANET WITH ME.
THAT'S THE ONLY DIFFERENCE YOUR ASSASSINATION WILL MAKE.

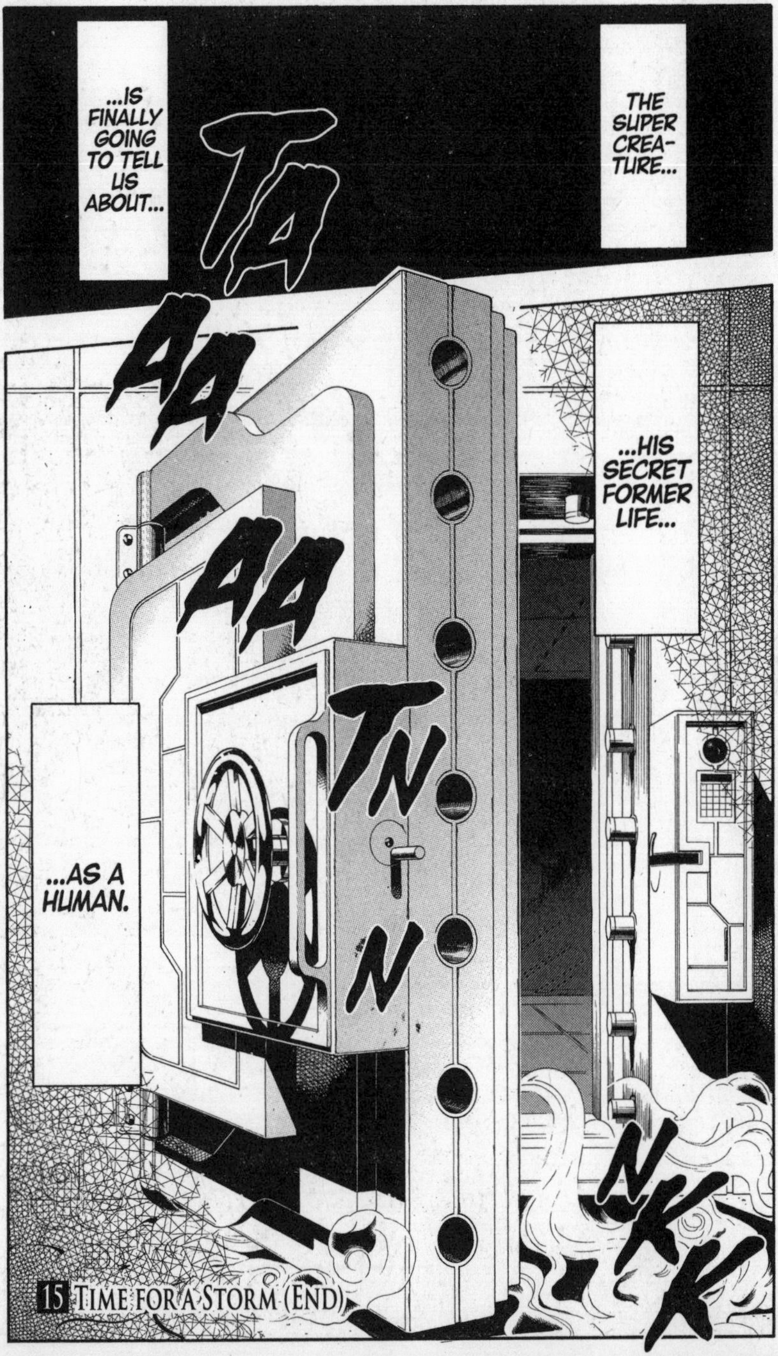
THE SUPER CREA-TURE...
...IS FINALLY GOING TO TELL US ABOUT...
TAAAAA
...HIS SECRET FORMER LIFE...
TNN
...AS A HUMAN.
NKK
15 TIME FOR A STORM (END)

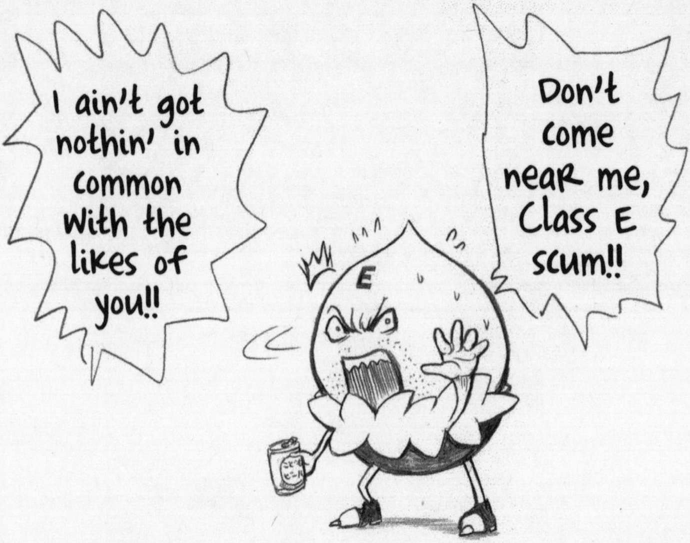
Don't come near me, Class E scum!!
I ain't got nothin' in common with the likes of you!!
E

A nation in Ruins...

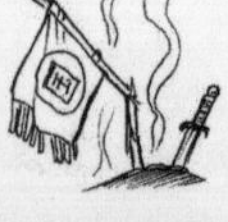

...peace
at last?

I use words that are typically used in everyday life so that they are easier to understand, even if they're slang or incorrect usage.

If you use proper words all the time, the dialogue in the manga ends up sounding weirdly stiff.

For example, I have the students use more slang and incorrect grammar than the teachers to make the conversations sound realistic.

On the other hand, I pay close attention to the grammar and spelling in situations where there wouldn't be mistakes, such as during school classes.

However... There are times when I make spelling mistakes in words I didn't intend to misspell...and that's just me being sloppy as usual...

—Yusei Matsui

Yusei Matsui was born on the last day of January in Saitama Prefecture, Japan. He has been drawing manga since elementary school. Some of his favorite manga series are *Bobobo-bo Bo-bobo*, *JoJo's Bizarre Adventure* and *Ultimate Muscle*. Matsui learned his trade working as an assistant to manga artist Yoshio Sawai, creator of *Bobobo-bo Bo-bobo*. In 2005, Matsui debuted his original manga *Neuro: Supernatural Detective* in *Weekly Shonen Jump*. In 2007, *Neuro* was adapted into an anime. In 2012, *Assassination Classroom* began serialization in *Weekly Shonen Jump*.

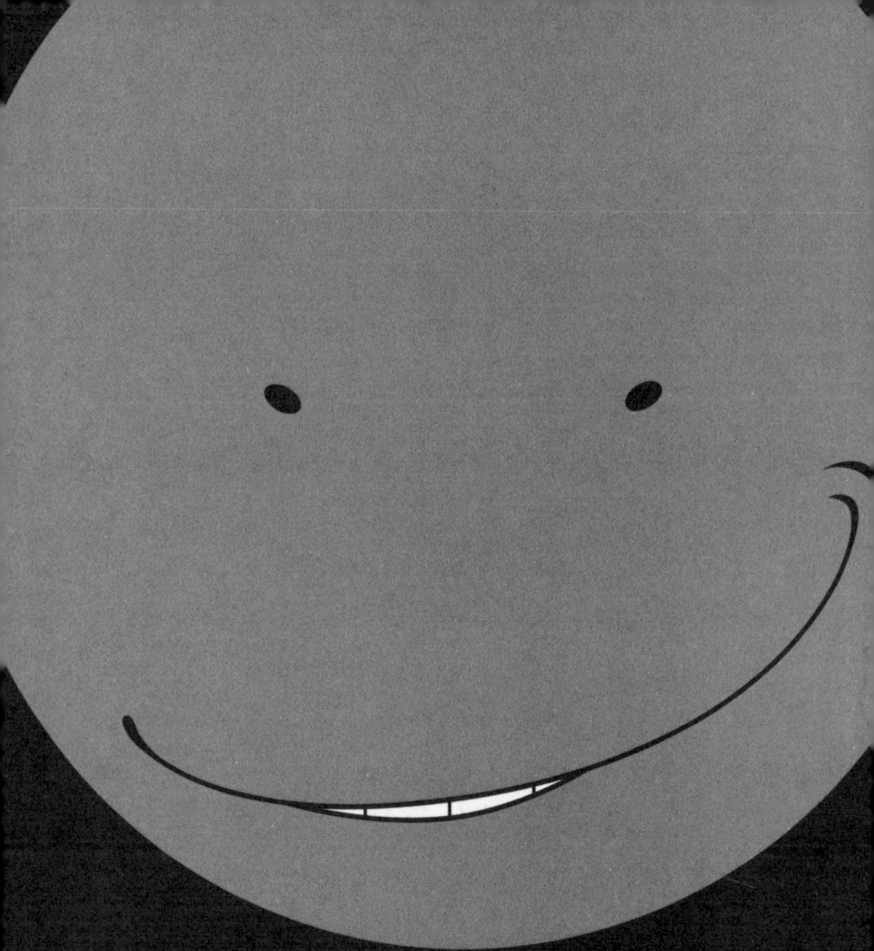

This new metallic purple appears when Koro Sensei is really smug or a touch conceitec
He loves himself as much as he loves his students and he calls this color "The Purple o
the Fateful Eternal Wind." This phrase really makes people want to kill him.

ASSASSINATION CLASSROOM

YUSEI MATSUI

15

TIME FOR A STORM

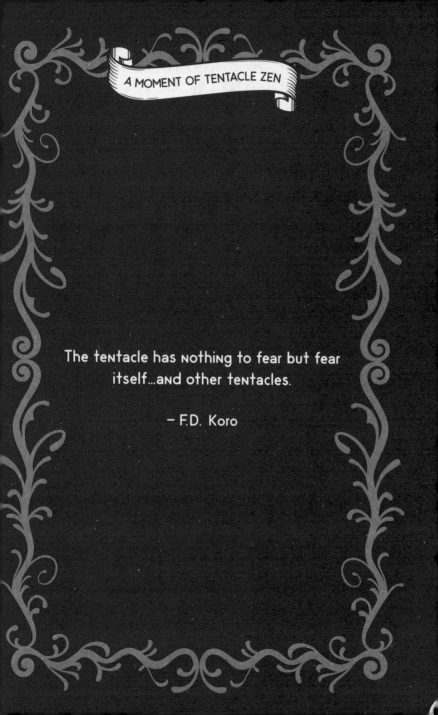

A MOMENT OF TENTACLE ZEN

The tentacle has nothing to fear but fear itself...and other tentacles.

– F.D. Koro

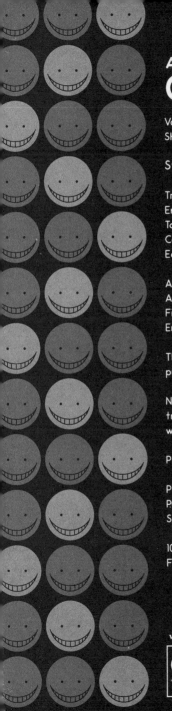

ASSASSINATION CLASSROOM

Volume 15
SHONEN JUMP ADVANCED Manga Edition

Story and Art by YUSEI MATSUI

Translation/Tetsuichiro Miyaki
English Adaptation/Bryant Turnage
Touch-up Art & Lettering/Stephen Dutro
Cover & Interior Design/Sam Elzway
Editor/Annette Roman

Published by VIZ Media, LLC
P.O. Box 77010
San Francisco, CA 94107

10 9 8 7 6 5 4 3 2 1
First printing, April 2017

www.viz.com
www.shonenjump.com

Syllabus for Assassination Classroom, Vol. 16

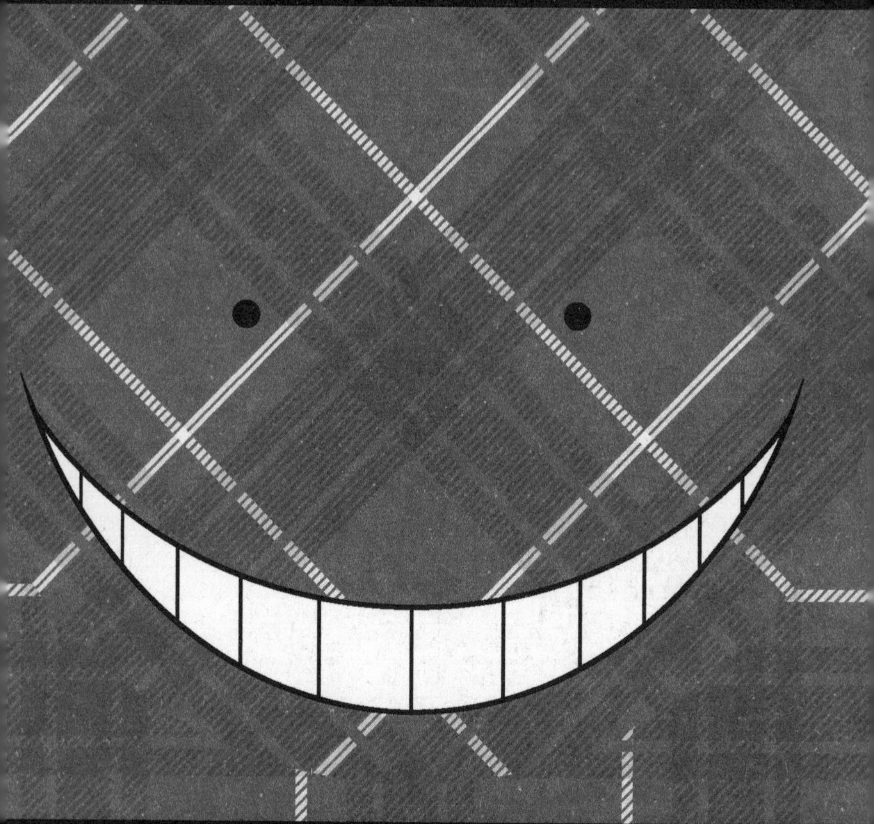

Koro Sensei tells all: his former profession, his nickname, the mad scientist responsible for his unique cephalopod physiognomy, the love of his life, and why he wanted to teach the 3-E students. New light is shed not only on his character, but on the reason he has vowed to destroy the earth in March. Will this intel change 3-E's commitment to assassinating their teacher?

Available June 2017!

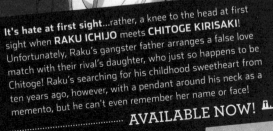

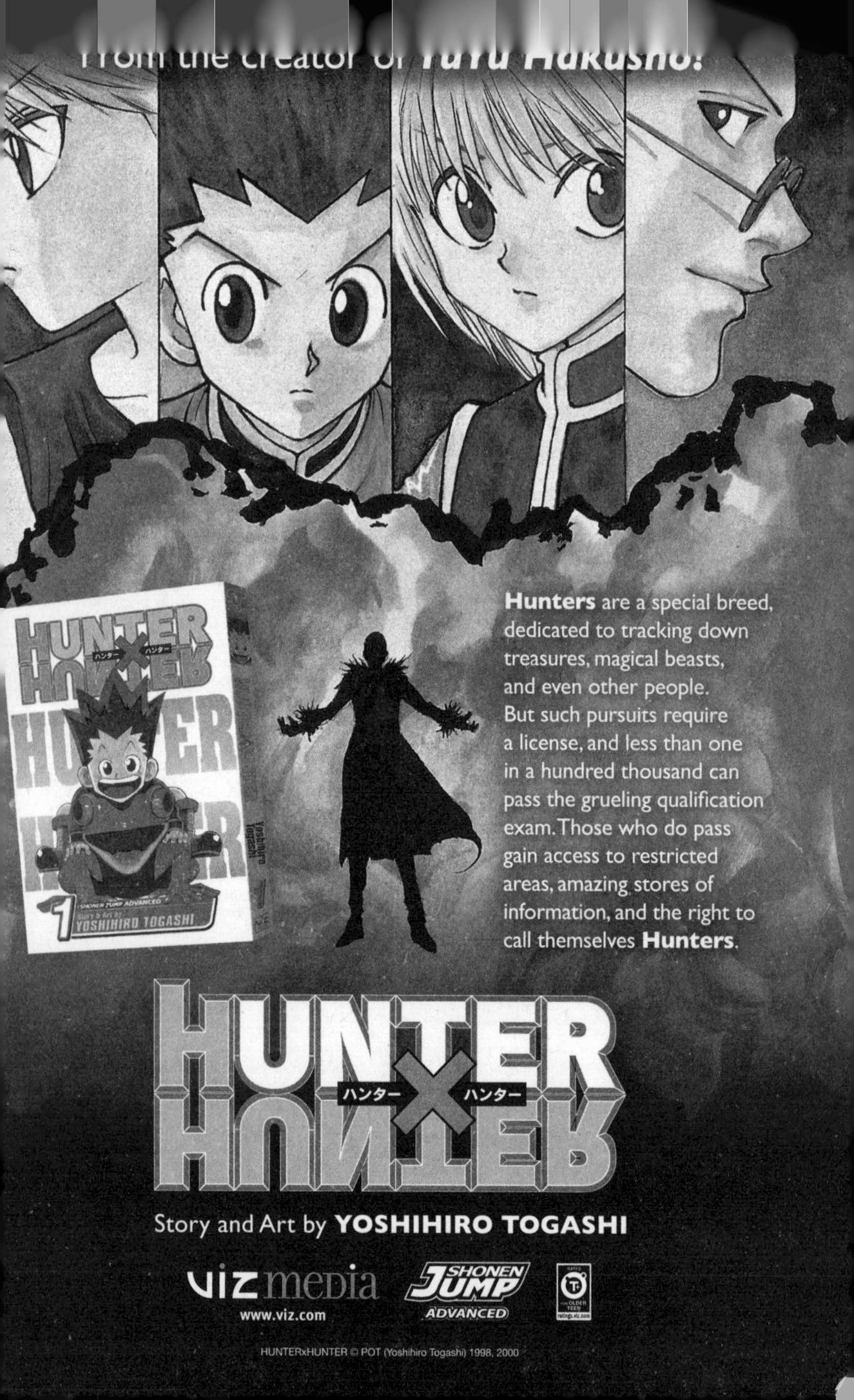

From the creator of YuYu Hakusho!
Hunters are a special breed, dedicated to tracking down treasures, magical beasts, and even other people. But such pursuits require a license, and less than one in a hundred thousand can pass the grueling qualification exam. Those who do pass gain access to restricted areas, amazing stores of information, and the right to call themselves Hunters.
HUNTER × HUNTER
ハンター ハンター
Story and Art by YOSHIHIRO TOGASHI
viz media
www.viz.com
SHONEN JUMP ADVANCED
HUNTERxHUNTER © POT (Yoshihiro Togashi) 1998, 2000

 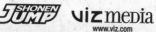

You're Reading in the Wrong Direction!!

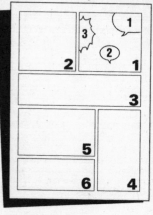

Whoops! Guess what? You're starting at the wrong end of the comic!

…It's true! In keeping with the original Japanese format, **Assassination Classroom** is meant to be read from right to left, starting in the upper-right corner.

Unlike English, which is read from left to right, Japanese is read from right to left, meaning that action, sound effects and word-balloon order are completely reversed… something which can make readers unfamiliar with Japanese feel pretty backwards themselves. For this reason, manga or Japanese comics published in the U.S. in English have sometimes been published "flopped"—that is, printed in exact reverse order, as though seen from the other side of a mirror.

By flopping pages, U.S. publishers can avoid confusing readers, but the compromise is not without its downside. For one thing, a character in a flopped manga series who once wore in the original Japanese version a T-shirt emblazoned with "M A Y" (as in "the merry month of") now wears one which reads "Y A M"! Additionally, many manga creators in Japan are themselves unhappy with the process, as some feel the mirror-imaging of their art skews their original intentions.

We are proud to bring you Yusei Matsui's **Assassination Classroom** in the original unflopped format.
For now, though, turn to the other side of the book and let the adventure begin…!

—Editor